Jean Mabillon, Samuel J Eales

Life and Works of Saint Bernard, Abbot of Clairvaux

Jean Mabillon, Samuel J Eales

Life and Works of Saint Bernard, Abbot of Clairvaux

ISBN/EAN: 9783742875112

Manufactured in Europe, USA, Canada, Australia, Japa

Cover: Foto ©Thomas Meinert / pixelio.de

Manufactured and distributed by brebook publishing software
(www.brebook.com)

Jean Mabillon, Samuel J Eales

Life and Works of Saint Bernard, Abbot of Clairvaux

LIFE AND WORKS
OF SAINT BERNARD

ABBOT OF CLAIRVAUX

EDITED BY

DOM. JOHN MABILLON

Presbyter and Monk of the Benedictine Congregation of S. Maur

Translated and Edited with Additional Notes

BY

SAMUEL J. EALES. M.A., D C.L.,
Vicar of Stalisfield, Kent.

VOL. III.

JOHN HODGES
BEDFORD STREET, COVENT GARDEN, LONDON
1896

TABLE OF CONTENTS.

PREFACE TO VOL. III.

This volume contains: —

The remainder of the Letters of S. Bernard, so far as at present discovered and tabulated. Of these Dom. John Mabillon included in his second edition 454: besides a number of letters "doubtful, spurious and written by others." These latter it has not been thought needful to translate: bearing in mind the great space that must be occupied by them, and the need of keeping the present edition within reasonable bounds. Two, however, No. 474 of the Appendix and No. 479, seemed of sufficient intrinsic interest to warrant their insertion: and are now numbered respectively 460 and 459

Five new ones were collected by D. Massuet and included in the edition of 1719.

In the fourth edition of Mabillon (Gaume: Paris 1839) from which, as before stated, we are here translating, there were inserted *thirty-six* new Letters of the Saint, transcribed by D. Martène from the Vedastine MS. and that of Anchin (Vol. i. pp. 74, 75.)

In our own time great services have been rendered to the study of S. Bernard, by the persevering labours of Dr. GEORG HÜFFER, formerly of Munster, Westphalia, and later Professor in the University of Breslau. He has published *Handschriftliche Studien zum Leben des heilig. Bernard von Clairvaux*,[1] and *Der heilige Bernard von Clairvaux. Eine Darstellung seines Lebens und Wirkens. Erster Band: Vorstudien.*[2]

Of these *Vorstudien*, i. e., Prolegomena, I have made great use in adding also letters to those already collected, and desire to express here my obligations to their learned and industrious Editor, though in several instances, especially in letters bearing on English subjects, I have been forced to differ in some respects from views which he has taken.

He has discovered in all *twenty-four* new letters: *six* in MSS. existing in the *Chapter Library* of Toledo, where he says "a rich store of MSS. is collected over the wide Gothic cloisters, which add so much to the stateliness of that noble Cathedral, the Primatial Church of Spain."[3]

---

[1] In Görres, *Ges. Histor. Jahrbuch*, 1884—5. v. 576—624; vi. 73—91, 232—270.

[2] Münster, 1886.

[3] The Parchment Codex of the library, bearing mark 9.26, is written in *duodecimo* form, and belongs to the end of the 12th century.

It is without index or page number, and contains as writings of S. Bernard: "*De moribus et officio episcoporum*" and his sermons "*super missus est;*" also a small number of his letters. The numbers 218—219—231 -221—116 of the editions are followed by an unknown letter to the Cardinal-Deacon Umbald—*Si vere diligis.* Then follow 168, 170, 164; then two new letters: to Innocent II. — *Si ego in testimonio,* and to the Cardinal L.—*Qui persecuntur Lugdunensem.* Following the now inserted number 179 is an hitherto unknown letter to the Archbp. Baldwin of Pisa, *Sancti desiderii vestri;* and another Suo—Vi—*Sicut depinxi me;* also a third to the Brothers of *Gratia Dei*, (Grâce Dieu), *Qui dabit me pennas.* The last

Closely allied to the Toledo MS. is Codex x. (F. 249) in the Library of the *Real Academia de la Historia* in Madrid, which contains, however, only three of the six new letters and these in a mutilated condition. [1]

One (No. 7) exists in the library of the old Cistercian monastery at Lilienfeld, near S. Pölten.

One (No. 8) from the Codex Monacensis, belonging to the monastery at Tegensee.

One (No. 9) from the Cartulary of Lonway.

Two (Nos. 10 and 11) in the Public Library at S. Omer.

Ten (Nos. 12 and 1—9 in Appendix) from among the MSS. in the British Museum, viz., No. 12 from the Additional Manuscripts No. 22634; and Nos. 1—9 of the Appendix, in No. 6047 of the same (Folio MS. on paper

is the well-known letter 174 to the Canons of Lyons, concerning the immaculate Conception of the Mother of God. Several sermons of the Saint follow, and on the last page some verses without any connection with Bernard (Hüffer, p. 190.)

[1] This parchment MS. which is in quarto of two columns, was written in the beginning of the 13th century, and has no page numbers. It belonged formerly to the Benedictine Monastery of S. Pedro de Cardeña, near Burgos, and was, according to the writer's note, *Frayre Guillelmo de Burgos escripsso este libro* etc., probably written there. His last note is at the end of the Codex, beginning the *Vita Bernardi*, which contains the usual 5 books.

Therefore the letters found are 174, 238, 218, 219, 231 etc., exactly as in the Toledo MS., but of the new pieces in Madrid, only the letter to Umbald is preserved; also the beginning of that to Innocent II. and the middle of the letter to Baldwin. The remainder was written on two leaves which have at a later time been cut away. The first words of the following leaf, *Et moti sunt sicut ebrius* etc., belong already to the beginning of the Tract *De moribus et officio episcoporum* which with the four sermons *super missus est* close the MS. (Hüffer, p. 191.

and a few parchment sheets: written in the 15th century). [1]

No. 10 appears among the Royal MSS. 5 F. 7, membr. S. 13.

Two others, Nos. 11 and 12, are found in a MS. belonging to the Library of Corpus Christi College, Oxford, (No. 137, 4° min. s. 12 *exeuntis*, fol. 99) and also in the Bodleian Library (c. 314, 4° min. s. 17 ex.). Farther details of each are given under the separate letters.

This brings the number of letters up to 484: and if the twenty-seven letters of Mabillon's Appendix be reckoned in addition to these, as has usually been done, the gross total will reach 511.

It cannot be said that these new letters (as Dr. Hüffer himself observes) are especially interesting in themselves.

[1] It also contains on Folio 1 to 161 a collection of Bernard letters, amongst which on Folio 125a, the first unknown letter is found, *Ad Treverensem Archiepiscopum*; the same is addressed to the Archbp. Albero of Montreuil (1131—1152) and admonishes him to energetic action in the miserable condition of the nunnery of S. Maur in Verdun.

A second new letter (Folio 160a) to Queen Adelaide, consort to Louis VI. of France, requests forgiveness for a bondman of hers, Wiscard. The letters immediately following, to the Chancellor S. and the nobleman Ebal de Florennes, request their help for the foundation of two monasteries. No 5 (Folio 160b) is a short letter of recommendation for a priest Eberhard, to the Count of Blois. No. 6 shows S. Bernard as spiritual guide to Count William II. of Nevers, who in 1147 had made a vow to retire as monk into the great Carthusian house of Grenoble. No. 7 must be addressed to him or his son, of the same name, if this letter is addressed to a Count of Nevers at all.

An eighth letter (Folio 161a) requests that great friend and admirer of S. Bernard, Theobald, Count of Blois and Champagne, to pardon the disobedient bondsman Anserich. The short following letter requests an unnamed friend to speak to the count in favour of the prayer of the above letter.

It is principally as having been written by (or addressed to) S. Bernard that they engage the attention of the student.

The letter from Clairvaux, however, to Pope Eugenius (No. 7) is *naive* and touching in its display of feeling: while that to Pope Lucius (No. 12 Appendix) throws a slight amount of light on the disputed election at York in connect.on with earlier letters of S. Bernard (which are referred to in the notes) on the same subject.

A letter has been recently republished as having possibly come from the pen of S. Bernard, bearing the superscription: "To the Knight RAYMUND, of Castle Ambrose." [1]

The title of this letter in the edition of 1640 (Paris: 1640, col. 1926.) is as follows.

"Letter of Bernard Sylvester, a man very learned indeed, concerning the management of property: it has been inserted in this volume, because some think it to have been composed by Saint Bernard."

The Letter is found in a MS. marked KK. I. 5 in the Cambridge University Library, and was edited in 1870 for the Early English Text Society by the Rev. J. Rawson Lumby, M.A.

In this MS. it is accompanied by a paraphrase in Scottish verse, by no means a close rendering of the original, and with frequent omissions.

This letter is not included in the edition of Mabillon: nor indeed could any one who had even a moderate acquaintance with the writings of S. Bernard suppose it to be from his pen.

[1] Or, of the Castle of S. Angelo.

It is entirely unlike his style and his manner of treating subjects; and finally, the sentiments it expresses are quite contrary to his opinions. There can be no doubt that it is from the pen of Bernard Sylvester, a cleric of Utrecht, who is probably the same person who is praised by Gervase of Tilbury as a poet of great merit. [1]

It would be difficult to account for the letter having been attributed to S. Bernard of Clairvaux by the anonymous scribe of the MS. into which it has been copied, were it not for his fame, which predisposed simple people who knew only of one person of eminence as a writer, who was named Bernard, to attribute writings which came in their way under that name, to him.

But the fact is there were not less than forty such persons named Bernard, and all distinguished enough to have left their names to the knowledge of history.

It is to be observed that in the latest edition of the collected works of S. Bernard (Paris; Migne. Third edition, 1879. Vol. i. cols. 645—651), this letter has been introduced. The present Editor has not seen his way to follow the example.

But he has derived from that edition, in all *six* Letters and documents: of which two (Nos. 485, 486) are examples of the circular letters sent by S. Bernard in great numbers to the sovereigns, nobles and people of the various countries in Europe, on the subject of the Second Crusade, when he had been entrusted by the Pope with the charge of inducing the nations of Europe to undertake it. These should be compared with Letter 363 (vol. ii. p. 906) and the note attached thereto, which refers to other circular letters of a similar kind.

---

[1] See Ducange, Glossary *s. v. Cisimus*

It is probable that further search in libraries may in the course of time, bring to light still more of such letters.

No. 488, again, is a very remarkable letter, as containing a "Mirror for Monks" in a very brief form, but with wonderful energy of expression. It is to be regretted that there is no clue to the identity of the person to whom it was addressed.

No. 490 is to be observed, as apparently speaking of Bernard, during his lifetime, as "of blessed memory" (*beatæ memoriæ*); as to which, see note *in loc.*

It would have been easy to increase largely this number, by including letters which are doubtful or certainly spurious; and those which are addressed by other persons to the Saint. But these would (1) have occupied much space; (2) they did not appear to be essential to the object of such an edition as the present. To a biographer of S. Bernard they are not without their usefulness and value: to an edition of the Saint's own works they do not seem indispensable.

There are other mentions of S. Bernard in the same Cambridge MS. already referred to, which are possibly of sufficient interest to be subjoined in a note.[1]

---

[1] "Item Sanct barnard sais that It is mar spedfull, needful and profitable to the manis saul heill to her mess, with clen hart and gud devotionne, na for to gif for the luf of god the fee of sa mickle laud as a man may ourgang quhill the mess is in doinge.

"Verteuis of the Mess" MS. KK. I. 5 Cambridge University Library.

Portions of this piece on "The Verteuis of the Mess" are like parts of "The Vertue of ye Masse" printed by Wynkyn deWorde.

But St. Bernard's testimony runs thus in the verse (Stanza 68): "herynge of masse gyveth a grete reward, goostly helth

Lastly the Percy Society reprinted in 1842 from a MS. in the British Museum, (Harleian MSS. 1845. ff. 15, 16,) the following:

Legitur in Vita Sancti Bernardi Abbatis Clarevallis, quod Demon sibi semel apparuit, dicens se scire octo versus in Psalterio, quosque cotidie diceret, tanti meriti acquireret, ac si totum Psalterium Davidicum decantasset. Et cum beatus Bernardus instaret ut sibi eosdem versus ostenderet, ille vero hoc facere recusaret; tunc beatus Bernardus, "Scio," in [quit] "quid faciam: nam quotidie legam totum Psalterium, deinceps; sicque predictos versus non obmittam." Quod cum audisset Demon, ne tantum bonum faceret, pocius sibi hos versus ostendit. Sunt antem qui sequuntur."

" Illumina oculos meos, ne unquam obdormiam in morte: ne quando dicat inimicus meus 'Prevalui adversus eum." (Ps xii. 4).

" In manus tuas, Domine, commendo spiritum meum; redemiste me, Domine Deus veritatis." (Ps. xxx. 6).

"Locutus sum in lingua mea 'Notum michi fac' Domine, finem meum."

" Et numerum dierum meorum, quis est: ut sciam quid desit michi." (Ps. xxxviii. 5, 6).

"Fac mecum signum im bono, ut videant qui te oderunt, et confudantur: quoniam tu, Domine, adjuvisti me, et consolatus es me." (Ps. lxxxv. 16).

." Dirupisti, Domine, vincula mea: tibi sacrificabo hostiam laudis, et nomen Domini invocabo." (Ps. cxv. 7).

agayne all sekenesse, and medycyne recorde of Saynt Bernarde, to people innocent that playne for weykenesse, to faythe, refresshynge in werynesse and to folke that gone in pylgrymage, it maketh them stronge set them in sykenesse, gracyously to explete theyr vyage."

(Early English Text Society. 1870).

"*Periit fuga a me: et non est qui requiret animam [meam].*" (Ps. clxi. 6).

"*Clamavi ad te, Domine: dixi, 'Tu es spes mea, porcio mea in terra vivencium.*" (Ps. cxli. 7).

ORACIO DICENDA POST HOS VERSUS.

Omnipotens sempiterne Deus! qui Ezechie Regi, inde te cum lacrimis humiliter, deprecanti, vite spacium protendisti! Concede michi indigno famulo tuo, ante diem mortis meo, tantum vite spacium, quo, ad mensuram, ut omnia peccata mea valeam deplorarem; ei veniam ac graciam, secundum misericordiam tuam, consequi merear. Per Christum.

ITEM ALIA ORAICO.

"*Domine Jesu C[h]riste! per illam amaritudinem mortis quam sustinuisti pro me in cruce, maxime cum anima tua egressa fuit de corpore tuo; miserere anime in gressu suo. Amen.*" [Royal MS. 17. A. xxvii. ff. 86b—88b].

We redenne in the Lyf of Seynt Bernard, that the Develle seyd to him, he knew VIII. versus in the Sauter tho wheche versus and a man sey hem wyche day, he schal never be dampnade. And Seynt Bernard askut whiche they were; and he sayde he schulde never wyte fro hym. And he sayde he wolde ellus say the hol Sauter uche day.

And he answerud and sayd, he wold razure telle him whiche they wer; and zese hit arne."

The above was known as the "PSALTER OF S. BERNARD."

In the present volume are also included the *Four Homilies* "*De Laudibus Virginis Matris,*" or *Super Missus est.*

The Sermons "*De Tempore*" from that for the First Sunday in Advent to the First for the Nativity; nineteen in all.

A Sermon discovered by Dr. Hüffer in the Royal Library at Brussels, and said to have been (partially) delivered before the Council at Chartres in A.D. 1151, will be included among those *De Diversis.*

S. J. E.

Soli Deo Gloria.

LIST AND ORDER OF THE LETTERS OF S. BERNARD.

III

COMPARATIVE TABLE OF THE NUMBERING
OF S. BERNARD'S LETTERS.

ENG. EDIT. EARLIER EDD. HORST AND MABILLON 2nd. HüFFER.

E. E.		HOR.	MAB.	HÜFF.
Letter	309 [1]	361 (Edit. Royal)	309	
	310	310	310	
	311	313	311	
	312	new	312	
	313	371	313	
	314	318	318	
	315	344	315	
	316	375	316	
	317	320	317	
	318	329	318	
	319	372	319	
	320	381	320	
	321	382	321	
	322	351	322	
	323	new	323	
	324	336	324	
	325	337	325	
	326	391	326	
	327	392	327	
	328	new	328	
	329	new	329	

[1] Up to this point the "received order" of the Letters has been retained by D. Mabillon. See Preface, Vol. I. pp. 14—16 (Eng. Edit.)

E. E.		HOR.	MAB.	HÜFF.
Letter	330	new	330	
	331	new	331	
	332	new	332	
	333	new	333	
	334	new	334	
	335	new	335	
	336	new	336	
	337	370	337	
	338	369	338	
	339	327	339	
	340	new	340	
	341	315	341	
	342	new	342	
	343	new	343	
	344	new	344	
	345.	321	345	
	346	377	346	
	347	378	347	
	348	388	348	
	349	330	349	
	350	331	350	
	351	new	351	
	352	new	352	
	353	379	353	
	354	new	354	
	355	376	355	
	356	316	356	
	357	317	357	
	358	374	358	
	359	new	359	
	360	380	360	
	361	383	361	
	362	334	362	

E. E.		HOR.	MAB.	HÜFF.
Letter	363	322	363	
	364	355	364	
	365	323	365	
	366	386	366	
	367	332	367	
	368	335	368	
	369	356	369	
	370	357	370	
	371	363	371	
	372	new	372	
	373	new	373	
	374	311	374	
	375	390	375	
	376	358	376	
	377	359	377	
	378	360	378	
	379	361	379	
	380	362	380	
	381	364	381	
	382	324	382	
	383	342	383	
	384	343	384	
	385	341	385	
	386	333	386	
	387	352	387	
	388	353	388	
	389	354	389	
	390	314	390	
	391	347	391	
	392	new	392	
	393	new	393	
	394	new	394	
	395	325	395	

E. E.		HOR.	MAB.	HÜFF.
Letter	396	365	396	
	397	387	397	
	398	312	398	
	399	319	399	
	400	320	400	
	401	338	401	
	402	336	402	
	403	340	403	
	404	345	404	
	405	346	405	
	406	new	406	
	407	348	407	
	408	349	408	
	409	350	409	
	410	366	410	
	411	373	411	
	412	new	412	
	413	389	413	
	414	328	414	
	415	393	415	
	416	new	416	
	417	new	417	
	418	new	418	
	419	new	419	
	420	new	420	
	421	new	421	
	422	new	422	
	423	new	423	
	424	new	424	
	425	new	425	
	426	new	426	
	427	391 See note to Ep. 420.	427	
	428	new	428	

E. E.		HOR.	MAB.	HÜFF.
Letter	429	316 See note to Ep. 420.	429	
	430	new	430	
	431	new	431	
	432	new	432	
	433	new	433	
	434	new	434	
	435	new	435	
	436	new	436	
	437	new	437	
	438	new	438	
	439	new	439	
	440	new	440	
	441	new	441	
	442	new	442	
	443	417 Id.	443	
	444	new	444	
	445	new	445	
	446	new	446	
	447	new	447	
	448	new	448	
	449	new	449	
	450	new	450	
	451	86 Id.	451	
	452	413 Id.	452	
	453	new	453	
	454	new	454	
	455	new	455	
	456	new	456	
	457	new	457	
	458	new	458	
	459	new	479	
	460	new	474	
	461	new	new	I

E. E.		HOR.	MAB.	HÜFF.	
Letter	462	new	new	2	
	463	new	new	3	
	464	new	new	4	
	465	new	new	5	
	466	new	new	6	
	467	new	new	7	
	468	new	new	8	
	469	new	new	9	
	470	new	new	10	
	471	new	new	11	
	472	new	new	12	
	473	new	new	1	Appendix.
	474	new	new	2	,,
	475	new	new	3	,,
	476	new	new	4	,,
	477	new	new	5	,,
	478	new	new	6	,,
	479	new	new	7	,,
	480	new	new	8	,,
	481	new	new	9	,,
	482	new	new	10	,,
	483	new	new	11	,,
	484	new	new	12	Migne.
	485	new	new	new	457
	486	new	new	new	458
	487	new	new	new	459
	488	new	new	new	460
	489	new	new	*sine num.*	
	490	new	new	,,	

IV.

INDEX OF SERMONS.

PREFACE

Of Dom. John Mabillon to the Sermons

OF

S. BERNARD.

1. THE sermons or homilies of the Fathers are, as a rule, less carefully constructed than the other monuments of their genius, and not so elegantly finished. The praise belongs to S. Bernard, beyond all, or nearly all other writers, that his sermons are meritorious, not less in polish and beauty of style, in variety of sentiments and in loftiness of thought, than his other writings, nor are they less endued with piety and gifts of grace. In seeking the cause of this superiority, I find it not only in the penetration, ardour and quickness of his intellect, which rendered it eminently suited for making truths clear to his hearers, and enabled him to touch and affect their feelings; but also in the very different character of the audiences for whose benefit they were delivered. For the ancient Fathers, having no other object but to instruct the people in general in the doctrines of the Faith, and the rules of Christian life, affected a style simple and less elevated, in the interest of the hearers themselves.

But Bernard, on the contrary, had most frequently for

hearers only men who were versed in spiritual things, and in the knowledge of the Scriptures, and many of whom had in the world been distinguished for their high rank, or their knowledge; and therefore he thought it proper to prepare and perfect his discourses, with the greatest labour and care, in respect to their knowledge and former rank. [1] That is the reason, I imagine, why not only his beautiful Sermons on the Canticles, which were finished with particular care, but also those which he has written for the great Festivals of the Christian year, or on various subjects, are generally preferred to the Sermons or Homilies of the Fathers, and of other pious and learned men.

II. Nor is this merely my private opinion of the Sermons of Bernard, nor is it confined to myself; it is also that of men who have a high name in literature, who have expressed themselves to the same effect, both in their discourses and in their writings: I shall cite two of the most distinguished only, whose authority, both in respect of doctrine and knowledge, is inferior to none. First, Justus Lipsius in his letter 49 to Albert le Mire, speaking of Sermons and sacred oratory, says: "Among the Latins, S. Bernard extorts my admiration and carries me away by his warmth and vehemence; he also instructs and impresses on account of the polish and acuteness of his sentiments, which he blends frequently to edification." Thus speaks this man of profound knowledge, after having sought out carefully from among the Fathers the perfect model of the sacred orator, whom he could put forward to be imitated: he is of opinion that there is no one who has realized more fully this ideal than Bernard, whom he therefore prefers to all the Latin Fathers. It may excite surprise if I give

[1] Life of S. Bernard B. iii. c. 3. 1.

to Bernard the preference, even placing him above the Greek Fathers, who excelled in that department of oratory; nor should I have ventured to express this opinion on my own responsibility, or if I had not in its favour the judgment of a man so eminent as Henry Valesius, whose brother Adrian, a worthy relative of so great a man, thus states in the life of him which he has written: "For three or four years before his death, as often as his disease obliged him to remain at home upon Festivals, he caused to be read aloud to him, ('*ab anagnoste suo*'=reader) the Sermons of Bernard, Abbot of Clairvaux : which he listened to with great attention and even eagerness. He was of opinion, and had been in the habit of saying to his friends, that they ought to devote Sundays and Festivals, not to the pursuit of literature but to the praises of God; and that for his part he found the Homilies and Sermons of Bernard more adapted to arouse and to strengthen feelings of devotion and piety in the soul, than those of any other of the Fathers, Greek or Latin." I adduce this testimony with the greater willingness, that the opinion of so great a man respecting the merit of these Sermons appears to me to be entitled to very great weight: and because it is a cause of joy to me to recall here the memory of that great man, who formerly deigned to honour me with his friendship and intimacy.

III. To the testimony of these two more recent authors, it would be easy to add many of an earlier age who have spoken of Bernard, not otherwise than as a preacher truly apostolic: among whom I ought not to pass over Erasmus, a man commonly more liberal with gibes than praises; he speaks thus of Bernard in his treatise, "On the Art of Preaching," B. ii.: "Bernard is an eloquent preacher, much more by nature than by art; he is full of charm and vivacity and knows how to reach and move the affections." But I fear lest in seeking to prove a fact, which few will wish to contest, I may be hindered in treating of matters of greater moment. Wherefore I pass on to treat of other things: and first, to inquire wherefore Bernard addressed his discourses to his brethren more frequently than the rules of his Order prescribed: secondly, at what time, that is to say, on what days and at what hours of the day, did he preach? Thirdly, in what language. Lastly, what principles of Christian and religious life was it his purpose chiefly to inculcate upon his hearers. Upon each of these subjects, I propose to enter into various particulars : both to exhibit the chief principles of his teaching and to lay down certain *criteria* by which to distinguish the Sermons which are really his, from those wrongly attributed to him.

IV. According to the *Use of Citeaux*, c. 67, it was the custom among the Cistercians that Sermons should be preached 'in Chapter' on the following days: "Christmas Day, the Epiphany, Palm Sunday, Easter Day, Ascension Day, Whitsunday, all the Festivals of S. Mary, the Nativity of S. John Baptist, the Festivals of the Apostles S. Peter and S. Paul, of S. Benedict, of All Saints; and on the First Sunday in Advent." There is no mention anywhere, as far I know, of preaching on simple weekdays or ordinary *ferias*, on which Bernard very frequently used to preach. Thus in his First Sermon for Septuagesima, n. 2, he says: "I speak to you very frequently, even beyond the custom of our Order."

V. I find two reasons why he who was emphatically a Religious and most observant of the discipline of his Rule, acted thus. The first was the command of the Abbots of his Order, who had imposed this duty upon

Bernard as an equivalent in *spiritua* labour for the labour
of body which he was unable to perform. This reason he
himself adduces in Serm. x. on Ps. xci., in these words:
"If I speak to you more frequently than is the custom of
our Order, I do this, not from any presumption of my
own, but from the direction of my venerable brethren and
co-Abbots who have enjoined this upon me; although they
would not permit its being done indiscriminately .... For I
should not now speak to you,if I were able to labour with you.
That would perhaps be a more efficacious Sermon to you:
it would certainly make my own conscience better satisfied.
But since that is forbidden to me for the present on account
of my sins, and by the numerous bodily infirmities which,
as you know, weigh upon me: may I, though I have myself
taught rather than acted, have the grace to be found in the
kingdom of God, though I be even the last there!" This was
the cause and occasion of his expounding Ps. xc. [1] on the
ferial days of Lent, which he continued to do in consecutive
Sermons, as frequently as the cails of pressing business and
the care of receiving guests permitted. Each of these hindran-
ces tended to withdraw him from preaching as frequently as
the authority of his co-Abbots and his own ardent charity and
zeal for the spiritual progress of his brethren, would have urged
him to do. This zeal was the second reason of which I
spoke. Thus he says in Sermon v. *De Quadragesima*, n. 1 :
"The charity with which I am animated on your account,
my brethren, presses me to address you: I should do so
more often were I not hindered by many occupations."
And again in Serm. viii. on Ps. xc. : "I should indeed speak
to you more briefly, beloved, could I do so more frequently .... but as often as, by the hard pressure of the
time, I am hindered most reluctantly, for many days per-

---

[1] *I. e.*, Ps. xci. according to the English version. [E.]

haps, from encouraging and consoling you; so often, when
the time again permits me to discharge the duty for which
I am so ready, my discourse may seem to be drawn out
somewhat long; but I think that none of you will wonder
at it." He calls the pressure of business and of guests 'the
hard pressure of the time,' and complains of it more than
once in his Sermons on the Canticles. But though Bernard
was thus hindered from preaching as frequently as he wished;
his Sermons were sufficiently frequent to make him fear
that he might cause in his hearers a distaste for spiritual
things. He says in his Sermon ii. on SS. Peter and Paul,
n. 1: "One thing I fear; lest you should hear the words of
salvation so often, that you should begin to regard them
as only words, and as of little worth." The holy Doctor
makes the same observation in Sermon xxxv. on the
Canticles, n. 9: "If you take the food of the body when
you are satiated and are without appetite, not only is it of
no benefit, but is even very hurtful; much more the food of
the soul, when it is taken with dislike and loathing,
becomes rather a trouble to the conscience than an increase in knowledge."

VI. As to the time at which this exposition of spiritual
things took place, Bernard himself indicates in various passages of his discourses when it was. There was scarcely a
day left vacant by these addresses, when he was not absent
or hindered by other duties. This is shown by many of the
Sermons *De Tempore* and *De Sanctis*, some of those *De
Diversis*, as well as by those very beautiful sermons *in Cantica*; without saying much of those brief addresses and
'Thoughts' which are, as it were, the first sketches of his
sermons.

For when some spiritual thoughts came into his mind,
which he had not the leisure to develop into a complete

Sermon, he confided those sacred germs to the wax of his tablets, in order to develop them when he should have time and leisure. We learn this from Ernald: [1] "The man of God used to dictate, and sometimes himself to write down on his waxen tablets the thoughts with which his mind was inspired from on high, and did not suffer them to perish."

VII. He chose for preaching, sometimes the morning hours after Prime and before the common labour, or before Mass; and sometimes the evening hours. He indicates the former time in Sermon x. on Ps. xci., n. 6 : "I fear to have overstayed my time. For that great man, your and my common Abbot, [2] is well known to have assigned this hour, not for preaching, but for manual labour." Sermon i. on the Feast of S. Michael, shows at the end that the time for Celebration was at hand: "but now the hour is expired, and we must go to Mass"; and on the Festival of All Saints, Serm. i. n. 3 : "But now we have to be fed by His acts and His words; for now we go to receive by His grace the pure and inviolable [3] Sacrament of the Lord's Body on the holy Table of His Altar." Again in Serm. ii., at the end: "But it is time to finish this discourse, for the Celebration of the solemnities of Mass summons us." As for evening sermons, we see that they took place sometimes, by his Serm. i. on S. Malachi, n. 8 : "Now the day has already fallen, and the sermon has gone on longer than I had expected." And still more plainly in Serm: xxxviii. *De Diversis*, n. 3. "We must separate : for I hear the bell, the time for evening prayer has already come." The Sermons *in Cantica*

[1] Life B. ii. n. 51.
[2] *I. e.*, S. Benedict.
[3] *Illibatum.* The word has both meanings.

show the same thing, as we shall see when we come to speak of them.

VIII. We have now to enquire whether the Sermons of Bernard were preached in Latin, or in [French,] the vulgar tongue. It is by no means easy to reply. For there seem to have been present as listeners to those sermons, the lay-brothers; who were men entirely ignorant, who knew nothing at all of Latin, who used only the idiom of the country, which was that corruptly called "Romana" universally among the authors of those times; particularly in Nithard, the historian of that epoch, in Gerard, author of the Life of Abbot Adalard, and in the Chronograph of Saint Tron, where we see that this idiom is corruptly called *Romana* and among the Germans *Walloon*. Thus Peter, chaplain of Louis le Jeune, King of France, says in his letter to the Abbot of Lagny: "a certain young man, a relative of mine, was sent to me out of England in order to learn *Romanam linguam*," [1] that is the common French of that day.

Those who spoke that language, did not understand Latin at all, not even in the ninth century, still less in the eleventh, as appears from the little book on the *Vision of Flotildis* or *Chlotildis*, in which certain presbyters are accused "who are not able to understand even the words which they read." [2] If, then, the unlearned brethren were present at the Sermons of Bernard, it is very improbable that those Sermons were preached in Latin. And indeed a copy of the Sermons of Bernard *De Tempore* exists in the convent of the Feuillant Fathers in Paris, [3] written in the French of the time of S. Bernard, as appears by the

[1] Duchesne, Tom. iv. p. 742.
[2] Duchesne, Tom. ii. p. 625.
[3] *Viz.*, in the time of Mabillon, *circa* 1690.

character of the writing and the antiquity of the idiom.
Add to this that Bernard in the beginning of Ep. 17 to
the Cardinal-deacon Peter, mentions that his scholars
had drawn up in their language (*stilo*) fragments of his
Sermons which they had heard, as they had understood
them; which seems to indicate that he meant, not in the
form in which they had been preached, but in another,
given to them by the hearers. He expresses himself in
almost the same terms in the following letter, where he
adds: "And perhaps they have them still." It may
perhaps be inferred from this, that Bernard had spoken
in the vernacular, to adapt himself to the lay-brethren,
and that his disciples had afterwards turned the sermons
into Latin.

IX. Many things show that the lay-brethren were entirely illiterate, and unacquainted with Latin. Those brethren were admitted to the choir, but had not the tonsure:
and they were quite distinct from the *Conversi*. Mention
is made of this matter in the *Life of S. Bernard*, B. vii.
c. 23, where we read: "this formula of the Divine science
viz., '*Let not the wise glory in his wisdom*' etc., has been
very perfectly imitated by those, who were trained in the
principles of heavenly philosophy at Clairvaux under our
holy Father Bernard: and there were of them not only
men well educated and acquainted with the mysteries of
the holy law, but also many laymen and uneducated, who
although they had not attained that degree of human
knowledge which would help them to attain the height of
perfection, yet they had illuminating grace and the life-
giving Spirit, who taught them all things that they needed
to. know, vastly more effectually than by any secular
learning. Of such was a certain lay-monk, learned, not
in grammar, but in the Spirit" etc. What was the con-

dition of ignorance of these lay-brothers, who were entirely unacquainted with the Latin tongue and scarcely
knew the Alphabet, we learn from John Eremita in his
letters to Peter, Bishop of Tusculum, respecting his Life
of S. Bernard. He says (n. 2): "A certain monk, a true
and sincere lover of the venerable Abbot, was, as it happened, walking about with a certain lay-brother, Humbert
by name, in a thicket beside the monastery of Clairvaux;
and holding in his hands a book of the miracles of the
holy father, was expounding it to him in the 'Roman' that
is, the vernacular idiom, for his own edification as well as
that of his companion." But why should he expound it
in the Roman or French tongue, unless that lay-brother
was ignorant of Latin?

Such also was that other layman, praised just below by
the same John (n. 3.), who although he had not previously
known even the alphabet, yet "by the grace of God which
enlightened his intelligence, and by the intercession of certain brethren, made such progress in a short time that he
learned not only to read passably, but also to sing fairly
as well. Later on, by practice, and the grace of God assisting,
he began to understand something of the signification of
words, and made some progress in that kind of knowledge." Which no one can help seeing is spoken of the
Latin tongue. It was not only of the Cistercians, but also
among other Orders that this class of lay-brothers was
received: such as he of whom Godfrey, Abbot of Vendôme,
B. iii. Ep. 8, speaks: who "because he was a layman,
spoke, not Latin, which he had never learned, but his native
tongue." I do not refer here to the brothers *conversi*,
although the same observations apply to them as to the
lay-brothers; and the same arguments go to show that
they also were ignorant of Latin. Which is also confirmed by the testimony of Herbert, in the *Miracles of*

Clairvaux: B. i. c. 16, where, in speaking of a certain *conversus*, he says, "who when he had come to the point of death, began to speak in the Latin tongue, though he had never learned Latin. Therefore it may be laid down as a general rule that the Latin language was not in common use among the vulgar, even if public documents were couched in Latin. It is true that Peter the Venerable, writing to Pope Celestine (B. iv. Ep. 18) to acknowledge his receipt of the letter announcing Celestine's election, says that he had made it known (*exposuisse*) in Chapter "both to the educated, and to the uneducated, whom we call *conversi*;" that is, had explained it in the vernacular, which would have been useless if they had been acquainted with Latin. Lastly, Ep. 67 of Bernard shows that in his day, as at the present time, the various provinces of France had each its peculiar idiom: for he says to the monks of Flay, near Beauvais, that they and his monks of Clairvaux spoke with unlike languages (*dissimilibus linguis*).

X. It is very true that this was the case: but it is none the less true also, at least it is our decided opinion, that the Sermons of Bernard were composed in Latin, preached in Latin, and in the same language reported by his disciples. This is shown in the first place by the constant and characteristic play upon words, which rests wholly upon the use of that language, then by the marked similitude of style in the Sermons to his other books and treatises.

Add to this that the Carthusians, who admitted lay-brothers as well, used all through that period the Latin language in public preaching to their brethren, and have continued the custom up to the present time. Besides, we must needs think that Bernard's other Sermons were composed in the same manner, as his *Exposition of the Canticles*: which Sermons were undoubtedly written in the same language in which they were preached, as we see from a passage in Serm. liv. n. 1: "They were written as they were spoken, and composed, like my other Sermons, with the pen in the hand, so as to recover more easily what perhaps might have escaped the memory."   .

XI. This passage explains the sense of the phrase quoted above from Ep. 18, where we saw that certain Religious of those who were in the habit of attending the sermons of St Bernard, reported them '*stilo*,' that is by the pen or simply in writing, not from their own recollection of their delivery. Thus Nicholas of Clairvaux in his Ep. 39: "the hand is not enough to hold the pen." In the same sense is to be understood that phrase in the end of Ep. 304: "He who reads this let them recognize my (*stilum*) writing, for I have myself written it." Where '*stilus*' (pen) undoubtedly is taken in the sense of *scriptura* (writing) and '*dictare*' (dictate) in the sense of *scribere* (write). So at the end of Ep. 310: "These words I have myself written (*dictavi*) so that by seeing my well-known writing, you may recognize the disposition of my heart!" Nothing can be more clear: for it is not from the pen, but from the handwriting, that the hand of a man is recognized. Add to this what is said by William (Life B. i. n. 70): "His writings are witnesses of this, either those which he himself wrote or which others have taken down from his mouth." All these testimonies bring me to believe that the sermons of S. Bernard have come down to us in no other language or wording than that in which they were delivered by him: and that the MS. of the Feuillants contains not the original, but only a translation from the Latin into the vulgar tongue. Indeed the manuscript which is looked upon as an autograph, was not written until after the death of Bernard: as the inscription shows in which he is called *Saint*, as we shall see later on. More than once too, he addresses his hearers as being men versed in theology; thus in Serm. iii. on SS. Peter and Paul, n. 6: "You no doubt remember, for I speak to men who know the Law," etc., and in Serm. vii. on Ps. xci., n. 5 : " I speak of Balaam : do you recall him, you who know the sacred histories !" In his Sermon for the Festival of Easter: "these are the words of the Apocalypse : let those learn them who have not read them : let those who have, recall them !" More plainly in Serm. iv. for the Nativity : "I speak to those who know the Scriptures." Compare also Serm. x. on Ps. xci., n. 2. From all these expressions we may infer that the hearers of Bernard were educated men and acquainted with Latin.

XII. Nor need we be shaken in this opinion, by the objection drawn from the case of the lay-brothers. To these, perhaps, other sermons were delivered in a language more familiar; if they did not rather attend with the *conversi* at a Chapter held specially for them, which by the custom of the Order was done each Sunday, with a Sermon in the vernacular. Nevertheless, Ep. 24 of Nicholas of Clairvaux (which we discuss below) raises some difficulties on this point.

XIII. It is without doubt that in those exhortations which the Saint delivered to *conversi*, or to strangers and men in the world, he used the vernacular. To the former class belongs that saying related of a certain *conversus* when dying, who having been encouraged by Bernard to hope in Christ, replied that he was secure of

Christ's mercy. Then having been cautioned by the Saint not to be too secure, he replies: "If all those things are true which you have urged upon us so often in your preachings, namely, that the kingdom of God is not to be obtained by the nobility or the riches of this world, but by the virtue of obedience alone; for this one sentiment, as a brief word from the Lord, I have kept in memory by careful endeavour," etc. Bernard therefore was in the habit of preaching to the *conversi*, and this he did on Sundays in their own Chapter, which is prescribed by the ancient rules of the Cistercians (Distinct. xiv., c. 4.)

XIV. Nor was the holy Doctor wanting in this duty even towards seculars and strangers, if ever the occasion so to do presented itself, or charity called upon him to do it; as Geoffrey testifies (Life B. iii. c. 3. n. 8): "He always strove to be useful to the people of God, but never consented to domineer over them. But he rarely went forth to preach except perhaps to places very near at hand. But as often as some necessity drew him forth, he would sow beside all waters, proclaiming the word of God in private and in public. He used to do this at the bidding of the Pope: and also at the wish of other Bishops wheresoever one of them happened to be present." The same Geoffrey describes in the same book of his Life (n. 7) the events which took place in the German territory, when Bernard went thither to preach the Crusade at the command of Pope Eugenius iii. He says: "Honey and milk were under his tongue.... Thence it was that when he spoke to the population of those countries, he produced a marvellous impression. Their piety seemed wonderfully edified by his discourses, notwithstanding that they, speaking another language, could not understand what he said:

indeed, more than they could have been by the most skilful interpreter who translated after him what he had said: and the power of his words moved them strongly, as was shown beyond a possibility of doubt by their shedding tears and beating their breasts. From the Germans, "inasmuch as they were men speaking another language," not understanding his sermons, we gather that he used his native language, that is, the French. Indeed the monk Philip in B. i. n. 16 of his *Miracles of S. Bernard*, says, that he spoke among the Germans the "Romana lingua," that is the French. Ekkehard Junior, in his book of *The Misfortunes of the Abbey of S. Gall*, speaking of a certain illiterate monk of the 9th century, says that Tutilo "spoke to his companions in the Latin language in order that this man might not understand him." The same remark may be made of the English, not to speak of others: for whose benefit King Alfred caused to be translated the *Fastoral Care* of Gregory the Great and the History of Bede into the Saxon language. About the same time the Gospels and the Rule of S. Benedict were translated into German.

XV. But perhaps I am delaying longer on these matters than their importance justifies; and yet I cannot regret it, since it all tends to show the apostolical zeal and care of the Saint. Furthermore, in his Sermons, as Geoffrey testifies in the passage already cited, "he used the Scriptures so appositely and with such facility, that it seemed not that he followed the text, but that he divined it, and led it, so to speak, whither he would, himself following as his leader the author of the Scriptures, that is, the Divine Spirit."

XVI. It will not be irrelevant now to consider briefly what principles, especially relating to the Religious life, he was wont to draw from the holy Scriptures, and inculcate upon his monks in his sermons. One of the chief was that, according to the Apostle, they ought to regard themselves as strangers and pilgrims in this world: upon which subject I may cite two passages; one from Serm. i. for the Epiphany, n. 1 : "Upon this subject, I have it at heart to remind you frequently, that we should never allow ourselves to forget that we are strangers and pilgrims, far from our fatherland, expelled from our inheritance. For whosoever has not felt this as a trouble cannot appreciate the (future) consolation : and whosoever does not feel the need of such consolation, it must be that he has not the grace of God." The other is in Serm. vii. for Lent, n. 1 : "Happy are those who show themselves to be strangers and pilgrims in this evil world, and keep themselves pure from it," etc.

XVII. Another axiom of Bernard was, that it was of the greatest advantage to monks, and to all who strive to lead a holy life, that according to the example of the Apostle, they should be forgetful of those things which are past, and press forward to those which are before. He says in Serm. ii. on the Purification, n. 3 : "For us, progress consists in this, as I remember that I have often said to you, that we should never think ourselves to have apprehended; but should always strive to go onwards, should incessantly seek to be better, and continually place our imperfections under the view of the Divine mercy." There is the same sentiment in Serm. iv. on Ps. xci., n. 3 : "It is a great virtue, and the height of security when leading a pious life, to take more heed of what is wanting in ourselves, than of that which we seem to have attained; to be forgetful of what is behind us, and desirous of what is beyond." Similar is the thought expressed in the same passage, that it is of much importance to perfection, that when we have fulfilled all the duties imposed upon us by religion and by our office, we should profess ourselves to be unprofitable servants; because that is the same thing as being unmindful of what is already done.

XVIII. A third axiom of his is this: that we should always fear, lest we should possibly fall from the grace of God. He says in Serm. v. for All Saints, n. 3: "For the present our whole blessedness consists in the fear of God.' And in Serm. i., after the Octave of Epiphany, n. 5, after having said that there are two kinds of fear, "the one lest we be cast into Hell, the other lest we be excluded from eternal life," he continues, "It is good to hold fast a third kind, which is known to those who lead a spiritual life .... For those who have tasted the food of the soul, fear to be deprived of it. In truth those who have put their hand to duties requiring strength, have need of food which gives strength .... This is the third urn ' which is significantly distinguished and separated from the others, to show that it is not for all: for the return an hundredfold is not promised to all, but only to those who have left all." That third fear, he adds in the following Sermon, n. viii. 9, "fills the soul with inquietude and care lest it should be abandoned by grace .... lest it should lose grace, so that it should become reprobate and fall daily from bad to worse, from a less fault into a greater." He develops still further his thoughts in Serm. liv. on the Canticles, n. 9. "I have learned in truth that there is nothing so efficacious for obtaining grace, for keeping and for renewing it, as to come constantly before God, not with lofty thoughts of myself, but with fear."

' An allusion to the incidents of the miracle at Cana [E].

XIX. To these axioms of Bernard, a fourth may be added, which is often found and earnestly urged in his sermons : namely, that we ought to avoid with all our powers the sin of ingratitude toward God, and to strive to show our thankfulness: especially those whom he has called out of the cares and troubles of the world. He develops that thought especially in Serm. ii. on the seven mercies of God, for the sixth Sunday after Pentecost, where he says (n. 2): "It is needful then that man should be grateful and devoted, if he desires that the gifts of grace which he has received should not only be continued to him, but augmented . . . . But we especially, whom He has separated for Himself, and chosen to serve him alone" etc. That very principle he enforces in Serm. 27 *De Diversis*, which is "against the worst of vices, ingratitude:" and among other things he writes in n. 6: "How many Religious we see and mourn over, who think that they are altogether safe, provided that they retain their habit and tonsure ! Those unhappy men do not consider how deeply their hearts are corroded by the worm of ingratitude, that it is only a mere husk of godliness they see, which hides the fact that they are penetrated entirely with this vice, so that they fail to recognize and blush for it, and to be saved by that salutary shame." And further on: "You see that those who are cleansed from the leprosy of worldly life, of which the evil qualities are manifest, do not in all points make progress in good; but that in some, the worse ulcer of secret ingratitude is formed, which is so much the more dangerous, as it is deeply seated." I should never finish, if I went on to show at as great length as I might, that this was one of the great principles of S. Bernard : but these will be at once a sufficient specimen and guide for pious readers.

XX. The doctrine of these Sermons is not only filled with piety, but is also plain, easy and presents no difficulties or cause of offence to the reader. If any less learned student should find any propositions more difficult to understand, such will be explained as they occur. I propose to examine here only one point of the doctrine of S. Bernard: namely, his opinion upon the state of holy souls after their release from the body, which he expresses in Serms. ii. iii. iv. for the festival of the Saints, in the fourth Sermon for the Dedication of a Church, and elsewhere. In the first place, the holy Doctor expresses his thought in such a manner as to show that he does so not lightly or without a feeling of his responsibility, but after laborious thought and earnest prayer: but "without presuming to judge any different opinion revealed to any one else," although "in thus believing" he thinks that he has "the mind of God" as he says in Serm. iv. for the Festival of All Saints, n. 1 and 2. Then having premised that there are three states in which souls may exist: 'in a corruptible body,' 'without body' or 'in a body that is already glorified;' he discusses the subject of the middle state, and declares his own opinion in four propositions. In the first, that those holy souls when delivered from the body, are forthwith admitted into heaven (Serm. iv. n. 1) and therefore are 'in the society of Angels' as he says in Serm. ii. on S. Malachi, n. 5. Secondly, that they dwell there "in the fulness of light" (Serm. iv. n. 1). Thirdly, that they behold Christ in His Humanity (*ibid* n. 2); but not His Divinity, because this is not given them to behold until after the Resurrection. In the meantime the holy dead are 'under the altar,' that is, they rest happily under the (protection of the) Humanity of Christ, into whose mystery the angels themselves desire to look. And in the fourth place, "they have joy in their spirit, a great gladness fills their hearts, though it is not complete" (Serm. ii. for All Saints, n. 4). Their happiness is not then 'without exception' (Serm. iii. n. 2) because of their desire to be reclothed with the body. But if this natural desire is still stronger in them, their entire affection is not yet directed freely towards God, "but is in a certain degree impeded, and causes an exception to their happiness, since their wish is drawn downwards."

The same view is expressed in the treatise *De Diligendo Deo* n. 32. Such then is the teaching of Bernard on this point, which, however, he has put forth as an opinion only, as appears from B. v. *De Consideratione* c. 4, n. 9, where he is considering the holy souls of the martyrs in the bosom of Abraham "under the altar, whatever is to be understood by that mysterious phrase, and patiently waiting in their first vesture of glory, their being clad with the second."

XXI. Although that was the opinion of Bernard, yet in various passages of his writings he attributes to them the vision of God; as when speaking of Malachi, he describes him rejoicing "in equal glory and fidelity with the Angels," (Serm. ii. on that Saint, n. 5); and declares that various Saints have merited to be admitted into the Holy of Holies "where they behold the Face of Him who there dwells, that is, the pure Glory of the unchangeable God," in one of the Sermons on the Canticles. Add to this what he says of the martyrs: that they are "plunged in the measureless sea of eternal light and luminous eternity"—(*De Diligendo Deo*, towards the end.) He speaks more clearly still in Serm. ii. on S. Victor, n. 4: "He has now entered into the heavens, which he had before had the privilege to see opened above him; but now truly beholds with open face the glory of God; and though absorbed in the contemplation of it, is yet not unmindful of the cry of the poor.—O blessed vision, by which he is transformed from glory to glory, as by the Spirit of the Lord."

But how are these expressions of Bernard to be reconciled with his former opinion, especially when he asserts in plain words in Serm. iv. for All Saints, n. 2, where he is treating professedly of this question, whether the Son after the Resurrection shall bestow upon his elect, "new and hitherto unknown delights, the delights of beholding Him face to face?" Shall we suppose that he has retracted and modified this opinion? We cannot at once affirm that he did so, since it is not possible to fix precisely the dates at which these sermons, which apparently conflict, were delivered.

XXII. Here I recall to memory a certain book of Thomas, an Englishman, on the "Middle State of Souls," in which (*Demensus* 4) he puts forth the opinion that Bernard is the first of the Fathers who has assigned a place in Heaven to the souls of the Blessed separated from their bodies by death, whilst the other and elder Fathers have taught that they would only receive this after the last Judgment; and that he again has denied to these souls the Beatific Vision of God before the Resurrection, which vision those other Fathers had believed that they would receive. Upon the former point, it is certain that Thomas was mistaken; and that he was wrong we bring forward only three witnesses, Cyprian, Alcuin, and Florus, the Deacon of Lyons, all long before the age of Bernard. Cyprian says (*Lib. de Exhortatione Martyrii* c. 12. towards the end): "How great is the glory and security . . . to close in a moment the eyes with which we have looked upon the world and upon men; and to open them immediately to behold God and Christ! You are taken away suddenly from earth to enter upon the realms of Heaven." More briefly, he says in *De Laude Martyrii*, "The martyrs taste the joy of Heaven." And he asserts in the former passage that not only the martyrs, but also the Patriarchs, the Prophets, and the Apostles are now possessors of Heaven. But Alcuin, in Ep. 81, bears witness to the doubt which existed in his time in the minds of some upon the question, but that it was secret and not openly expressed; as if they feared to be suggesting that which was erroneous, since it was against the opinion of all. These are his words: "There is a hesitation and doubt in some minds, as to whether the souls of the holy Apostles and martyrs, and of the other just made perfect, are received into the Kingdom of Heaven before the Day of Judgment," which opinion Alcuin disapproves and reckons among Spanish heresies. The opinion of Florus is more explicit still. He gives it in his Exposition of the Mass, in commenting upon those words of the Canon: *Remember, O Lord, Thy servants* etc., where he says "It is clearer than the daylight, that the souls of the Saints, as soon as they go forth from the prison house of the flesh, are received into celestial habitations." Nothing can be more conclusive than these testimonies against the theory of the Englishman Thomas, and in favour of the opinion of Bernard, or rather of the Church.

XXIII. As to the second point, that is, respecting the Beatific Vision of God: it is not clear to me whether the ancient writers who consider that the souls of the saints are not in heaven until after the last judgment, but are retained in certain secret resting-places, do or do not, allow that they have the Essential Vision of God before that same time. But, not to wander into an unnecessary discussion, Bernard indeed attributed to them the manifest vision of the Humanity of Christ: but even in this he disagreed from the common opinion of John xxii. and his followers. Yet he seems not to differ as to the fact, from those who ascribe to the blessed a certain contemplation and sight of the Divine, but imperfect until after the Resurrection; since the entire reason, on which Bernard bases his opinion, is precisely the same as causes those authors, of whom I have just spoken, not to assign the Perfect Vision of God to the disembodied souls; namely, the vehement desire which they have to be reunited to the body. They thought with Bernard that the Perfect Vision of God is of such power and virtue, that it absorbs and altogether extinguishes all other affections: which consummation will not take place even with the Saints themselves, until after the Resurrection. See on this subject, S. Augustine, Serm. cclxxx. n. 5, and cccviii. n. 5 and 6. The words of Bernard also in Serm. xix. *De Diversis*, n. 3, where he is explaining the privileges of the Blessed, are worthy of remark. There he says: "In this they for the third time, draw with joy the pure waters from the wells of the Saviour, and contemplate with unveiled eyes, so to speak, the Essential Divinity; nor are they deceived by any imagination of corporeal appearances." He says this, as it seems, in speaking of the present state of souls: and without doubt ascribes in this passage the direct vision of the Essential Divinity to the Saints before the Resurrection.

XXIV. But now dismissing this subject, I come to the last point of this Preface, that is to say, to the critical identification of the genuine Sermons of Bernard. The discussion of this matter will not be very long, since there is a general and well-ascertained agreement with regard to most of these. Out of the Sermons *De Tempore* which

Horst had admitted, I have relegated among the spurious the second for Maundy-Thursday [1] upon the words, *Sedisti ad mensam divitis.* It recalls in no respect the genius of Bernard; nor is it found in any of the old MSS. which I have been able to consult: nor even in the old Lyons edition of 1514.

XXV. This sermon was followed by a *Meditation on the Life and Passion of our Lord*, beginning with the words "Jesus of Nazareth," etc., which is equally wanting in the ancient MSS. and the old Lyons edition. Trithemius and Bellarmine attribute it more correctly to S. Anselm under the title "*Stimulus amoris.*"

XXVI. A Sermon on the combat of David with Golia (so it is written), for the Fourth Sunday after Pentecost, is placed at the end of the Sermons of Nicholas of Clairvaux in that MS. which was used by the Religious Bertrand Tissier, the author of the *Bibliotheca Cisterciensis.* But since that sermon is found in a large number of Codices of good note, as those of Clairvaux, Anchin, Paris, and of the Blancs-Manteaux; and it is also cited in the *Flores Bernardi* compiled four hundred [2] years earlier, it seemed proper not to remove it from its place.

XXVII. Since I have been led to mention here the Sermons of Nicholas of Clairvaux, it seems in place to mention that this Nicholas became a monk at Montier-Ramey and thence migrated to Clairvaux. There he became secretary to Bernard, whom he afterwards deserted.

---

[1] Cœna Domini.

[2] The copies read '*quadringentos.*' There is probably some error. The *Flores* was published in A.D. 1499; Tissier's *Bibliotheca Patrum Cisterciensium* in A.D. 1660.

He dedicated to Henry Count Palatine of Trèves nineteen Sermons composed by him; and which were published in Vol. iii. of the previously mentioned *Bibliotheca Cisterciensis*, with a Preface from the same Nicholas to Count Henry, in which are these words: "For the rest, I send to your Glory nineteen Sermons, from the Festival of S. John Baptist to that of S. John Evangelist; some other Sermons and certain verses of the Psalter commented upon in my way, and written down with my own pen, except that in a few places I have followed the comments of another;" namely, of Bernard his teacher, whose manner he had set himself to acquire. For he speaks thus of Bernard in his Sermon on the Nativity of our Lord: "I have borrowed the entire sense of this statement from that ark of the covenant, whose judgment is as the judgment of God. Him I refer to, whose piety and discretion, whose wisdom and eloquence, whose life and reputation, are deservedly known throughout all the Latin-speaking lands." A high eulogy of Bernard indeed. If Nicholas speaks so coldly in the Preface which I have quoted above, it is only because it was addressed to the Count of Trèves after his desertion of Bernard. And to these nineteen sermons are subjoined in the MS. four more, which the same Nicholas refers to not obscurely in his Preface: (1) on the words of Wisdom, *Justum deduxit Dominus*, etc.; (2) on the five stones borne against Goliath; (3) on flesh, skin, and bones; (4) on those words of the Apostle, "Whoso glorieth, let him glory in the Lord," which are all attributed to Bernard; the second indeed, as I noticed just now, for the fourth Sunday after Pentecost, and the three others placed among those *De Diversis*, not only in the first Lyons edition, but also in all or almost all the MSS. These I have thought it unadvisable therefore to disclaim for Bernard, especially because Nicholas being his Secretary, and a man not particularly scrupulous, as was observed in the notes on Ep. 298, may have arrogated them to himself.

XXVIII.   In the Sermons for Saints' Days, the second on the Conversion of S. Paul is wanting in most of the MSS., even in the French one at the Feuillants.   But it is included in the Vatican MS. No. 663, and I have no doubt is really the work of Bernard.   That for the festival of S. Mary Magdalen is one of the nineteen of Nicholas, and is relegated to Tom. vi., having been omitted from Tom. v., where are included with other Sermons of Nicholas, both Serm. v. on the Assumption and a Sermon Panegyric on the B. Virgin.   Furthermore, I have purposely passed over not a few sermons attributed to Bernard, as well in the new edition of Cologne as in the supplement of the Fathers of Homey, and in some MSS., both of which were quite different from the style and genius of Bernard: nor did it seem worth while to include them in the class of spurious works.

XXIX.   Among the sermons *De Diversis*, those which in some MSS. are entitled "Collections from the Discourses of S. Bernard," are some of them assigned to Guerric Abbot of Igny, and others to Nicholas of Clairvaux.   To Nicholas three, of which I have spoken above; viz., the 6th, 7th, and 21st. To Guerric six, Nos. 8, 28, 71, 73, 76 and 79.   But since these sermons (which are found in the Cologne MS.) are as Horst reports, wanting in the collections of those of Guerric, and are found in many copies of Bernard, it seemed advisable to retain them among the Sermons *De Diversis:* especially as all these little rivulets (so to speak) have flowed from Bernard as a fount, as we read at the end of a MS. in the

Royal college of Navarre at Paris, containing the Sermons of Bernard *De Tempore* and *De Sanctis*, with this little note at the end: 'There follows a Sermon to the Clergy on Conversion, which has thirty-one Sections; and certain *Collections Abridged* out of various Sermons of this Saint, which he delivered at various places and times : these abridgments have been very usefully made by those who were at his side night and day. After these follows the tract of Dom. Geoffrey his secretary, which he composed and sent to Dom. Henry, Cardinal Bishop, upon *"Simon Peter said to Jesus."* Last of all follow the letters of S. Bernard which he wrote to various persons. All these writings, though they come to us from another hand than his, were rivulets which flowed from him as a fount.' Those 'collections' are the Sermons *De Diversis*, of which many are rather abridgments or analyses than Sermons proper.

XXX. Of the five Parables ascribed to Bernard and placed after the Sermons *De Diversis*, the first is genuine : the second and third seem constructed in imitation of the first : the fourth and fifth are in the ancient editions placed among spurious works. The Ode Exhortatory to Rainauld seems to me quite unworthy of Bernard. I have set out in another place my reasons for thinking that the Rhythm on the Name of Jesus and the other brief poems should not be attributed to Bernard.

XXXI. What I have said with respect to the Sermons of the holy Father, has the support as well of the *Books of Flowers* (Florilegium) which William, a monk of S. Martin at Tours, composed and entitled 'Bernardinus:' as of the MS. Codex in French, which Nicholas Faber, preceptor of Louis *le Jeune* presented to the Feuillant Fathers, of the convent of S. Bernard in Paris. In the former are mentioned almost all the Sermons *De Tempore* and *De Sanctis*, with most of those *De Diversis*, and certain brief discourses which I shall point out in their places. One single Sermon for Maundy-Thursday and one on the Passion of our Lord for the fourth day, appear to be genuine; not so two others which I have rejected. There are in this collection also two passages extracted from the first sermon for the conversion of S. Paul; which mention of 'the first' indicates a second, but from this no passages are quoted.

XXXII. However, a single Sermon on the Conversion is included in the Feuillants MS., namely this first. It contains in all 44, which I enumerate here on account of the singularity and the great age of the MS., which is nearly as old as the time of S. Bernard. There are six for Advent, the same number for the Vigil of the Nativity of our Lord, five for the Nativity itself, one for SS. Stephen, John, and Holy Innocents; three for the Circumcision, three for the Epiphany, one for its Octave, two for the Sunday after the Octave, one for the Conversion of S. Paul, three for the Purification, two for Septuagesima, six for Lent, the first four of which are in the same order as in the editions, and the fifth on "Suffered, Dead and Crucified." After this, is inserted a sermon for 'S. Benedict,' and after this, the sixth for Lent on 'the threefold prayer,' the fifth in the editions, omitting that on the Lord's Prayer. which is usually the sixth. Then follows one Sermon which is called 'Common to the Abbots,' which is No. xxxv. *De Diversis*. Also another 'Common' Sermon, which is nothing else than the Preface to the Exposition of Ps. xci.; and finally, three on the Annunciation.

XXXIII. Nicholas of Clairvaux sent all these Sermons, and others also of the third volume, in two volumes to Peter Abbot of Celles, as we see in his Ep. 24: "I who had renounced writing, I who am worthy only of solitude and a hiding-place, yet anticipating and feeling your eagerness for the discourses of a man whose eloquence and wisdom, whose life and reputation, have not undeservedly spread to all Latin speaking countries, have taken my tablets, and copied what I had of his." The same Nicholas has expressed himself in a similar way in his Sermon for the Nativity of Our Lord.

XXXIV. The words which follow in the former letters seem to me worthy of remark, "But you say: you were able to do all that, and more, without breaking silence. I am surprised that you should seriously think so. For who is more in the midst of the press than he who is entangled in the task of correspondence? What a variety of words clash, as it were, around him, when he strives to vary their use and yet to use them with preciseness and accuracy, when he asks himself how best to reach his conclusion, and seeks what, where, when, and in what manner he should preferably speak. Will you now regard this as silence and quiet, especially for an unskilled writer, who is wanting even in ideas, and who knows still less how to clothe them in a flowing and ornamental style?" In these words Nicholas seems to intimate that he himself spent much time and labour in writing, in balancing the style, and in arranging the arguments in order, of the sermons which he transmits. But what sermons does he transmit? Manifestly those of Bernard; as he says a little further on: "Yet I have put force upon myself, and send you two volumes of the sermons of the man of God; one of the two I have written, which begins thus: 'The *Apostle Paul* is *usually brief in words, but deep and pregnant in his meaning.*' There is another volume long since written, now both worn and rubbed. [1] But seek some one to copy it diligently and intelligently; for it is full of deep teachings." Now if I take the sense of these words correctly, Nicholas means to imply, that he had written the sermons collected in the second volume in his own, (that is Latin) words : which volume began with '*Solet Apostolus* etc., which is the commencement of Serm. xix. *De Diversis.* If so, the arguments recur, which I endeavoured to treat at length above, and which go to prove that Bernard did not deliver his sermons in the Latin language, but in the French ; and that his disciples afterwards clothed them in Latin. I must confess that there is a great difference occasionally between the sermons, especially those *De Diversis* : which difference might be conceivably caused in this way, that different persons had turned them into Latin of various styles. Add to this that Geoffrey, who was secretary to the Saint, composed his little book on the *Colloquy between Simon and Jesus,* 'out of many Sermons,' he says, ' of our Father.' Why should not other secretaries also have done the same ? But if that were the case, why did they not (as Nicholas did) make a claim upon these sermons which they had translated ?

XXXV. To me, after mature consideration, it seems that the perplexity expressed by Nicholas with regard to composing and writing, has reference not to the sermons of Bernard, but to his own letters. Nicholas endeavours by all this winding of words to excuse himself from correspondence. I am confirmed in this interpretation by the title of his letter "To the Abbot of Celles, to excuse

---

[1] *Rosum et rasum.* Possibly, "revised and corrected."

himself from writing and composing." Or perhaps he wished
at the same time to express that he was desirous of being
relieved from the duty of writing letters and of copying
sermons from MS.; or at least to put a higher value upon
his labours in these departments. Finally, Nicholas has
borrowed that phrase, almost word for word, from Ep. 89
of Bernard to Oger (n. 1), in which Bernard excuses himself from writing : nor is Nicholas to be understood in
any other sense in this passage. The faulty text of Nicholas may then be restored after this letter of Bernard;
which furthermore was written twenty years before
Nicholas migrated to Clairvaux: and the latter was in the
habit frequently of appropriating the words of Bernard for
his own purposes, as I have observed elsewhere. As the
knowledge of this man's career throws great light upon
the history of Bernard, it seems worth while to describe
him here as he really was.

PART II.

Respecting Nicholas, the Secretary

OF

S. Bernard.

XXXVI. Nicholas was French by birth, and at an early age became a monk at the Abbey of Montier-Ramey in the Diocese of Troyes, and about four leagues distant from that city. He was a man of quick and versatile talent, insinuating in gaining the favour of others, remarkably accomplished for that time. He was entrusted with the charge of the schools in that Abbey, and was on terms of friendship with many important men of his time; such as Atto, Bishop of Troyes; Peter the Venerable Abbot of Cluny; Peter of Celles; Henry brother of Louis le Jeune, and others.

XXXVII. The reputation and genius of Bernard, not less than his sanctity, drew him to Clairvaux: he liked the life of the monks which he saw there, and solicited the favour of the elder brethren that he might be admitted into their community: declaring that he was dissatisfied with a luxurious rule, and desirous of one more severe. He carried his point almost at the first attempt: and on his return to his own monastery, he pressed on the matter, and Bernard being absent, he wrote to the Prior and

elder brethren a letter, which is No. 7 among his, addressed thus: 'To my lords and reverend Fathers the Prior
R. (that is, *Rualene*) and to his council.' In this he runs
through the entire round of winning entreaty. He bepraises
the devotion of the monks at Clairvaux, urges his wish to
see them again, and hints his strong wish to join their
company.—"Your humility and my own necessity," he
says, "inspire me with great confidence, and a third reason
also arouses my hope; namely, the welcome which you
gave to so humble a person as myself." He fixes the time
at which the letter was written a little farther on, in these
words : "What joy can there be for me, who am sitting
among the shadows, since I no longer see the light of
heaven, the light of Clairvaux! O light coming down from
the Father of lights! where shine the stars of the firma-
ment, whence was taken that greater light, which enlightened the earth, I mean Pope Eugenius." This was done
then in the pontificate of Eugenius, and indeed in the
first year of it : since Rualene was in that year taken
from being Prior of Clairvaux, to rule over the monastery
of Aquas Salvias, of which Eugenius had been Abbot before
his elevation; and at that time Nicholas had already been
admitted at Clairvaux, as his Ep. 43 shows. Although
these words "I mean Pope Eugenius" seem to have crept
into the text from the margin.

XXXVIII. Besides this former letter to the Prior and
elder brethren of Clairvaux, he wrote two others afterwards : one to brother Gaucher of Clairvaux, into whose
good graces he had insinuated himself, the other to Fromund, who was in charge of the guests at the same place ;
Nos. 44 and 46. In the former he states his wishes at
great length and with much eagerness : and says that the
desire with which he is burning, is so strong, that "a day

seems like a year" until it is attained: that he has not failed
at the time fixed, but has had much to endure from the
brethren at Montier-Ramey, both by way of entreaties,
of caresses, and of threats, so that he has with difficulty
been able to detach himself from their community: that
at length he has torn himself out of their hands "without
clothes, without coin, without servants, without horses, and
has arrived at Rivaux," which is a Cistercian monastery
in the district of Troyes, and from thence will come into
Clairvaux. But he says that he was taken from thence
to be sent "to the ends of the earth" at the demand of
the Abbot of Montier-Ramey (that was Guy, at whose
request Bernard composed the office for S. Victor), who
had put him back into a certain Priory, from whence he
wrote this letter full of expressions of most eager desire:
and he sent also another to Fromund by a certain clerk,
who was in the same place as he. In the former one to
Gaucher, he describes himself thus: "Though under the
vestments of the humility of Christ, I threw myself into
the gulf of pleasure, and though of the inheritance of the
Crucified, though purchased by the wounds of my Lord,
I showed myself a monk without discipline, a Presbyter
without dignity, not only in the Sanctuary, but in the Holy
of Holies! While going to and returning from the Roman
Curia, guided too much by curiosity, I made for myself
a name great among the great of the Earth; but in my
whole life I cannot remember a single day in which I
really lived." If he said this sincerely, nothing could be
more humble.

XXXIX. "At length an agreement ('*Concordia*,' such is
the title and subject of Ep. 40) having been entered into
with his Abbot, he was admitted into Clairvaux together
with Prior Theobald, who afterwards left the Abbey, and

whom he endeavoured, in his Ep. 6, to no purpose to recall. His conversion induced Brocard or Burchard, Abbot of Balerne, of the Cistercian institution, to write him a letter of congratulation upon it, which is now found as No. 9 among those of Nicholas, in which we read these words: "I thank God, the doer of all new things, for the new and wonderful thing he has done in the new change of a Nicholas become new. In making you change the black habit for the white, he has done a new and wonderful thing; but what is still more wonderful among these new things, is that such a white monk is made out of such a black!" These were the applauses of the Cistercians over their proselyte.

XL. Scarcely was he confirmed in this community than the office of secretary to Bernard was committed to him. The Saint had many Secretaries, because of the great number of different matters which were referred to him. The chief of these was Geoffrey, after whom came Nicholas. He complains, if he speaks sincerely, of the duty required of him in his Ep. 15 to a certain friend of his at Montier-Ramey: "You know that I am now among men who are distinguished by the severity of their discipline, the gravity of their manners, the wisdom of their counsels, the weight of their authority, and their rigorous silence. I do not wish to be accused of singularity; but while they remain in the contemplation of God, I ply pen and tablets, I marshal and exercise squadrons of words. From the morning watch on until night I do nothing else. Let it not be imputed to them, who have laid this burden upon me, and have made it my duty to write and reply to many people."

XLI. In another letter, his No. 35, he describes thus

his little writing-room: "I have in my Clairvaux a little writing-room *(scriptoriolum)* surrounded on all sides by offices *(officinis)* of heavenly labour, which almost hide it. It has access by a door into the chamber of the novices, where a crowd of young men, noble and well educated, are putting on the new man in newness of life .... On the right side is the cloister of the monks, where that growing assembly promenades to and fro .... There the Religious, according to the precepts of severe discipline, open one by one the books of the Holy Scriptures, not that they may winnow and garner the treasures of Divine wisdom, but that they may learn in them the love of God, penitence, and devotion.

"On the left rises the house and ambulatory of the sick, where their bodies, wearied and exhausted by the discipline of the Rule, are restored by more generous food; until cured or at least benefited, they come back to the mass of those who labour and pray, of whom the Kingdom of Heaven suffereth violence, and they, as violent, take it by force. And do not think that my little domain is to be disdained; for it is pleasant in aspect, comfortable as a retreat, and altogether a spot to engage the affection.

"It is full of books well selected and divine: on perceiving which my heart is rejoiced, I feel a more confirmed scorn of the vanities of the world, considering that they all are vanity, yea, vanity of vanities, than which nothing can be more vain. These books have been delivered to me to read, copy, and dictate; there I meditate, pray, and adore the Majesty of the Lord." But Nicholas did not pass his time wholly in transcribing books, but also in transacting business, as is shown by his Ep. 49 to Peter of Celles, to whom, among other things, he writes thus: "I have written these words to you, my dear friend, by little and little, because a multitude of interruptions prevented me from doing it all at once: and I have done it all with my own hand. For all who have business come to me. I alone am able to say with holy Jacob: 'All these evils have fallen upon me.'" (Gen. xlii. 36).

XLII. From this we may infer that Nicholas had scribes under him. One of these was Gerard of Peronne, his special friend, "the trusted and intimate sharer," he says in Ep. 10, "in my writings," who is praised by him in many other letters. It is to the same Gerard, and to the monk Henry, who was of royal birth, that Nicholas has dedicated his letters.

XLIII. He was frequently occupied in traffic about sales of books with Peter of Celles and others. His letter 34 to Amadeus, Bishop of Lausanne, is of that kind. In it occur these words: "I send you the book of the Magister Anselm *On the Holy Spirit* well corrected and pointed, if I do not mistake." But he was in the habit of lending books only upon this condition, that when they were sent back a second copy of each also should be sent with them, free of charge. This in fact, in Ep. 24, he demands of Peter of Celles, to whom he had lent two volumes of Bernard: "Hasten to have a copy made of this, according to my agreement, in return for the trouble I have taken. Kindly send me also those others which I have sent you, and the copies of them as was covenanted; and see that I do not lose an *iota*." This is to Peter. He borrowed also books from others in turn, as in Ep. 17, written to Peter, Dean of Troyes. "Kindly lend me the letters of the Bishop of Mans, which I am anxious to copy." Again he writes to Philip, Provost of Cologne and Chancellor to the Emperor; in the name of the brother of Philip he congratulates him that he was about to undertake a pil-

grimage to Jerusalem, and makes this request with regard to
his library, which was very rich: "But pray leave with the
poor of Christ that treasure of yours which is so valuable.
I mean the noble library which you have collected with such
great judgment and taste; and the poor brethren will intercede for you with prayers and tears, that the God of our salvation may make your journey safe and prosperous (Ep. 29)."

XLIV. Nicholas, that he might show himself a perfect
religious, not only declined after the example of his brethren at Clairvaux, to read verses, but also sent back a
tunic presented to him by a friend, as being unsuitable
for his order. As for verses, he thus expresses himself
with regard to them in Ep. 15: "I have not yet the
verses of my friend, or rather of our friend, Walter, in
my hands. But even if I had seen them, I should not
have read them, for I do not receive anything which is
tortured into metrical lines." The tunic had been presented to him as a sign of friendship, by Odo, Abbot of the
Black Monks of Pottières; but, in Ep. 37, Nicholas sending it back with many thanks, says, "That it is too costly
and beautiful for him: in this respect only," he says, "is
it not good, that it is too good." Then he adds, "I do
not wish, I am not able, and indeed I ought not to wear
it. In the midst of my brethren who are clad only in
patched and scanty habits, (*semicinctiis*; see below), I cannot
be seen clad, as it were, in purple and wrapped in a tunic.
No, by no means can I fit a vestment doubly splendid on
my sinful flesh, lest I be carried away altogether by its
follies. I send back to you then the tunic, since no one
among us dares to put it on, or ought to do so. But do
you, Father Abbot, to whom it is permitted by your Order,
and whom it befits because of your dignity, wear it. For
when you wear the tunic, you do only in accordance with

the custom of your Order. But you know who has said: 'If thou spendest more, when I come again I will repay thee.'" (S. Luke x. 35).

XLV. There are three things in these words worthy of notice. The first is respecting "*semicinctiis*," a word which Nicholas uses in its proper sense; and thus we infer that the Cistercians used *semicinctia*. What the *semicinctium* was, we learn from Herbert, Book i. *de Miraculis Cisterciensium*, c. 6, where, speaking of Schocelin, a recluse in the environs of Trèves, he says: "This man, although very rich, had only a common and very scanty apron *(semicinctium)* bound around his loins, which scarcely fulfilled the requirements of modesty in a covering, when he was obliged to appear in the sight of men." The ancients called them *lumbaria (loin cloths)*. And indeed it seems likely that the Cistercians used similar *semicinctia* from the first: especially as they wore a single tunic for their only garment, and such an article was required by decency, when the nature of their labour obliged them to lay aside this habit. Another fact is worthy of notice; that Nicholas says that it would be in accordance with the custom and order of the Abbot of Pottières to wear the tunic. The latter had professed the Rule of S. Benedict, which allowed to his monks, among other things, the use of the tunic (c. 55). That is true; but at this period it was the custom among monks to wear the cassock *(toga talaris)*, not the tunic, which only descended to the middle of the leg, such as the Cistercians then wore. Was it then that tunic, no doubt a white one, which Abbot Odo had sent to Nicholas, and (which is in the third place to be noted) he considered the Abbot was at liberty to wear "both by his Order and by his dignity!" Did then black monks use white habits? If so, why was there so great a controversy between them and the Cistercians about the white and black vestments? The Benedictines used the white tunic, at least in certain places; but the cowl was black, whereas the Cistercians wore white. Thus in the Ceremonial of Aniano, which was at that period in use for the black monks, monks are depicted in various places, wearing the white tunic and black cowl; each of which I have remarked in other pictures, especially in the book of Rabanus Maurus *de Cruce*, where he is represented in the white tunic. Although the controversy between the Cluniacs and the Cistercians was about the colour, not only of the cowl, but also of the tunic, as appears from the letter of Peter the Venerable No. 229, 2; but the usage is not uniform in this respect among ourselves at this time. But since the custom has been established among those who wear the white tunic, to add the toga to the tunic, and to lay aside the cowl when not in choir, which formerly was not permitted except in bed. The toga alone, with the scapular, seemed sufficient to be retained as a mark of the monastic state: then at length, when the toga was made of black cloth everywhere, and the white colour preserved for the tunic. Later still the *Staminea* [1] replaced the toga, over which was worn the tunic, which in our times was worn of a black colour, but in the earliest times the Cistercians wore only the tunic and the cowl, or were content with the scapular in place of the cowl; while the toga, whether simple or trimmed with furs, and *Staminea* they rejected.

XLVI. Let us return to Nicholas, who spared no trouble to keep himself, by constant correspondence, in the

---

[1] A worsted under garment. (E.)

memory of the friends, which he had been able to make when he was in his former monastery of Montier-Ramey, especially with the two Peters, the Abbots of Cluny and of Celles. We have two letters only from him to Peter of Cluny, before his defection from the Cistercian Order, which are the last two among his collected letters; but many more to Peter of Celles.

The first is Ep. 20 in the person of a monk, Adam, who had migrated from the Abbey of Celles to Clairvaux. The next is Ep. 24, under his own name, "To the Lord Peter, Abbot of Celles, the dearest among his friends." The title of Ep. 28 is very similar: "To Peter, Abbot of Celles, his special and most intimate friend." Also Ep. 48. That of the following letter is briefer and more familiar, "From a friend to his friend," and (to omit Ep. 51) that of Ep. 52 runs, "From a friend of Clairvaux to his friend at Celles, as his most devoted." I note these details with the more care, to show, in view of events to be mentioned below, that Nicholas, before his desertion of Clairvaux, was well known to Peter of Celles, and regarded as an intimate friend: so that he was quite distinct from that Nicholas of England, against whom Peter of Celles wrote in defence of Bernard, who was then dead; and which Nicholas he declared was quite unknown to him.

XLVII. Nicholas of France, during his stay at Clairvaux, wrote various letters in the names of different persons; namely, of Bernard himself, of the Prior Rualene, and of other monks, in all fifty-five, which he dedicated to his "very dear brethren Gerard and Henry," that is, Gerard of Peronne, and Henry, son of Louis le Gros and brother of Louis le Jeune, then monks at Clairvaux, in whose names also he wrote some letters. Among those which he composed in the name of Rualene, the title of one is erroneous, viz., Ep. 23, of which the inscription is couched in these words: "To the Right Reverend the Lord Hugo, Archbishop of Tours, Brother R." The mistake in this title is in this sentence: "In the person of the Prior of Rievaulx to the Archbishop of Tours." And John Picard notes in the margin that Rievaulx is an Abbey of the Cistercian Order in England, in the diocese of York. That is quite correct; but what had the Archbishop of Tours to do with Rievaulx? And it is quite certain that the letter was written in the name of Prior Rualene, whose name is found in an abbreviated form in the inscription of the letter, which has given occasion for the error as to the author. The same error is found in Ep. 25.

XLVIII. Peter the Venerable, Abbot of Cluny, had, as I have said, a strong affection for Nicholas, whom Bernard sent to him from time to time, to communicate confidentially his most private thoughts by his means. On this subject a letter of Peter should be read, which is No. 264 among those of Bernard. But at length it happened—O unhappy condition of mortals!—that Nicholas, abusing the indulgence and confidence of Bernard, made use of his seal for bad objects, and at length brought about a discreditable separation from him, which it is doubtful whether he ever seriously repented. Bernard sent information to Pope Eugenius, in Ep. 284, respecting the improper use which had been made of his seal; but without naming Nicholas, for the holy man was charity itself. "I have been in perils among false brethren; many letters have been forged and fraudulently sealed with my seal, and have gone forth into many different hands. I very much fear that this treachery may have reached even to you." He deplores this sad fall in another letter, No. 298, to the same Eugenius; there, as the crime was public, he does not conceal the name of the offender: "Nicholas has gone out from us because he was not of us, but he has left behind him foul footprints. I long ago knew what he was, but I had been waiting either for God to convert him, or for him to show himself a Judas:" note the long suffering of the good man. "This he has done. Besides books, silver, and much gold, there were found upon him when he left, three seals,—one his own, one the Prior's, the third mine .... The earth is stained with his disgraceful deeds, they have become proverbial amongst all; I refrain from polluting with them my lips and your ears." Bernard adds that if he should dare to come to the Court of Eugenius, as he had boasted he would do, no one better deserved "life-long imprisonment." This fall of Nicholas took place in 1151, as appears from the letter here quoted, which is dated in that year; and from one of Peter the Venerable, No. 388, written in the same year, about the election of a Bishop of Grenoble, in which Nicholas is still praised as an intermediary faithful and dear to both.

XLIX. It is the common opinion that he fled into England and was received in the Abbey of S. Albans: and also that he was that Nicholas who, after the death of Bernard, published and attacked his opinion upon the conception of the B. Virgin, and was opposed by Peter of Celles. It is true that his opponent was also named Nicholas: but he appears to have been of English birth, from two letters of Peter to him; viz., B. vi. Ep. 23, and B. ix. Ep. 10. In the former Peter says, "Let not English shallowness be indignant, if the sound and mature judgment of France is more reliable than it ...... I have experienced that the English are more prone to theories than the French." And in the latter: "The Frenchman will hold the Englishman

imprisoned and bound in his caverns." These words show
that this Nicholas was English: while the last words of
the letter prove, further, that Peter had never seen him:
"Would that I might see you face to face, you whose
eloquently expressed works it has more than once been a
pleasure to me to hear." I put aside the difference in their
styles; that of the Englishman is harsher and more for-
cible; of the Frenchman more polished, ornamented and
agreeable. But it is clear from the facts adduced that Nicholas of Clairvaux was well known to Peter before his
flight, and a personal friend of his; and that he was not
English, but French: he is therefore to be distinguished
from the English Nicholas.

L. Whither then it will be asked did the French Nicholas
betake himself? After having carried here and there his
wandering steps, he settled at length in his old Monastery
of Montier-Ramey, where, after Bernard was dead, he was
allowed to live in peace and security. This appears
both from Letter 59 of Arnulf, Bishop of Lisieux, to
this Nicholas himself, and from that of Nicholas himself to
William, Archbishop of Rheims, which Stephen Baluze
has lately published in Tome ii. of his *Miscellanea* (V.CL.)
This letter was written not earlier than 1176, in which year
William succeeded to the See of Rheims. In it Nicholas
praises him, because he had received him into the sanctuary [1] of his friendship, and because he had not given
way to the calumniator and whisperer. (Nicholas greatly
feared these). Then he excuses himself, because he had
so long deferred paying his respects to him.

He adds these words, which are of interest for us:
"Shall I excuse myself by pleading the difficulty of the
road and the length of the journey which separates the

[1] *Sacrarium.*

city of Rheims and the Abbey of Montier-Ramey?" It is evident then that at the time when he wrote he was staying at the latter place. "But the journey is short, the road easy, and lined by many of my friends."

LI. What he was doing in that Abbey, and in what character he had gone there, he indicates in the following sentences, from which we extract only these words: "Shall I add that I have not permission to come to you? But I go and come as I please. I go out and return the whole day. These reasons I might plead, if I were placed under the authority of any and were not perfectly free." Thus, then, Nicholas lived at Montier-Ramey in complete independence. An unhappy condition certainly for the man who had been the disciple and secretary of Bernard! But who can wonder at his fall, when the angels fell from Heaven itself?

But in this respect he chiefly exhibits his vanity, that he boasts, as he was in the habit of doing at other periods of his life, respecting the number of his friends. Thus, in a certain letter which he wrote about the same time as that last quoted, to Henry, Count of Champagne, and which is published in the same volume of the *Miscellanea*, he says: "From my earliest youth I have been favoured by the great, and by the chief princes of this world; but to you I owe especially all that I am, and all that I have the faculty of doing, both by the right of birth and by the duty of friendship." From this it may be inferred that Nicholas was born in Champagne, of which Henry was the Seigneur. His fall, like that of many others, can be attributed to a vain sentiment of petty pride and conceit. It is clearly evident how devoted he was to Henry, Count of Champagne or Troyes, by two of his letters, in one of which he dedicates to him his sermons which have been published in the third volume of the *Biblio-theca Cisterciensis;* this is inscribed "To Henry, my own Seigneur and my benefactor," and the other inscribed to the same person, as "The most Serene Prince and his very dear Seigneur." It is also printed in the second Tome of Baluze, where we read these words: "I send to your Highness certain letters which I have had occasion respect-fully to address to the Lord Pope, to the Chancellor of the Roman Curia, and to other persons of consideration on various occasions during the last two years." But it appears from Ep. 59 of Arnulf, Bishop of Lisieux, to the Monk Nicholas of the Monastery of Montier-Ramey,[1] that he abused the authority of that Prince, in fact in this letter he speaks of a certain Canon of bad life, a disciple of Nicholas, whom Nicholas says that he had received "for the last time and by favour" on the intercession of Ar-nulf, which the latter denies that he has given.

LII. From all these facts which I have noticed, it is very clear what was the character of Nicholas; namely, vain, inconstant, restless, and such that scarcely anything good could ever be expected of him; but what was the end of his career we do not know.

It remains for me to give here, as I promised above, a fragment of the first sermon of S. Bernard, rendered into the French language, in that very ancient copy which exists in the house of the Feuillants Fathers at Paris, as a specimen, of which the following is the title and the beginning.

[1] *Arramato*, but read Arremaro.

VII

Ci en commencement Li Sermon Saint Bernart
Kil Fait de L'avent
et des Altres Festes Parme Lan.

1. Nos faisons ui, chier Freire, len comencement de l'avent
cuy nons est asseiz renomiez et connuiz al munde, si cum sunt
li nom des altres sollempnitiez, mais li raison del nom nen
est mies paraventure si conue. Car li chaitif fil dadam nen
ont cure de veriteit, ne de celles choses ka lor salvateit
apartienent, anz quierent . . . . les choses . . . . faillanz et tres-
pessaules. A quel gent . . . . nos semblans, — les homes de
ceste generation, ou a quei gent evverons nos ceos cui nos
veons estre si ahers et si enracineiz ens terriens solaz, et
ens corporeiens kil repartir ne sen puyent? Certes sem-
blant sunt a ceos ki plongiet sunt en aucune grant auve,
et ki en péril sunt de noier. Tu varoyes kil ceos tienent
kes tienent, ne kil par nule raison ne vuelent devverpir
ceu ou il primier puyent mettre lor mains quels chose
ke ce soit, ancor soit ceu tels choses ke ne lor puist niant
aidier si cum sunt racines derbes ou altres tels choses.
Et si ancune gent vienent a ols por ols asoscor si plon-
gent ensemble ols ceos kil puyent aggrappeier ensi kil a
ols nen a ceos ne puyent faire nule ajué. Ensi perissent
li chaitif en ceste grant mer ke si est large, quant il les

choses ki perissent ensevent et les estaules layent aleir,
dont il poroyent estre delivreit del peril ou il sunt . . . .
prennoyent et salveir lor airmes. Car de la veriteit est dit,
et ne mies de la vaniteit, vos la conesseriz et ele vos
deliverrat. Mais vos, chier Freire, a cuy Deus revelet, si
cum a ceos ki petit sunt celes choses, ke receleis sunt as
saige et as, senneiz vos soiez entenduit cus encenousement
envor celes choses ke vrayement apartient a vostre
salveteit : et si pensiez di merrement a la raison de cest
avenement, quariez et encerchiez, ki cest soit ki vient,
et dont il vient, ou il vient, et por kai il vient, quant il
vient et par quel voie il vient. Certes molt fail aloeir ceste
curiositeit, et molt est saine. Car tote saint Eglise ne
celeberroit mies si devotement ces avenement, saucuens
granz Sacrement ne estoit en lui receleiz.

2. Tot a premiers sesvu . . . dez ensemble—lapostle ki
de cest avenement est toz enbahy, etc.

3. Por Deu, cheir Freire, fuyez orgoil, et forment lo
fuyez. Orgoilz est commencement de toz pechiez, ki si
hisnelement abattit enparmenant Luciferum ki reluisoit
plus kler ke totes les estoiles, ki un Engle ne muat
mies en diaule mais nes lo prince des Engles, qui apar-
memes ot envié de lomme, et si mist en luy la felonie, kil
avoit conceut en luy mismes quant il li semonut kil
seroit si cum Deus saichanz bien et mal, s'il maingieuet de
larbre ki defendus li estoit. Chaitif malaurous ke promis
tu, cum ce soit ke li Fils del haltisme ait la cleif de
science. Anz est il mismes li cleif David qui clot, et nul
ne avuret. En lui sunt reponuit tuit li tressor de sapience
et de science.

Embleras les tu dons por doneir a lomme. Or puez
veor ke menteires est cist et ses peires selon la sentence

de notre signor. Il fut menteirez quant il dist hil sem-
blanz seroit al haltisme et peires fust de la menzonge
quant il lenvelimeié semence de la falseteit gittat assi . . . .
en lomme, quant il dit quil seroient si cum Deu. Et
tu assi o tu homme tu vois lo lairon, et si cours ensemble lui. Vos aviez oït, chier Freire ceu cum leist anuit en
Ysaié la Profete lai ou nostre Sires dist, Li prince de ton
peule sunt inobedient et compaignon de lairons.

4. Por veriteit nostre Prince furent inobedient et com-
paignons de lairons.

Cest Adam et Eve ki firent li encomencement de nostre
lignieié, ki par le consoil del serpent mais del diaule par
lo serpent vorrent malement traire en ols ceu kapartient
solement al Fil de Deu, Nen a ceste ficié ne mist mies
li Peires en respit la torture cum faisoit al fil. Car li
Peires aiment le Fil, anz lo venuit aparmêmes assi de lome,
ot si apoese sor noz toz sa . . . . Car nos pechames
tuit en Adam: et en lui receumes tuit la sentence de
dampnation.

Et ke feroit li Fil . . . . il por luy avengier veoit. si eument
lo Peire kil a nule creature neu espargnieuet assi cum il
desist. Por me pert mes (Peires) tottes ses creatures.
Li premieres Engles se voit eslevir à ma haltesce et si
ost grant compagniéé ki a lui consentit: mais li amors ke
li Peires at vers mi prist a parmêmes venjance de luy
ensi kil luy et toz les siens ferit de cruyer chastiement:
et de plaié ke sancié ne puet estre. La science ke meye
est ausi volt ausi entrepenre li hom. Et il de lui nen
ot mies assi pitiet ne lespar gnat ses oils. At dons Deus
cure des beestes? Il n'en avoit fait mais ke dous nobles
creatures ke renaules estoient et ke dovoient estre bien-
aurouses, cest Lengle et lôme. Mais por me at parduit
une grant partie dengles et toz les hommes. Donkes

porceu kil saichent ke ju aimme ausi lo Peire si est droiz
qu'il rezoivet parmi ceos qu'il at parduit assi cum en une
maniere parmi. Si por mi est leveiz cist tempez si cum
dist Jonas, prenneiz me et si me gittiez en la meir.' Tuit
ont de mi envié,—mais ju en vois, et si me demonsterroy
teils a ols, ke tuit cil qui lor envie acoyserant et insevré
me vorront, seront bien aureit, etc.

The above is the Preface of Dom. John Mabillon.

In the fourth edition (1839), from which we translate,
the following editorial note is appended to it:

"In our times the same question has been raised again,
whether the Sermons of S. Bernard were preached in Latin
or in the vernacular; but with the same issue as in the
time of Mabillon. As for me, having duly and carefully
weighed the reasons which are brought forward on either
side, so convincing do those adduced in favour of the
more usual opinion appear to me, as to leave no doubt
whatever in my mind, that all the Sermons of S. Bernard
which we have, were written and preached in the same
Latin in which we possess them. And it is also sufficiently
clear to me, that what the codex of the Feuillants
Fathers contains, is a translation into the vulgar tongue:
a translation, which to all experts, seems not even to go
back so far as the age in which Bernard lived; some even
contending that it is not earlier than the thirteenth century: but which of these two opinions is nearer the truth,
is a matter still under discussion.

                                        N. E.

Such, with the exception of a few lines of only tempo-
rary interest, which I have omitted, were the prefa-

tory remarks of the latest editor of S. Bernard. The question of the language of S. Bernard's Sermons, on which he expresses so decided an opinion, may now be considered as closed. No student of the Sermons in the original, can fail to acquire at length an assurance that he has before him, not the mechanical diction of a number of unknown translators, but the utterances, vivid and characteristic, of the Saint himself.

The perpetual play of phrase is a habit with S. Bernard, as it vanishes, or nearly so, with a translation out of the Latin, so it could not have been transferred into Latin out of a rude and unformed language, such as were then all the provincial dialects of France.

2. The specimen above given will show in what state were the vernacular idioms at that period: and how little susceptible of fineness of literary workmanship. It is not the nervous and powerful French of modern times, flexible to all purposes of the speaker, capable of expressing the slightest shade of meaning, and especially wealthy in significant phrases, whose paragraphs are luminous and persuasive beyond those of any other language, in their logical clearness. That is what it has grown into; the Greek of modern times.

.But in the time of S. Bernard the French language was obviously only in its rudimentary stage. It could express simple ideas in a simple manner, but was not at that period adequate, with its harsh structure and rudimentary spelling, to be a fitting exponent of ' the thoughts that breathe and words that burn ' which are found in all S. Bernard wrote.

3. Few, therefore, will be found to doubt that, whether or no S. Bernard may have preached on occasion in the

vernacular [which is likely enough and indeed almost certain], the language in which he thought and studied was Latin, as it was that in which he read and prayed: and consequently it was that in which he composed his sermons and other works.

The index prefixed to the Sermons in this edition is new, and adapted for more general use than the previous one upon which it is founded.

S. J. E.

VIII.

LETTER CCCLXXXI. [Formerly No. 364: the former No. 381 is now No. 320] (*Circa* A. D. 1150).

To Abbot Suger.

Bernard assures him that he himself is far from attributing the evils under which the Kingdom suffers, to him: and that he regrets that others should do so. He advises Suger to decline to share (by associating with them) the unpopularity of those who are the real cause of these evils.

To the Reverend father, and my very dear friend, Suger, by the grace of God Abbot of S. Denys, Brother Bernard, called Abbot of Clairvaux, wishes health and gives assurance of his humble prayers.

I reply briefly to the letter of your Paternity, being somewhat pressed for time: it was towards evening when I received the letter, and I have to set forth to-morrow to attend the general chapter at Citeaux. In few words then, I beg you to put entirely out of your mind the idea, which had not even occurred to me, that I could think you responsible for the evils under which we are labouring.

It is true that in my zeal I have written to you with an eager warmth: but this was only because I was striving to impress your Holiness with my sentiments and to induce you to share them. Another reason for it was, that

although I was quite sure of your good intentions, yet I
was greatly pained by the evil reports dealing with your
name, which have given scandal to the Church. Why do
you continue to have relations with people who are not
willing to conform to your manner of life and especially
in matters of this kind? Why do you shelter them with
your name? Is it not your bounden duty to separate yourself altogether from those sacrilegious, and to keep them
at a distance; so that you may be able with good conscience, to say with the Psalmist: *I have hated the congregation of the wicked, and will not sit among the ungodly*
(Ps. xxvi. 5): and thus the entire Church and all the
Saints may know that you are entirely guiltless,
and free from their company and their companionship.
Remember the opening words of the Lord by the Prophet:
*Blessed the man that hath not walked in the counsel of
the ungodly* (Ps. i. 1.) But pray believe that I have never
thought any harm whatever of you: for I know you well,
and the purity of your intentions. Farewell; and pray for us.

LETTER CCCLXXXII. [Formerly No. 324; the former
No. 382 is now No. 321] (*Circa* A. D. 1150.)

To Leonius, Abbot of S. Bertin.

[That monastery has already been mentioned in Ep.
149; and Thomas in Ep. 108. As for the Abbot Leonius,
he is described by Hermann of Laon *De Miraculis B.
Mariae* B. iii. C . 4, as "a very religious man, skilled not
less in secular learning than in theological." He was Abbot
from 1148 to 1163].

*Bernard expresses his gratitude to Leonius for his
kindnesses to him and to his monks, and requests him*

not to hinder the monk Thomas, who was desirous to mi-
grate from S. Omer to Clairvaux.

To the beloved and venerable Lord Abbot LEONIUS and
the whole community of S. Bertin, Brother BERNARD, called
Abbot of Clairvaux, wishes health and the presence of
the Spirit of truth whom the world cannot receive.

I have received your letter, beloved brethren, and the
statement of your wish which you request of me. Nor
can I ever forget the kindnesses which you have rendered
with gladness and liberal hand, to me and mine. But what
if, though not forgetful, I am found ungrateful? Will my
mindfulness of them be held as an excuse? On the contrary, it will make the ingratitude worse. But I am
not forgetful of, nor ungrateful to my friends, even
though I am unable to recompense you for the benefits
which I have received at your hands; but wherein I am
unable, the Lord will recompense you in my stead. I am
liberal of that which belongs to another, since I myself
am poor and needy. He who knows the depths of man's
heart, He knows how greatly I love the honour of your
Abbey and the splendour of the house of the Lord, for
He is among you. In this matter I do not fear that I
am saying anything but the truth. I love those who
love me; yet I am not hereby justified; for even Pagans
do this. Thus I have no great merit in returning your
affection: I should even be blamable if I did not do so.

But I loved you, before you rendered me any service:
how then could I not love you, after you had done so?
If it was my duty to love you, even before you had laid
me under obligations: it would be worse than an injury,
should I not do so, after you had conferred benefits upon
me. Always then, brethren dearly beloved, I am bound
to love you for the Lord's sake: and will serve you in Him,

whose servants ye are: yea, I will honour Christ, whose
members ye are, always in you.

2. Nevertheless, as the honour and service is unques-
tionable which I am bound to render towards you, so it
is to be rendered with prudence and reasonableness,
because *the honour of the King loveth judgment* (Ps.
xcix. 4). Upon the matter therefore, respecting which
you write to me, I reply to your Charity that I do not
dare to hinder, nor ought you to hinder, from good, one
who wishes to do it. For what have we to reply to the
Apostle, who says *Quench not the Spirit* (1 Thess. v.
19). For it is not a safe thing to put out that light,
which when extinguished, we cannot light again. And
what again to this: *Let every one remain in the same
calling wherein he is called* (1 Cor. vii. 20)? Thomas
has been called, I say: not by me, but by Him who
calls those things which are not, as though they are (Rom.
iv. 17).

Why do you look askance at me in this matter, as if it were
the work of man and not of God? That call is not from man,
nor by man, but from the LORD. For it is not man, but God,
who works upon the hearts of man, and directs their inclinations, whithersoever He will. That call, I say, is from the
Lord; and therefore it ought not only to be admirable in our
eyes, but we ought to respect and uphold it. For who or what
is man, that he should come to the assistance of the
spirit, or of the work of God? It is only He who seeks
his wandering sheep, who knows what He seeks, and
where He seeks it: who knows also whence He recalls it,
and in what manner and to what spot, so that it may not
be lost at the last. See then that you do not call back
him whom the Lord has summoned; do not bend down again
him whom the Lord has raised up; nor place the least stumbling-block in the way of one to whom God has stretched

forth His Hand, in order that he may ascend towards Himself.

3. But now we have to examine what weight should be allowed to that fact which you refer to, that he was offered to your house by his parents. I refer it to your good sense, which has the greater strength of reason and ought to prevail, that which has been done by parents for their child without his knowledge, or that which he has done on his own account, knowingly and prudently. Or rather I should say, to speak with exactness, that it is not he but the grace of God which, while he was unwilling, influenced him preveniently that he might will what was good, and when he willed it, sustained him, that he might not will in vain. But I maintain that the vow of his parents remains entire, and that their offering is not annulled but crowned. For both the same person is offered now who was offered before; and to the same [God] to whom he was before offered; only he who had been previously offered by his parents alone, is now offered by the son himself. Beyond this expression of opinion, I have nothing to say in the matter by way of direction; but I give you my advice. A word has come forth from the Lord; do not hinder the course of God's grace, do not repress the first impulses of a good disposition; for that which is begun in him is from the Holy Ghost. And do not overlook that you have done an injury to me, in the accusation that I desired to take away from you the Religious whom God had sent you; because I have never done you wrong in this way. Thomas himself knows, that if he should ever violate his vow, which he made with me as its witness, and any one else who has advised him to do so knows also, that I shall arise to bear witness against them in the day of the Lord. But in the meantime it is better for him, for you, and for me too, that we should keep the unity of the Spirit in the bond of peace. Farewell.

LETTER CCCLXXXIII. [Formerly No. 342. The former No. 383 is now No. 361]. (*Circa* A. D. 1150).

To the same Abbot of S. Bertin.

Bernard begs him to continue the kindness hitherto shown to his brethren.

To his very dear friend Leonius, the venerable Abbot of S. Bertin, Brother Bernard, called Abbot of Clairvaux, wishes health in Him who desires the salvation of Jacob.

Your charity shows sufficiently well how much reason I have for relying upon you; since it lets no occasion pass for making itself known, nor hides its light under a bushel. And I feel exceedingly grateful for all the kindnesses, which you do to my brethren, who are settled near you.

[These were the monks of Clairmarets, near S. Omer. Manrique refers the foundation of this house to A. D. 1138. According to the Chronology, A. D. 1140].

What you do for them, you do for me: and indeed I feel more grateful on account of what is done for them, than if it were done for myself. I pray you then to continue your kindness to them, since they are so far from us that I cannot assist them as I ought. Let your kindness supply my place: be to them a father, and let them be to you as sons. If ever the occasion presents itself for me to manifest my gratitude, rest assured that I will give you convincing proofs of it. Farewell.

LETTER CCCLXXXIV. [Formerly No. 343; the former No. 384 is now No. 273]. (*Circa* A. D. 1150).

To the Monks of S. Bertin.

Bernard thanks them for their kindness towards his brethren, and assures them that God will repay them abundantly.

To his dear brethren, all the monks of the Abbey of
S. Bertin, Brother BERNARD, called Abbot of Clairvaux,
wishes health, and that they may serve God with joyfulness.

I feel obliged to express to you my lively gratitude for
your kindnesses. For since benefits received ought to be
held in everlasting remembrance, I am bound to be neither
unmindful of, nor ungrateful for the many kind actions
which you have done to my brethren, or rather to me.

What is laid out upon those who are mine, is laid out upon
me; the bounty lavished upon my very bowels, is a bounty
to me. I know in whom I have trusted, and am well
assured: I know, I repeat, that you love me, not in word
or in tongue merely, but in deed and in truth. The proof
of your affection, and of the favour which my brethren
have found in your eyes, is shown not by mere words, but
in your actions: therefore it is the purer in the eyes of
God, and the more agreeable in that of men, inasmuch as
they come from disinterested goodness in the giver, and
are beyond the deserving of those who receive them. For
these, therefore, I return thanks to the whole of your community: for all these good deeds both I and my brethren
are your debtors in all that we are, and to the extent of
our powers. But lest it should appear a little thing to
you to be accepted by men, by my God also you are
accepted. For that which you have done to one of the
least of His brethren, you have done unto Him (S. Matt.
xxv. 40), and still more for that which is done not to one
only, but to many of His.

For all these benefits little return is to be looked for
from me, for I am needy and poor: but the Lord shall
make return for me. He who is the rewarder of all good
deeds shall reward you, because you have presented His
poor with the blessings of sweetness, with an example
of charity. I thank you then for your past gifts: and for

the future I entreat that you would not desist from your good deeds. For from the seed of good works you will reap in God's good time the harvest of peace and of glory; which may God vouchsafe to us also. Amen.

LETTER CCCLXXXV. [Formerly No. 341: the former No. 385 is now No. 418.]

To the same.

Bernard congratulates them on their better observance of their Rule, and exhorts them to preserve an earnest desire for religious perfection, and to make continual efforts to attain it.

To the whole community at the monastery of S. Bertin, most dear to him in Christ, Brother Bernard, called Abbot of Clairvaux; health and the assurance of his prayers.

1. Thus, thus act, I pray you, my dearly beloved. The disciple who makes progress is the glory of his master. Whosoever does not profit in the school of Christ is unworthy of His training: especially when we consider that in the present life no one remains in the same condition, and that therefore not to make progress is without doubt to fall back. Let no one therefore say: It is enough for me: I wish to remain as I am: it is sufficient for me to be to-day what I was yesterday and the day before. He who is of that mind is, so to speak, sitting down on the road; he is halting on the ladder on which the patriarch saw angels, but all either ascending or descending. (Gen. xxviii. 12).

I say then: *Let him that thinketh he standeth, take heed lest he fall* (1 Cor. x. 12). Steep and narrow is the way to salvation, not a spot to halt and settle down upon: and in the House of the Father only is it that

there are *many mansions* (S. John. xiv. 2). Therefore
he who says that he abides in Christ *ought himself also
so to walk, even as He walked* (1 S. John ii. 6). Now
Jesus Himself, as the Evangelist declares, *increased in
wisdom and in 'stature and in favour before God and
men* (S. Luke ii. 52). He instead of coming to a stand-
still, *rejoiced as a giant to run his course* (Ps. xix. 5):
and we also, if we are wise, shall be attracted by the
fragrance of His virtues, and follow swiftly in His footsteps. Otherwise, if it shall happen that we allow Him
to pass far away into the distance, the road shall become
far more laborious and even dangerous to the slothful
soul, when it cannot be quickened by the influence of
His virtues, nor perceive the clear traces of His footsteps
because of the distance in front at which He is.

2. So then, brethren, run that ye may obtain (1 Cor.
ix. 24). This indeed you may succeed in doing, if you
clearly understand that not yet have you attained, if
*forgetting those things which are behind, ye press forward
to those things which are before* (Phil. iii. 13), if ye faithfully carry out your Rule, lest God be displeased with
you, and so *ye perish out of the right way* (Ps. ii. 12).
*He who eateth me, saith Wisdom, shall still hunger, and
he who drinketh me shall still thirst* (Ecclus. xxiv. 29).
Let then the slothful soul, who deserves to be polluted with
the filth of the oxen (Ecclus. xxii. 2) understand that the
distaste which it feels [for that which is spiritual (E)]
comes not from being filled and satisfied with it, but from
the abstaining from spiritual food.

3. Finally, since all things work together for good to
those who are called to be saints according to the Divine
purpose (Rom. viii. 28), let the example of those who
are influenced by worldly ambition, move us to imitate it.
For what man who is ambitious of worldly honours do

we ever see content with those he has obtained, and not
desirous of more? So also the eager and inquisitive,
whose eye is not satisfied with seeing, nor his ear with
hearing. What! do not those who are the slaves of
avarice, who are lovers of pleasure, who strive to gain
the empty praises of men, by their eager and passionate
desires, reprove our negligence and lukewarmness? Is it
not plainly a disgrace that we should be found less ardent
in the pursuit of spiritual good? Let the soul which has
been devoted to the Lord blush to follow after righteousness with less earnestness than at an earlier time it
followed iniquity. For what a difference in value between
the one cause and the other! The wages of sin is death;
but the fruit of righteousness, eternal life (Rom. vi. 23).
It should shame us to go onward to eternal life with less
eagerness than we used to go towards death; and to be
less desirous to augment our portion of salvation, than of
condemnation. For we are all the more inexcusable, the
more easy it is to run quickly along the way of salvation:
and the light yoke of the Saviour is the more easily borne
the heavier it seems to be. Does not the very number
of the wing-feathers of little birds help to bear them up,
not to weigh them down? If you take them away, then
the rest of the body sinks by its own weight. Thus it
is with the discipline of Christ, with His easy yoke and
light burden; the more we put it off our shoulders, the
more we are borne down towards the earth, because
it bears us up, rather than is borne by us. The discipline of silence, for example, is weighty and painful to
some; but yet the Prophet regarded it as a source of
strength rather than a burden, for he says: *In silence
and in hope shall be your strength* (Isaiah xxx. 15, Vulg.)
In silence, he says, and in hope, because *it is good that
a man should both hope and wait in silence for the Lord*

(Lam. iii. 26). In truth, the consolation and sweetness of the present life weakens the soul, while the expectation of the future life strengthens it. You have therefore done well, dearest brethren, in adding something to your former rule of silence, [1] since, according to the Prophet previously quoted, *silence is the work of righteousness* (Isaiah xxxii. 17, Vulg.). You have also done well in withdrawing yourselves more and more from the doings of the world, which constitutes *pure religion and undefiled* (S. James i. 27). *A very little leaven, my brethren, corrupts the whole mass* (1 Cor. v. 6), *and dead flies destroy the sweetness of ointment* (Eccles. x. 1). Would it not be pity to endanger, or even to render less acceptable the merits of a life filled with so much labour and discipline both of soul and body, by mixing it with some worthless consolation, or rather desolation? Who knows what obstacle may be put in the way of the sweetness of the interior consolations, or of the graces of Divine visitation, by some fugitive and trifling solace of this kind? Especially we monks, whose life is, whether we will or no, to be passed in labour, should be the most miserable of all men, if for such trifling gratification we should incur losses so great. What foolishness, what even insanity would it be, should we who have renounced matters of more importance, cling to those of less at such great risk to ourselves! If we have held the entire world as a worthless thing, if we have renounced

---

[1] Bernard regarded the practice of silence as eminently favourable to religious perfection, as we see in Epistle 91, to the Abbots assembled at Soissons, and in many other passages of his works. Nor is this surprising. It would be, on the contrary, very strange to suppose that the religious life could subsist without the strict observance of silence. It is called by Bernard "the guardian of religious life." Ser. ii. for the Octave of the Epiphany, No. 7.

the affection of relatives, if we have immured our own selves in monasteries as if in a prison; and far from doing our own will, have subjected ourselves to the command of others: what ought we not to do, in order that we may not lose by our foolishness or lukewarmness the fruits of our sacrifices?

Be of good courage, then, dearest brethren, and study to persevere in those things which you have begun, and to abound in them more and more; and that the fruits of your righteousness may increase day by day. Remember *that he who sows sparingly, shall reap also sparingly; and he who sows bountifully shall reap also bountifully* (2 Cor. ix. 6). And be ye certain of this, that even a little increase in the seed shall be followed by an increase in the harvest by no means little. These few words, brethren, I have deemed it my duty to write to you, in the joy and gladness of my soul, at hearing of your progress in holiness, and with the wish to admonish you to practise willingly and gladly those holy and salutary observances which you have embraced, and which are able to save your souls. For you know that *the Lord loveth a cheerful giver* (Ibid. v. 7). Pray for me; and may Jesus Christ have your whole community in His holy keeping.

LETTER CCCLXXXVI. [Formerly No. 333: the former No. 386 is now 366]. (A. D. 1150).

JOHN, ABBOT OF CASAMARIO [1] TO ABBOT BERNARD.

He consoles Bernard for the unfortunate issue of the [Crusade] expedition to the Holy Land.

[1] Casamario was a Benedictine Abbey in the neighbourhood of Veroli, in Italy. It was founded in 1005, and the first Abbot

To his dear father and venerable Lord BERNARD, Brother JOHN, his servant and Abbot of Casamario, such as he is, wishes health, and prays that he may run well and attain a happy end in the grace and love of Christ.

1. I am mindful of the sweet and familiar affection with which at one time, you in your kindness honoured me, though unworthy: and therefore I presume to lay open the thoughts of my heart to your Paternity, as if I were présent with you: trusting in your goodness that I shall not be suspected of the least intention to wound you. For I hope that the feelings of reverent affection, which I have towards you, are not unknown to you: and if I should say anything foolish or ill suited to the occasion, I trust that you will forgive it, in your kindness and gentleness, as a father forgiving a son. It has been told me, dearest father, that you grieve much over the issue of that matter, which has ended so differently, I fear, from your wishes, (I mean the Crusade), that it has not added to the glory of God and the advantage of His Church, as you desired it should do. Wherefore, after long meditating over this matter, God has put into my heart (as I verily believe) these thoughts which I humbly communicate to you, reflecting that the Lord often reveals somewhat to a person of small importance, which He does not permit to be discerned by His servant who is great and fulfilled with many gifts: just as the stranger Jethro gave counsel to Moses, that holy man who spake face to face with God (Exod. xxxiii. 11, and xviii.).

2. It seems then to me, that the glory of God has been

was named Benedict. Bernard visited it many times, and was united in a close friendship with Abbot John, the writer of this letter. He was a man of great piety; and in 1140 he affiliated his monastery to the order of Citeaux and observance of Clairvaux. See Ughellus, *Italia Sacra*, Tom. i. col. 289.

much advanced in this expedition, although not in the manner which was supposed by the Crusaders themselves. If they had been willing to prosecute to the end the enterprise which they had taken in hand, piously and religiously as it became Christian men to do, God would have been with them, and would have certainly done great things by their means. But since they gave themselves over to evil courses, and this could not be hidden from the Lord, the Author of the expedition from the commencement: He that His Providence in the ordering of it might not fail, turned their perverseness into an occasion for His clemency, and by the misfortunes and troubles which He sent upon them purified them, that they might gain the Kingdom [of Heaven]. And I have known some of those who returned, to declare that they had heard many who died in the Holy Land, when dying, protest that they did so willingly, nor desired to return, lest they should fall back into their former sins.

3. But not to leave it doubtful what I would state, I affirm as to my spiritual father in confession, that the patrons of my house, S. John and S. Paul, have deigned often to visit me: and in reply to my questions respecting the Crusade, they have declared that the places left vacant by the multitude of Angels who had fallen, had been filled up by the souls of those who died in the Holy Land. Know this also, that they had an intimate knowledge of you, and have predicted to me that the end of your course will come speedily.

Since then the matter has been ordered according to the will of God, although not as men desired: it will be wise in you to be consoled respecting it in Him, whose glory alone you seek and desire. It was He therefore, who bestowed on you the grace to forward the matter by speech and action, since He foresaw the good which should come out of it. I pray that He will fulfil your course in happiness, and may establish me with you in His Glory.

LETTER CCCLXXXVII. [Formerly No. 352 : the former No. 387 is now No. 397] (A. D. 1150).

To Peter, Abbot of Cluny.

Bernard begins by protesting his friendship and affection for Peter, and begs him to excuse anything that he had written with too much sharpness in a former letter.

To the very Reverend father, and his very dear friend, Peter, by the grace of God, Abbot of Cluny, brother Bernard, called Abbot of Clairvaux, wishes health in Him who is the true Salvation.

Would that I could send you my heart to read as you read my letter that is before you! Then I am sure you would read most clearly the affection for you which the finger of God has graved deeply on my heart and in my whole being. What then? do I begin again to commend myself to you? By no means. Long since did my soul cleave to yours : and an equal affection has rendered equals two men very unequal in other respects. For if your humility had not deigned to stoop to me, what could there have been in common between your dignity and my littleness? But thus it has happened that your greatness and my humility have been united in reciprocal affection : so that neither I, without you, are humble; nor you, without me, are exalted.

Nicholas, one of my Religious who is particularly attached to you, has astonished me in no small degree by saying, that to his surprise and regret he had noticed in a letter which I had addressed to you, various sharp and bitter expressions. [1]

Believe me, who love you, that nothing which could wound your Beatitude ever proceeded from my mouth, or was harboured in my heart. The great pressure of business is the cause of the mistake : for when my secretaries have not quite understood my meaning, they are sometimes apt to employ expressions too sharp; nor am I able to read over what I have directed to be written. [2]

For this once, pardon me : henceforth I will read over whatever I shall write to you by the hand of others, and will trust only my own eyes and ears. Other things, my son and yours, who bears this letter, shall tell you by word of mouth. Kindly listen to him as being to me another self; to me, who love you, not in word or in tongue only, but in deed and in truth. Salute your holy community on my behalf, and beg them to remember their humble servant in their prayers.

LETTER CCCLXXXVIII. [Formerly No. 353, the former No. 388 is now No. 348.] (*Circa* A. D. 1150.)

LETTER OF PETER THE VENERABLE TO BERNARD, ABBOT OF CLAIRVAUX.

He rejects titles and praises and declares how much he values Bernard and his friendship.

[1] The letter here referred to is not found amongst the published letters of S. Bernard. Peter the Venerable mentions it in the following letter (No. 4). Letter 270 shows that the monks of the Grand Chartreuse had been similarly wounded by a letter from S. Bernard.

[2] It is clear from what Bernard says here, that many of the letters, if not of those which remain to us, were the work of his secretaries. Such were those of Nicholas, which we give in the Appendix.

He freely accepts his apology for the tone of his letter.

Brother PETER, the humble Abbot of the Cluniacs, to the venerable BERNARD, Abbot of Clairvaux, a man renowned among the members of Christ, loved after God and in God.

1. What shall I say? I am accustomed to speak : but now I am stricken dumb. Why so? you ask. Because your letter, which would ordinarily have made me eloquent, has made me dumb. Wherefore? I read so much in it, although it was so brief, that if I should try to pour myself out in answer I should seem rather taciturn than talkative. But I am speaking to a serious and religious man. Therefore we must act, as gravity demands; as your profession if not mine, directs. What! is not this true? The letter is short, but contains much to be answered. Pardon me, I pray, if I have said other than was befitting. For it is the part of true friendship, not only to endure the amenities of a friend, but also to hide or tolerate even words that are unsuitable. I have received, as I said, from you a most excellent letter, a letter breathing most tender love, and honour more than I deserve. You call me "most Reverend", you address me as 'Father', you call me 'dearest friend'. I rejoice at it : but in respect to truth, which has passed from Christ into your soul, I am unable to accept the two first, but I say nothing against the third. For I know not that I am most reverend; I cannot be styled Father with regard to you : but to be dearest friend to you I gladly assent with lips and heart.

2. So now I may be silent about the names of most reverend and dearest friend, of which, as I said before, the one does not befit me, but the other I gladly accept; about the name of Father, O reverend brother, I say to you, what Dom Guigo, Prior of the Grand Chartreuse, a

man renowned in his generation, and a most illustrious
flower of the Religious of his day, once wrote to me. I
used often to write to him, and often in conversation, or in
familiar correspondence, used to call him Father. He bore
this at first, thinking I was about to make an end of
writing. But after he saw me to persist in it, and in
frequent letters to reiterate the name of Father, the good
man at length broke out into these words. For he wrote
me a letter, in which amongst other things he inserted
this : "I entreat you by that love, with which your heart
is filled for me all unworthy of it, that when your Serenity deigns to write to my humble self, you would so
think of my spiritual interest, as not to puff up my
weakness with dangerous complacency." And presently :
"This I seek above and before all things, and entreat
you with bended knees, not to honour my unworthy
self with the name of Father. Enough and more than
enough, if he is called brother, friend, and son, who is
not worthy even of the name of servant." Thus he wrote
to me : and I write the very same to you. Let it suffice
if I enjoy the name of brother, dear or dearest friend
from you; or whatever name like those befits you to
send, or me to receive. So much about your salutation.

3. But what about that which follows? "I would," you say,
"I could send my mind to you to read as I do this present letter!" And farther on : "I am sure you would read
very clearly the affection for you which the finger of God
has written in my heart and in my whole being."

These words in truth, setting aside the deeper and mystical meaning of the words [of the Scripture] are as the
ointment upon the head, which descended from Aaron's
beard even to the skirts of his clothing : they are like the
dew of Hermon, which fell on mount Sion : even thus do
the mountains pour forth sweetness, and the hills flow

with milk and honey. Do not wonder, that I so carefully ponder and weigh your words.

For I know they are not uttered from a careless mouth: but from his, who knows not how to speak except from a pure heart, a good conscience and an unfeigned affection. I know, I say, and all the world knows with me, that you are not of the number of those, who, according to the Psalm, *Have spoken vanity, to each to his neighbour;* you are not of those, *whose lips are deceitful, they have spoken from a deceitful heart* (Ps. xii. 2). Therefore as often as it pleases your Holiness to write to me, I receive and read and welcome your letters not negligently or carelessly, but eagerly and gladly. For who would not read carefully? who would not receive with much affection the words I have before cited, and those which follow? " Now indeed," you say, "my soul is joined fast to yours and the equality of love has made equal souls in differing persons. For what was there in common between your highness and my humility, if your worthiness had not waived your worth? And so it has come to pass that your greatness and my humility have been united in reciprocal affection: so that neither I am humble without you, neither can you be exalted without me." Can words of this kind be negligently read? Ought they not to hold fixed the eyes of the reader, to seize his heart, to unite our souls? You see, dearest friend, what you have written, what you felt about this: I cannot do otherwise than take the letter in the simple and literal sense, and accept what so great, so truthful, so holy a man has been pleased to say. Neither, as you yourself have said, do I begin again to commend myself to you. While yet young men we began to love in Christ: shall we now when we are old men, begin to doubt about so sacred, so lasting a love? Far be it from me, (trust one who loves you) so to use your words, for it has never occurred to my heart, nor gone forth from my mouth, to doubt words which you have uttered so seriously. So I embrace, I keep and guard all that you have written in the letter of which we speak. Far rather would I be deprived of a thousand talents of gold, than have these words by any means torn from my heart. But enough of this.

4. As concerning the matter about which your prudence thought me hurt, the fact was this. In respect to the matter, which is well known to you, of a certain English Abbot, your letter said: "They speak as if judgment was overturned, and justice had perished from the earth, and there were none to snatch the weak from the hand of the strong, the needy and poor from those who oppress them." [1]

But believe me, I was moved at this, as the Prophet says of himself, although I am no prophet: *I as one deaf did not hear, and as one dumb that openeth not his mouth.* And again: *I am become as a man that heareth not and as one that has not an answer in his mouth.* (Ps. xxxviii. 13, 14). I was not offended indeed at this, but if I had been, full satisfaction was made when you said: "My excess of business is to blame; for when my secretaries do not quite catch my meaning, they of their own accord, are apt to sharpen the expressions, nor am I able to read over what I have directed to be written. For this once pardon me; henceforth I will read over whatever I shall write to you by the hand of others, and will trust only to my own eyes and ears." Therefore I forgive and easily grant pardon. For it is no great labour to me (I speak humbly) even in great offences, to forgive one who asks, to give pardon when entreated: and if it be no trouble to forgive in grave matters, how much less, rather none at all, can it be in light ones?

[1] This letter is not now extant.

5. Concerning the will of Dom Baroni, the Roman sub-deacon, which when at the point of death he is said to have made in favour of your abbeys at Clairvaux and Citeaux, those things which he had left with us; I was made aware of this by certain persons who said that this was enjoined upon them by him. Yet I wish you to know that, according to the opinion of persons worthy of credit, you will find that you owe those things more to the kindness of the Abbot of Cluny, than to the will of Baroni. I know indeed, I am not so unskilled in divine or human law as to be ignorant, how by a will both legacies and trusts are binding at death. But yet I read elsewhere: "Nothing is so agreeable to natural law, as to hold as a binding disposition the act of a possessor who himself transfers his property to another person." I say this, because as the before-mentioned witnesses confess, whatever he had deposited at Cluny he intended to leave to Cluny, unless he removed it in his lifetime. Yet I was unwilling to use this privilege: and that, which, according to their testimony, I believed to be mine, I gave [1] up to you and yours. What I think about the election at Grenoble, which our friends the Carthusians oppose, I have confided to my dear friend, your faithful Nicholas, to be related to you. You may believe what he tells you from me to be my opinion. If any requests have escaped my mind, when I remember them, I will ask them of my dear friend in Christ. To conclude, I ask as much as is possible, and desire, what I have already requested of certain of your Order: that in this great body of holy men, who have assembled at Citeaux, you will make mention of me as your sincere friend, and that you will commend earnestly me and the whole congregation at Cluny to their prayers.

[1] See notes to Ep. 270.

LETTER CCCLXXXIX. [Formerly No. 354: the former No. 389 is now No. 413] (A. D. 1150).

To Peter, Abbot of Cluny.

Bernard expresses the pleasure which the letter of Peter had given him, and regrets that the burden of his occupations prevents his writing at greater length.

To his very dear father and lord, Peter Abbot of the Cluniacs, Brother Bernard, called Abbot of Clairvaux, health and the assurance of his prayers.

I have had but a little moment to read your letter, but I have been affected by it in no small degree. Though I had been occupied as much as you know, or may suppose, dearest father, yet I was able to withdraw for a moment, and escape from a crowd of people who had business with me, and to whom I was to give interviews. Shutting myself up with that Nicholas whom your soul loves, I read and re-read your letter, in which I found so much sweetness. Your affection was so manifest in it, that it aroused my affection in return. I regretted that I was so tormented with business, as not to be able to reply. There could not have been a worse day for that: for a great multitude had come together, from almost every nation under heaven. It was necessary that I should give an answer to all. It was no doubt, for my sins that I was born into the world for these cares without number, by which my life is weighed down and consumed. In the meantime I write to you, my dear friend, these few words of reply: and when I shall get the time, I will write you more carefully, to open to you more clearly the heart of one who loves you. With respect to the will of Baroni which you have sent to me, I may most truly say that I receive as a gift on your part, and not as a legal right, the legacy made by it. I am glad to know the exact facts regarding the election at Grenoble,[1] and I assure you that I am very sensible of that which our common son reported to me upon that subject on your behalf. I am quite prepared to do willingly what you wish in that matter. In your General Chapter at Citeaux, special mention was made of you, as of an eminent father and prelate, and also a dear friend: and prayer made for all the Religious of your Order, whether living or dead. [2]

The Bishop Elect of Beauvais [3] as being yours, salutes you: for he is yours.

I Nicholas, your son (who have written this letter) salute you for ever and beyond; and also all that saintly community who are united to you both in body and in spirit. [4]

LETTER CCCXC. [Formerly No. 314: the former No. 390 is now No. 375] (A. D. 1152).

To Eskilus, Archbishop of Lund, and Legate of the Apostolic See in Denmark and Sweden.[5]

Bernard declares himself humbly grateful for his friendship, and offers his own in return.

To his very dear lord and father, Eskilus, by the grace of God, Archbishop of Lund,[6] Brother Bernard, called Abbot

---

. [1] See Ep. 388, 5.

[2] These prayers were customary between congregations of Religious which were united by the band of mutual intercession.

[3] Henry. See Ep. 307, and notes.

[4] This postcript is added by Nicholas, secretary to S. Bernard, on his own account.

[5] Dacia et Succia. But read Daniâ et Suediâ (E.)

[6] Lund was the metropolitan See of Denmark, of which Eskilus was Archbishop. This prelate received many letters from Peter of Celles, who at his request, sent Carthusian monks into Denmark, and who praises him (B. i. cp. 23) because by his means "the Order of Citeaux or Clairvaux, and also that

of Clairvaux, health in Him who is truly our Saviour.

1. I have received your letter and greeting, or rather the assurance of your heartfelt affection towards me as gladly, as I return a similar affection towards you. I cannot read the account of all your troubles, without sharing them as if they were my own: nor am I able, very dear father, to see you grieved without myself grieving, nor to hear of your troubles and anxieties without being also troubled and anxious. Whatever disturbs your heart touches and pains mine: and the enemies of your peace trouble not you only, but me also. For, all the thought and affection which friends owe to each other in absence, I consider that I owe to you, and you to me. I am bold in thus expressing myself, but I am sincere: and to this boldness the condescension of your Greatness has compelled me. When, without that, should I have thus presumed? or being a poor and humble Religious, have dared to hope for the friendship of a man so highly placed? But if I cannot repay you wholly, I am not without one who will undertake my debt; for the Lord will repay for me (Ps. cxxxviii. 8); the Lord, I say, in whom and for whose sake

of Prémontré, entered those countries not only in the blade, but in the ear, and that great increase of their brethren took place there." I find that Eskilus was not only Archbishop of Lund in Denmark, but also Primate of Sweden by a decree of Pope Adrian IV. He came from Denmark to Clairvaux to visit S. Bernard. (Mabillons Note).

It may not be superfluous to add to the above that Lund (*Londinum Gothorum*) is actually in Gothland, a province of Sweden, but which was long the chief seat and the capital of the Danish power in Scandinavia, and thence said to be in Denmark. The metropolitan power of the See extended over all Sweden, Norway and Denmark: but this dates from 1104. Pope Adrian IV. (Nicholas Brakespeare, the only English Pope) sat only from A. D. 1154 to A. D. 1159. (E.)

you have embraced me with such warm and devoted friendship.
Blessed be thy holy Angel, who has suggested that to thy
pious heart; blessed be our God, who has given the suggestion good effect. I am honoured by the privilege of
your friendship: I have been refreshed by the abundance
of your kind messages delivered to me also by my very
dear brother, your son William: your messenger, as by
your letter and by those also who proceed from your
country to ours, and from this country to you.

2. Would that it were given to me to say these things
to you by word of mouth instead of writing them, for
thus I should be much better able to express my feelings
towards you. The word spoken is certainly more welcome
than the word written; the tongue better able to express
the sentiments of the soul than the fingers to write them.
For the eye of the speaker wins acceptance for his words
and the countenance would express the disposition of the
heart better than the fingers. But since I am at a distance
from you, and not able to speak for myself, I do so as
well as I can by means of a letter, which is the next best
mode of communication. I have received your messenger
with great pleasure, and have supported your business with
all the credit that I have with my lord, the Pope. [1]

As regards the secret purpose [2] which your heart so
ardently nourishes, William, your devoted servant in the

---

[1] See Ep. 280. n. 4.

[2] He had the design of taking the monastic habit at Clairvaux. S. Bernard was still living when Eskilus paid a visit to
Clairvaux. See *Life of S. Bernard*. B. iv. C. 4. No. 25 and onwards,
where there is also mention of two monasteries founded by
this prelate. Peter of Celles (B. vii, Ep. 17) congratulated him
on having succeeded in his purpose. It was in 1178 that he
finally became a monk at Clairvaux, where he passed in pious
exercises the last five years of his life, and died there in 1182.

bowels of Jesus Christ, will tell you what I think of it:
I have placed my words in his mouth, and you may listen
to what he says respecting it as to myself.

Alas! I am obliged to close, and cannot write further.
The hard duties of the day summon me, a crowd of visi-
tors requires my presence, and I am enforced to break
off abruptly my letter rather than to finish it. But although they prevent me from writing to you at the length
I could wish, they cannot make my affection for you any
less; I cannot express it at leisure, but I feel it just as
strongly. My heart is always with you, although my time
is employed elsewhere; and it will be with you always,
most reverend and pious father, who art the object of
my entire friendship.

LETTER CCCXCI. [Formerly No. 347: the former No. 391 is now No. 326.]

To the Abbess of Favernay.[1]

*Bernard warns her that not only the walls of her
house but the characters of its inmates should be reformed;
and urges upon her diligent care of the hospital attached
to the Abbey.*

Bernard, called Abbot of Clairvaux, to A..., Abbess of
Favernay, health and the double merit of purity and grace.

Those brethren who have come to consult me for their
soul's health have given me no little pleasure in speaking
of the good purpose and earnest zeal which you display
in reforming the institution over which by the grace of

---

[1] This was an Abbey of Benedictines situated in the diocese of Besançon, and County of Burgundy. Archbishop Anséric
entrusted the reform of it to the Religious of Chaise-Dieu
in 1132 the date of this letter. See Ep. 190.

God you are placed; but I warn you and entreat you that you show as much care in forming the characters of your nuns as in repairing the walls of your monastery. It is equally your duty to take diligent care of the hospital also, which those brethren I referred to, carry on under your direction; and that you should keep it safe and free from any exaction or spoliation on the part of your servants and vassals. It was by their evil advice as I hear, that certain things given to that house by the Abbesses who preceded you, have been taken away by you, and these I entreat you to restore. For as it is a part of your care to undo or correct the ill-doing of others, so you ought to preserve and maintain and even to increase and multiply the possessions of those who have done well. The Presbyter also, who, while dwelling in that house, seems to have at the same time property outside, you ought to oblige either to give up the care of that property or leave the house. Farewell: and rely on my assistance in anything which is in my power, because of the good which I have heard of you.

LETTER CCCXCII. [A new letter: the former No. 392 is No. 327].

To Ralph, Patriarch of Antioch.

Bernard urges upon him the duty of humility.

To the very reverend lord and father, R., by the grace of God, Patriarch of Antioch, Brother BERNARD, Abbot of Clairvaux, wishes all that the earnest friendship of a poor Religious can desire, or the prayer of a sinner can obtain for him. If notwithstanding my lowly station I dare to write to your Greatness do not impute it to presumption but to a confiding simplicity; for both Brother Hatto has suggested that I should do so, and charity has determined me to follow the suggestion. Therefore, after having briefly expressed my respect and devotedness and having rendered to you the greeting and reverence which is due, I pray the Almighty God that He who deigned to place Peter in that See may render you also a worthy successor in it. But as your prudence well knows, no combatant *will be crowned, unless he shall have striven lawfully*. Hence that blessed Apostle himself, whose words these are, when he wished to say that a crown of righteousness was laid up for him, prefaced his declaration by saying *I have fought a good fight* (2 Tim. iv. 7). If it be the case that the life of man upon earth is a continual warfare (Job vii. 1), what then ought to be the life of a Bishop, who has double cause to combat, for himself first, and then for the flock committed to his charge? It is his duty in fact to struggle against the desires of the flesh, against the devices of the world, against spiritual wickedness in high places. And who is fit to do this? this threefold cord is not easily broken. These are the three bands which the Chaldeans made, in order to fall upon the herds of Job, and carry them away; namely the flesh, with its vices and its evil desires. But *let God arise, and let His enemies be scattered* (Ps. lxviii. 1). Let Him arise, I say, whom we need; Who has said *Without Me ye can do nothing* (S. John xv. 5). But as to when He is with us, what says the Apostle: *I can do all things through Christ which strengtheneth me* (Phil. iv. 13). Be thou also strengthened in Him, my father, and thou wilt be strong: gird thyself, stand fast in the fight, combat with courage on behalf of the flock entrusted to thee, and which thou art bound to restore in safety to Him who entrusted them to you; but combat on your own behalf also, since you will have to give account for your own soul. You have been raised to a very lofty position; be also the more vigilant in it: lest (which may God forbid) you should fall thence, and the fall be the more crushing, as the station was the loftier. So you shall hold your exalted post in a fit manner, without conceiving feelings of pride; according as the Apostle says: *Be not high-minded, but fear* (Rom. xi. 20). To a thoughtful and wise man, a lofty station is much more a cause for fear than for pride. If the Church confers dignities, it fears nevertheless the ruin of those on whom they are conferred: but it is not the high rank, only the pride of rank, that is blameable. Who should so much fear and suspect a headlong fall, as the man who sits on high with lofty look and frown of pride? The fear of a possible catastrophe represses the haughtiness of dominion. Whatsoever we wish that men should do unto us, let us also do the same unto them. Who does not wish to have deference from his inferiors? would that we equally rendered it to those who are superior to us. If not, we are as those who use two weights and two measures, a thing which is abominable before God (Prov. xx. 10). We are then in the same condition, if we do not render to our superiors the same weight or measure of dutiful obedience as we require from our subordinates. I cannot sufficiently admire the cautious and humble faith shown in the reply of the Centurion, who said to the Saviour: *For I also am a man placed under authority, having soldiers under me* (S. Luke vii. 8). O prudent soul and heart truly humble! before speaking of his own power over his soldiers, he repressed any arrogance in his speech by a recital of his own subjection to authority, and so laid more stress upon the fact that he was under the rule of others, than that he was placed to rule over others. For the order of his sentence shows the sequence of his thoughts, and the well-arranged method of his earnest request. I should wish to enlarge on this subject, and to

6

make distinctions more clearly: but modesty withholds me.
I will do so, when I shall have leisure to write to greater
length; provided that I am assured that these few words
have given you pleasure. In conclusion, I earnestly entreat,
that if I have as much favour and interest with you as is
generally supposed, those soldiers of God, who dwell in
the Temple at Jerusalem, may find that they are still more
in your favour henceforth because of my commendation
In so doing be assured that you will act acceptably towards
God and at the same time agreeably to men.

LETTER CCCXCIII. (A new letter).

To W., Patriarch of Jerusalem.[1]

Bernard exhorts him to humility.

To the venerable Lord and beloved Father, W., by the
grace of God, Patriarch of Jerusalem, BERNARD, Abbot of
Clairvaux, wishes health and the Spirit of truth, who proceedeth from the Father.

1. Having an opportunity of sending by a trustworthy
man, a friend of ours, who is the bearer of this, I, although
busied about many things, write a few words to you, who
art also busy. If indeed it seem to any presumptuous
and I be judged for this, yet it is a light presumption
that proceeds from affection. But that I may not write
much when I, promised little, let me come to the point.
When it pleased the Creator of the universe to make
known the depth of the wisdom of his plan for the salvation of the human race, He so loved the world, that
He gave His only begotten Son, who was made man for
men, and He called to Himself those of the sons of men
whom He would; both chosen out of the rest, and beloved above the rest. And again one of these, as if elected

---

[1] William, to whom letter 175 was written; which see.

from the elect, and beloved beyond the beloved, He separated for the special favour of his love: to whom,
when lifted up from the earth, He offered with out-
stretched hands His evening sacrifice, before He commended
His spirit into His Father's Hands; He, like a Brother to
a brother, a virgin Himself, committed His virgin Mother
to a virgin in His stead. To what end such a beginning?
Listen carefully.

2. The Lord has chosen many, and made them princes
among His people, that they might have the dignity of the
Episcopate; but thee by a special grace He placed in the
house of His servant David. To thee also of all the
bishops in the whole world has been committed that
land, whence sprang the green herb, and the fruit of the
earth after its kind; from which sprang also the Rose of
Sharon and the lily of the valley. Thee alone, I say, the
Lord chose above thy fellows, to be to Him as it were
a bishop for His household, day by day to enter into His
Tabernacle, and to adore Him in the very place, where
His feet once stood. We read that it was said to holy
Moses when he received a command from the Lord to
make known to the sons of Israel: *Loose thy shoe from
off thy feet, for the place whereon thou standest is holy
ground* (Exod. iii. 5). That place is also holy, but it was
sanctified by type and figure; while this has been hallowed by
the very Truth Himself. That spot was holy, but this is
holier. What comparison is there between the figure of
the truth, which is seen only as in a glass and darkly,
and that glory which shall be revealed when the veil is
at length taken away. And yet when all these things were
shown in figure and as still future, it was said to Moses:
*Loose thy shoe from off thy feet; for the place whereon
thou standest is holy ground.* And I say to you: loose
thy shoe from off thy feet, for the place where thou

standest is holy ground. If hitherto your affections have
been in any degree set on dead works—give them up
quickly : for the place whereon thou standest is holy
ground. O how fearful is that place, in which first through
the mercy of our God the Dayspring from on high hath
visited us! O how fearful is that place, in which first the
Father met the Son returning from a region so little
worthy of Him, and falling upon His neck clothed Him
with a robe of glory! O how fearful is that place, in
which the sweet and righteous Lord poured into our
wounds both oil and wine, in which the Father of mercies,
and the God of all consolation, made with us a covenant
of peace. Thanks to Thee, O Lord, thanks to Thee, because Thou hast worked a good work in the midst of the
earth, in the midst of the years, making this a mark of
law and grace. For when Thou wert angry, Thou didst
remember pity. Behold a place far more sacred than
that on which Moses stood, and far more noble : for it
is the place of the Lord, the place, I say, of Him who
came by Water and Blood; not only by water, as Moses,
but by Water and Blood. Behold the place, where they
laid Him! Who shall ascend into the hill of the Lord,
or who shall stand in His holy place? He alone ought to
ascend, who has learnt from the Lord Jesus Christ to be
meek and lowly of heart.

3. The humble can alone ascend securely; because humility has no exaltation from whence it can fall ; the proud,
although he climb, yet cannot stand for long, like one
who wishes not to stand on his own feet, but has taken
to himself that of another, like him of whom the Prophet
says in detestation: *Let not the foot of pride come against
me* (Ps. xxxvi. 11). For pride has only one foot, the
love of its own excellence. And so the proud cannot stand
for long, like one who only leans on one foot. For who

can stand on that foot, on which have fallen those who worked
iniquity as an Angel in heaven, and a man in paradise?
If God spared not the natural branches; the man, I mean
whom He crowned with glory and honour, and set over
all the works of His Hands; nor a angel, who was the
beginning of His works, full of wisdom and of perfect
beauty: much more is it to be feared lest He spare not
me when I boast myself; being no longer in the garden
of pleasure, nor in the realm of heaven, but in the vale
of tears. Therefore that you may stand firm, stand in humility; stand not on the one foot of pride, but on the
feet of humility, that your footsteps be not shaken. For
humility has two feet, the consideration of Divine Power,
and of its own weakness. O beautiful feet and firm,
neither wrapped in the darkness of ignorance, nor stained
with the slippery soil of luxury! Do you, then, who are placed
on high, refrain from high thoughts, but fear; and humble
yourself under the powerful Hand of Him, who will bow down
in His strength the necks of the proud and lofty. Think
of the Church committed to your hands, not as a servant into
those of a master, but, to go back to the beginning of
my letter, as a mother to the care of a son, as Mary to
John, so that of thee also it may be said to her, *Mother,
behold thy Son.* And of her to thee, *Behold thy mother.*
For so shalt thou be safe in thy coming in and in thy going
out; and in thy approach to His Majesty, who although
He be high and inhabiteth eternity, yet has regard to the
humble both in heaven and in earth.

LETTER CCCXCIV.

To the Archbishop of Lyons.

On behalf of the Abbot of Aisnay near Lyons.

To the Archbishop of Lyons, Legate of the Apostolic See,

BERNARD, Abbot of Clairvaux, health and earnest desire that he may be enriched with good works both before God and men.

I shall not see without profound grief that the high reputation which you have enjoyed, and the odour of sanctity which by your means has been shed over our Mother Church [1] in whose garden you have flourished and bloomed as a lily, should be forfeited and changed. As a cedar is exalted in Libanus, so are you now in the Church of God; amiable, praiseworthy and dear to all. We have already had great actions from you; but hitherto we have been in expectation of still greater ones. Now, however, I say to you: Hold fast what you have already gained; do not allow your fame to decay. Better is a good name, than much riches. How have you treated the Abbot of Aisnay? [2]

It has taken you but an instant to judge him, to condemn him, to depose and deprive him at once of his title and office. You have acted far too hastily in the matter: the thing was done in a moment, in the twinkling of an eye, as it were: absolutely as it shall be at the Resurrection of the dead. Permit me to speak to you with freedom, for the fulness of love casteth out fear. What was the fault of that poor man? His praise is in the Church; and what wrong had he done?

I say what I know for a fact, that both from those who are dwelling in the Abbey and those who are without comes one only opinion; and that in praise of him. Whether he has been guilty of any fault is as yet unknown: for

---

[1] I. e. Lyons: in which province Clairvaux was. See Epp. 172, 174 and note on the latter (E).

[2] Aisnay was an ancient and famous Benedictine Abbey situated near Lyons, at the confluence of the Saône and the Rhône. Later on it became an Abbey of secular canons.

no inquiry according to the canons has been held. It seems to me that he ought to have been left undisturbed, or to have been deposed by a formal and regular judgment. What then! he has confessed no crime, he has been proved guilty by no one, nor convicted in either way, and yet you have condemned him?

But you reply to me: When his cause was in question, he allowed it to go by default. He was not able to produce those witnesses, which I had written to him to bring forward. Very good: according to you, those were against him who did come forward in his favour: it is as if it had been said to them: Either come forward against yourselves, or he will be deposed. Those I allow, he could not have: but he could have others, whose testimonies would have been not less trustworthy than those whom he could not have. But now let us look at the affair from another point of view. Granted that he is wrong: he has made default at the bearing of his cause, his plea has failed, he has no longer the right to call himself innocent. But do you not know that principle: 'It is permitted to revive a faulty process by the remedy of an appeal?' And if you were unwilling to take any notice of the appeal which he has lodged, at least you ought to have deferred further proceedings against him until the issue of his appeal to another tribunal was known. It is unbecoming in the head of a diocese to let rash words and inconsiderate judgments come forth from his lips: hastiness, especially in a cause of such a nature that it cannot remain secret, but must be generally known, is unfitting for a prelate.

I tell you that in injuring that Abbot you have injured many people, who will not be indifferent to the persecution of which he is the object: and not to conceal anything from you, I have been earnestly requested by many persons, whose wishes are not to be disregarded, to write

on his behalf to the Apostolic See. But how could I
resolve to do that, without having first addressed myself
directly to you, my lord and very dear father? I address
myself to you then in the interest of peace, you whose
honour and reputation have always been a matter of interest to me; and intreat you to recall that hasty sentence
and to restore the Abbot to his station, until his cause
shall be re-examined with greater care. This I advise as
your servant, and in your interests. I have no desire to
declare against you, but to be on your side both before
God and before men.

LETTER CCCXCV. [Formerly No. 325].

To Alvisus, Bishop of Arras.

*Bernard represents to the Bishop that there would be
injustice in requiring him to send back to the monks of
S. Bertin, Thomas of S. Omer, who had made profession
at Clairvaux, but whom they made claim to as having
been destined to their Abbey by the vow of his parents.*

To his venerable father and friend, Alvisus,[1] by the grace
of God, Bishop of Arras, Brother Bernard, called Abbot,
health and the assurance of his poor prayers.

1. You have made a request of me on behalf of the
Abbey of S. Bertin, which you love, and which I love too,
and have loved from its foundation. Would that your Prudence had more carefully considered what it is that the

---

[1] The same person who, as Abbot, is addressed in Ep. 65.
He was Bishop from 1131 to 1148, and died the 8th October
of that year at Philippopolis, according to the necrology of
S. Denys at Rheims.

Mention is made of his death in a letter of Louis le Jeune
(*Epp. Sugerian.* no. 22. See Ep. 339).

venerable Abbot of that monastery asks; and what a thing it is, I do not say to do, but even to ask to be done? For I do not doubt that you would have blamed him as one who was doing a grave wrong, not only to us his friends, but to the man whose soul he seeks for: yea, and also against God, whose Providential counsels he seeks to alter. What my lord and father, could he persuade you, to make such a request as that, of your friend? God makes his voice heard from heaven by Thomas, bids him leave his country and his friends and his father's house, and come to the place where He shall show him. Who am I that I should thwart the Spirit of God? What right have I to hinder Him, who calls His own sheep by name, who Himself leads them forth, so that they may follow Himself and no other? Thomas has chosen poverty; am I to send him back to riches and pleasures?

2. I am not ignorant that at S. Bertin the brethren are able to work out their salvation: let those whom God has called thither remain in that vocation in which they have been called. I know well where I have read: *No man having put his hand to the plough and looking back, is fit for the Kingdom of God* (S. Luke ix. 62). For no reason whatever would I be willing to put a stumbling-block in the way of my dear son Thomas, or to grieve a soul which God has entrusted to me. And I am beyond measure astonished, that a prelate of such good judgment as yourself, should allow himself to be persuaded to make such a request of me. For I am tempted to reply, presuming on your friendship, as you know, as the Lord did to the sons of Zebedee: *Ye know not what ye ask* (S. Matt. xx. 22). But I reflect that my affection must not make me presume so far as to forget that I owe deference to the dignity of a Bishop.

3. Act then as you are accustomed to do: honour your function in this matter also, and bravely give assistance

to those souls, the spouses of Christ, whom He has called
to Him, that they may attain to enter in without
hindrance or delay. Act I say, as the friend of the Bridegroom, who stands and rejoices greatly when he hears
the Bridegroom's voice: and as you are accustomed to
help others, so help these, as not to smother (which God
forbid) the inspiration of the Spirit, but to show yourself
a faithful worker together with Him. For your Paternity
may be quite sure of this: that [those souls] shall never
fall from their profession at my advice or by my permission. For I know that I should myself sin, and should
cause them to sin, should I either advise or permit them
[to leave and go elsewhere]. Let them then fulfil the vows
which have gone out of their lips. Let those beware who
lend an ear to the teachers who say: Behold, here is
Christ, or there is Christ. For it will behove them one
day to give account before the tribunal of Christ of the
vow they have made, and of which I am the witness.

LETTER CCCXCVI. [1] [Formerly No. 365].

To Ricuin, Bishop of Toul.

*Bernard excuses himself for having unknowingly received
one of his professed Religious.*

To the venerable Ricuin, by the grace of God, Bishop
of Toul, Brother Bernard, called Abbot of Clairvaux, with
the little flock committed to his charge, wishes health,
safety and peace.

I thank the Author of Salvation, that you have deigned
to honour me with a letter. But I must confess that the
pleasure which your salutation gave me was tempered by
the obedience required of me to your order: nevertheless,
I have done what you directed. At the same time I protest

---

[1] [Ep. 61 is addressed to the same Ricuin].

before God and your Holiness that I received the monk who had made his profession with you, quite unknowingly; and I appeal to the testimony of Brother William himself in proof of this fact. So that if there is anything to blame in his reception; it is not ours. Now that I have given full and sincere satisfaction, I count upon your favour and benediction. Farewell, holy and most reverend father: I trust that your career may be as full in years as in virtues: and that it may be crowned by a holy and peaceful death.

LETTER CCCXCVII. [Formerly No. 387.]

To Odo, [1] Abbot of Marmoutiers, near Tours.

The monks of Marmoutiers were striving about certain tithes with the secular clergy: S. Bernard thinks that they ought to submit to the decision of arbitrators.

To the most reverend Father and Lord Odo, by the grace of God, Abbot of Marmoutiers, and to the Community under his charge, holy and united in the love of Christ, Hugo, Abbot of Pontigny and Bernard of Clairvaux, wish health, and pray that they may walk in the Spirit and seek with all zeal the face of the God of Jacob.

1. Charity, brethren, bids us write to you and for your good, because although we are absent from you, it is only in place not in heart. For the sweet and fragrant odour of your well-known holiness has led our minds to the same desire of your society. But we have seen with deep regret for some time past, that this happiness and peace, which we have shared, has been diminishing day by day. For suddenly a cloud of sinister report has arisen, doubtless from the face of the north [2] wind, and

---

[1] Odo was Abbot from 1124 to 1137.

[2] See note on Ep. 165 (E).

covered our faces with confusion, since we were far from expecting to hear of you a thing quite unworthy of your high reputation. Fearing therefore lest both your fame be imperilled and our glorying on your behalf hindered, unless the reports which spread so quickly were replaced by a breeze of happier character; we, by an impulse of fraternal solicitude, have undertaken by this letter to urge upon your Reverences promptly to apply a remedy to the harm done to your reputation by the reports which are daily flying abroad.

We wonder that some of you (for indeed we do not suspect all) have been so simple or so blinded with avarice, as not so spare your own high reputation in preferring the petty offerings of one altar (See note 1 at end of letter) to the esteem of the world. You ought not, my brethren, you ought not to put on a level with any earthly gain, the testimony to your high character which you have long since deservedly gained, even from those who are without. But perhaps you say : We are doing wrong to none. We are only maintaining our rights, and are ready, if anyone contests them, to submit to the decision of the judge. Very good. But what would you reply if another should answer and say : *This is the very fault which is in you, that you have lawsuits ; why do you not rather suffer wrong?* (1 Cor. vi. 7). What if another has also written: *"If any have stolen thy goods, seek them not back"* and further, *If a man strike thee on the right cheek, offer him the left also ; to him that taketh thy coat offer also thy cloke* (S. Luke vi. 29, 30).

2. These and the like objections we might make to you, we did not prefer to correct rather than to condemn you. But this we say, that it is safer for every Christian and especially for a monk, to possess a little in peace, than much with strife. As we sing : *" a small thing that*

the righteous hath is better than great riches of the ungodly
(Ps. xxxvii. 16). What then is the reason that you
strive about the altar and against the sons of Levi, i. e.,
against the clergy? It is the part of clergy to serve the
altar and to live by the altar. Our profession and the
example of the monks of old tell us to eat the good of our
own labours, and not of the sanctuary of God. Here, it
happens that the clergy serve this very church, about
which is the present dispute, and you desire to partake
with them the recompense, when you have performed
none of the duties. Paul claims for the clergy, and Moses
did so before him, *Thou shalt not muzzle the ox that
treadeth out the corn* (Deut. xxv. 4) again: *Who planteth
a vineyard and eateth not of the fruit thereof; or who
feedeth a flock and eateth not of the milk of the flock?*
(1 Cor. ix. 9).

But we ask you, on the contrary, "with what boldness,
O monks, do you claim wine from a vineyard you have
not planted, or milk from a flock which you have not
fed? by what agreement do you make a demand where
you have given nothing? Certainly if you will, baptize the
infants, bury the dead, visit the sick, unite those that
will be married, teach the ignorant, rebuke sinners, excommunicate the scornful, absolve the penitent, reconcile the
sorrowful; in a word, let a monk, though it is his part to
sit still and be silent, open his mouth in the midst of
the church, then perchance will also the labourer prove
himself worthy of his hire. But it is a hateful thing to
wish to reap where you have not sown: while to gather
what another has sown, is absolutely unjust."

3. Yet let that pass: it is permitted by the gift of the
Bishop, and no wrong must be considered to have been
done, when it is sanctioned by a lawful investiture. However, what are you doing respecting your agreement? Now

that the canons are exclaiming and complaining, if we mistake not, of injury done to them, you will not deny that you have allowed your cause to be placed in the hands of the Bishop of Chartres as well as of Count T., so that whatever reparation is assigned by the judgment of these two, either party will be finally bound by it. That is the best and wisest course. Such mediators have been chosen, and you may have full confidence, not only in their well-proved integrity, but also as we know, in their private kindness of feeling towards you.

What, therefore, good men and your own friends have determined on both kindly and faithfully for restoring peace, why do you not abide by?

Are they to be thought not to have acted faithfully because the award seems not equitable, in that it gives the wealth of the greater to the less? So it may seem indeed, to one who seeks only his own advantage, one who values his coins more than his friends, wealth more than justice, earthly possessions more than brotherly love. If you were of the world, and the world loved that which was her own; that would seem neither wonderful nor unexampled, but now the sons of light and peace, love darkness rather than light, things temporal better than peace. Such as these the lament of the prophet bewails: *they that were brought up in scarlet embrace dunghills* (Lam. iv. 5).

4. Are we not right, they say, not to accept an award which is against our interests? But suppose that it had been against the interests of the other side? The matter then should be decided with equal and just determination. Yet this warning ought to have been given before the agreement was made. For where there is no law, there can be no breach of it. Now that you have given your adhesion, it is no longer a question of your interests, but

of the terms of the agreement. What have you to say
to this, and why do you make difficulties? When you
object to the decision of the arbitrators you show yourselves as turbulent, unfaithful and breakers of covenant.
Either deny the agreement or fulfil it.

What then? You do not deny the agreement, but you
evade it, and lay the blame on the Bishop, as if he had
not acted fairly with you; but had taken you with craft
and guile, and led you into that agreement which now you
deplore? You can say so: but it will be wonderful if you
persuade anyone of it, even if you believe it yourselves.
By no means, they say; but what was done without our
consent, that is, without the consent of the whole Chapter
ought not to stand. What? ought not that which the Abbot
has determined with the consent of the elders to stand, if
you do not all agree? Either you do not regard or you
despise that plain sentence about this very thing in your
Rules. For it decrees "that when the brethren are called
to Council, they shall one by one answer what they think,
provided that they shall not presume to defend their answers: but when the Abbot shall have heard the opinions
of each, whatever he pleases to determine all shall acquiesce
in without contradiction." [1] If therefore in arranging all
things the authority of the Abbot be decisive, the Rule
prescribing it, because on the opinion of the Abbot hangs all
the management of the monastery; it is evident that you
are proving yourselves disobedient and rebellious, who are
trying to overthrow an agreement that the Abbot has made,
and acting against his will. Unless indeed he has said from
his heart, that what he has openly established and determined, he secretly destroys through his monks, and thus
constitutes himself also a covenant breaker. Which be it

[1] Rule of S. Benedict, C. 3.

far from us to believe. For even to suspect so good a man of such a thing, is evil. For that suspicion of some who, more than befits honest people, were seeking evil where none is to be found, does not affect us, when they think that without sinning of this kind there can be no agreements between churches. But, as you inquire very anxiously, we judge that this matter has been satisfactorily dealt with by the answer of catholic and learned men; or even if it should not be so, we are ready to declare on the authority of the canons that as exchanges may be rightly made in ecclesiastical properties, so they seem to be right for churches. These views we express in order to put to silence those who presumptuously introducing themselves into matters which concern them not, are always ready to stir up strife and disorder. [1]

LETTER CCCXCVIII. (Formerly No. 312).

To Guy, Abbot of Montier-Ramey, and the Religious of that Abbey.

Bernard having been requested by the Abbot and monks to compose an Office for the festival of their patron S. Victor, pleads the difficulty of the task and his own scanty qualifications for it: he expounds the qualities needed in forms intended for public worship, and traces the rules of the Ecclesiastical Chant.

To the venerable Guy of Montier-Ramey, [2] and to his

[1] The name of Altars was given to parish-churches which had the right to tithes. At that period, it was not rare to see them conferred on monasteries, even by members of the secular clergy. See letter 316.

[2] A Benedictine Abbey in the diocese of Troyes. It had for patron the Confessor S. Victor, whose Acts are among the works of S. Bernard. The monk Nicholas, Secretary of S. Bernard, was of this Abbey. Respecting him see Ep. 298.

holy community, BERNARD, the servant of their Holiness, health and the power to serve God in holiness.

1. You ask me, my dear Abbot Guy, in company with all your good brethren, to write for you an Office to be solemnly said or sung on the Festival of S. Victor, whose sacred body rests among you. You urge me to do this, in spite of my reluctance and feeling of insufficiency, which you overrule, though it is so well founded. And as if there could be any more powerful motive to me to comply with your wish, than the wish itself, you employ also the intercessions of others with me. But it seems to me that you ought to have consulted your own judgment, to have reflected, not merely on your affection for me, but on my (obscure) position in the Church. For a task of that importance needs not merely a friend, but a learned and able man : whose greater authority, sanctity, and more polished style would both adorn the work and befit its holiness.

2. Who am I, the humblest among Christian people, that my compositions should be read in Churches? And how little eloquence or faculty of invention have I, that I should be called upon to produce a chant suitable to be used and listened to on a Festival? What! can I begin anew to sing on earth the praises of that Saint, who is now being praised, and that worthily, in heaven?

·To wish to add anything to the celestial praises is to detract from them. Not that men may not praise here below, those whom the Angels glorify above; but because on a solemn Festival, the praises of the Church ought to have nothing of novelty or of lightness; but to be authentic and serious, redolent of hoary antiquity, of grave and Church-like character.

But if there was a desire, and an occasion, for the composition of an Office: I should have thought (as I have already said) that it should have been entrusted to some one whose reputation, and whose eloquence, would have enabled him to treat it both more agreeably to the ears of the worshippers and more profitably to their hearts.

The author's aim should certainly be to glorify the truth, to inculcate righteousness, to recommend humility, to teach justice: it should enlighten the mind, elevate the heart, mortify the passions, discipline the senses, crucify evil desires and inspire devotion. The Chant, if one is used, should be full of solemnity [1]; and equally distant from rusticity and luscious sweetness.

Yet let it be sweet, so that it be not trifling; and let it so please the ear, that it may touch the heart.

Let it be such as to lighten sadness, to lower the fire of anger; and let it not obscure but heighten, the sense of the words. It is of no small detriment to the spiritual sense, to have the attention withdrawn from the intention of the words by the levity of the chants, and to be more attracted by the flexibility of the voices, than by the sense of the words they dwell upon.

Such are the qualities which, it seems to me, are needed in the Offices of the Church: and such the ability which those require who undertake to compose them. Am I such as this, or are these qualities to be found in what I have written for you? And yet out of my poverty, as you continued to knock and to call upon me, I felt constrained to rise up, and according to the word of the Saviour, not because you were my friends, but because of your importunity, to give you that which you asked. I send you then, at your earnest request, if not what you wished, at least such as my hand was able to compose. I have made use of facts from ancient writers, which

---

[1] See note ɩ at end of the letter.

you have sent to me, and have written two discourses on the life of the Saint [1] as well as I was able, avoiding in the one hand such brevity as to make them obscure, and on the other a tiresome prolixity. Then as regards the musical part of the Office, I have composed a hymn, taking more heed of the meaning of the words than of the rules of the metre. I have arranged in their proper places twelve Responsories [2] with twenty-seven Antiphons: adding one Antiphon for the first Vespers, and two others to be sung according to your Rule, upon the Festival itself, the one at Laud, the other at Vespers. Now for all these things I expect a return, I ask payment. What then do I expect? Whether you are pleased with them, or no, it matters not; because I have given you what I could. And the price I ask for it, is your prayers for me.

The sentiment which Bernard expresses here with his usual elegance, merits serious attention. It would be easy to supplement it with those of other Fathers, and to show what they have thought respecting Church Music, did the length of a note permit. Nevertheless as the rule here laid down may seem somewhat severe and rigorous, to the opinions and tastes of the present age, I may be permitted to quote the opinion on this subject of a man confessedly pious and religious, who has treated, in a style full of elegance and charm, of subjects important equally to piety and virtue. To musicians he writes thus: "Here permit me to observe to you, that a new kind of singing rules in our Churches; unusual in character, rapid and dancing in time, and in no way suitable for religious purposes, but rather fitting for the theatre or the concert-room.

In the search for artifice, we lose the ancient manner of praying and singing: we follow a secular taste, and neglect the interests of piety. What else is this novel and dancing

---

[1] These will be given later, with the Office of S. Victor.
[2] See note 2 at end of the letter.

kind of chant, in which the singers are made like actors, to take now solos, now duets, and anon choruses : or that in which they reply to each other as in a dialogue, then leaving all of a sudden the field to one who expatiates alone, the others speedily joining in?"

A little farther, the same author continues : "In the last age there were musicians of surpassing genius, as you your-selves allow, who have composed a kind of music very differ-ent from yours, and (if I may say so) much more religious. But your disdain has long since buried their books of music. Restore to us, I entreat, somewhat of the ancient religious-ness in our sacred music ; take to heart, and spend your care upon, the addition of beauty to Divine worship, by composing chants more in harmony with the meaning of the words which they are to interpret. What is the use to me in Church of varied airs and harmonies in many parts, if there be no unity in the Chant, and if I am unable even to distinguish the words, which the music ought to make an entrance for into the heart?" (Jerome Drexelius *Rhetor. Celest.* B. i. C. 5).

2. A *Responsory* was a versicle sung by the choir in an-swer to the priest or other officiant ; or as a refrain between the verses of a Psalm or Lection, also before or after a Lection.

An *Antiphon* was of a similar character, but before or after a Psalm. Generally only a few words were said *before*, and the whole *after*, the Psalm in question : but on great Festivals this was altered. (E.)

LETTER CCCXCIX. (Formerly No. 319).

To Lelbert, Abbot of S. Michael. [1]

Bernard sends back to him a monk who had quitted his cloister under a false pretext of pilgrimage.

To his father and friend, Lelbert, Abbot of S. Michael, Brother Bernard, the unprofitable servant of the servants

---

[1] There were many Abbeys of this name in France : Mount S. Michael otherwise called *in Periculo Maris*; S. Michael on the Meuse ; S. Michael de Tonnerre in Burgundy; de l'Ermi-

of God who are in Clairvaux, health and due affection.

This your son returns to you, having renounced, by my advice, the pilgrimage which he had undertaken, although it was with your leave. For on enquiry I find that the permission to set out upon this enterprise was only asked by him in pure frivolity of mind, and only granted by you because of his importunity : I have sharply reprimanded him, as he deserved, and persuaded him to return. He is as far as I can tell, sorry for his instability, and resolved to correct it. I believe that it is better for a Religious, whatever fault he have been guilty of, to do penance in the interior of his monastery, than to go abroad and wander over one province after another. The object of monks is to attain, not the earthly Jerusalem, but the heavenly : and we reach it, not by wandering upon our feet, but by reaching out towards it by the affections. But you, my father, will I doubt not, make him welcome at his return, even although you suspect the sincerity of his conversion : and will rather rejoice because this your son was dead, and is alive again: he was lost, and is found [1] (S. Luke xv : 32).

tage in Poitou; and S. Michael in Thiérache (Terascia) which latter is thought to have been the Abbey of Lelbert. He is .perhaps confounded with Elbert who conveyed in 1121 to Bartholomew, Bishop of Laon, a piece of ground on which to build a Cistercian Abbey at Foigny. Or it may be that Gilbert, his successor, is meant. He is mentioned in a Cartulary under 1130 and called by the monk Hermann of Laon, the Plato of his age. (Mirac. B. V. M. B. iii. c. 19). After the death of Simon Abbot of S. Nicholas (who is mentioned in Ep. 83) Gilbert was recalled to the latter Abbey, whence he had been taken. A diploma of Pope Innocent II. in 1138 is granted to his successor.

[1] These are similar expressions to those used by Hildebert on the same subject (Ep. 33). The language of Bernard may

LETTER CD. [Formerly No. 32*b*].

To the Abbot of Liesse. [1]

*He begs that Brother Robert may be received and kindly
treated : and enquires respecting the Abbot's health.*

To the venerable father of the monastery at Liesse,
and to his sons, Brother Bernard, the unprofitable servant
of the servants of God who are at Clairvaux, health and
prayer that they may serve the Lord with fear and rejoice
unto Him with trembling.

I send back brother Robert; entreating for him and
with him, in the first place, that he may be welcomed with
a greater degree of kindness and clemency, than is ordi-

be compared with that of Abbot Theodomir, in a treatise
of Jonas, Bishop of Orleans, against Claude of S. Taurin, about
the pilgrimage of monks.

[1] Some copies have *Lesciensis*. This was a Benedictine
Abbey, on the borders of Hainault and Thiérache, and already
celebrated even at that time, by the cultivation of sacred
literature, as we learn from Philip de Eleemosyna (Ep. 24.
Bibliothec. Cisterc. Vol. iii.). It became famous again at a
later time by the piety and foundations of one of its Abbots,
Louis de Blois. It was built up from the ground in 1080 by
Thierry d'Avesne (Heriman in *Spicileg.* v. xii. p. 423). Gun-
ther was the first Abbot; and after twelve years was succeeded by Reiner, who died 1124. Gedric followed as Abbot;
he founded the library, and drew around him out of Hainault
pious and learned men. It may have been Gedric to whom
this letter was addressed.   (Mabillon's Note.)

The conjecture thus made is confirmed by the following
observation of Edmund Martène : "Ep. 400 in the copy at S.
Martin at Tours which is very ancient, is headed *Epistola
Bernardi ad Werricum* (for which name it is easy to read
Wedricum) *Letiensem Abbatem.*" The name had not been
known previously.

narily shown to returning fugitives. For the penalty ought not to be the same, where the [cause of the] offence is different. In the next place, I earnestly request that he may be removed from the Obedience [1] where he has been long constrained to stay, at the peril [as he says] of his soul; and transferred to another house, where he may dwell more safely and happily. Otherwise, I fear that you may lose the man irrevocably, for I have penetrated his secret intentions.

I have heard that your Lord Abbot is dangerously ill; and am most desirous to hear how matters are with him, whether tending towards life or death, and to rejoice over his continuance in life, though it be mortal life, or grieve for his death, though the death be an entrance into life; or to speak more accurately, that I may experience in either case both joy and grief. For in the former, I shall condole indeed with him, because he is kept back from life, but rejoice with you, because he is preserved to us; while in the latter, I shall congratulate him on having attained his reward, even while I mourn with you on the loss of a friend so needful to us.

LETTER CDI. (Formerly No. 338).

To Baldwin, Abbot of Châtillon.

He reassures this Abbot, who from a false report, feared that he had offended Bernard.

Since you fear so much that you have offended me, I infer that you love me much. But lay aside this appre-

---

[1] The name of Obedience, cell, priory or villa, was given to a country house occupied by two, three or more Religious, who were charged with the care of it. These houses are called cellules (*cellulæ*) in Ep. 254: *n*. 1.

hension; for what you feared is not the case. I have looked carefully into the report, as you advised, and I find that the mischief was in the mouth of the person who told this to you. You may be sure that one of two alternatives is the fact: the man spoke to you out of suspicion, or else from mere malignity. Doubtless the fraud of which he has been guilty, shall recoil upon his own head, this iniquity fall upon his own path. For he is the culprit in this, which he falsely imputes to another.

LETTER CDII. (Formerly No. 336).

To Baldwin, [1] Bishop of Noyon.

Bernard recommends a young man to him pleasantly.

To Baldwin, Lord Bishop of Noyon, Brother Bernard, called Abbot of Clairvaux, health and a recompense even greater than his deserts.

I send you a young man, the bearer of this letter, to eat of your bread, that I may make proof, by seeing whether you permit this reluctantly or no, of your avarice or liberality. Do not mourn over it, do not weep: he has but a little stomach, he will not eat much. Yet I (shall) thank you; if he returns from you fatter in body and more instructed in mind as well. Let the manner [2] of speech

---

[1] About his election there is a letter of the Chapter of Noyon among those of Abbot Suger (No. 44); and in the same collection are found many of the same Baldwin, then Bishop, about the Church of Compiègne; they are No. 157, 158 and 162. From Ep. 44 it appears that Baldwin was Abbot of Châtillon before being Bishop. It was to him that Bernard wrote Letters 279 and 401; and he is himself the writer of Letter 426.

[2] *Maneries*: Low Latin for Modus, used here in the sense of manner, or *mannerism*. Mod. Fr. *manière*. John of Salisbury uses the word (Metalog. C. 17) and other authors, but it is rare. See Du Cange, *Sub voce* (E.)

I have used stand instead of a seal, for mine is not at hand, nor is your friend Geoffrey. [1]

LETTER CDIII. (Formerly No. 340).

To the Archdeacon Henry. [2]

Bernard discusses whether Baptism would be valid if administered in the form:

'Baptizo te, in Nomine Dei, et sanctæ et veræ Crucis!'

To his friend HENRY, the Archdeacon, Brother BERNARD, called Abbot of Clairvaux, health and the assurance of his prayers.

1. I reply briefly to the question you proposed to me; yet with all respect to the opinions of persons wiser than I. A child just born, and in danger of death, was, you tell me, baptized by a certain layman, who did not employ the ordinary formula, but instead of it the words: *Baptizo te, in Nomine Dei, et sanctæ et veræ Crucis!* and you inquire whether the child is really baptized, or if it lives, should be baptized again. [3]

I think the child has been truly baptized; and I do not think those words (which were wrong or superfluous) had the power to nullify the truth of the faith, and the piety of the intention (of him who used them). For not to speak of the fact that in the name of God is implicitly expressed the one Substance of the Holy Trinity, those which follow manifestly refer to the Passion of Our Lord.

---

[1] The secretary of S. Bernard at this time, who had therefore the custody of his seal (E.)

[2] Henry, brother of King Louis the younger, was at that time Archdeacon of Orleans. (Chartulary of S. Martin des Champs.)

[3] p. 98.

Unless we suppose that the Apostle contradicted himself when having said in one place, *He who glories, let him glory in the Lord* (1 Cor. i. 31 and 2 Cor. x. 17), he says in another, *God forbid that I should glory, save in the Cross of our Lord Jesus Christ* (Gal. vi. 14) as if he referred to the wood of the Cross, and not rather to the grace of Him who was crucified.

Similarly, when, pronouncing that ordinary Baptismal formula of the Church, we say: *In the name of the Father and of the Son and of the Holy Ghost* is it to be any otherwise understood, than as a making confession of faith in the Holy Trinity. Further, a confession of faith in the Holy Cross, is only a confession of faith in Him who died upon the Cross. We read in fact in the Acts of the Apostles that Baptisms were performed not only *In the name of the Father, and of the Son and of the Holy Ghost*, but also that some were baptized *In the name of Our Lord Jesus Christ* (Acts. x. 48).

3. You go on to inquire whether the person who performed that baptism did wrong, or whether (if he did not) his formula of Baptism may be imitated by others. But it does not follow that though the extreme simplicity and absence of wrong intent in the act of any individual, shields it from all blame, or at least from severe blame, those persons are to be excused who should have the temerity to introduce into the Church a new formula of Baptism And if it shall be urged that the Baptism in question was after all wrong; yet I hold it for certain that the baptizer was not so far wrong as to endanger either his own salvation or that of the child baptized. For it does not seem to have been through contempt of the Church's formula, that he broke forth into the words in question, but through the precipitation of a faith which was living and full of piety.

This question had been put to Bernard: if the letter before us is really his, which many editors deny, and which I should not venture positively to affirm *(Note of Horst)*.

But Mabillon observes:

This Ep. appears doubtful to some. Yet it is found in the most ancient editions: in that of Lyons in 1520 and all following ones: also in the MS. Codex in the Sorbonne: nor does the style differ from that of S. Bernard. He was asked, I say, whether Baptism administered under the form "I baptize thee in the Name of God and of the holy and true Cross" would be valid; he replies that it is; and supports his opinion by a reason not wanting in force. But at the present day that reason is not accepted by divines; it is opposed to the tradition of the Apostles, of other Fathers, and to the authority of S. Augustine himself: and these all teach with one voice, that the express invocation of the Most Holy Trinity, made with distinct mention of the name of Each of the Three Persons, is of the essence of the formula; and that Baptism administered without this is invalid. So also *Canon. Apostol.* No. 49, which interpreting S. Matt. xxviii. 19 of the Baptismal formula, rejects a Baptism administered 'in the name of the Lord', and continues thus: 'For the Lord does not say to us, Baptize *in my death*; but *Go ye and teach all nations, baptizing them in the Name of the Father and of the Son and of the Holy Ghost."* The statement of S. Augustine is clear, that the words of the Gospel are precise, and that without these Baptism cannot be validly administered (*Contra Donatist.* B. vi. C. 25) Similarly Ep. 23 *ad Bonifacium;* and *contra Faustum* (B. xix. C. 16). What he understands by the words of the Gospel, he explains *Contra Donat.* B. iii. C. 15. "If Marcion administered Baptism with the words of the Gospel, *In the Name of the Father and of the Son and of the Holy Ghost,* the Sacrament was complete and valid." See also *contra Maximin.* C. 17; Ep. 20; and *Enarrat: in Ps.* lxxxvi. Hence also the opinion of Cajetan, that Baptism administered in the name of Christ is sufficient, is shown to be erroneous. (Thus far Mabillon).

The argument of S. Bernard, from the 'truth of the faith and piety of the intention' of the person using the erroneous formula for Baptism, is virtually an appeal to 'the uncovenanted

mercies' of God: an appeal which would have been rightly
made had the child died, and if the debate had been respecting its salvation: but which does not seem to be to the
point when the question is respecting the conditions of the
Sacramental covenant, of which the prescribed formula is one.

The expedient of conditional rebaptism does not appear to
have been thought of by either S. Bernard or his corres-
pondent.   (E.)

LETTER CDIV. [Formerly No. 345].

To Albert, a Recluse.

*He advises him to take food only once in the day; and
not to permit women to enter his cell.*

Brother Bernard of Clairvaux, to Brother Albert, a
recluse, health and prayer that he may be enabled to
fight the good fight.

You ask me to sanction I know not what kind of fast, of
which you had spoken to me within your cell; and also that
you may have conversations with women, which if you remember, I expressly forbade; and you say that because of your
extreme poverty, you cannot avoid these. I do not wish to arrogate to myself any authority over you. I gave you a counsel,
not a precept : to eat only once in the day; not to admit at
all the visits and conversation of women; to maintain
yourself by the work of your own hands; and many other
things which it would take too long to remind you of.
If you foresaw that you would not be able to supply
needs so costly as yours, you should not have attempted
what you cannot carry out. The advice I gave I thought
safe for you; you are not obliged to follow it : but I have
nothing to change in it. Farewell.

LETTER CDV. [Formerly No. 346.]

To the Abbot G.

Bernard assures him that one of his Religious has sufficiently good health to live according to the custom of the community.

To the Abbot G., Brother BERNARD, health and assurance of his friendship.

Be assured that Brother G. since his return from La Chreste [1] where he took various remedies, has performed all the observances of his community, as a man in perfect health, nor has he been indulged in food more than others: also he has attended the night offices as they have done. If he shall do otherwise when with you, do not yield to it. You may be sure that anything wrong with him is not weakness of body, but lukewarmness of soul. Farewell.

LETTER CDVI. [A new letter.]

To the Abbot of S. Nicholas. [2]

To his valued friend and co-abbot of S. NICHOLAS, Brother BERNARD of Clairvaux wishes health and the spirit of piety.

The enemy of Christ, the devil, has acted according his manner, in seducing a soul: as for me, to whom the man seduced happened to come, I have done what I could, as I always strive to do, to correct and bring him back. There remains therefore, that you should do your

[1] A Cistercian monastery in the Diocese of Langres.
[2] This was no doubt Simon, Abbot of S. Nicholas des Bois, to whom are addressed Letters 83, 84.

LETTER CDVIII. [Formerly No. 347].

To W., Abbot of Troyes.[1]

Bernard recommends to him an ecclesiastic who was desirous of quitting the world, but whom he feared would be unequal to the life at Clairvaux on account of his delicate health.

The ecclesiastic whom I send to you was desirous of quitting the world and entering our House, but I, fearing that our Rule would be too severe for him, have persuaded him to take refuge with you. Him therefore I recommend to you as a man well known to me, respectable and learned; and lastly as a servant of God who cannot fail to become, I think, by the grace of God, a trustworthy support and great comfort. It is rather in your interest than in his that I wish him to come to you, whom I love as myself. I would willingly keep him with us on account of his merit and good character, were it not that I fear to accept an ecclesiastic of delicate health and unaccustomed to labour. Farewell.

LETTER CDIX. [Formerly No. 350].

To Borgon of Abbeville.[2]

Bernard tells him that he ought not to attach too great importance to seeing him with the bodily eye: he makes request

[1] This was William, Abbot of the Regular Canons of S. Martin of Troyes.

[2] Borgon of Abbeville, which town is on the Somme, is praised with his wife Elizabeth in an old MS. Breviary in the library of Corbie, written five hundred years before, as being the founder of the house to which this Breviary first belonged, viz., the Priory of S. Peter at Abbeville.

for a certain piece of uncultivated ground for his Religious.

To the illustrious Lord who is dear to me, BORGON of Abbeville, BERNARD, called Abbot of Clairvaux, health and the assurance of my prayers.

It has been mentioned to me that it would be agreeable to you to see and have some talk with me; because you are so kind as to regard me as one of the servants of the Highest. And I reply that I am touched by this proof of your humility and by the good report of your nobleness, of which I have heard; so that I too should have great joy in seeing you.

But this feeling of merely human kindness which we share, although good, is not altogether perfect. For this sight of another with the bodily eye is brief and fleeting, and is such as other living beings may also have. But we ought to look for and sigh after that most joyful vision of the Heavenly society, and to labour for it by good works, so that we may at length attain unto it.

You possess in the parish of Courrenne, a piece of ground which is deserted and uncultivated and altogether useless to your predecessors and yourself until now, and of which my dear and intimate friend, the Abbot of Anchiles-Moines,[1] has spoken to you: if you would have the great kindness to bestow this as an alms upon the Church of Anchiles-Moines, this your bounty shall benefit both your own soul and the souls of your ancestors and of your descendants.

---

[1] This was a Benedictine Abbey which was then in the Diocese of Térouanne, and which was afterwards in that of S. Omer. It was founded at Térouanne on the river Lis, about A. D. 700: at first for nuns, who were afterwards replaced by monks when the Monastery was re-built after the invasions of the Normans.

LETTER CDX. [Formerly No. 366].

To Gilduin, Abbot of S. Victor.[1]

Bernard recommends Peter Lombard to him.

To the reverend lords and fathers, his very dear friends, G., by the grace of God, the venerable Abbot of S. Victor at Paris, and to the entire community of the same, Brother Bernard, called Abbot of Clairvaux, health and the assurance of his humble prayers.

I am forced to ask much of others, since much is asked of me: nor am I able to refrain from putting my friends under contribution, as I am myself made to contribute by other friends. The Lord Bishop of Lucca, my father and

---

[1] The Abbey of S. Victor *extra-muros* (of Paris) was for Regular Canons of the order of S. Augustine. Gilduin was abbot of it from 1133 to 1155. Bernard recommends it to Abbot Suger in his letter 369. The Abbey possessed the *cowl* of S. Bernard, as a proof of the attachment which he always felt towards it. This abbey was founded by Louis le Gros in 1113 and first organized by William de Champeaux, who was removed from it to be Bishop of Châlons. The Abbot of this house was nominated by the King. The Abbey became so flourishing that it had thirty other Abbeys, and more than eighty Priories, in dependance upon it. James de Vitry praises it thus in his *History of the West* C. 24; "This is a holy house, filled with Religious worthy in all respects to be called soldiers of the Lord: it is a refuge for the poor and a consolation for the unhappy, a place of retreat for sinners and a peaceful refuge of scholars .... There have adorned it since its foundation, like stars shining in the sky, or like the precious pearls of a rich coronet, many doctors of the University of Paris, learned and honourable men; at the head of whom is to be named the celebrated Hugh of S. Victor, the lute player (as it were) of the Lord and organ of the Holy Spirit."

friend, has recommended to me the venerable Peter Lombard [1] and begged me to provide, by means of my friends, for his subsistence, during the brief time that he is pursuing his studies in France. This I have done while he was at Rheims. Now he is at Paris, and proposes to remain there until the Nativity of the B. V. Mary,[2] so that I venture to commend him to you, because I rely more on your friendship than on others, and to entreat that you will provide for his subsistence during this time. Farewell.

LETTER CDXI. [Formerly No. 373.]

To Thomas, Provost of Beverley.[3]

Bernard in this sweet and winning letter invites Thomas to enter the Religious life, notwithstanding the sins of his past years. He reminds him that nothing in the world is to be preferred to a good conscience.

To the young man of good promise, Thomas the venerable Provost of Beverley, Brother Bernard, the servant of the poor of Christ who are at Clairvaux, health, and apostolic holiness as his name gives promise.

1. Although I have not the pleasure of being known to you, I venture to write to you in obedience to the impulse of charity and the suggestion of your friend Ivo. He has acquainted me with what he knows of you and what he wishes for you : and charity which *believes all things*

---

[1] Peter, called by theologians the 'Master of the Sentences', was born in Lombardy, and thence called 'the Lombard'. Leaving the school of Bologna he went to study in France. The Bishop of Lucca was Uberto or Gregory, to whom was written Letter 3 of Nicholas of Clairvaux in the person of Bernard.

[2] September 8.

[3] See Letter 107, to the same person.

(1 Cor. xiii. 7) did not suffer me to remain indifferent.
So little in fact is that the case with me, after what I
have heard of you, that it did not require much reflection
to induce me to write to you, to exhort you and even
to pray for you : do you see to it that this be not
ineffectual.   What I have heard of you from those who
know you, does, I must assure you, please me much : not
indeed the nobleness of your descent, your distinguished
manners, your personal beauty, ample means or distinguished position : all these, and whatever resembles them,
are only as a flower of the field, a glory of the mortal
flesh : but it is the quickness of intellect, the frankness
of character and above all the love of holy poverty which
I am told that you have conceived even in the midst
of riches, upon which I greatly congratulate you, and
they give me good hopes respecting you, which I trust
in God will not be confounded.   Would that the Angels
may soon partake our joy, and celebrate with gladness
in the Heavens your penitence and your conversion, as
they do of other sinners.   How happy should I think
myself if it were granted to me to cultivate the flower
of your youth, to train a nature of such rare excellence,
to preserve it for God as a costly perfume, and offer it
to Him as a pure and acceptable gift.

2. Perhaps your conscience will reply to what I have
said, that your life cannot be offered up in complete
purity, since you feel that it has been defiled with many
crimes   Yet this does not affright me, nor, being a sinner, do I shrink from another sinner : nor do I disdain
one sick with sin, since I feel myself similarly diseased.
But even though you think me whole, I do not refuse to
become weak with the weak, that I may gain the weak ;
willingly following the counsel of S. Paul in this : *Ye who
are spiritual, restore such an one in the spirit of gentle-*

ness, considering thyself, lest thou also be tempted (Gal. vi. 1).

I count as nothing the fierceness of the disease when I consider the skill of the Physician, and His kindness which I have so oft experienced in my own times of great spiritual feebleness. Whatever may be the sins with which you are defiled, and however burdened your conscience ; though you feel your youth rendered vile by shocking offences : even though you have been hardened by a long continuance in sins, as a beast of burden in his litter : without doubt you shall be cleansed, you shall be rendered whiter than snow, your youth shall be renewed as that of an eagle. Can I doubt, when it has been said : *Where sin abounded, grace did much more abound?* (Rom. v. 20). The Good Physician healeth all our infirmities of soul and crowneth us with loving kindness and tender mercies. (Ps. ciii. 3, 4).

3. A good conscience is an inestimable treasure: more valuable and more sweet, more sure and secure, than anything else in the world. A good conscience does not fear the loss of possessions, the attack of evil tongues, or the pains of the body ; even death is more a cause of honour to it than of defeat and shame. What good upon earth, I ask, is to be compared to the happiness it gives ? What has the world, with all its false and flattering promises, to offer to those who foolishly love it ? Are wide estates, stately palaces, the insignia of high rank in the Church or in the world? Without speaking of all the cares and dangers without which these things can neither be acquired nor retained, are they not all swept away together from the possessor when death comes to him? For is it not written : *They have slept their sleep and none of the men of might have found their hands.* (Ps. lxxvi. 5). But the blessings of a good conscience

are ever green: they do not wither in time of trouble, they do not pass away at death, but flourish anew: they make their possessor full of joy during life, they console him when dying, they raise him up again when dead, and they fail not for evermore. But why do I linger upon words, when I am prepared to support them by facts? It only depends upon yourself to prove, either that I have borne false witness, or that true riches are in your power. So much I have seen and experienced. With what joyful steps shall I come to offer bread to the fugitive, with what joyful embrace shall I receive a son, who has come to his right mind. The best robe shall be quickly brought forth for him, the ring put upon his finger, and it shall be said: *This my son was dead, and is alive again: he was lost and is found* (S. Luke xv. 24).

LETTER CDXII [A new letter].

To T., a young man, who had vowed to enter the monastic life.

To his very dear son T., Bernard, Abbot of Clairvaux, health and that he may go forth to meet the Bridegroom and the Bride.

·1. I will speak to you in simple words: man is a being rational and mortal: the one of these qualities he owes to the grace of his Creator; the other is the consequence of sin. In the one we are companions of the dignity of the Angels; in the other, of the weakness of the brute creation. Yet each ought to be a motive to us to seek the Lord; both the dignity of reason and the fear of death. Be thou mindful of the promise that thou hast given to me, and in which I repose full confidence. I ask its performance; the time to redeem it approaches; have no fear, where there is nothing to fear. It is not a burden, but an honour, to serve the Lord in joy and gladness I cannot grant to you a long delay: for while nothing is more certain than death, nothing is more uncertain than the hour of death. Your tender age is no safeguard against early death. The fruit is often torn from the tree by the hand or by a tempest, even while it is still green. Why do you rely upon your health and your comeliness?

O beautiful youth, trust not over much to your bloom. The flowers of the white privet fall, the dusky hyacinths are gathered (Virgil. Ecl. ii. vv. 17, 18).

Come forth, come forth with Joseph from the house of Pharaoh and leave your mantle, that is, the glory of the world, in the hand of the Egyptian mistress; come forth from your country and your kindred; forget your own people and your father's house; and the King shall be charmed with your beauty. The Child Jesus is not found among relations and acquaintances. Come forth from your father's house to seek Him; for He came forth on your account from the house of His Father. His coming forth is from the height of heaven. Deservedly was He found of the Syro-Phœnician woman, who came forth from her own land and cried to him, saying: *Have mercy upon me, O Son of David!* For He upon whose lips is grace found, quickly replied to her: *O woman, great is thy faith: be it unto thee even as thou wilt* (S. Matt. xv. 22—28).

2. Satan perhaps may be hostile to Satan: but can the Spirit of truth possibly be contrary to Himself? It was He, I fully believe, who spoke to me by your mouth to tell me of your conversion. See then that you do not turn aside to the right hand or to the left; but come to Clairvaux according to your promise. This I have written to you briefly and in private, and send it by my dear son Gerard, your friend. Do not put forward any excuse. If your earnest desire is in the matter, if you still wish to be taught

and to be under a master; the Master is come and calleth for thee; He I mean in whom all the treasures of wisdom are hidden. It is He who teacheth man knowledge; who makes the tongues of infants eloquent, who openeth and no man shutteth, and who shutteth and no man openeth.

LETTER CDXIII. (Formerly No. 389).

To Abbot Rainauld.[1]

Bernard requests him to receive kindly a novice whom he sends back to him with his resolution renewed and strengthened.

To the Lord Abbot Rainauld, Brother Bernard, health and spiritual graces to the fulness of his desire.

I praise the prudence which has made you reluctant to distress a monk on account of a novice; and still more I approve the humility with which you have borne so patiently the injury (and so great an injury) which has been done to you: but I place incomparably above all the charity with which, being unwilling to break a bruised reed, you have thought of resorting to my counsel to see if I could bring him to a better mind. O prudent humility and humble charity! so to spare an insolent monk as not to discourage a novice wavering in his purpose. I have then strengthened his mind as much as I could, and sent him back to you, prepared as far as I know, to amend all those faults of which he is accused; and I advise, and if it is necessary I entreat, your benignity so well proved, that the man be kindly received; and to bring, if it be possible, the brother in question, to whom also I have written a letter of entreaty, to an entire change of feeling. Farewell.

---

[1] Abbot of Foigny, I think; and the same to whom are addressed Ep. 72 and those following.

To the Monk Alard on the same subject.

Bernard blames him for obstinately opposing the return of the before mentioned novice when expelled, although he was disposed to return and amend.

To his dear son ALARD, Brother BERNARD, health and paternal affection.

1. Brother Adamar complains that you have shown yourself too bitter against him: not only because he was expelled from the convent by your influence, but because the exercise of the same influence prevents his being re-admitted. I am quite willing to believe that you have acted throughout this matter only from the purest zeal; but when I recollect that (former) obstinacy of yours which my friendly zeal for you causes me often to reproach you with, as you know, I fear lest this same zeal of yours is not according to knowledge. For even to lay aside the words of the Rule, what audacity is it in any one to strike and to excommunicate, much more to expel, any person when the Abbot was absent and knew nothing of it.[1] Would it not have been more a proof of your humility not to do to another what you would not wish done to yourself? And ought not the pursuit of your perfection to have brought you rather to imitate the Apostle when he says, *To the weak become I as weak, that I might gain the weak* (1 Cor. ix. 22) and again: *If a man be overtaken in a fault, ye which are spiritual restore such an one in the spirit of lenity, considering thyself, lest thou also be tempted* (Gal. vi. 1)? But the

---

[1] Rule of S. Benedict, c. 70.

Prior, you reply, expelled him and not I. I know that well, but he did so at your persuasion, and indeed yielded to your strong representations. But now when the Prior himself pitying him, wishes, as I have heard, to recall him, because you remain in the same harshness of feeling he is not suffered to amend a step taken without sufficient reflection, and under pressure from you. I demand of you how you dare, without fearing, to remain alone implacable, so that while all the others pity him, and the Lord Abbot himself is disposed to recall him, you cannot be brought to agree he shall be received again? Have you not read, *He shall have judgment without mercy who has showed no mercy* (S. James ii. 13)? or again, are you forgetful that *With what measure ye mete, it shall be measured to you again* (S. Matt. vii. 2)? Do you in truth despise that which is promised to the merciful, *They shall obtain mercy* (Id. v. 7)?

2. But you do not know, you reply, how justly he was expelled. To this I say, I do not inquire whether he was expelled justly or unjustly; that is not the point. That which alone I complain of, that which I blame, that which I wonder at extremely, is that when the man humbly acknowledges his fault, when he asks pardon, when he patiently awaits your decision and promises amendment, he cannot obtain a favourable hearing; although the Apostle in such a case, would *have love confirmed towards him* (2 Cor. ii. 8); and according to the giver of our Rule, he should have a new probation with all patience.[1] At all events: if he were unfairly expelled, it is fair that he should be recalled; but if fairly, even then it would be a pious action to receive him again. Wherefore without wishing to go to the bottom of the affair, the course which I advise

---

[1] Rule of S. Benedict C. 58.

will, I consider, be a safe one for you: and thus whether you act from a sentiment of justice or of mercy, you are sure to act in union with our just and merciful God. I entreat you then, my dear son, not to refuse to my entreaties, which this man has come so far to ask for, that benefit, which you did not think fit to grant to his own.

LETTER CDXV. [Formerly No. 393.]

TO A CERTAIN MAN, WHO HAD BROKEN A PROMISE HE HAD GIVEN.

Bernard exhorts him to break through the yoke of carnal pleasures, and to fulfil his promise to enter into religion.

You may be forgetful of yourself, but I am not forgetful of you: because I love you; and my grief on your account is equal to my love. I love you too well not to be grieved on your account: and my grief keeps me from forgetting you. But alas! how bitter and sorrowful is that remembrance to me! I cannot but wonder what has withheld you, that you did not come to us, as you had promised. For I could not believe that you had broken your promise, and such a solemn promise too, for any light reason: since I had ever found you, even from your boyhood, thoroughly faithful and truthful. Nor was I wrong: the reason which withheld you was emphatically a grave and a weighty one. It was the very same as overcame David, in spite of his valour, and deceived Solomon, in spite of his wisdom. But what! shall one who falls, never be helped to rise again? How many and needful things I have to say to you! but to write them would take too long. This only I will say shortly. If any spark of your former affection for me remains: if

you retain the least hope of ever breaking through that
miserable captivity in which you are held; if finally, you do not
wish to destroy and render useless the confidence, which it
is said, in all your irregularities, you have ever had in my
prayers and in the friendship of this community; do not
put off the revisiting Clairvaux, if you are still sufficiently
free, and sufficiently master of yourself, to be absent even
for a time from that cruel beast which revels daily on
your goods and will one day take the life of your soul.
Otherwise there will be no more henceforth of your
friendly intimacy with our brotherhood, and it is in vain
that you plume yourself on the society of good men: it
is certain that they will think you unworthy of their
society, if you refuse to follow their counsels. But if
you do not delay to come, I trust that through the mercy
of God, you will be freed from the fetters of death,
before you depart from us.

LETTER CDXVI. [A new letter.]

To a person unknown.

*Bernard assures him that he has not been charged
with the distribution of Count Theobald's alms.*

A biting letter, such as you sent me lately, according
to your habit, shows that you are irritated against me.
I thought at first that it was a form of pleasantry in
which you were as usual indulging, and that you did not
mean seriously what you said: but a monk who happened
to come here from your neighbourhood, disabused me of
that idea. He knew nothing previously of those letters of
yours, except what he had heard from me: but without
knowing it he repeated to me the exact sense of them,
though in other words: so that I could no longer doubt

that you had been indulging suspicions against me with respect to the almsgiving of the Count of Champagne, that I had in some way done injustice to absent friends.

And you thought this, because you imagined that the gifts of the Count passed through my hands. But anyone must be very ignorant both of the Count and of me, to suppose that he acts or determines his gifts, according to my advice. Now that matter is settled. Furthermore, I have permitted myself to request importunately, I might almost say impudently, that some gift might be made to various monasteries, and in particular to that very bishop, in whose cause (for I suppose you did not write to me openly on your own behalf) you have spoken so harshly; and I have failed. The Count himself has made distribution of his means, what he chose, and to whom he chose; partly indeed in my presence, but not by my hands; and I am far from complaining of this. I might perhaps have been able to obtain something for myself, had I chosen to do so; but I thank God that by His help, I was so far from doing this, that I declined what was offered to me. At present you may, if you think fit, believe me rather than common report, in matters concerning myself; there is no reason that I know of why you should think the Bishop or me unworthy of the bounties which you have been accustomed to bestow up to the present time. Be sure of this, that we are prepared to go without, whatever we are not considered worthy to have.

LETTER CDXVII. [A new letter.]

To the Abbot of Saint Tron.

He requests that a certain Brother Dodo may be kindly received.

To his dear brother and co-abbot, G., of Saint Tron, Brother BERNARD of Clairvaux, wishes health in the Lord.

This is my opinion, or rather my judgment about the question in which Brother Dodo has come to seek my humble understanding. Since he has alleged no sufficient cause why he wishes to desert his place and his Order, there appears to me no reason why he should be permitted to do it. His scruple rests principally upon a vow which he says he has previously taken, but which seems to have been only a somewhat hasty word, followed by no consequent action. Such a vow cannot possibly take precedence of another which though taken later, was deliberate, and not left as a mere word, but rendered farther binding by making profession and taking the habit; especially when the former seems to have been neither stricter or more severe than the latter. Wherefore I think that you, who have to render account for his soul to the Lord, cannot safely give him the licence which he calls for; since it is written: *The Lord shall count among the evil doers those who consent to their iniquity* (Ps. cxxv. 5. Vulg.)

Receive him kindly as a son, and watch over him carefully as one committed to your charge; you will find him, if I do not mistake, willing to follow your counsels, and to submit himself to whatever you shall direct.

LETTER CDXVIII. [A new letter, from the Archives of Savigny (*Circa* A. D. 1152)].

To HUGH, ARCHBISHOP OF ROUEN.

He requests that a donation made to the Abbey of Savigny may be confirmed by the Archbishop.

To his dear father and lord, HUGH, by the grace of God, Archbishop of Rouen, and to the whole Church in that

place, Brother BERNARD, called Abbot of Clairvaux, health
and the assurance of his prayers.

I wish your Benignity to be credibly and certainly assured,
that Philip,[1] Lord Bishop of Bayeux, has at my request
granted a tilled field,[2] situated before the farmhouse[3]
of Ecurie, and containing four acres[4] of land, to your sons,
my brethren at Savigny, in my presence, and in that
of the Reverend Father Lord Henry,[5] now Archbishop of
York, Guy, Lord Abbot of Charlieu, and others of your
brethren. Wherefore I beg and earnestly entreat your
Piety, being very dear to me as you are in the Lord, to
take measures as regards them, your sons before mentioned,
in your fatherly care and kindness, that they be not dis-
turbed or troubled henceforward, in their possession of
this field. If anyone, now or at any time, shall attempt to
impugn their title to this field, or to eject them from it:
let it be the task of your charity to interpose in their
defence and on behalf of the Abbey which is yours, and
so to defend their right, that they may possess it without

---

[1] Philip Harcurius (Harcourt?)

[2] *Cultura*. The word is only used in this sense in very late
Latin. The classical and proper meaning is *Culture*. (E.)

[3] *Grangia; only found in low Latin: 'dicuntur a granis quæ
ibi reponuntur'* (Lyndwood). (E.)

[4] *Acra*: not a promontory or headland, which is the classical sense, but '*certa terræ portio mensurata.*' The amount of
it varied extremely in different countries, and even in the same
country at different times. Cowell says: '*apud Anglos acram
esse quantitatem terræ sexdecim perticas in longitudine conti-
nentem et totidem latitudine.*' The Roman *pertica* or *decempeda*
was a measuring rod ten feet in length, however: while the
English 'rod, pole, or perch' is $16\frac{1}{2}$ feet. Spelman derives
Acra no doubt rightly, from *Ager*. (E.)

[5] This must have been Henry Murdach, previously Abbot
of Fountains. He died in 1153. See letter 106, and note. (E.)

molestation: for the facts, as I have written them to you, are true and without question.

LETTER CDXIX. (A new letter: from the Library of Celles. (A. D. 1152).

To PETER ABBOT OF CELLES.

Bernard transfers an oven to the monks of Celles.

To the venerable PETER, by the grace of God, Abbot of Celles, Brother BERNARD, called Abbot of Clairvaux, health and his earnest prayers.

I grant and confirm to your house an oven placed near Troyes, which was the property of our house at Mores. For since our brethren there are not able to profit by the proceeds of the same, they therefore, who built the same oven, having received repayment of forty-four livres which they had expended in the erection of it, do by my hand trans fer it to you and to your house, to be freely held. Which we sanction and confirm by the impression of my seal. The following brethren of your house are witnesses:

PETER the Prior.

JOSCELIN the Subprior.

STEPHEN the Provost.

and also Walcher, Rainauld, our Cellarers, and Fromund, who erected the building in question.

Given in the year 1152 of the Incarnation of Our Lord.

LETTER CDXX. [1]

To MAR. AND HIS WIFE.

He exhorts them to almsgiving and good works.

BERNARD, Abbot of Clairvaux, to his beloved MAR. and

[1] With respect to the thirty-six letters next following, Dom Edmund Martène gives the following note in his work *Vete-*

his wife, health, and that they may so love each other, as that Christ may be loved still better by each of them.

Whatever you possess upon the earth, it is certain that one day it must be lost to you, unless you have taken the precaution to send it before you into the heavens, by gifts put into the hands of the poor.

Therefore, dearly beloved, lay up for yourselves treasures in heaven, where neither moth nor rust doth corrupt, and where thieves do not break through and steal (S. Matt. vi. 20), where, in fine, no enemy however great, can do any harm either to us or to you. If you are anxious to hear of fit bearers [of these treasures] you have at your doors not one only but many, who will faithfully convey whatever you choose to entrust to their charge. For at this present time God has multiplied their troubles and calamities, that you may have opportunity thereby of storing up treasures in the place of so great happiness and safety. Do you, on your part, make known and recommend the same course to T. my good

rum Scriptorum Monumentorum Historicorum, dogmaticorum, moralium Amplissima Collectio, Vol. i. p. 725: "The following letters, hitherto unedited, of S. Bernard Abbot of Clairvaux, I have copied almost all froma MS. of good rank in the famous Abbey of S. Vedast at Arras; and although written at various times, I refer them to the same hand, following therein the counsel of [qualified] friends." Of these the first thirty-four, viz., from 420 to 453, were extracted from the Vedastine MS.; the thirty-fifth, which is now No. 454, from a MS. at Anchin; the thirty-sixth, now 455, from one at Verdun. All these we refer to the same hand, as does Martène; but he, though most learned, was in error in asserting with respect to five of these, that they had not been edited before. For those which stand now as 427, 429, 443, 451, 452, had appeared before, almost word for word, as 391, 316, 417, 86, 413.

Note by Editor of the fourth Edition (of Mabillon).

brother and your nephew: and to W. who has married
your granddaughter, and to any others whom you know
who will not despise this counsel so advantageous to
them; those especially who are in the house of God. I
wish the blessing of a visit from you soon.

LETTER CDXXI.

To a certain Abbot.

*He excuses himself for the shortness of his letter, and
sends back to him a young man whom he was quite unable to admit among his monks.*

Health and best wishes.

I am not unmindful that the brevity and dryness of the
letters I send to you has been disagreeable to you. But
much occupation obliges me to be curt in writing, and
too little devotion makes me cold and dry. Grant me
indulgence for this: and still more that the urgency of
present calls obliges me to make proof again of your
consideration. I have only space to add what it is needful to say: that this young man from your neighbourhood
who comes, desiring to join us for his soul's sake (passing
over you, for what reason I know not), I cannot receive,
as you are aware, and therefore have persuaded him to
return to you. He will, unless I mistake, be serviceable
to you in the future, if you are willing to receive him:
which I earnestly beg that you would do.

LETTER CDXXII.

To a certain Bishop.

*He recommends to him the cause of the monastery of
S. Martin.*

Health, and that he may do the will of God in all things. Is it pleasing to you that the poor monastery of S. Martin should lose that alleviation of its poverty which God has conferred upon it, and that for the lack of friends more than of justice? For otherwise, if it is supposed not to have a just cause, it will be of great service to the house, that such an unfounded report should be set at rest, I am desirous therefore that you would not mind the trouble of inquiring diligently into their case, and of trying to bring it to a settlement either peacefully and by common consent, or at all events with justice and judgment.

Farewell, my very dear father: be mindful of me.

LETTER CDXXIII.

To a certain friend.

He excuses himself for not being able to go with him to the Legate.

The reason why I have not come to you, as you bade me, is so grave, that although as yet you know it not, I am sure you will be sorry for it when you do. I earnestly [1] entreat you to offer your supplications to Almighty God on its account.

What we two were about to treat of with the Legate, carry out alone, as well as you can.

LETTER CDXXIV.

To a certain Judge.

He recommends to him the cause of the Abbey of Fontenay. [2]

[1] In the text is *simplex*, but we should probably read *supplex*.
[2] Fontenay was a distinguished monastery in the Diocese of Autun, not far from Montbar, and founded by the relations of S. Bernard about A. D. 1118. It was the second daughter-house of Clairvaux, and its first Abbot was Godfrey.

I have up to the present so confided in you, as to suppose it not necessary for me to be, wheresoever I knew you were, in respect of matters which affected our interests. I wonder therefore that you have been so inactive about the Abbey of Fontenay, which I left under your guardianship, and frequently begged you to be watchful over it. I hear that in suits on behalf of the same abbey which you have accepted for your determination, you have not yet come to a conclusion. Let me know how long you will delay to do this: how long you will neglect to visit and encourage those brethren, as you are accustomed to do; I shall not cease to complain on their behalf.

LETTER CDXXV.

To a certain friend.

He commends to him the bearer of this letter.

I commend to your charity the man who bears this, who is very dear to me on account of his love for religion; he is in need of your interest with the Count. Let him have the benefit, I entreat, in favour of his suit, which he will explain to you, of all my humble interest with you, and of all the interest which your Reverence has with the Count.

LETTER CDXXVI.

To the Bishop of Troyes.

He disapproves that he has bestowed the office of Arch-deacon upon a very young man.

To the venerable father H., by the grace of God Bishop

of Troyes, [1] Brother BERNARD, health, and his respectful duty.

The courtesy of your Highness is the cause that emboldens me when needful, to write to you with what is undoubtedly presumption about your affairs. I undertook to make request to you on behalf of your excellent son G., or rather to give a piece of advice in your own interest. I wonder then that you, whose high character I have warm respect for, should, for what reason or at whose opinion that it was advisable, I cannot conjecture, have thus acted respecting the Archdeaconry, of which G., whom I mentioned, is so well able to discharge the duties, as to prefer to bestow it upon a mere boy, who is not able to discharge the duties himself; [2] so wrongly and in defiance of your duty, as it seems to me.

For if you have built up anything of good, you have again (which may God avert!) destroyed it. But sufficient has been said to a man of understanding. If you fear men, the Gospel teaches you whom you ought to fear still more. If you wish to please men, yet it is better to be the servant of God: if you owe anything to Cæsar, to God you owe still more.

LETTER CDXXVII.

To a certain Abbot.

He praises him : and urges upon him the reformation of his Abbey, and chiefly of the hospital attached to it.

[1] [This was Hatto, to whom were written Epp. 23 and 203 of Bernard, and a greater number among those of Peter of Cluny.]

[2] [The holy Doctor was always greatly indignant at the bestowal of ecclesiastical dignities upon boys. That is shown by Ep. 271, in which he blames Count Theobald for endeavouring to procure them for his young son William: as also by *Tractat. de Offic. Episcopor.* c. 17 and *De Considerat.* III. 5.]

With desire that he may have the spirit of grace and modesty.

Those brethren who have come to me for spiritual advice, in speaking of the good desire that you have for the amendment of your house, which may God's grace enable you to effect, have given us no little joy. But I warn and entreat you in your pious desire, that as you labour to repair the material fabric, so you should strive to reform the characters of its inmates. Most watchful care is necessary, not only with respect to the monastery, but also to the hospital or Refuge, which these brethren administer under your charge: to the end that you should keep it secure and free from any exaction or malpractice on the part of your servants or dependents: and those properties which by the evil mind of Abbots before you have been, as I hear, taken away from the same Refuge, I entreat you to restore. For as it belongs to your office and charge to correct and counterwork the evil doings of others: so you ought, not only to preserve secure and uninjured, but also to increase and multiply, the means of those who do well. Let the Presbyter also, who is resident in that Refuge, and who, it seems, has property at a distance, be obliged, either to give up the management of that property, or to leave the house. Farewell: and rely on my assistance in anything which is in my power, because of the good which I have heard of you. [1]

LETTER CDXXVIII.

To a certain friend.

He thanks God for the prosperous issue of certain affairs.

I know that you are desirous of the information which

[1] Compare with this letter No. 391, to the Abbess of Favernay.

I now write to give to you. I thank Him who has worked
all our works for our good. We have done a great work
and have completed a difficult journey gladly and prosper-
ously, we have dismissed our brethren in joy and peace,
abounding in friends and resources, and in favour as I
think, both with God and with men. I have brought back
Brother G., though not without danger of offending both
the Bishop and his brethren. After the time of harvest,
which is now in progress, if you have need of him, or
rather because you have need of him, he will be at your
disposal.

LETTER CDXXIX.

To a certain friend.

*That ecclesiastical benefices are to be accepted not from
a lay hand, but from the Bishop.*

When laymen are desirous of relinquishing abbeys or
ecclesiastical benefices which they hold unlawfully, that is
one good thing. But when they wish to transfer them to
the use of the servants of God, the good is doubly great;
nevertheless, since this cannot be done except by the hand
of the Bishop, a prelate will approve himself either the
author of evil or of good according to that which he gives
or denies his assent to. That which a knight asks of you,
this ought to be asked of him by you. What! Do you
think it better for a church of God to be in the possession,
as a family estate, of a man of war, than of the Saints of
God? It will be strange if all who hear of it do not
wonder. Desist I pray you, lest the sons of the uncir-
cumcised hear and rejoice. Granted that you are able to
deliver the captive church from the hand of the powerful,
and to obtain her right, which, nevertheless I think by no

means probable: whom, I, ask you would you choose the more willingly as your heir and successor in it? One who serves in the King's army, or one who is employed in intercession for your sins? Do then what is just, what is worthy of you, what will be the cause of rejoicing to God and men; what, finally, though it be no small matter, I might confidently ask of you on the ground of our friendship.

LETTER CDXXX.

To Pope Innocent II.

Bernard having been chosen by the Pope as arbiter, in order to decide a dispute between two contending rivals for the Archbishopric of Tours, he declares the election of Philip null and void.

For the purpose of deciding the dispute at Tours, venerable Father, I called a meeting at Blois, which is a place fitting by its nearness, and its security for those who were to be present. There, when those who were opposed to the election of Philip had objected to it on many grounds, which I pass over on account of brevity; there appeared at length to be two chief grounds for these objections, namely, that he was below the canonical age; and that he had neither been elected by the persons whose duty it was to elect, nor even by a majority. The higher officials of the Cathedral were absent at that time, having been driven both from the Church and their own houses; namely, all the Archdeacons, the Dean and the Precentor, and all the other Presbyters of the Church, as well as a number of clerics of various orders. It was urged on the contrary, that the election of Hugo was valid and canonical, because those whose authority was of the greatest weight for the choice, combined in agreeing to it: nor was it a fatal objection that it was held in an unusual manner, that is, beyond the precincts of the Church and even of the city, since this was due to the necessity caused by the persecution; nor again, that the opposite faction had taken no part in the election, for although forewarned and summoned by their brethren, they refused to come.

For a place was fixed for it, and that the very place which by common consent was suitable : but those others anticipated the day, forced on the election, and chose Philip secretly, rashly, and entirely without the knowledge of any but themselves. Nor did they wait even for any of the suffragan Bishops : but these are said to favour the election, and to have assented to it. To this the party of Philip replies : "We are able to give good and sufficient answer to the objections made, if only another day be named convenient to us : not that we deny this present day to have been appointed, but our Archbishop-elect has not been warned of it. For the person ought certainly to be summoned by name whom the entire cause concerns." Their opponents rejoin : "By no means : the contention is not between the persons elected, and for the See, but between the electors, and respecting the validity of the elections. The litigants, whose the cause is, ought alone then to be summoned to the hearing ; and it would be a thing grave and indecent that the person elected should, as you contend, be counted among the litigants. It is sufficient if he be summoned generally with others. For none is excluded from letters of citation who had part in the cause ; although you cannot deny that it was openly announced by you that (Philip) was being sought for. He had disappeared, he could not be found, and it was very possible that he would not be present on the day appointed.

But he will profit nothing by his absence ; for even if

he should not come, the cause will nevertheless be brought to a close without him. If, as you say, the cause is his, and the man is wanted to answer for himself, the blame for his being without a citation, is surely his who disappeared, or yours who neglected to find him. What does it matter to those whose duty it was to issue general letters of summons to your city and your Church, whether this man absented himself or no, not merely from the city, but from the neighbourhood, or even from the realm, or what his intention was in so doing? What is wanting of all that is needful for a fair trial of the matter, unless perhaps he distrusts the justice of his cause? We see that he is fortified by a multitude of wise men and skilled lawyers, attended also by a number of armed men, as if there were any need of them.

He has also Bishops with him, and an excellent proctor.[1] Would he then have come so unprepared? or if he did not propose to come, what did he want with so great a company of needless assistants? Would not his own friends have been sufficient for him? The judge offers all that was needful in this way. And these things we should say, if it should appear that Philip really knew not the day appointed for the business. But now, can he deny that both the place and time of the hearing was signified to him by the Abbot of Clairvaux, who eighteen days before when passing through the See of Cambray, happened to meet him in hiding there? and if so, is it not manifest that what he really seeks is not a peaceful decision but farther delay? These then being the pleadings brought forward, it seemed just to me and those who were with me, being religious and learned persons, Bishops and Abbots and clerics, to

---

[1] *Procultorem.* Query, whether an error for *Procuratorem,* or to be derived from *Procultator* (Collocare). [E.]

put an end to the long and harassing suspense of the
Church: and therefore not any longer to endure the delays and procrastinations of those who seek only their
own interests, and under that pretext to ruin and destroy
the Church. Judgment, therefore was pronounced by me,
that justice required that the cause should be gone into,
and that there was no canonical excuse (for delay) brought
forward: when those others, fencing according to their
usual custom, and as if they had but little confidence
in their cause, appealed.

Whereupon the Apostolical letters were brought forward, in which I was directed to bring the cause defini-
tively to an end, and (the parties) were directed to
yield full obedience to my decision; but they refusing to
listen, left the Court. Being called a first and a second
time, they refused to come. Then turning to the other
side, I proceeded with the hearing in judicial order, according to your mandate: and after obtaining Canonical
proof upon each of the heads before mentioned, after exam-
ining witnesses, and completing all formalities, I quashed
the election of Philip by the Apostolic authority given to me.

As concerning Hugo, since he seemed to have been
elected while below Holy Orders, I have left, as is proper,
the decision of his case to your clemency.

LETTER CDXXXI.

To the Lord Pope.

In favour of the Bishop of Troyes.

I entreat you in your justice, to give a favourable
hearing to the Bishop of Troyes; and my great desire is
that by the good offices of your Blessedness, such a
concordat should be arrived at between him and his
clergy, that the latter should cease any longer unfairly to

vex a man who is old, and of whom they have no well-founded complaints to make. There is one among them not worth consideration, on account of his youth, but troublesome on account of his insolence, whose presumption ought, I consider, to be chastised, nor he be allowed to tread his Bishop under his feet : the bearer of this letter will inform you who he is. Let your judgment deign then to make fair decision respecting him and the others, so that the Bishop, who is a lover of your honour, may himself be honoured, and no one be oppressed by lack of justice. It is not to be borne with that the hatred of anyone should be allowed to injure a man who is defended by his innocence.

LETTER CDXXXII.

To the same, on the same subject.

In the matter of the Bishop of Troyes and his clergy, I entreat you to be very cautious, that both the Bishop may receive the honour to which he has a right, and the clergy may not be deprived of due justice. Let peace be renewed between them, and a curb imposed upon the ill-disposed, so that for the future they may not be able to rise up against their already aged Pastor.

LETTER CDXXXIII.

To the same, on the same subject.

It is needful that you should be the friend of my friends : and I am anxious that you should assist Brother N. in the cause which he has on hand; yet with such discretion, that the clergy should be rendered subject to their own Bishop, as is meet, and that they should not be oppressed in his awarding of justice : and as to every thing else, there should be peace between them.

to the well known fountain of loving kindness. This then, is my request, that your Apostolic Piety would not permit a good man, whose white hairs have already deserved peace and quiet, to be unjustly harassed : and that you would deign to grant the petitions which he makes by his messenger.

LETTER CDXXXVII.

To the same, for the same purpose.

You heap favours upon me and increase my glory, when my friends for my sake find favour in your eyes; and the greater their number, the more must I think of your affection for me. Yet I seek not glory from man; but desire the Kingdom of God and His righteousness; and I think this is the case with the Bishop of Troyes also. With confidence therefore do I desire to recommend him to you under either character, that of a good man and of my friend. I would recommend to your Charity not him only, but also the bearer of this letter, who is sent by him : a young man of good disposition and dear to me.

LETTER CDXXXVIII.

To the same on the same subject.

I commend to you the cause of the Bishop of Troyes, which his messenger, a man dear to me, has in charge : uphold it, for I believe it to be just. The man himself is a friend of my friends. Pray do not listen to any evil report against this Bishop; but assist his suit, and his messenger, as much as you can.

LETTER CDXXXIX.

To a person unknown.

He exhorts him to prefer the care of his soul to anxiety about the body, and to renounce the world.

The lord Bishop of Aveia [1] has done me a great kindness, after giving me his acquaintance, which I much desired, in making mention of me to your Charity, and gratifying me by informing me of your safety. And indeed, what the Bishop said of my soul I accepted the more willingly as he spoke thus of my body: 'I love your body indeed, but I love your soul more: for I love not my own body, except for the sake of my soul, according to that rule which you know is held dear by me: *Thou shalt love thy neighbour as thyself* (S. Matt. xxii. 39), and as I prefer my soul to my body, so do I likewise with yours. For take away the soul, and what will the body be, except what all human bodies are said to become: *Dust thou art, and to dust shalt thou return* (Gen. iii. 19). But the soul is in a state to be preferred when it is released from the body, only if it is not weighed down with sins so great, that this which was taken from the dust hinders, in returning to the dust, the spirit from returning to God who gave it (Eccles. iii. 7). It is evidently not just that that which is moved should be loved equally with that which moves it; that which is ruled with that which rules; that which imparts life and that which receives it; that, in fine, which is dust and comes from the dust, and that which comes from above, and is made in the image of a higher nature. Yet how frequently, alas! is this herb of the field and its ill-savoured flower, the flesh, and the pleasures of the flesh, held not only equal to, but of greater worth than the reasonable soul, capable of eternal blessedness! I know well that you are wiser, but I grieve that you do not yet live

[1] [There were two places of this name: one in Spain, a town of the Basques, in the Tarraconensis: the other of the Vestini, in Italy, now destroyed; the See being removed to Aquila.]

according to your wisdom; do thou therefore, beloved of God, *have pity on thine own soul* (Ecclus. xxx. 23). Why should you live as those with whose opinion you do not agree? Either change your life, or hide your sentiments. But this is the better course, not to contradict in your actions, what your reason has understood, and your heart embraced. A wise man does not think lightly of the counsel of the wise : *What shall it profit a man if he shall gain the whole world, and lose his own soul!* (S. Matt. xvi. 26). What does it help you to retain the truth in your mind, when you still act according to vanity in your life? Depart, I pray you, from among the sons of the strangers, whose mouth talketh of vanity and their right hand is a right hand of iniquity. These indeed call such a people blessed : but do you with the Prophet not only cry out in word, but realize in practice that *Blessed is the people whose God is the Lord* (Ps. cxliv. 15). Let those whose doom it is to perish with the world, take their pleasure in it : but do thou delight thyself in the Lord, and He shall give thee thy heart's desire : it is good for thee to hold fast to Him, so that you too may be able to say with Jeremiah, *The Lord is good unto the soul that seeketh Him* (Lam. iii. 25) and if to one that seeks Him, how much more to one who finds?

LETTER CDXL.

To a certain Prior. [1]

Bernard sends to him a young man, whom he requests may be admitted into the Order.

The young man who brings you this letter I found

[1] [Perhaps to the Prior of Clairvaux, as Martene supposes.]

waiting for me at Châlons sur Marne : and when he saw me, he asked very simply and modestly that he might become a monk and be received into our Order. He related to me that Thomas de Maren, whose esquire he had been, wished to make him a knight for the warfare of this world, but that he preferred the warfare of Christ; and had therefore left him and come to us. Upon this consult with some of the brethren, and if they approve, and it seems good to you also, receive him to probation. I make known to you that leave has been obtained from the Bishop, not by any request of mine, but by the entreaties of the lady Beatrice, [1] for me to winter near you, yet not in Clairvaux itself, but in the plain of Menthe. In the meantime, be watchful; arouse the slothful, repress the presuming, encourage the fearful: become all things to all men, make the virtues of all yours.

LETTER CDXLI.

TO A CERTAIN ABBOT OF THE BENEDICTINE ORDER.

He sends to him two young men not sufficiently vigorous for the Cistercian Order, but who would perhaps be serviceable to him.

That he may strive after peace and good will. These two young men who have a good will, but whose bodily powers are far from being sufficient to our Order, I have thought well to send on to you : because, if they continue to be such as we have found them during their probation, I have great hope that they will be of use to you. But receive them and put them yourself under probation,

---

[1] Letter 118 of S. Bernard was written to this Beatrice, a noble and religious woman, whose kind care and helpful charity he there highly praises.]

so as to ascertain the truth of what I say; nor be in any haste to allow them to make profession, until you have recognized that they will be of service.

LETTER CDXLII.

To a certain friend.

Concerning a certain man, whose vicious propensities he describes, and who was endeavouring to make marriages for his children from among the nobility.

I have done what you wished, though it was a matter which did not at all concern me, except that you wished it. For what concern have I with your lands, your lawsuits, your marriages? Then that man, for whom, at your earnest request I was obliged to intercede with the Duchess, I have always known from his youth to be ill disposed and far removed from all good : insomuch that I believe that the matter will turn out badly, not by any greed of the Duchess, but by the just judgment of God. I never see that he makes any pilgrimage to any of the Saints, though he is a sinner : nor hear of his giving alms, though he is rich; nor of his giving protection to the widow or the orphan, though he has been long in high authority. And now, above all, he is constantly seeking to exalt himself beyond his measure. Consider, you who are his friends, that the society of the nobles can hardly come to any advantageous issue for him, since, not regarding his own mediocrity, he is so anxious to unite his sons and daughters to them in marriage. But I hope and strongly wish that as to this matter, which on your account I have goodnaturedly undertaken to ask for him, he will make good use of it.

LETTER CDXLIII.

To a certain Abbot.

*Respecting a certain monk who wishes to migrate to
another order: which Bernard disapproves of his doing.*

A brother when he came to consult my simplicity, took
back with him the following advice or rather opinions. [1]
He adduced no suitable reason for wishing to desert his
place and his order; there seems to be no reason why he
should be permitted to migrate to another. His scruple rests
principally upon a vow which he says he had previously
taken, but which seems to have been only a somewhat hasty
word, followed by no consequent action. Such a vow
cannot possibly take precedence of another which, though
taken later, was deliberate, and not left as a mere word,
but rendered farther binding by making profession and
taking the habit; especially when the former seems to
have been neither stricter nor more severe than the latter.
Wherefore, I think that you who have to render account
for his soul to the Lord, cannot safely give him the licence
which he asks for: since it is written: *The Lord shall
count among the evil doers those who consent to their iniquity* (Ps. cxxv. 5 *Vulg.*) Receive him then, kindly, as a
son, and watch over him carefully, as one committed to
your charge; you will find him, if I do not mistake, willing to follow your counsels, and to submit himself to
whatever you shall direct.

LETTER CDXLIV.

To a certain Abbot.

*Bernard recommends to him L., a returning fugitive,
whom he begs may be kindly received.*

[1] The rest of this letter is the same as No. 417.

I entreat you by the mercy of God, and by our mutual affection, to receive kindly Brother L., who is repentant of his error, who promises amendment and is desirous to return; and that in his reception and reconciliation he may be gently and clemently treated, as is usual with other fugitives: and permit him to think that my entreaties and interest with you have done something to better his position.

LETTER CDXLV.

To a person unknown.

He writes that he has recovered from a severe attack of illness, having escaped from the very gates of death.

Health and every good thing he could wish.

I have long known your anxiety for me, which you have expressed so kindly in your letter, and I am grateful for it. Nor was I purposely neglectful to let you know in what state I was: but up to the present opportunity has been wanting by which, when I began to be better in body, by the mercy of God, I could relieve your anxiety of mind. But now be of good cheer; for the Lord hath chastened and corrected me, but He hath not given me over unto death. On the First Sunday in Advent I first approached to the Altar in my own person and attained to the reception of the Holy Communion, without the assistance of another (priest): I have myself written this letter: by which two signs you may understand, how greatly, by God's goodness, I am strengthened both in body and mind. I would gladly see you, if it could be managed conveniently and without hindrance to your work.

LETTER CDXLVI.

To Amadeus, Abbot of Hautecombe.

He begs him to send messengers to Montpellier to go on board the ships of the King of Sicily and convey his excuses for not having sent brethren to Sicily.

To his dear brother in the Lord, AMADEUS, Abbot of Hautecombe, Brother BERNARD called Abbot of Clairvaux: Health and brotherly love.

I request that you would send your father [1] or some other intelligent and discreet messenger on my behalf to Montpellier, so as to be there on the Octave of the Assumption [2] B.M., for on that day the ambassadors of the King of Sicily [3] ought to be there, with a fleet to convey the daughter of Count Theobald to the son of their lord. If then they have brought ships, as they perhaps will have, for the conveyance of our brethren, and ask for the [completely organized] Abbey which I was to send, let your messenger present the excuse thus: [4] 'That the brethren were ready and the Abbey organized: but that the lord Alfanus [5] the ambassador of the King of Sicily, said that the King required only two brethren, who were to be sent in advance to view the proposed site; but that

---

[1] *Patrem:* but should we not read *priorem* (prior)? (E.)

[2] Aug. 15; so that the date named would be Aug. 22 (E.)

[3] Roger, the first King of Sicily; to whom Letters 207, 208, 209.

[4] Bernard afterwards sent brethren to found an Abbey in Sicily, over whom he set "Magister Bruno, formerly his own companion for many days, and at a later time the father of many souls rejoicing in Christ." See Ep. 209 which is said to have been written in that or the preceding year.

[5] ? Alfonso.

when the King shall signify his will to me, the whole Abbey shall forthwith be sent: for it is dangerous to religion and to the Order, as your Wisdom knows, for brethren to be lingering in a strange land, without discipline, and without the oversight of their Abbot or other brethren.'

LETTER CDXLVII.

To a person unknown.

He recommends to him the Abbot of Farfa, a Cardinal of the Holy Roman Church.

I recommend to you a man noble, both by birth and character, a Cardinal [1] of the Apostolic See, that you may receive him in an honourable and friendly manner. He has come down from the side of the Pope to the court of the King and at his summons, and is entrusted with secret business concerning both state and church. Receive him honourably, as a man of good will, and in him do honour equally to two very noble Princes of the world, namely him from whom he has come and him whom he has come to meet; the Pope and the Emperor. There is something bold in so humble a person as I daring to recommend to you so great a man, but the very humility of your petitioner excludes shame in this matter, and if I have acted foolishly, yet humility itself has been my motive.

[1] I supposed at first that this was Gerard a Cardinal deacon created by Innocent II., who became afterwards a monk at Clairvaux, and lies buried in the cloister there. But, since he had not the dignity of Abbot, it seems better to suppose that it was Adinulf, Abbot of S. Maria at Farfa, a Benedictine, created a Cardinal presbyter in 1130 by Innocent II.

LETTER CDXLVIII.

To the King of France.

Bernard excuses himself from undertaking a dignity to which he had been elected.

To the King of France, Brother Bernard, health.

I rejoice sincerely, I confess it, that you take such a sincere interest in the things which belong to God. For to pass over other proofs of it, you would not interest yourself [1] so greatly in the promotion of a poor and humble man, and all to no purpose, if it were not in the cause of God: by what other advantage can you be moved so to act, seeing that I am a poor and helpless man? You do not merely assent to my elevation, but you have the goodness to ask me to accept it. You show to me your royal favour, you pour upon me the treasures of your kindness, and that I, insignificant as I am, should not tremble at the weight of honours, you assure me of your royal assistance and protection. What condescension in a sovereign, what ripe wisdom in one who is so young! But I, O best of Kings, can by no means agree to put forth my weak hands, my poor and paltry spirit, my body broken down so that scarcely anything remains for it but the grave, to the duties of the strong, nor do I, thus un- worthy and insufficient, dare to enter upon those holy functions. This the electors ought to have considered; but if they are unmindful of it, yet I am not able to assent

---

[1] This letter seems to have been written on the election of S. Bernard to the Archbishopric of Rheims, after the death of Archbishop Rainauld, when the vote of all the electors fell upon the Abbot of Clairvaux; which dignity he refused, as he did many others. After the See had been vacant for two years, Samson was elected in 1140.

because I read: "Have mercy upon thine own soul, thou who art dear to God" (Ecclus. xxx, 23 *Vulg.*). Or if they believed me to be worthy because of the habit of religion which I bear, yet in this habit there is an appearance of holiness, not holiness itself.

No one is better known to me than myself; to no one so well as to myself am I known; nor assuredly can I believe those who see only my face and judge of me only from the outside, against the testimony of my conscience. Behold I, and the children whom God has given me, pray here, although sinners, for your kingdom and your person: it would be a hard and cruel thing to separate us one from the other; you would provoke us not to pray but to weep. The above is sufficient as regards men: but now on behalf of the Church, deign, I entreat you, to give attention to a few words about what I have in my mind. The mistress of churches sits in sadness and her tears are upon her cheeks: her beautiful colour is changed, her former comeliness faded, her costly and precious ornaments trodden under foot, her nobleness brought into contempt and her liberty into servitude. I am tormented in this flame, nor can there be any thought of consolation for me, until a deliverer comes to console her. Let reverence for her Spouse touch your heart, by whose Blood you have been redeemed, by whose likeness you have been adorned, by whose heritage you have been made rich, and let your pious proposal be carried out; that the Spouse who is so dear to our one Lord may no longer be left to struggle with a crowd of evils, with which her eyes are pained. I say to you, and I say it as one truly faithful, that it is not expedient for you (to permit this to go on). May it be granted to you, O noble and most illustrious King, so to govern the Kingdom of France, that you may thereby gain the Kingdom of Heaven.

LETTER CDXLIX.

To a friend.

He writes that he is at length regaining health, having escaped from the very jaws of death.

Health and happiness.

You have industriously drawn out a work useful, and as far as appears to me, Catholic. Yet I should like, if my life endures, to go over it in your presence, and to discuss various passages with you : and then, if there is any phrase or sentence rightly open to objection, it may either be expunged altogether or so altered, as no longer either to be calculated to move the objections of readers, or to be removed [1] itself. For the rest, rejoice with me that though *the Lord hath chastened and corrected me, yet He hath not given me over unto death* (Ps. cxviii. 18). For when the axe was already laid at the root of the barren tree, and I feared instantly to be cut down, I was restored by the prayers of my friends, who, promising that they would render fruitful with the most precious soil of their tears, the sterile soil of my heart, obtained some extension of time for me from the bountiful Lord of the vineyard (S. Luke xiii. 6).

LETTER CDL.

To the Brethren * * *.

Bernard exhorts them to give alms in that time of famine.

You are not ignorant, brethren, who has said *Blessed are the merciful, for they shall obtain mercy* (S. Matt. v.): and this, *Blessed is he that considereth the poor and needy* (Ps. xli. 1): and again, *If thou seest the naked,*

---

[1] [*movere; moveri:* We frequently notice this play upon words in S. Bernard, as in other writers of this time. (E.)]

cover him; and despise not thine own flesh (Is. lviii. 7)
and in holy Job, *Thou shalt visit thy habitation and shalt
not sin* (Job v. 24). The occasion of my recalling to you
these texts, a few out of many such, from Scripture, is
this : that it appears the poor and needy are in greater
need than usual at this time ¹ of famine.

Therefore if there is in you any bowels of mercies, any
pity and compassion, these poor people are fitting objects
for its exercise : inasmuch as they are humble and suffering, they are your bone and your flesh, and it is right
they should know that you think thus respecting them :
that they should know it, I say, if not by material benefits,
at least by kind words; that you should I mean, direct your
chaplain to urge and exhort the people with all earnestness
publicly and privately, to be charitable to the poor.

LETTER CDLI.

To a certain Abbot.

*He requests him to receive kindly a fugitive : and begs
him not to lay down his abbatical dignity.*

Health and friendly greeting to his friend.

No one who has read this letter and recognizes whence
I have taken the formula of salutation ought, I consider, to
be angry with me, because I have presumed to prefer myself by association with one who is my superior and have
ventured to call him mine, as if he were inferior and
dependent in some way upon me, whereas I justly belong

---

¹ [In the year 1146, as we learn from the short chronicle
of Châlons in Labbe "there was a severe famine in all lands,
such as never had been before." This famine, if we give
credence to the *Chronicon Lobiense*, which was included in
my *Thesaurus Anecdotorum*, Vol. iii, began in 1143, and lasted
seven years. (Martène's Note)].

wholly to him and am below him in every respect. Yet
we are accustomed not improperly to call ours not only
those who are our inferiors, but also those frequently to whom
we know ourselves to be inferior, as in this: *Thou art my
refuge and my portion in the land of the living* (Ps. cxlii.
5). For this indeed I have done concerning you but not for you·

But now I have to reply in few words, for the present,
to your letter which came to my hands on the Festival
of the Conception [1] of the Blessed Virgin, the observance
of which rightly demanded my whole time, and did not
suffer me to think of anything else; but then also the
messenger was in · haste to be on his way homeward,
so that he would scarcely wait until to-morrow, and give
me time, already worn out as I was with the Festival, anyhow,
to write back even these few words to you. This fugitive
brother then, I have thought there was nothing better for
me to do than to send back to the place whence he came,
having sternly reproached him, inasmuch as he was hard
of heart: since according to our customs I have no right
to retain him from his house without the consent of his
Abbot. Your course then will be sharply to chide him in
a similar way, and to drive him to an humble apology, and
after that to encourage him with my letter on his behalf
directed to his Abbot.

Respecting my weakness of body I can make no certain reply
to your kind solicitude except that I have been, and still
am, in poor health: neither any less nor more than I am
accustomed to be. The cause why I have not sent what
I had proposed to send, is that I feared scandal and injury
to souls, more than the danger to the body of one person.
Not to pass over entirely any of the subjects upon which
you touch, but to respond to each, though briefly, I come

---

[1] "Natalis animæ Dominæ nostræ dies festus."

to yourself. You have written that you wish to hear, what I, since I know all your circumstances, would advise you to do. But this which you are contemplating, if I do not mistake, I could not advise: nor if I may say so, would you be able to carry it out. But I wish that you would not hide from me what you really desire respecting yourself. Putting aside, however, your own wishes, and mine equally, as is right, I think the question is more what the will of God is concerning you; and this, the safe path, I would persuade you, as I would myself, to follow; nor is it disadvantageous to you, if I could induce you to think so. If you will take my advice therefore, hold fast the duties which you have, remain in the post in which you are, and strive to be of service to those over whom you are in authority; nor do you try to avoid a position of rule, as long as you are able to be of service to those you rule over. Woe indeed to you if you rule over others without profiting them, but still deeper woe, if you fear the responsibilities of rule, and avoid the possibility of doing service to others.

LETTER CDLII.

To a person unknown.

Bernard praises his prudence and humility.

Health and spiritual grace according to his desire.

[This letter is word for word the same as No. 413 "To Abbot Rainauld" which see].

LETTER CDLIII.

To a person unknown.

He promises to Stephen worthy fruits of penitence, if he shall persevere.

Who can sufficiently admire the warmth of your charity? But since I know that you are anxious and it is not a right thing to do to allow you to remain longer than is needful in that anxiety, Stephen your son and mine, if he shall complete his course with conduct worthy of its beginning, if he shall attain to offer the tail of the sacrifice with equal devotion to that with which he has offered the head, I offer my testimony in his behalf that he will bring forth worthy fruits of penitence.

LETTER CDLIV.

To the Aunt of the Emperor of Spain. [1]

He promises to her the intercessions of the brethren, and begs that the controversy which existed between them and the monks of Careda, may be determined by the Bishops.

I return thanks to God, on hearing from my brother Nivard of your devotion : and pray that He may render to you a rich return according to His goodness, with respect to the faith and confidence which you have in us. We gratefully concede to you the right of brotherhood in our house and a share in our prayers, as you have desired : and trust it may be of as much benefit to you, both in life and in death, as to any one of us. Of another matter : I have necessarily to call the attention of your

[1] [This letter seems to have been written on the occasion of the founding of the monastery at Spina, in the diocese of Palencia of which Sanchia, sister of King Alfonso, was the founder. See Ep. 301 which is said to have been written about A. D. 1149.]

Highness to the matter of the monks of Careda[1] because they spread calumnies against us by your niece and also by themselves.   Concerning the monastery   .   .   .   .   .

It behaves us to provide things good then not only before God, but also before men, and we desire by all means thus to proceed in this business, that our good be not evel spoken of, nor that those men should have any occasion for speaking ill of us.   Therefore we remit the matter to you, that you may kindly take steps to put an end to that scandal; and if they should not be willing to desist by any other means, that you would be so good as to bring the controversy to an end by the award, as is proper, of the Bishops of Zamora[2] and Astorga.   And when it shall be made clear, either by their own acknowledgment, or by the award of the Bishops, that they have nothing to complain of and no claim to make against us in this matter, we shall be prepared, by God's help, so to organize the place, as that it may be a cause of rejoicing to your pious mind; and so that God may be glorified in your work.

LETTER CDLV. [A new letter: from the MS. Copy in the Abbey of S. Sepulchre, Cambrai.]

FRAGMENT OF A LETTER TO NICHOLAS, BISHOP OF CAMBRAI.

To the venerable lord and dear father N.,[3] Bishop of Cambrai, BERNARD, called Abbot of Clairvaux, health and

---

[1] [Or of Carracetta, a Benedictine Abbey in the diocese of Astorga, founded by King Bermund about A. D. 990. Alfonso VII., King of Spain, gave it to the Cistercians. See Epp. 361, 373.]

[2] *Zemorensis:* but read *Zamorensis.*

[3] [Nicholas de Chievres, who is mentioned in Ep. 214.]

prayer that he may provide things good before God and before men.

I seek a new instance of an old friendship; not to remove a doubt, but to make new assurance of it. For I am sure that you have affection for me; but just as your friendship has been displayed to me. [1]

No. CDLVI. Letter or Charter of Bernard on behalf of the Abbey of S. Tron.

BERNARD, Abbot of Clairvaux, to all to whom the present letter shall come.

It happens that the Abbot of Saint Tron [2] and Baldwin de Wasia who are on their way to Rome, that their controversy may be decided, are passing by this place in the course of their journey.

Having heard the cause that was between them, and pitying their labour and expense, I have, by the help of God, brought them to a peaceful and friendly composition in this manner. The Abbey of Saint Tron shall possess for ever, according to its privileges, Werrebroeck and Saleghem, with the undivided parochial right. We have determined also that the church of Saint Tron shall give to Baldwin twenty shillings yearly on the Feast of S. Remigius. Baldwin has also at my entreaty resigned to the same church of Saint Tron the [right to] oblations which he had in that church.

Simon, Bishop of Tournay, also has thus understood the agreement.

---

[1] [The rest is wanting; nor has it been found anywhere else.]

[2] [This was Goswin, Abbot of Saint Tron, a monastery near Ghent, from whose autograph this Schedule has been extracted.]

No. CDLVII. Letter or Charter of the same Bernard
on behalf of the monasteries of Luxeuil and
S. Èvre. [1]

This is the compromise between the Abbots of Luxeuil
and Saint Èvre concerning the church of Galdouis-Curtis.

I, BERNARD, called Abbot of Clairvaux, to whom the lord
Pope [2] has committed the cause between the Abbots of
Luxeuil and Saint Èvre [3] for decision; have brought that
cause to a close by way of agreement in the following
manner.

It is agreed that they of Saint-Èvre should have the
entire tithe of Galdouis-Curtis; but that those of Luxeuil
shall have the church itself, and all things belonging to it
except the tithes, resigning any right that they may have
in the church of Basigni which they held of Saint-Èvre.
But all the annual dues which the church of Galdouis-
Curtis owes, whether to the Bishop or his assistants, those
of Saint-Èvre shall discharge entirely each year. This
was done under the advice of the venerable Bishops
Godfrey of Langres and Hatto of Troyes, and of the
religious persons who were invited for this purpose by
me, whose names are:

> William, Abbot of S. Martin at Troyes,
> Baldwin, Abbot of Châtillon,
> Stephen, Abbot of Trois Fontaines,
> Baldwin, Abbot of La Crète,
> Guy, Abbot of Charlieu. [4]

---

[1] [From the original at Saint-Èvre. Written A. D. 1140.]

[2] [Innocent II.]

[3] [The Abbot of Luxeuil at that time seems to have been
Josceran; that of Saint-Èvre Peter or Durand.]

[4] [To this document was appended a seal, but it is worn
away by time.]

No. CDLVIII.[1] Charter of the same Bernard on behalf of the monastery of S. Amand de Boisse.

I, BERNARD, called Abbot of Clairvaux, state publicly and give notice that I have conveyed the place of S. Amand de Boisse[2] and whatever I have in it by the gift of the Count of Angoulême, and of the church of Angoulême, and of Peter Austensius, to the church of S. Amand to which are witnesses: Hugh, Bishop of Angoulême; Junius, Abbot of La Couronne; also Brother Philip, our Prior, and Brother Gerard and Brother Geoffrey, monks of our House. Done at Clairvaux in the year of the Incarnation of the Lord 1153.

These are all the Letters of S. Bernard which have as yet come to light. It is probable, for the reasons given by Dom John Mabillon in the General Preface (Vol. 1. p. 17—19 of the English Edition), and considering farther that the "certain Letters which have not yet been brought to light" are represented in the fourth edition by an addition of forty-one Letters in all, which had been discovered by the research of D. Massuet and D. Martène, the list is now in all probability as nearly complete as it is ever likely to be.

An Appendix to the fourth Edition above mentioned contains some letters doubtfully ascribed to S. Bernard, and some others that are certainly spurious; some also written by Nicholas of Clairvaux, his untrustworthy secretary, in his name; and certain Letters by other persons, which have no necessary or even very close connection with the Saint. These (twenty-seven in all) it has not been thought needful to include in this Edition; but an exception has been made for the interesting letter of the Novice,

---

[1] From the muniment room of that place.
[2] See notes to Ep. 299.

love me in Jesus, you ought not to feel such apprehensions on my account. For these things are the burden of the Lord, and His yoke is easy, and His burden light. I am far from being able to imitate the multitude of good examples, which are brought under my notice day by day: but in order to reassure you respecting my condition and my wishes, I wish to send to my dear friend a description of Clairvaux in few words; of the poor of Christ who dwell in it; of the manner and routine of their life, to emulate which my soul earnestly aspires.

2. First of all then, I will describe to you in some degree and measure, my former life: in some measure I say, though there was seldom or never any measure in it. But I desire that you should know from the description, if you will give it your attention, from how many and frightful deaths the goodness of the Lord has delivered me, and may glorify Him, who in truth will in no wise cast out any sinner that cometh unto Him. If in the course of my history, you should remark faults which you have fallen into as well as I, I advise you faithfully as a brother, in the interest of your salvation to correct them without delay, while you have still time, since you know not what a day may bring forth. I then, my dear friend, when I was at Noyon, used to sit frequently in an embrasure of the windows of the Bishop's house, either alone, or with you or other companions: and often contemplated the order and stateliness of that house, then in the freshness of its beauty, now already growing old: and while doing so I used secretly to turn my mental vision upon that most exquisitely ordered house which is in the heavens, whose fairness, glorious, indestructible and ever new, transcends the imagination of man. When I reflect that I unfortunately pursued a road which led me farther away from that celestial home instead of bringing me nearer to it, I seem to

myself most miserable. By that, if I had not speedily fled from it, I should have been quickly and infallibly hurried to that house far different, the abode of misery and of extreme and unmeasured iniquity, where not order but horror dwells for ever, where is the worm that dieth not and the fire that is not quenched.

How rightly did I then realise with anxiety, whither the love of the world would carry me, as it had already begun to do. By it I was devoured and consumed by loose and foolish desires, being, as it were, drunken with them: nor had I any desire nor power to resist fleshly pleasures. One thought only still followed me everywhere, that I must die; and that I should not be able to escape paying eternal penalties for the fleeting pleasures of this world.

3. For when I sat at the table of our lord the Bishop, our fellow-citizen and our host, I fed daintily off silver plate, and healthfully also, as far as the dishes were concerned: and while I helped myself with my bodily hand, to these dainties, I often took from the same plates, with the hand of my mind, a far different food. And you, my dear friend, did not know that I was doing this, though I sat tolerably near you. What then? have I anything to say against these daily festive banquets, or the innocent plates and dishes? against the good wine, of which the soft colour charmed the eye, and the pleasant flavour the palate, or against the silver goblets which contained it? By no means. There was no fault in the food, in the wine, nor in the silver vessels: but in the earthen vessel of my body were the seeds of thorns, of which the growing crop pierced and wounded my soul, and which the sight and hearing of outward things strengthened and made to grow. Often then at table and elsewhere, these thoughts passed through my mind, as I gazed upon the costly and sumptuous dinner services of the Episcopal table.

sumption! I was quite sure that the Lord was righteous, and that He was able to destroy me for ever in hell: and yet knowing this, and fearing it, I yet did not cease to offend Him. I had indeed, that the Lord might be my portion, received the sacrament of order, [1] but the course of my life since I had done so, had rendered me very unsuited, by the very fact, for the sacrament. O how strange, how foolish and shameless was my state of mind! The testimonies of God are pure: and I presumed to read and preach them out of a polluted heart, and with a mouth defiled and insincere, though I knew that the Lord had said to the sinner: *Why dost thou preach my laws, and takest my testimonies into thy mouth?* (Ps l. 16). If ever I read or cited these laws in the church, from any other motive than the love and honour of God, I knew surely that I was guilty of a kind of sacrilege, because I offered to vanity the worship which was due to God. And therefore I was not the servant of God: for of this the Apostle says: *If I pleased men, I was not the servant of Christ.* (Gal. i. 10) and the Prophet: *God will scatter the bones of those who please men.* (Ps. liii. 5 *Vulg.*). But to speak truly, it was frequently my chief preoccupation, a most lamentable one, to please men, or to please myself, not to please God.

6. I was at that time nothing but a bad servant. By what right then should I occupy longer my place in the field of God, being a root of bitterness, good for nothing, even hurtful to many and more hurtful to myself, since I produced only bitter fruit? What example did I give to the living, or what sacrifice did I offer for the dead, I who ate of the fat of their offerings, and drank of the wine of their libations? since, with whatever cloak I concealed the fact, I

---

[1] *Clericatus*; i. e., minor orders, or at least the tonsure. (E.)

I

was only a pilferer and robber of the goods of the Church,
and an expender of them for culpable purposes. O how
wicked and hateful to God was my perversity! I had
heard that S. Jerome had written: 'Whosoever abuses the
goods of the Church to improper purposes, commits the
sin of purchasing falsehood, and is guilty of the Blood of
the Saviour.' Thus since I was in this, as in many other
respects, guilty of abuse and of rapine, that true and terrible declaration of the Apostle was often sounding in my
ears: *Robbers shall not possess the Kingdom of God* (1 Cor.
vi. 9, 10): and in reply came from the depth of my heart
the fearful, sorrowful, and crushing conclusion: Therefore
they will be precipitated into the prison of unclean spirits,
where they will be consumed for ever in the fire that is
never quenched! Yes, I arrived at that instant conclusion,
as well by the law of argument and reasoning, as because
the day of the Lord in which this shall come to pass,
rapidly approaches; as says the Prophet: *The day of the
Lord cometh, for it is nigh at hand: a day of darkness
and gloom* (Joel ii. 1, 2?) Therefore is it strange if these
and many similar sayings rendered me thoughtful and full
of care: since I could not recall from my infancy a moment
of my life, in which I had not been guilty of some dis-
honesty or other action worthy of death. Nothing pleased
me better than the vain occupations and meetings of
vanity, plays, jests, games, works provoking to mirth, not
to profit: frequently did I utter falsehood, rarely the
truth. I swore falsely, I flattered, I complimented, and
such like: and in consequence of common and habitual
custom, I thought them scarcely sins at all, but only a
compliance with politeness and the usages of society. Yet
I knew that all these things, when they make separation
between God and man, are only falseness and foolishness.
I am silent about my greater faults, my feelings of pride

and envy, hatreds, quarrels, slanders, evil speakings. I am silent about those wicked thoughts and works of mud and filth in which I was unhappily absorbed in secret; all that was in me from one moment to another was but mire, and my actions were hurrying me unto the punishment of eternal death. But the Father of Mercies looked upon me, and at length He visited me, and drew me to the feet of His Son.

7. You see then how great a thing the Father of goodness did for my soul when He mercifully drew me from the waters of Babylon, and still more mercifully placed me at Clairvaux beside the fountains of Salvation. Although Clairvaux is in appearance situated in a valley, its foundations are upon the holy hills, whose gates the Lord loves more than all the dwellings of Jacob. Glorious things are spoken of it, because in it the glorious and wonderful God doeth glorious and marvellous works. There those who have been long insane return to themselves: and although their outer man perisheth, yet their inner man is born again, and to use the words of the Apostle, is *renewed from day to day* (2 Cor. iv. 16) in the likeness of him, who has been made a man according to the will of God (Eph. iv. 24). There the proud are humbled, the rich are made poor, there the poor have the Gospel preached to them and the darkness of sinners is changed into light. To this place then had assembled a great multitude of men poor but blessed, gathered out of various regions and nations from the very ends of the earth; yet have they one heart and one soul, so that of that house especially it may be said: *Behold, strangers of Tyre and them of Ethiopia, these were there.* (Ps. lxxxvii. 4. *Vulg.*) Rightly then the residence of all the joyful dwellers in that place has no empty or ill-founded joy; but it is everlasting, and they have a sure hope, which they have found in Clairvaux, of their ascension

into Heaven, which has already begun. There they find the
ladder of Jacob with angels upon it ; some descending, who
so provide for their bodies, that they may not faint in the
way : and others ascending, who so rule over the souls of
these happy ones that their bodies also may hereafter be
glorified with them.

9. For the more diligently I watch from to-day those
poor men of a life so blessed, the more do I believe that they
follow Christ perfectly in all things ; and I infer by certain
signs that in all things they do they are shown to be true
ministers of God. For when they are occupied in prayer,
they speak to God in spirit and in truth ; and as well by
their trustful and attached tone towards Him, as by their
humble posture of body, they show plainly that they are
the near and dear friends of God. But when they are busied
in singing the praises of God more openly by psalmody :
how pure and how fervent is the disposition of their mind
towards it, the entire posture of their body sufficiently
shows by their holy fear and reverence : while their lingering and careful pronunciation and modulation of the words
of the Psalms shows how sweet to their lips are the praises
of God, sweeter even than honey to their mouth. And
while I watch them singing so piously and unweariedly the
Psalter in the daily Hours and nightly offices, from before
midnight right on to the break of day, with only a brief
interval, they seem to me a little less indeed than Angels,
but much more than men. It is not in mere human power to
perform this task with such steady cheerfulness and constant
endurance, as well as with such great fervour and desert,
but must be a divine gift. During the reading of the
Scriptures too, they seem to drink in gently and softly
the waters of Siloah which flow in silence, and spring up
unto eternal life. Their posture and demeanour show that
they are disciples of one Master, who teaches their hearts,

saying: *Hear, O Israel, and be silent.* They are still then, and listen, and increase in wisdom: since the wise man who listens and learns shall become still wiser.

9. And these poor men who lead so saintly a life, what effect do you suppose, my dear friend, that they produce on the spectator, as they go and come from their work, or carry on their various manual labours? It is quite evident that they are acting on motives higher than earthly, even upon the prompting of the Divine Spirit; so patiently and placidly, with such quiet countenances, and in such sweet and holy order, do they go through all things, that though they exert themselves very much, they never seem to be distressed or overburdened in any thing, however great their labours. Whence it is manifest, that in them works that Holy Spirit, who sweetly disposes all things: in whom also they are refreshed, so that they rest even while they labour. Of these men, now so poor, some, I hear, have been Counts, others Bishops, or holders of other dignities, or men illustrious for their great knowledge; and some, young men of noble birth. But now, by the grace of God, every distinction of person among them has expired: and the higher was the previous rank of any one of them in the world, the less he considers himself in this flock, and the lower in all respects. When I look at them working in the garden with the hoe, in the meadows with fork and rake, in the fields with the hook and in the woods with the axe, and with other tools at different descriptions of labour, to judge from their outward appearance, the work they are about, their tools, their uncared-for persons, their ill-arranged and common clothes, I should suppose them to be not persons of consideration, but a kind of people stupid, speechless, and uncultured, the scorn of men, and the offscouring of the people; but a sound and trust-

worthy intuition within my heart tells me that their life
is hidden with Christ in the heavens. Among them I
rejoice to see Geoffrey of Peronne, Rainauld of Picardy,
William of S. Omer, Walter of Lisle, all of whom I
knew formerly in the old man : but now, thanks to God,
of that old man is no trace any longer. In their former
state I knew them proud and puffed up, with haughty
looks and airs of extreme importance : but now I see
them humbled under the merciful hand of God, and with
a humility surprising to those below them and to themselves. In their former time I knew them as sepulchres
outwardly whitened, but within full of the bones of the
dead : now on the contrary, I see that they bear, as it
were, the earthen vessels of the Lord, which though plain
outwardly, are filled within with the costly perfumes of
Heaven.

When, then, the whole community goes to or returns
from the accustomed work, quietly, one after another and
step by step, as it were, in order of battle and with the
humble arms of peace displayed, do not the Angels of
God look upon this little band of men converted to Christ
out of the darkness of sin, and thus urging their way
onwards, with joy and gladness ; and sing, as it were :
*What company is this which cometh up from the wilder-
ness as the morning star at its rising, beautiful as the
moon*, etc. (Cant. vi. 9). The devil is frightened and en-
raged to see himself excluded : knowing (would that he
might always see and lament) that the loss to his
kingdom is not small by the renewal of so many souls.
Therefore he arms himself with all the resources of his
sharpest malice ; so as to capture in the nets of subtle
and involved reasoning those whom he can no longer
hold captive by the blandishments of this world. But
not even thus shall the enemy prevail ; for they have

placed their most safe refuge in the Cross of Christ, their dear and only hope of salvation, which they embrace with all their heart.

10. Finally, my dear friend, what idea would you form of these same poor of Christ, did you see them at the time of their meal? What sobriety, what self-restraint! I believe that in their demeanour there is nothing visible that displeases God, or enables man to find fault. So modestly, so holily do they behave themselves, as to appear without question that which they are: righteous men, who fear God. Therefore they receive with attention their spiritual food, the Word of life, for which they are always a-hungered: therefore they eat and drink reverently the other gifts of God which are set for them: no exquisite delicacies, but that which they have culti-vated with their own hands; vegetables and pulse. Their drink is a kind of beer; if this is wanting, they use plain water instead. Wine they seldom use; and then mixed with much water. They eat and drink then, as rendering due nourishment to the body; not as in indulging in good cheer or in gluttony; but only, as yielding to the necessity of nature and to God, as it is written, *Meats for the belly and the belly for meats, but God shall destroy both it and them* (1 Cor. vi. 13). For the Kingdom of God is not food and drink, but righteousness and peace and joy (Rom. xiv. 17) which form the only object of their desires, and the end at which they aim. For the great mistress of their entire life is obedience: which they follow so faith-fully in all respects that there is not a single moment even of the day or night which is not devoted to obe-dience and Divine worship among them. Therefore I verily believe that (to pass over actions which are of greater merit and importance) there is not a single step which they take nor a movement of their hands which is

directed otherwise than to the obtaining remission of sin or
an increase of glory in eternal life. Those who perhaps
sometimes fall, as they are not able entirely to avoid doing
while they bear the burden of weak flesh, are nevertheless
not crushed, because the Lord supports them with His Hand.

11. Here then, my dear friend, you have those few
particulars which I promised to set down in this letter
for your edification respecting the poor monks of Clairvaux. Many greater and better things remain untold : but
for the present these suffice. My strong desire is that I
may be worthy to be united in body and in spirit as far
as may be with those poor in Christ, so that I may be
helped by their intercession, may feel a more fruitful
penitence, and be able to cry with greater faith to the
Lord. *Lord, I have fled unto Thee, teach me to do Thy
will, deliver me from my enemies, O my God* (Ps. cxliii.
9, 10). *Unto Thee, O Lord, do I lift up my soul. O my
God, I trust in Thee, let me not be confounded* (Ps.
xxv. 1--2) or similar prayers. For I am so far under
probation, and by the grace of God, am being trained in
their rule and manner of life; so that when I shall have
been admitted into their body, I may know how to watch
with them, and to slumber only in the spirit. For the Kingdom is promised to the vigilant, and he who sows in the
spirit shall in the spirit reap life eternal. To which I pray
that by the mercy of God, I may happily attain, and the
whole Church of Noyon, my mother and patroness; so that
I may see Christ and reign with Him. Amen. Farewell.
God willing, on the Sunday after the Ascension of Our
Lord, I shall receive the equipment of my profession,
through the grace and blessing of Jesus Christ, which I
trust He will deign to grant unto me by the merits of
His Mother and by your prayers. Amen. Again farewell;
remember thy last end and have pity upon thy soul.

LETTER CDLX (Formerly No. 474, from Spicilegium.
Tom. iii. p. 501. A. D. 1152).

LETTER OF HENRY, BISHOP OF TROYES TO S. BERNARD.

*He puts the Abbot in possession of the Abbey of Bou-
lancourt, which the Augustinian monks who then possessed it, willingly ceded.*

To the venerable and most Reverend Father BERNARD,
Abbot of Clairvaux, and to his successors regularly appointed, I, Henry, Bishop of Troyes, wish health for ever.
If we employ care and vigilance to ensure the benefit
and improvement of the monasteries and churches established in our Diocese, we hope for help and wait for
reward, from Him whom the care of all belongs. In our
Diocese there is a certain collegiate Church, Boulancourt
by name, having an Abbot, Canons, lay-brethren, and
nuns (*mulieres*), all of whom had vowed themselves to a
holy life, where since discipline had altogether failed, arrogance was prevalent' and honourable conduct was entirely wanting : and having been summoned by the dwellers
in that institution. who were not able to maintain themselves by their own efforts, I made a visitation of it. There
I earnestly entreated the Abbot, and all the inmates as
well Canons, as lay-brethren and nuns, that I might grant
the Abbey itself and all its possessions, which could not
be maintained by themselves, to God and to the Order
of Citeaux, and especially to the venerable Abbot and
Monastery of Clairvaux, that they might reform and possess the same for ever, according to be custom of the
Order of Citeaux. And the Abbot of the before mentioned
house delivered up the Abbey into my hands, and conveyed it to the house of Clairvaux.
Seeing then that Almighty God has enlightened and

amended almost the whole world by your care, wisdom, and piety: I give this Abbey to the Cistercian Order, to your Paternity and to the Abbey of Clairvaux, with all its possessions, for ever. The chief possessions are these which I set down under their several names: the land adjacent to the Abbey, the farmhouse at Froide-Fontaine, the lands [1] of Haymo, in Rosteria, the Dry Lands, Domni peruclum, Brueil; with all dependences and appurtenances of the said granges, and all things which the before mentioned Abbey had, in full possession. This grant I have confirmed and authenticated by my seal; so that no lapse of time, nor perversity of any man whatever might either change or altogether destroy it. Done in this year of the Incarnation of our Lord MCLII, in the reign of Louis the Younger, King of France

---

[1] *Pertam, qu.* for *perticam?* (E.)

APPENDIX.

LETTER CDLXI. (A. D. 1138).

To Cardinal U. [Humbald.]

He entreats his help in the matter of the disputed election to the See of Langres. [1]

To his very dear lord and friend MAGISTER U., by the grace of God, Cardinal, Deacon of the Apostolic See, Brother BERNARD, called Abbot of Clairvaux, wishes health, and that he may hunger and thirst after righteousness.

If you truly love me, let your love be *not in word nor in tongue, but in deed and truth* (1 S. John iii. 18). Or rather I should say, if you are a lover of justice, as you have hitherto either shown yourself or appeared to be, have pity upon the melancholy position of the Lord Christ, who in the church of Langres, is being at the present time unworthily treated by the wicked, and who cries out to you: 'Help me, O Humbald, for wicked men have persecuted me.' There, in short, He suffers and is oppressed in His members, to whom a man is given for a Bishop,

---

[1] For a full account of this dispute, see Letters 164, 166—170 of S. Bernard: and for the arguments used in favour of the other claimant, who was a Cluniac monk, see Peter the Venerable, Abbot of Cluny, Letters B. i. No. 29, B. ii. No. 28. S. Bernard succeeded in having the election annulled, and a relation of Bernard, Geoffrey, Prior of Clairvaux, was made Bishop of Langres.

not rightly nor orderly, but by fraud and force. That man too, is neither of worthy life, nor of honourable character, nor has he the qualities requisite to be of use to the Church. Lastly, he was neither canonically elected nor lawfully consecrated. Therefore if you can do anything, have pity upon us and help us. [1]

LETTER CDLXII. (A. D. 1139). [2]

To Pope Innocent.

He defends the testimony he has given respecting the election at Lyons.

[1] This letter is found in the Chapter Library of Toledo (MS. IX. 21, 12mo) and the *Real Academie de la Historia* of Madrid (Div. of S. Pedro de Cardena: Codex x. F. 249). The latter MS. belongs to the beginning of the thirteenth century. The person to whom this letter is written, Cardinal Humbald or Hubald, cannot be identified quite certainly. There were two of that name: the one, *Tituli S. Adriani* mentioned *in Bullen*, Feb. 13, 1139 to May 21, 1141: the other, *Tituli S Mariæ in Via lata*, Jan. 7, 1135 to Dec. 9, 1143. The former letters on the same subject were written in A.D. 1138, and this was in all probability carried to Rome by the same messenger. It was probably therefore the latter Cardinal to whom it was addressed.

[2] See Letters 165, 171--173. The testimonial which S. Bernard refers to as having been given by himself is evidently that in Ep. 171. Not long after the disputed election to the See of Langres, mentioned in the last letter, died the Archbishop Peter of Lyons who had been opposed to S. Bernard in that matter. He was succeeded by the Dean of Lyons, Falco, who had been on the contrary the chief supporter of Bernard, and the Prior of Clairvaux, Geoffrey, then Bishop of Langres (Ep. 165). But his election being disputed, Geoffrey in his turn wrote to the Pope (Ep. 172), using, however, the practised pen of Bernard, to recommend him, and ask for him the grant of the pallium. (E.)

To his very dear father and Lord, INNOCENT, by the grace of God, Supreme Pontiff, B(ERNARD), called Abbot of Clairvaux, sends his humble greeting.

If in the testimony which I gave respecting the Archbishop of Lyons, I have lied unto my lord, God forbid that I should do so knowingly. But if I have been deceived in the matter, how many persons there are who are either deceived with me or deceiving me! And that which above all, renders [1] me excusable, is that the Religious themselves who are very near neighbours of the man, and to whom he is exceedingly well known, are nevertheless either deceiving me or themselves deceived. And finally, that both his election was unanimously agreed to by the whole clergy and people, and his consecration solemnly performed by the provincial Bishops, is shown by the fact, that not an enemy appeared to open his mouth and object. What is the use now of objections coming forward so late? If they are people from a distance, they could not know the man as well as his neighbours do: but if they are neighbours, they should have objected before. All the proceedings respecting that man were carried though as I said, deliberately and formally, and nothing was done in secret. Which is the more credible, that a few calumniators have lied respecting a man whom they hate, or that the whole body of the electors, or I should say, the Holy Ghost, who has caused so many of the faithful to be of one mind in electing this man? Let the person who has vainly endeavoured to persuade you of the contrary, bring forward proof of his statements. If he fails to do this, what else can I think about him, than that *an evil man out of the evil treasure of his heart brings forth evil things* (S. Matt. xii. 35). Let him see to

[1] (*redit*).

it that this threatening does not touch him : He who gath-
ereth not with me, scattereth abroad (S. Luke xi. 23).
But I have confidence in the successor of the first pastor,
that because he fears and loves Him who is the Gatherer,
he will not feel able longer to give heed to a disperser.

I remember that in writing to your Holiness, I commended the person of our Archbishop, nor am I ashamed of having done so. For I have almost as many
witnesses in favour of my testimony as there are people
who know him. And if I commended his election as
having been rightly made, I commended that which the
entire body of electors with one voice authenticated.

But if the popular judgment should appear not to be
regarded, yet the opinion of Religious men should, if it
seems good to you, be asked for. If neither do they
differ, then I judge it to be clear that you should determine judicially which of two things it becomes you to
approve : namely, the opinion of all, or the delivering of
the man to the will of his enemies.

LETTER CDLXXIII. (A. D 1139).

To Cardinal Luke. [1]

On the same matter.

To Magister L(uke), by the grace of God, Cardinal of
the Apostolic See, a man who loves him much sends greeting : with the prayer that he may abide in the love of
God.

Those who persecute the Archbishop of Lyons [2] are
influenced by their own evil passions, and do not observe

---

[1] The Cardinal Priest Luke was of the *Titulus S. Johannis
et Pauli.* He is mentioned in Ep. 144 (E.).

[2] Falco. (E.)

the limits of fairness. It is needful for you to exert yourself not feebly, but vigorously, on behalf of that man, for
he is powerfully attacked. Let the love of me add something to your zeal, for it is an injury to my own Archbishop, [1] as you know, that I am witnessing.

LETTER CDLXIV. [2]

To B. [Baldwin], Archbishop of Pisa.

*He expounds the text "Ille erat lucerna lucens et ardens",
with reference to the Episcopal office of Baldwin.*

To the Lord, and most intimate friend B., by the grace

---

[1] See Letter 171. (E.)

[2] This letter is a reply to a letter (which is lost) from the
Archbishop. Baldwin had been a monk at Clairvaux, and had
apparently accompanied Bernard into Italy. At all events he
was with him there in A. D. 1137, as is shown by Ep. 144 to
the monks at Clairvaux, which Baldwin wrote at Bernard's
dictation, as they were both in the suite of the Pope on his
march to Apulia. One phrase in the letter shows that he had
been raised to some dignity; apparently shortly before to the
Cardinalate. He afterwards was made Archbishop of Pisa; he
retained this post till Oct. 1145 or 1146, when Bernard mentions
(or rather implies) his demise in Ep. 245 to Eugenius III. The
high esteem in which Baldwin was held, appears in two other
places besides these letters. In the second book of the *Vita
Bernardi* he is praised as the glory of his fatherland, Pisa, and
in the *Exordium Magnum Cisterciense* an entire chapter is
devoted to him as to other celebrated *alumni* of Clairvaux.
Another person belonging to the Church in Pisa, however, the
Frater Angelus to whom Bernard sends greetings in the above
letter, cannot be further traced. Similarly with regard to the
execution of the project announced of sending a Cistercian
colony to Pisa, which is mentioned in the concluding phrase
of the letter; for so far as is known no cloister of this order was
created there during the course of the 12th century; therefore

of God, Archbishop of Pisa, Brother BERNARD sends greeting: with the prayer that he may abound in hope, and in the power of the Holy Spirit.

I have received your letter, which is a proof of your strong affection towards me and holy desire for my presence. In which certainly your affection is not without return, since those whom you love, love you, and those whom you wish for, wish for you also. If a return is due from me for the letter which I gladly read, to you, I would most willingly make it. Would that I were never absent from you. But that is not to be hoped for: would then that I were worthy to have your presence even occasionally. But that too is in the hand of God. We are the servants of one Lord, whose will is to be obeyed by both of us: nor must we do whatsoever we will. And you indeed He has set for a light of the Gentiles. If you let your light shine, it is not hidden: nor on the other hand, if you do not, can that be hidden either. For *a city set upon a hill cannot be hidden, nor can a light set upon a candlestick* (S. Matt. v. 14): its darkness and its light are each entirely visible, and of necessity they are a mark for the admiration or the contempt of all. It is even rather preferable to be hidden under a bushel than to be raised upon a candlestick, and then not to give light. A lamp when extinguished, not only casts a dark shadow, but emits evil smelling smoke. Paul did not travail unavailingly, nor was

unless we suppose that the plan failed owing to unknown impediments only the possibility remains to connect this passage with the founding of the monastery *Caput Aquæ* in Sardinia which took place 1149 from Clairvaux, when the Archbishop of Pisa presided as Primus and Legate. How much time intervenes is beyond calculation, as no point of time is given to enable us to place this letter, further than that it was between 1139 and 1146. (E.)

he as salt that has lost its savour.. And therefore he was a good savour of Christ in every place: even at the present time he is a savour of life unto life to very many. (2 Cor. ii. 14—16). Blessed is He to whom it is said: *For the fragrance of Thy perfumes we will run after Thee* (Cant. i. 3, 4). That is as if he said: In the light of Thy beams we will go forward: and that is nothing else than saying: We profit by the example of Thy character and actions. From Him do the Saints derive the odour of sanctity: from Him also do they shine as lights. How many sinners has Saint John brought to penitence by his example! For he, whose fame was widely spread and his life most ascetic, shone as a light in the world and diffused a sweet fragrance. *He was a burning and a shining light* (S. John v. 35) placed on high; and thence, as from a lofty candlestick, he ministered the light of his virtues to all, and diffused a sweet odour everywhere. I desire that you may be an imitator of S. John. *Let your light shine before men* (S. Matt. v. 16): yet so that it shall shine and glow also before God; and that of you also it may be said, He was a burning and a shining light. The one thing is necessary on your own account: the other on that of your flock. He shines well who is kindled by his own fire. How many are there who do not shine by their own light! Hypocrites wish to shine [outwardly], but have no wish for an inward fire. Yet of the two things, it were better to have the inward fire without the outward light, than to have the light without the fire. *What do I wish*, said Our Lord, *except that the fire should burn?* (S. Luke xii. 49). The moon shines, but it has no inward fire, and therefore it suffers obscuration; since it shines not by its own light, but as they say, by the light of the sun. Wherefore perhaps the Scripture saith: *A fool changeth as the moon: but a godly man is stedfast in wisdom as the sun*

(Ecclus. xxvii. 11).[1] It compares excellently the wise man to the sun, who bears within himself the fire which is the source of his light, so that it cannot fail. Similarly, *charity,* without which a man is not wise, *never faileth* (1 Cor. xiii. 8).

He who is content with the testimony of his own conscience does not need to appear great by the praise of another person. But what am I doing? for I am making these reflections as if I thought them of great importance *(necessaria)* to you. *But out of the abundance of the heart the mouth speaketh* (S. Luke vi. 45), and I know not how it is, that to an anxious and solicitous affection nothing is sufficiently safe. On that account I venture still to add a particular fact which has come to my knowledge. It is said that there are with you persons who are fond of gifts, so that a person of your house is reported to have accepted money for the transfer of a bailiff. Although transactions of that kind do not wound the conscience of one who [like yourself?] has given no personal consent to them, yet they may tend to blacken his character. For it behoves us *to provide things honest not only in the sight of the Lord, but in the sight of men* (2 Cor. viii. 21); though I know not in what manner the compliance could be excused of one, who, when he has the power to correct such abuses, does not do so. I salute in all humility Brother Angelo (?) with all the Church in your house. By him, whom, God willing, you will send to the Chapter, I will send if you require it, the whole Abbey.

---

[1] The reading of the *Vet. Lat.* is: *Homo sanctus in sapientiâ manet sicut sol,* on which the quotation is apparently founded. It differs somewhat from both the Greek and the Syriac. (E.)

LETTER CDLXV. [1]

To his friend Vi. Brother Bernard.

As I have depicted myself in a letter, so I am, except that the hand is but ill able to express the disposition of the mind. Not only is there nothing for you to fear from me, but there never has been. And so for me, if I have ever felt perchance any apprehension of you, I do so no longer. So that I do not demand my friend [1] anew, but hold him fast with all confidence: nor do I regain him, because I have not lost him. I bind him to me by the affections of my heart wherewith he is held as it were with arms: and there is none who is able to tear him from my breast. I embrace a new friend from an old, because true friendships do not grow old, or if they do, they were not true. *I will hold him and will not let him go, until I bring him into my mother's house, and into the chamber of her that conceived me* (Cant. iii, 4). When I say that he is at leisure, I do not mean that he is unprofitable, but highly favoured. For his times of leisure

---

[1] It is altogether uncertain to whom this letter is addressed. If it were William, Abbot of S. Thierry, and afterwards a monk at Signy (as Dr. Hüffer thinks) we should naturally have expected 'To his friend G.' for *Gulielmus*, as in the various letters undoubtedly to that person (See Epp. 85, 86). All that can be said is that the Letter before us contains allusions, as will be seen, suiting sufficiently well the case of an Abbot who had resigned his office and become a simple monk, for the sake of greater leisure and retirement. Among S. Bernard's other correspondents there is another W. (the Vi. may be really meant for W.), Abbot of Troyes, to whom Ep. 408 is addressed (E.).

[1] *In Cod*: antiquum: but Hüffer (Vorstudien p. 213) reads *amicum*, no doubt rightly).

are not so truly leisurely, as that they are plainly assiduous in the pursuit of good objects, and fruitful to salvation. Unhappy am I who am entangled in such a multitude of affairs, an exile from my own thoughts, unworthy of holy leisure, void of sacred stillness. Yet since you deign (to request it) I am yours, and will be, as long as I live. The sermons which you ask for, were not ready: but shall be prepared, and you shall soon have them.

LETTER CDLXVI. [1] (*Circa* A. D. 1135).

To the Monks of Grâce de Dieu.

To all the very dear brethren who are at Grâce de Dieu, BERNARD, called Abbot of Clairvaux, desires health: and that they may be rendered strong in the Lord, and in the power of His might.

Who shall bestow upon me *the wings of a dove* (Ps. lv. 6) that I may fly to see the earnest endeavours of my sons, and their progress in spiritual things, their peace and order and discipline? I desire to behold those new settlers in a new spot, how among strangers and foreigners they fight (a good fight), how they *sing the Lord's song in a strange land* (Ps. cxxxvii. 4). Already I have flown to you in mind and am with you in spirit: but according to the saying of the Lord, *The spirit indeed is willing but the flesh is weak* (S. Matt. xxiv. 41), nor can the latter follow the former at this time. But it shall follow at a later

---

[1] During S. Bernard's life two Cistercian monasteries of this name were founded; the one in Franche Comté, the other in Poitou. However, here only the latter is meant, which was founded in 1135 from Clairvaux. The writing of the letter falls in the first year of the monastery, when the expression *novae incolae* still applied to the monks. (E.)

time, if ever it shall regain from the Hand of God its former strength. But in the meantime, do ye, beloved, stand fast in that work wherein ye are, yea, rather make progress in that to which you have put your hands : because where any one ceases to strive to go onward unto perfection, there he begins to be deficient.

LETTER CDLXVII.

To Pope Eugenius. [1]

Bernard replies to the Pope's letter to the community at Clairvaux on his election.

[1] This letter should be read immediately after Ep. 238, which was Bernard's first letter to his former pupil and subordinate after his elevation to the Papal Chair. (For the details of Eugenius' career, see note to Ep. 237). He was elected Feb. 15, 1145, and Bernard had already saluted him in his first letter, the joyful tone of which, however, was somewhat qualified by surprise, anxiety and earnest admonition ; a little, it would seem also, by not receiving any direct communication from Eugenius, to inform his former chief and his brethren of the great charge which had been conferred upon him. That letter could scarcely have reached the Pope when the two brethren, whose return from Rome was expected when the letter was sent, came back to Clairvaux and brought the desired letter from Eugenius. This was delivered ; and its comfortable contents, as also the Apostolic blessing of him who was once a humble monk of the cloister was read to the Abbot.

Then revived the spirit of the Saint ; and praising God, he fell on his face and adored, he says, with his brethren, the new Pope as if he had been personally present. This letter was unknown until now. It is preserved in MS. in the old Cistercian monastery at Lilienfeld, situated near St. Polten, in an adjoining valley of the Danube. This letter is there named as the last of 110 of S. Bernard in the Parchment Codex 55 on leaf 94 a.-b. Unfortunately this folio MS., which dates from

As cool waters to a thirsty soul, so is good news from a far country (Prov. xxv. 25). I have gladly [1] received our brethren Gg. and G. coming from your presence,[2] and in their words have become as it were consoled. And sometime since I had heard by others the news of what has taken place, and of what the Lord has done with respect to His son. *But they who went by did not say: The blessing of the Lord be upon you* (Ps. cxxix. 8). Now, however, when the letter was read over containing a picture of your goodwill towards us, from its fulness we all received good words, consoling words, health and apostolic benediction. When I had heard this, my spirit lived again, and giving thanks to God, I fell prone upon my face, and I and your brethren rendered homage [3] to you upon the earth. I do not tell you this in order to anoint your head with the oil of the flatterer, that they may deceive the poor and needy, who are deceivers and deceived, but as those who are blessing him whom the Lord hath blessed. For it behoves me to speak with you both in another tongue and on other matters. The words which I speak to you are not as the caresses of a flatterer.

He is rash who meddles with the strife of another (Prov. xxvi. 17). Like a potter's vessel adorned with drossy silver, so are swelling words joined with an evil heart

the 13th century, contains only a fragment of the letter: the above description is followed by a few phrases in which S. Bernard denies every idea of flattering the Pope. Then the text breaks off in the middle of the phrase, *blandientis oscula* and then follow without any context a number of texts out of the book of Proverbs and Ecclesiastes which have no connexion with the letter. (Hüffer).   [E.]

[1] Hüffer reads *leti*: but qu. *laete*? (E.)

[2] *(a latere vestro)*.

[3] *(adoravimus)*.

(Ibid. xxvi. 23). Boast not thyself of to-morrow; for thou knowest not what a day may bring forth (Ibid. xxvii. 1) . . . . It is better to be rebuked by a wise man, than to be deceived by the adulation of fools (Eccles. vii. 5).

LETTER CDLXVIII [1].

To Berald, Abbot of S. Benignus at Dijon.

On behalf of a fugitive monk.

To his venerable friend, Dom Berald, Abbot of S. Benignus at Dijon, Brother Bernard, unworthy Abbot of Clairvaux, wishes health and the spirit of piety.

[1] This letter is taken from the Codex Monacensis 1860, a paper MS. of the monastery at Tegensee, written in the 15th century. Here it follows at the conclusion of a series of well-known Bernard letters, one to the Abbot B. of S. Benignus in Dijon, in which the Saint associating with his request "a certain venerable Brother Henry," intervening on behalf of a monk who has twice deserted the cloister, or at least requests for him a letter of dismissal. This letter, however, does not show the excellent penmanship of S. Bernard, and the age of the MS. causes some mistrust concerning its authenticity, as at that time with other writings a number of spurious letters were circulated under Bernard's name. On the other hand it is evident on the authority of the Abbot himself that his letters were not unfrequently written by others at his direction: the one now under consideration employs the phraseology often used by him, and above all, not only the person of the receiver, but also another direct connection between him and the Abbot can be proved by documentary evidence. In the first place a peculiar link connected the Saint with the venerable Church at Dijon, which had been intimately associated with the history of his family, and in which his mother Alith was long buried, until the translation of her body to Clairvaux. The castle of Fontaines, the home of the

I knock suppliantly at the door of your Piety on behalf of this wandering lamb of yours, insomuch that you
may be pleased, after the example of the Good Shepherd,
piously to compassionate and have mercy upon him. I
do not at all lose sight of the levity of the man : and
that twice he has escaped from the monastery and has been
received again. But yet as your Paternity well knows,
mercy is to be exalted above judgment ; and especial deference ought to be rendered to the blessed Benedict,
who orders that an absconding monk is to be received again,
even till the third time. This also the venerable Brother
Henry entreats from your goodness. But if you come to
the conclusion that in this matter it is not expedient to
grant our request : then in the last place the brother himself makes this petition of you ; that you would give him
letters dimissory, to this effect that by your licence he
may be permitted to seek the salvation of his soul in
some other monastery. For the rest, your affection for me
will be glad to be made aware in an unceremonious way,
that *the Lord hath chastened and corrected me, but he hath
not given me over unto death* (Ps. cxviii. 18). Farewell.

family, was situated near Dijon. Letters xiv. xv. xvi. were
written by S. Bernard on behalf of this monastery to Pope
Honorius II., Cardinal Haimeric and Cardinal Peter. Abbot
Berald sat, as far as we can ascertain, from 1122 to 1129,
in which latter year he appears, in company with the Abbots
of Citeaux and Clairvaux, as witnesses of a deed of gift by
Hugo, Count of Champagne (See Vol. i. pp. 200—202, *Note.*)
to S. Benignus. The year 1129 therefore is the latest date
that can be assigned to this letter.   [E.]

LETTER CDLXIX. [1]

PETER, ABBOT OF CLUNY, TO ABBOT BERNARD.

To the venerable, and every way most worthy of deep respect, Dom. BERNARD, Abbot of Clairvaux, Brother P., the humble Abbot of Cluny, wishes the fulness of health and true affection.

That you have acceded to my earnest requests, and at my instance, have undertaken and succeeded by continual and wise pressure in accomplishing a peaceful settlement of the quarrel which had broken out between our brother H., Prior of Arche, and the canons of Lonway, I gratefully accept, and render true thanks to you therefore. But that you may be assured that the issue of your efforts is agreeable to me, I express definitely on this page my sanction and confirmation, with the consent of my whole Chapter, of the award: viz., the receiving of Ten Solidi yearly from the Canons above named by this prior of Arche and his successors for ever: promising you that because of this coöperation, our thanks and service shall never fail wheresoever it shall be needful. To our beloved brother W., Prior of Arche.

[1] This is a merely formal letter of approval and official sanction, from that intimate friend of S. Bernard, Peter the Venerable, Abbot of Cluny. Bernard, as we learn, had at the request of the latter interposed in a quarrel between the Cluniac Prior of Arche and the Canons of Lonway, and Peter willingly sanctioned the conditions of agreement. A second short letter to that Prior contains with reference to the former letter the conditions for placing in the place of the canons monks from Clairvaux.

These letters were discovered in the Cartulary of Lonway by the late Vicar (Merle) of Fontaine-lez-Dijon, who conjectures the date of the first to be about A. D. 1145, of the second A. D. 1149. He points out also that it is the Priory of Arche-en-Barrois that is here referred to.   (E.)

The canons of Lonway, as we hear, held from you a
certain plot of land of the estimated value of Ten Solidi
(yearly), which sum I understand has been paid by the hand
of the lord (Abbot) of Clairvaux, as my letter now existing is found to attest : (he directs the land to be peace-
ably yielded to the brethren of Clairvaux :) who have entered into possession of it.

LETTER CDLXX [1]

Dom Galandus, Abbot of Regny, to S. Bernard.

To the most kind father and lord, BERNARD, the most
Reverend and religious Abbot of that very holy community, dwelling as to the body indeed in the Bright Valley

---

[1] This letter is one numbered 138 in the Parchment Codex
in the Public Library at S. Omer. The Codex is a Fólio MS.
in two columns, of the beginning of the 13th century, which
according to a note on the last page (which is half destroyed),
folio 185*b*, belonged to the Cistercian Abbey of Clairmarais.
It contains five books of the *Vita Bernardi*, many sermons,
most of the treatises of the Saint, up to 157*b* 158*b*. Then follows
this letter of a monk Galandus of Règny to the Abbot of
Clairvaux, to which is added a *parabolarium*, as it is called,
or writing of the same author. These theological treatises *)
run to the end of that codex, and are submitted by the accom-
panying letter to the judgment of the Saint before publication.
Abbot Julian of Regny whose help has considerably aided the
work, advised this.   Such a reminting of the roughly expressed
phrases of Galland is not only intended for the correction of
anything that might be against faith and good morals, but
also of grammatical slips, although that point does not appear
of importance to the author.   Whether Bernard responded

---

* These begin 'De reparatione humani generis.' 'Novimus primos
parentes nostros a Deo beneconditos in paradyso positos' (2) De
misericordibus; (3) De luxuria et castitate. (MIGNE).

(Clairvaux), but spiritually built up in brightness and beauty of character : Brother GALANDUS sends most devoted greeting and humble obedience.

At the persuasion of a certain friend and adviser, whose name and office the brief preface which follows to this little treatise will at once reveal, since I had a scanty treasure in silver, I, though an inexperienced and unskilled minter, have made out of it certain coins. And although I was hampered by the smallness of my stock of silver ; yet nevertheless I ventured to adopt [for my work] the form and semblance of that made out of pure silver; while it is enough for me, if I could hammer out coins of a lower kind and less value. But yet since I fear that I have transgressed the rules and prescriptions for legitim-

to the request is not clear. Possibly Ep. 449 may be looked on as the answer of the Saint. This modest writing does not seem to have had a large circulation; it appears not to have been printed, and the name of the monk is not elsewhere known. When Galland in the title of his letter says "a monk of Regny" he is not strictly accurate. The Cistercian monastery of this name in Auxerre was founded in 1128 * when the brethren of the adjoining Abbey of Fontenay, in the diocese of Autun, removed to Regny. Six years previous to this Fontenay, which was founded in 1104, submitted itself to the rule of Clairvaux, and besides receiving brethren from that Order, obtained in Stephen a new 4th Abbot; his predecessor is that Julian referred to by Galland. Julian appears first in the year 1123 and as the 1st Abbot. Gerard occupied the position for a long time, and it would not be safe to predate the election of Julian. Therefore the letter and the composition of Galland must fall during the 2nd decade; a result which corresponds with the whole tone of the letter. At that time Bernard was not the celebrated Abbot who in 1130 decided in the Synod of Étampes the burning question respecting the double election to the Papacy. (E.)

* This is Mabillon's date. But Dr. Hüffer puts it in 1134.

ate coin, and especially since the fraud of false moneyers, when detected and as it is sometimes, brought before the judges, is usually met with severe blame and punishment; therefore I determined to send my humble little penny pieces to be subjected to your examination, inasmuch as I know well your skill and experience in this art, having both seen and held in my hands, pieces of various denominations, which were the work of your skill, and have heard them praised by those who were wise, before mine were offered to the public notice. From both the workmanship and the inscription [of yours] I acknowledge that I have taken some hints, while I was at work upon my coinage, such as it was.

And this I believe will not be concealed from your Holiness, when you shall have carefully examined the coins which I send. In these, although the rudeness of the composition and turning may rightly displease you, yet the metal of which they are made does not lose its value. And thus perhaps the costliness of the material may obtain acceptance for that which might be otherwise rejected on account of the want of grace in the workmanship.

But now briefly to make clear what I have said : the coins founded by me are the little propositions of the treatise. Which, because they treat of virtues indeed and divine subjects, but do so in too simple and unpolished a style, have manifestly a costly material, but a design wanting in grace. For I both point out the scantiness of my intellectual wealth, by the smallness of my stock of silver, and just as coins of lesser value are not made entirely of silver, nor yet are wholly without it, so also my utterances are neither resplendent with the cleverness of intellectual power, nor by the mercy of God, are they altogether wanting in spiritual grace and fulness. If (which may God forbid) I have possibly said anything in them which is against the rule of a right faith or piety, then truly I have transgressed the law and rule of legitimate composition. [1]

But whether this has in fact happened to me in any case, your judgment and experience will when you run through the book, speedily be able to pronounce: and if you shall discover any such instance, I humbly entreat you with earnest prayers, that you will either correct it yourself, or point it out to me for the purpose of correction. If you shall find, that I have here and there transgressed grammatical rules, although I think this kind of offence of small importance, yet these also I will correct as you shall think best. I entreat that indulgence may be shown to my ignorance in case of error in the statements or absurdity in the opinions offered: though I have followed the instructions to me of that most reverend father and my Abbot, Dom Julian: and though being the least of all his scholars, have presumed to pen certain treatises in this book; following everywhere as well as I could, the method and mode of speech delivered to me from him. In fact he bade me to speak, by various similitudes or parables; and if I have, in many passages, endeavoured to use figurative phrases rather than plain words, it has been that people might listen more willingly, being addressed in tropes and parables. Although this was a method unaccustomed and unusual to me, yet as I have great reliance on the good effects of obedience, I have not refused to adopt the method recommended to me. In which, if there shall be, by the gift of God, anything found useful or edifying, it is to be ascribed to the merits of my teacher; but whatever is said in it with too little care, that I confess is to be ascribed to my want of wisdom. For that I do

---

[1] Monetae.

not employ decorated [1] discourses, nor go deeply into philosophical niceties is in no way strange, since I am scarcely able to express my subject itself in the most simple and unpretending words. But just as certain persons are accustomed, after they have well drunk of the best wine, to drink willingly a little water, or after the most delicious and succulent viands to delight in the eating of herbs and fruit, or after they have long treated of serious objects, to bring forward something witty, as if for a screen to other labour, so also you, Reader, are able to do if you are ever able to descend to these trifling and little readable lines, and thus afterwards to return, as it were, the more refreshed, to the lofty sentiments of the learned, which are worthy of close attention.

The end of the letter, and beginning of the Book of Similitudes [2] of Dom Galandus of Regny.

LETTER CDLXXI.

GERULF TO S. BRENARD. [3]

To the venerable B., Abbot of Clairvaux, Brother GERHOCH: Klagenfurt.

---

[1] *faleratis* = phaleratis.

[2] Parabolarium. The word is not to be found in either the lexicon of Forcellini, or the Glossaries of Ducange or Spelman.

(E.)

[3] This letter is preserved in the Parchment Codex, No. 138, in the Public Library of S. Omer, a folio MS. in three columns, of the beginning of the 13th century, partially defective (from fol. 185*b*) and which originally belonged to the Cistercian Abbey of Clairmarais in the diocese of S. Omer, which was founded in 1140.

The author of these letters is the celebrated Augustinian Abbot, Gerhoch of Reichersberg. This man occupied an important position in the German Church of the twelfth century; and

To Dom BERNARD, the venerable Abbot of Clairvaux, Brother GERULF, health in Christ.

his share in the spiritual movement of that time, can in many ways be compared with that of Bernard, although in extent and brilliancy is does not approach the latter. Like Bernard Gerhoch was consumed by a burning zeal for the House of God. His whole outward activity was devoted to maintaining the purity of the faith and practice of the Church. His accusations against the worldly conduct and the covetous grasping at money of the Papal Court are expressed with the same honest openness which adorns Bernard's letter *De Consideratione.* A similar courage made him maintain to the face of the Emperor Frederick the correctness of the election of Alexander III., although the swords of the princes are lifted against him as they were against Bernard, "*mucro barbaricus*" on the court day at Lüttich. The likeness between these two recurs in various circumstances of their lives. Like Bernard Gerhoch drew a number of his brethren and relatives with him into the monastery; and like him he enjoyed the friendship of Eugenius III. On the other hand, differences between them are not wanting. The undercurrent of self-love in the one is contrasted with the disinterestedness of the other (Bernard). The dispositions of the two are entirely different. Gerhoch's nature shows an inclination to extremes: his incessant contests against error and corruption led him to onesided doctrinal statements and impracticable reforms: the many writings in which he contends for these ideas are wordy and not always clear, yet emphatic and able. They show great learning, as also great knowledge of ancient, as well as of contemporary literature; so much so that the writings of Bernard in this point cannot stand in comparison. These writings of Gerhoch bear witness to the reverence the author had for Bernard. Words like—*vir sancte Abbas—nominis ac vitæ illustris columna ecclesiæ ac luminare fulgidum, oraculum divinitatis,* are in the mouth of this sincere and celebrated man, of double weight These expressions are accompanied by a large knowledge and use of the tracts and sermons of Bernard. Lengthy portions of them were mixed up with his texts, with or without a reference. Gerhoch, besides the reform of the Clergy, had his

In the Court at Babenberg[1] I was unable to enjoy your longed-for presence according as I wished. For the tumult

thoughts and his pen incessantly occupied on two difficult doctrinal points, of which the second has become a watchword in the theological disputes of that time. It is this: the question of the efficacy and authority of the Sacraments dispensed by simoniacs and schismatics, and also of the Eucharistic sacrifice, as well as of the Christological question, *de gloria et honore filii hominis*. Gerhoch's assertions, which cannot be exactly discussed here, are directed on the one part against the teaching of the schismatics from the time of the dispute respecting the investitures, and of *Peter Leonis*; and on the other hand against the ideas of the celebrated Abaelard who in so dangerous a manner influenced the French, German and Italian dialectics. Gerhoch not only opposed those false doctrines most strenuously, he also by the harsh expression of his opinions, caused serious scruples to moderate Realists, as also to Bernard. The Saint has in none of his writings taken up a definitive side in these questions. Gerhoch was under the impression that there were certain contradictions in the teaching of the schismatics respecting the Sacraments, when he resolved to fully explain his teaching to one whom he venerated so highly as Bernard.

The writing resulting from this, called *De Simoniacis*, has up till now only been known in fragments, for in the MS. of the Belgian cloister, *Les Dunes*, from which Martène printed, the commencement of the tractate is missing. Fortunately, however, the mixed Codex 261 of S. Omer, a Quarto from the Monastery of S. Bertin, of the 13th century, contains the complete writing as also Gerhoch's letter of dedication to Bernard. The letter, here placed in the fifth position, after a Gospel history and several works by Bernard, commences with a complaint of the mass of business on the Babenberg court day—which made it impossible to have a quiet exchange of opinion. This was the more to be regretted, as it often estranged friends, and they had not in all things the same opinions. He must at least

[1] Habebergensi: *Codex.*

of causes was such a hindrance, that but few things could be touched upon, and of many upon which I was desirous of your fatherly advice, so that by my questions and your answers in turn, my inquiries by your kindness, might be brought to a final issue; and we might be able to think and to speak the same thing until, if in anything we thought otherwise, God should reveal it to us. But I do not say this, because I suppose that you think in any way otherwise than corresponds to the truth of the case, but, because it greatly disturbs many persons that we who have been sent forth, as it were, as forerunners by Our Lord, do not on all subjects hold one and the same language. For as formerly when Joshua and Caleb were encouraging the people of Israel to exterminate the dwellers in the Land of Promise, other forerunners who had been with them said: *We be not able to go up against the people for they are stronger than we.* (Num. xiii. 31); so also now when Nicholas II. Leo IX. Alexander II. Gregory VII. and other Popes of the Roman See, their successors, down to Pope

ascertain what was Bernard's view relative to *Simoniacs*, as the latter in the discussions of that question had not clearly expressed himself for or against. He therefore sends this treatise under seal to Bernard, so that his judgment through Dom Adam, may decide what shall be done with it. In the introduction Gerhoch goes back to the Babenberg contest of words. Bernard had in that laid stress upon two texts, probably as a warning against self-conceit, that everyone should well weigh what fruit their own labour had ripened in the service of God. This admonition causes Gerhoch to doubt himself, but also directs his look to the highly meritorious work of Bernard, etc. The time of the writing of the letter and treatise *De Simoniacis*, most probably is 1135, as both directly refer to the meeting at Babenberg. What reception this writing found with Bernard, whether he sent an answer through Adam of Ebrach, is not known.   (E.)   .

Innocent in our time, were encouraging the people of God
to the extermination of Simoniacs and others to whom
ecclesiastical offices and other benefits are now forbidden,
as from those others the Land of Promise was taken away
by the judgment of God; when those Popes, I say, were
encouraging the people of God to the driving forth of
such persons, there were not wanting learned readers of the
Scriptures, as it were explorers of the Land of Promise,
who said in agreement with those other explorers: We
be not able to go up against the people, for they are
stronger than we. There we saw certain giants, the sons
of Anak, which are of the race of giants, compared with
whom we seemed as grasshoppers (Num. xiii. 33). Notwithstanding against these, by the mouths of a few, cried
out the spirit which was in Joshua and Caleb: *Fear not
the people of this land; for as bread are we able to devour
them; every defence is departed from them, and the Lord
is with us, fear them not* (Num. xiv. 9). As then I am
desirous rather to be in agreement with truth with a few,
than to err with many, I am anxious to be instructed by
your fatherly wisdom, whether in what the following treatise shall contain, I speak the words of sobriety and truth
or whether it seem otherwise to you, as it is thought by
some, on which account in the Court at Babenberg you
supported neither me, nor my opponents very strongly.
For I wish that this treatise, which is enclosed by my
seal, should come to you thus untouched, that you may be,
if you so determine, the only reader of it. But if it
should seem good to the Spirit of piety which dwells in
your breast that it ought to come to the knowledge of
many persons, then I earnestly beg that whatever in it
ought to be corrected, you would either yourself correct
or suggest to me how it should be done. For you are
able to transmit to me whatever writings you wish through

Dom Adam. And I earnestly beg that you will not find it too great a trouble to do this, since I love your writings and am accustomed to give thanks to the Spirit of Truth which convinces the world by your means. From this expression of thanks, then, let the introduction of my treatise commence, and may God rule my mind and my pen.

The beginning of the Treatise of Brother GERULF to Abbot Dom BERNARD respecting simoniacs.

I give thanks to the Spirit of Truth, who by your writings *convinces the world of sin and of righteousness* (S. John xvi. 8): of sin, because they believe not in Christ, since while confessing Him in words, they deny Him by their actions; and of righteousness, because you so attribute it to Divine grace, that it is no more permitted to man to boast respecting the righteousness conferred upon him from above, than of the obedience of Christ, from which hangs all our righteousness. For what is that obedience except that which He Himself points out when He says, *I go to my Father and ye see Me no more* (S. John xvi. 10). For this He said in the same night in which He was betrayed; going to His Father through this very obedience unto death, and leaving the whole advantage of His obedience to his followers. For in that obedience of Christ consists the entire righteousness of Christians, according to the saying of the Apostle : *For as by one man's disobedience many were made sinners, so by the obedience of one, shall many be made righteous* (Rom. v. 19). What righteous man, then, will boast of a righteousness of his own which he has in himself, when neither human effort nor freewill, but the obedience of Christ alone, has brought about his righteousness? That obedience without doubt in which He went to the Father and now we see him no more. On account of that obedience then which was so great, grace is bestowed upon those who believe in Christ by their own freewill, and for the sake of this obedience itself, upon those who love Him, that a spontaneous intention may be implanted in them, to follow of their own freewill that which is both discerned by their freewill, and approved, as the right action to be done, by the free working of their mind : so that the righteousness of men itself is undoubtedly derived from the præsignalized obedience of Christ. Wherefore the Spirit of Truth rightly convinces the world of this righteousness, not only in those who neglect it, but also and even much more, in those, who ascribe it to their own powers : namely, because they are inexcusable on account of their will, which as you assert in a certain treatise, is constrained by no necessity, and because of their desire for a vain glory, they are liable to condemnation. For truly, after Christ drew near to the Father by the way of obedience, and because He exists as the fountain and efficient cause of our justification ; whosoever, now that the history of Christ is made known, hereafter serves sin, acts just as if, when the giant Goliath had been overthrown and the whole army of the Philistines put to flight, the people of Israel had preferred to submit to and serve the Philistines, rather than enjoy the liberty acquired for them by their brave champion David. But those who arrogate to themselves the victory of Christ, or ever so little of the righteousness which followed that victory, or even of the praise and glory which is due to it, are found to be like the proud Saul, who envied too much the humble David, and desired to arrogate to himself the glory which was David's. For Saul was wroth and said : *To me they have ascribed but a thousand, and to David ten thousand* (1 Sam.

xviii. 8). Thus many are angered also now, if the glory which is due to God alone is not offered to them, because they receive glory from one another, and neglect the glory which comes from God alone. These, as I have said, the spirit of truth convinces, as well in your words as in your writings : showing that the righteousness of man is to be attributed solely to the grace of God. I recall that saying of the Apostle which was vehemently pressed upon me by you in the Court at Babenberg : *Now unto the King eternal, immortal, invisible, to God alone, be honour and glory* (1 Tim. i. 17), and that of the Angels : *Glory to God in the highest* (S. Luke ii. 14). Which two testimonies, drawn from Apostolic and Angelic lips, you perhaps pressed upon me under the idea, that I unhappy, in grasping at the glory due to God alone, might lose the grace of peace, pronounced upon *men of good will* (S. Luke ii. 14. *Vulg.*). I rejoice, most pious and reverend father, in your solicitude for me, but yet I thank God that I am not conscious to myself of any greedy desire for human and vain glory. I am not conscious to myself, I say ; yet am I not thereby justified : for He that judgeth me is the Lord, whose is this very gift which is in me, so that to me it is a very small thing, that I should be judged by you or in the day of man. For neither do I judge my own self (1. Cor. iv. 3--5), but await in fear and trembling the Divine judgment upon all my actions, words and even thoughts : a trembling which is increased by your admonition, reverend father, in which you say that each of us ought to consider, how much fruit, and of what kind, comes of his labour in the word of God. This you are able securely to say, as being conscious of the abundant fruits which have come of your planting and watering ; God giving truly the increase to your labour which you have undergone in preaching the word of God. But I reflect

with trembling on this your saying; for I recollect out of
much labour which I have done, but a few scanty bands
[of converts], in comparison with those who draw after
them a great flock of disciples either to the eremitic life
or to another manner of life, very different from that in
the world, and similar to the life of those who, with
Elijah the Prophet, lived in solitude upon the herbs of
the field, when, because of the many fornications of the
wicked Jezebel, they could have no place for living holily
in the cities. Or as when idolatry was reigning in Jerusalem itself, the city of God, the holy city, through Atha-
liah, the daughter of the before mentioned Jezebel and
wife of Joram, King of Judah, because of whose uncleanness, while she raged in the Kingdom of Judah, three kings,
viz., Ahaziah, Joash and Amaziah, were cut off from the
book of the generations of Jesus Christ according to Matthew,
where it is said : Joram begat Ozias (S. Matt. 1. 8).
At that time then such great ungodliness of kings and
queens ruled in the cities of Judah and Israel that under
them preachers of the word of God had not liberty to
teach nor even to live, as is shown by the complaint of
Elijah and by the death of Zecharias the Prophet, who
was slain between the temple and the altar, and by the
fact that there were many prophets, of whom Elijah and
Elisha were the chief, who wandered about in mountains,
in dens and caves, whose example you, my father, and
those like you seem to follow, in dwelling apart in the
woods and inviting those whom you are able to persuade,
to do the same thing. For if the austerity of dress and
simplicity in food which you practise be considered, why
should the example of Elijah be supposed to be wanting
to you of ancient precedents? Unless perhaps the excessive zeal, with which he himself pursued the priests of
Jezebel, of whom he slew in one day eight hundred and

fifty, [1] yet not before he showed that their sacrifices were wanting in the Divine fire, be considered too extreme. For neither the king, nor the people being deceived by the same false prophets would have easily permitted so many priests to have been slain unless it had first been shown how great a difference there was between the sacrifice of Elijah and that of these men. But this being demonstrated by the fire of God not consuming their sacrifice, neither the King nor the people defended them: and as they were deprived of all help, Elijah slew them Would that you had his zeal, in the first place in rendering useless the sacrifices of the heretics, and in the next in slaying them with that same sword of the Word, with which you are so powerfully armed. For to mention one leader [2] of the schismatics or heretics: in what way do you intend to separate from Peter Leonis, the people who adhere to him as long as, though he himself is cut off from the Church, he is believed to offer the same sacrifice which we offer, and not to differ from us more than good and evil priests differ in the Church; and these appear indistinguishable in sacrificing from the good, efficiency unto salvation only excepted? For it is not sufficient for the expulsion of heretics that we distinguish them from evil Catholics by this, because their sacrifices neither profit themselves nor those who communicate with them, whilst in the Church there are evil priests not yet interdicted, and whose ministrations are not beneficial to themselves, yet are means of grace and salvation to those who hear or communicate at their Masses. This does not, I say,

---

[1] *Octingentos.* This is apparently just a mistake on the part of the writer; as the Vulgate reads like other versions *quadringenti* et *quinquaginta*, = four hundred and fifty. (1. Kings xviii. 22) (E.)

[2] [Vexillifer.]

suffice, since the heretics glory in that alone in which the Magi of Pharaoh also formerly gloried, namely, that they are entirely similar in outward signs, except in so far as the finger of God alone distinguishes them. For what are sacraments, except the signs of sacred things with which Pharaoh and the whole of Egypt are deceived by the Simoniac heretics and others separated from the Church, that is, etc. [Migne 194. Col. 1335. sqq.]

LETTER CDLXXII.

Brother G.[erhoch] to Abbot Bernard.

To the venerable Abbot of Clairvaux, Brother G., health and the assurance of the prayers of a sinner, if they be of any service to a Saint. [1]

[1] This second letter treats of various matters. Gerhoch repeats in the first place a request, which he had already preferred to the Saint in a letter which has not been found. A plan worked out by Pope Eugenius when Abbot of Trois Fontaines for a division of clergy-funds by law and to prohibit all irregular sharing of them had not yet been introduced. He requests Bernard in the sense of his admonition which he gave to the Pope in his first letter to use the power of his sharp and living word on behalf of this important matter. He further says that the completion of the timely exposition of the Song of Solomon is desired by many. He also says there is current under Bernard's name an Ascension Day Sermon, which not only contains strange expressions, but also teaches a christological error which Gerhoch repudiates, referring to Holy Scripture and a passage of Leo the Great. Should the sermon have come from Bernard, which the writer doubts, he advises it should be withdrawn; — if not, he advises that the fact should be distinctly declared, in honour to his other writings. He then again refers to the Babenberg controversy. He calls to mind that in the warfare there he was sustained only by the acquiescence of Innocent II. and hopes to get some definitive answer from Bernard on this presumably changed

I wrote lately to your holiness, with respect to that community which the Roman Curia founded in the times of

opinion. Finally, Gerhoch is like others astonished that Bernard should not have included a main error in the list of Abælard's heresies. To this second letter of Gerhoch so far as is known, no answer was ever sent by Bernard.

A law of Eugenius about division of clergy-funds was either already promulgated at the time of this letter or followed very soon after. The letter, which presupposes a personal intercourse of the Pope with Bernard, must fall in the spring of 1147 or 1148, when alone this condition prevailed. From the conclusion of the 4th book *De Consideratione* which belongs to the latter years of Bernard, it is clear that then at the beginning of the fifth decade of the century that early plan had become law. The purpose of this special canon does not seem to be known. The remarks concerning the *sermo de Ascensione Domini* Bernard settled by referring to his genuine sermons on the Ascension and Glory of the God-man; thereby proving that it was impossible for him to have originated the one in question. How the Saint would have replied to the request about his present opinion as to the schismatical sacrament remains an open question; his writings containing no help: the question perhaps would not have been satisfied in the end. Bernard would easily dispose of the last reference as it was grounded on an incomplete knowledge of the documents. His writing *contra quædam capitula errorum Abælardi*, which Gerhoch probably had before him, did not indeed contain the missing point of accusation. It was, however, included in his *capitula hæresum P. Abælardi*, to which the first writing distinctly refers. The text of this letter of Gerhoch is taken from two MSS. which, but for some minor details, verbally agree. The one MS. is No. 22634 of the Additional MSS. in the British Museum, a Quarto belonging to the 2nd half of the 12th Century, written in 2 columns of 36 lines each. The Codex contains 13 leaves of which this letter fills fols. 3*b* to 4*a*. A second copy *e coævo codice Ottenburano* in 4to is the so-called codex *apogr. Mellicensis* which has been brought forward by the well-known scholar Bernard Pez, and beside this letter contains two other works of Gerhoch of Reichersberg. (Hüffer.) (E.)

Popes Celestine and Lucius of blessed memory, according
as the then Abbot, now Pope, Eugenius advised. Whose
counsel then was this, that the privilege should be
confirmed; just as lawful favours should be distributed
for the common advantage, but unlawful rejected with
disapproval, great care being taken to use discretion,
in the Roman Curia: respecting the details of which it is
not for me to write to you, as your Prudence can easily
learn through the lords Cardinals who had unanimously
approved that determination, which was then proposed
at the advice of your disciple then Abbot, but which
now the same person, made your master and ours,
proposes to subvert. But it is not becoming, that now
he is Pope, he should destroy what then as Abbot, he
began to build up. For perhaps it was for that reason
that God raised him up, and gave to him, who was little
in his own eyes, a great name, that now being Roman Pontiff
he might bring to perfection what he had up to that time
as Abbot counselled. I believe then that to that end he
requires intimate advisers, of whom you, holy father, are
believed to be the chief, because you speak in such manner in the first letter which you sent to that son of yours,
then by so great an exaltation, become to you a father, as
to strive to render him attentive and prompt to plant and
to root up, to destroy and disperse as well as to build
up. There is indeed in that letter of yours to which I
refer, the word of God in its strength: but still more is
there in your lips the word of God, living, and able to
pierce even as a two-edged sword, and penetrating even
to the division of soul and spirit (Heb. iv. 12). Wherefore it is greatly to be desired by us, that the same things
which you have written, you should now urge upon him
by word of mouth, and continue to press them upon him
until success shall attend your persuasion. If you do not

complete before your death the exposition you have begun of the *Canticles* your epithalamium [1] will be turned into great mourning for many.

If a certain sermon on the Ascension of Our Lord is from your pen, as it is said to be, it will be worth while for you to examine it diligently, and if it shall seem good to your prudence, to modify it in part. For there it is said that a follower of the Lord, whom the Father Augustine lays down should be called the Lord rather than one of his followers, holds in heaven that place in which Lucifer would have been placed, if he had not fallen but had stood fast in the truth. *But we believe and therefore also speak* (2 Cor. iv. 13) that the Man born from the Virgin Mother is truly called, and is, the Most High, not only in the Nature of the Word which is always the Most High, but also in His Human Nature, which is exalted even to sit (at the Right Hand of) God the Father, according to that saying: *A Man was born in her, and the Most High shall stablish her* (Ps. lxxxvii. 5). Which exaltation, that we should not take it to be attributed in Christ only to the Person, Pope Leo attributes to the Human Nature, saying in his sermon on the Lord's Ascension: "Great and unspeakable was the cause of rejoicing, when the Nature of the human race ascended, in the sight of the saintly host, above the dignity of all the dwellers in Heaven, passing [2] beyond the ranks of the Angels, nor placing any bound to its progress in those lofty heights, until it was received at the Right Hand of the Eternal Father, and associated with His throne of glory, to whose nature it was united in His Son." Since

---

[1] The pious author seems to have meant *encomium* or *panegyric*. The use of *epithalamium* in this sense is without precedent. (E.)

[2] *Supergressura* or *supergressa*: Mellic.

then that sermon of yours to which I have referred, holy
father, does not agree with this sermon emanating from
the Apostolic See, you will do well to retract the same,
if it is yours, or to declare that it is not from your pen,
that the rest of your most excellent writings may not be
dishonoured thereby; if those things which are there
wrongly expressed, as it appears to many persons, should
either be not corrected, or (not) shown to be not written
by you. For this would be shown in a fitting manner,
if another sermon should be put forth by you, holy
father, on the Ascension of Our Lord, in which the
subject of (His) Human Nature being, although not changed
into the Divine Nature, yet exalted into the glory of God
should be so treated, as is fitting. He said: *Glorify Me, O
Father, with Thine own self* (S. John xvii. 5) and the Father
replied: *I have both glorified it, and will glorify it again*
(Ibid. xii. 28). Perhaps it has been reserved for thee, O
Abbot of Clairvaux, to declare in clear language, something
of His glory, for which you too shall be glorified in a
dwelling of light and peace. Would that I may see your
writings on this subject of His glorification, which if you
are not able for the present to complete at full length,
at least, holy father, make known to me, a sinner, in few
words your meaning, which is, I doubt not, most sound
and correct. For even if in anything you were otherwise
minded, when you wrote the sermon referred to, God
has since revealed to you, that which then was hidden. [1]
I have once betaken myself to the oracle of Divine know-
edge, and I hope not to cease my knocking, until the door
be opened to my summons; and although not because I
am a friend, yet because of my importunity which pro-

The text has *non velatum*: but according to the context'
this must be an error.   (E.)

ceeds not from rashness but from necessity (S. Luke xi. 8).
For your fatherly piety may remember, what a struggle
with impiety I sustained in the Court at Babenberg for
him, because I said that those sacrificing without the Church,
or within it, having been deprived of their office do not
produce [1] the Body of the Lord. In truth if Pope Innocent had not supported me, or rather *if the Lord had not
been with us, when men rose up against us, they had
swallowed us up even living* (Ps. cxxiv. 1—3). Of necessity then I have enquired your meaning upon this subject,
which then you will find that I remember well. For I do
not doubt that you are of those of whom the Apostle
says: *If in anything ye be otherwise minded, the Lord
shall reveal even this to you* (Phil. iii. 15); and I entreat
your piety, that briefly, and with the crumbs falling from
your table, you will indulge me, in my hunger, so that I
may know what you now think about this matter. I wonder greatly, holy father, that in the List of Heresies of
Abaelard, you have passed over this, which he asserted
both in his words and writings, that the man who was
born of the Virgin is to be called God [2] and that Christ
is to be called God not properly but figuratively, not on
account of His whole self but on account of part only,
since there is nothing in which he, perverse as he is, is
found to have erred more perversely than this. From
this you may understand that it is desired by many that
light should shine forth from your lips against that cloud
of falseness.

---

[1] *Conficere.*
[2] *Dominum*: is the reading of the London MS.

LETTER CDLXXIII.

To the Archbishop of Treves.

To the venerable lord and very dear father ALBERO, by the Grace of God, Archbishop of Trèves and legate of the Apostolic See, BERNARD, Abbot of Clairvaux, wishes health, and that he may find grace before God.

You comply with my wishes if I seek those things which are my own: how much more ought you to do so, if I seek not my own advantage, but that of Jesus Christ! but those things which are Christ's are mine also, for He is our Brother and our flesh. And my [salvation] is in the mercy of Christ, who bore my injuries unto death, even the death of the Cross. The servant is not greater than his Lord. I consider no part of His reproach as alien to me, since He on my account, was made the reproach of men and the offscouring of the people. I lament His condition, who lamented mine, and gave up His own self for me.

God has sent women into your heritage: they have polluted your holy temple: I speak of the Church of S. Maur at Verdun. Lo! the heritage of the Lord, the very heritage, itself a temple, but a temple polluted, is violated by a double sacrilege. They have withdrawn that which is sacred from its sacred place: that is, they have alienated their own selves from Christ. Holiness becomes Thy House, O Lord; but the House of Prayer has been turned into a den of thieves and of fornication. The place of the habitation of Thy glory, has become a lair for dragons: and no man lays this to heart. Is this then pleasing to you, that God should suffer the loss of His heritage in your diocese and in your time? Do you then render to

Him evil for good? God has exalted you above your companions: stand up in defence of that which is His. If you say, How does the matter concern me? in what way do you profit by that opinion? for without doubt he is blameable for an evil action who is able to correct it, and neglects to do so. The Virgin of Israel has fallen to the earth: but cannot one who falls be helped to rise again? Put on a kindly willingness: stretch forth your hand; if you are the friend of the Bridegroom, draw forth the Bride of Christ from the abyss of misery, and the mire of pollution. Use your influence by letters with these people that they may acquiesce in the election which has been made by those to whom the election was entrusted to be carried out, for otherwise there will be confusion both as to the person elected, and as to those by whom the election was made, and to the whole Church of Rheims whose daughter it is. Otherwise if you do not influence them by your threats and entreaties, I assure you that your reputation will be in great danger in these parts. But I do not venture to judge of your conscience. May the Spirit of Truth teach you to discover the evil and to choose the good.

LETTER CDLXXIV.

To Adelaide, Queen of France.

To the illustrious QUEEN OF FRANCE : B[ERNARD], Abbot of Clairvaux, health and the assurance of his prayers.

I venture to submit a request to you, and that with confidence, though not as relying upon any knowledge or intimacy which so humble a person as myself may have with your Highness, but rather upon your well-known kindness and liberality. Wicard, your servant, complains of you, that although he knows of no offence of which he has been guilty, he has been deprived of all his goods unjustly and sent into exile by you. And since I have learned that this man has the good resolution of deserting the world and turning unto the Lord. [1] I consider it not an unsuitable thing for me to ask or for you to grant that you should both take him back into your favour, and restore to him the whole or at least a part of his property.

I also commend unto you, if he or I have found any favour in your eyes, this pious man, the Abbot of [2] Beaulieu, who from interest in this matter has taken the trouble to bring this letter of mine to you from a great distance. Let it be your care then, that he has not endured this fatigue to no purpose. Farewell.

LETTER CDLXXV.

To the Chancellor S.

To the honourable and noble S., the Chancellor, B(er-nard), Abbot of Clairvaux, health in the Lord.

God has bestowed upon you much property in this world.

But among things temporal and earthly the great danger that you have to fear is lest, if you make no provision for the safety of your soul by means of these things, you should lose those things which are heavenly and eternal for the sake of those which are transitory and perishable.

---

[1] [I. e. of entering a monastery.]

[2] [There were two Abbeys of this name : one in Flanders (Nord) the other in Champagne (Aube). The latter is proba-bly) meant here. (E.)]

Allow me simply to suggest to your prudence that I am desirous to separate some [1]. . . . from the rest of our brethren and to construct an Abbey. If then you are willing to build, retaining both them and their habitation, which you are easily able to do, be so good as to notify me by a letter from you by the bearer of this. And in truth you ought to bear in mind that it is for no other end that you have lately been warned from above, by the great weakness of which I have heard, that by this, or some other good work, you should provide a means of help for your soul, which is struggling among the deceptive pleasures of this world.

LETTER CDLXXVI.

To a certain nobleman named Ebal.

To his friend Ebal of Florennes, Bernard, Abbot of Clairvaux, health, and that he may avoid evil and do good.

You have bestowed upon me a degree of confidence in remonstrating with you when it should be necessary, from the fact that you have commended yourself so humbly to my prayers, that you have associated yourself so fervently with our community, and especially that you did not hesitate to incur lately the great fatigue of a long and fruitless journey [to visit] me. But of what advantage do you suppose my prayers can be to you when you daily oppose them by your bad actions! For you, as I heard, besides other innumerable bad actions which you do not cease to commit, interfere with the free action of the monks of Liesse, [2] which monastery your pious mother built, not for the purpose that. . . . and that they should

---

[1] The MS. is illegible here.

[2] [Lætiensis or Lesciensis; a monastery in Flanders (Nord). See Note to Letter CD.]

relinquish it again and depart.   Of what advantage would
that be to you? This liberty which you seek with respect
to that monastery is worse than any servitude.   If you
have any confidence in me, or will acquiesce in my advice; if you desire the benefits you have already obtained
by my prayers, I do not say to be of any advantage to
you, but not to do you harm instead of good, you will
lay down this obstinate disposition of mind and without
any delay, and putting aside every objection, you will
confirm the free gift, just as it was made by your mother
to the holy brethren : yet in such a manner that they
promise always so many monks out of their number, to
the same monastery, as may be sufficient to perform the
accustomed duties fully and fittingly.

Do you also and your mother, make provision from
your own resources, for their clothing and sustenance in
the service of God.   Farewell.

LETTER CDLXXVII.

To the Count of Blois.

To his beloved son in Christ, the Count of Blois,
B[ernard], Abbot of Clairvaux, safety and peace.   .

I commend to your Highness this man, the Presbyter
Eberhard, as a person most faithful to me; and to whom
you may entrust without hesitation, as to myself, any
communication you may wish to make to me : and likewise
receive what he may say to you on my behalf.

LETTER CDLXXVIII.

To the Count of Nevers.

To his most dearly beloved in Christ, Wilhelm, B[ernard],
called Abbot of Clairvaux, health.

The more prepared you show yourself to obey, the more careful and cautious it behoves me to be in advising or correcting. It was indeed proper and becoming that you should carry on and complete that praiseworthy beginning of your conversion: and that was so much the more becoming to you, that you had bravely treated all that was yours as of no account, going on to perfect that which remained, namely, the giving up of yourself also, and thus no longer living according to your own sole will: inasmuch as you are a true follower of Christ, who became obedient unto His Father, even unto death: and though He was able to do all things, yet confessed that He could do nothing as of Himself. [1]

But since, as you represent to me, both the exigency of the present time and compassion for the poor, and the care of your House which you have assumed, seem to hinder the completion of your [good purpose] at the time intended: neither do I, as far as concerns me, prohibit whatever course charity may have prescribed to you: yet so that you do not delay beyond the limit already fixed by yourself. And take heed of this also: that during this period of freedom thus conceded to you, you do not misuse the time by employing it, not in the Divine things, but in the fulfilment of your own inclinations, or even perhaps (which may God forbid) in secular pleasures and business. Farewell.

LETTER CDLXXIX.

To the Count of Nevers.

To J., [2] Count of Nevers, his friends the brethren of Clairvaux, health and their prayers.

[1] S. John. v. 30.
[2] Perhaps the successor of him to whom Letter CDLXXVIII was addressed.　　　　　　　　　　　　　　　.　(E.)

You abound, as we suppose, in the substance of this world; the servants of God at Molesmes are enduring great penury, so that, as we have heard, they are in want of bread: and they have great difficulty in purchasing sufficient grain for their number. We have taken this step to suggest privately to you, without their knowing anything of it, or expecting any such action on our part, that, if it should be in your heart to bestow an alms as unto God, you may be aware that there is great need of it in that monastery. If, however, without any ill feelings towards them, you are either unable or unwilling to make a gift to them, it is free to you to decline; since in fact, they are quite unaware of the request which we are making bold to urge upon you. Farewell.

LETTER CDLXXX.

To a Certain Prince (Theobald, Count of Champagne.)

To the laudable Prince T(heobald), Bernard, Abbot of Clairvaux, health and his prayers.

I fear to be tedious to you, since I intrude upon your many occupations with so frequent letters. But since it is the very love of God which obliges me to do this, I fear still more, if I should fail to obey. If then I have found any favour in your eyes, if there is still in you that justice and kindness which hitherto I have been able to trust to, I entreat you by the Lord Jesus, and by that bond of brotherhood which you took upon you in our Chapter: I entreat you with my whole heart, and prostrate as a suppliant at your knees, to act according to mercy with Anseric, who is prepared to submit himself in all things (faithful and lawful) to your will. Consider the kindness which you may show to him as done to me. That his castle has come into your hands, is in consequence of my advice. Nor do I regret to have thus advised, so much confidence have I in your truth and goodness.

LETTER CDLXXXI.

To a person unknown.

To his friend, B(ernard), Abbot of Clairvaux, health in the Lord.

I beg you, my very dear friend, to use your utmost diligence both diligently to explain and faithfully to commend as far as you are able, this sealed letter [enclosed] to the Count; that so I, although a sinner, may be able to offer my prayer to God for your sins with greater eagerness and confidence. Be thou on my behalf to thy lord, that I may be on thy behalf to the Lord of all.

LETTER CDLXXXII.

To David, King of Scotland.

To the Lord David, the most illustrious King of Scotland, whom he embraces in the bowels of Christ, B(ernard), called Abbot of Clairvaux, health and eternal life.

Long since, O most illustrious sovereign, have I been drawn by your high reputation to regard you with affection and to desire to see you face to face. I desire it, I repeat; and I know that it is written: *The Lord hath heard the desire of the poor: Thine ear (O Lord) hath heard the preparation of their heart* (Ps. x. 17). Fortified with this confidence then, I trust in the Lord that I shall some time behold you even in the body, and even now I view you in mind and spirit with satisfaction, and often recall the

memory with sweetness and joy. Our brethren who are
at Rievaulx had felt the bowels of your first kindness; and
to them you opened the treasure of your goodwill, you
have cherished them with the anointing of your mercy
and pity, and the palace of the Heavenly King was filled
with the fragrance of the ointment. I am not ungrateful
for these kindnesses, which are as welcome to me as if
they had been bestowed upon me in my own person. But
there are still others of our brethren who have lately become neighbours of yours. I think you are not ignorant
of the manner in which (some of the monks) of S. Mary's
Abbey at York, where they had lived too carelessly, received an inspiration from on high and went forth into
a solitary place: how they endured persecutions and injuries inflicted on them both by guile and by open force;
how when they were rich, and abounded in the things of
this world, they became poor Religious for the love of
Christ, true seekers after the apostolic life and holiness.
The world would love them, according to the saying of
the Lord, if they were of the world. But now, because
they are not of the world, it persecutes them as strangers
and aliens. And they indeed, by the help of God, bear
patiently whatever the world attempts against them. But we
and whosoever fears God, ought to assist the servants of
God in their tribulation. To you then, most compassionate
King, I commend these servants of Christ of whom I
speak: I supplicate you on their behalf, that you would
afford to them some solace in their poverty: and I hope
that you will receive for your reward an everlasting Kingdom from Christ the King of Kings, in the day of the
recompense of the righteous. Amen.

LETTER CDLXXXIII. (A. D. 1144).

To Pope Lucius II.

To his very dear father and lord, Lucius, by the grace of God, Supreme Pontiff, Bernard, called Abbot of Clairvaux, health, and his humble duty.

We have rejoiced in the Lord and given thanks in every thing, being strengthened by the grace of Almighty God, who judges in equity, and by your efficacious coöperation, in this as in all things, and having great delight by that Curia so distinguished.

We were then expecting the hoped-for issue of the matter; we were expecting that the flowers of Roman wisdom should by a faithful administrator, be converted into fruits, that our joy might be fulfilled: since rejoicing over flowers must be with fear and is more full and perfect when the flowers come to the birth, wherefore it is said in the Canticles: *Let us see if the flowers have brought forth fruit* (Cant. vii. 12). We were expecting that this vine of Winchester, or rather of that which is commonly called in songs a second Rome, should form grapes, but changed into bitterness it became a wild vine, and brought forth wild grapes. O happy Winchester, chosen to be decked with the ornament of a great name, that it should be called a second Rome! O powerful one, who makest of none effect the commands of the powerful among the fathers, changest their opinion, pervertest their decisions, pourest disgrace on the truth, and sanctionest with loud and unhesitating voice, the judgment which Rome had pronounced should not be sanctioned, without consideration and weighing of the prescribed oath! For the Dean, having been invited to take the prescribed oath, not only declined the oath in public, but was prepared to swear to the contrary. Yet that Philistine was not ashamed in his wilfulness to raise up the idol Dagon beside the ark of the Lord. Was not this because his face was become as that of a harlot? He stands shamelessly, he offers himself for sale to every passer-by, he sits for the hire of a harlot. What does not the evil hunger for gold enforce? Winchester has usurped the worthy name of Rome, and nothing is suffered to be done without him. Absolution and the dignity of the Church are made matter of hire, and are thought to be voluntary. Not happy Winchester therefore, but unhappy; which debases costly pearls, which gives that which is holy to dogs, which does not drive out of, but introduces into, the temple the sellers and buyers of doves, and opposes (for shame!) in a marvellous way the Curia, the unconquered senate of Rome. O father, O glory of Rome, defender of righteousness, who alone sustainest so many and so great affairs, who guardest the state with the arms of righteousness, and adornest it by thy character, whom my dull mind may call the avenger of these infamies, who makest the scourge of cords, and with the strong hand of Roman power overturnest the table of those buying and selling! If the chiefs of Rome had cast lots, your discretion would have assigned the lot of this office to you beyond all others. O happy are we, in the first place, with so righteous a protector for so great a cause! Happy are we, again, in there being so powerful an avenger of such great presumption! If then the spear is in your hands, we call upon you to lift up this spear against those who resist the Roman power. For behold, behold I say, that man, that enemy, a forerunner of Satan, a son of perdition, an adversary of law and right, he lifts up on high his head; and the judgment pronounced by the apostolic mouth which speaks in equity, which was spoken and promulgated, and lucidly determined and made firm by you in common audience all for the defence of righteousness alone; that judgment he has repudiated, blamed, blackened, unsettled and contemned : and has set up that pretender, that dullhead, a man such as the sins of the people have deserved. Rome is indignant and Phineas is fired with zeal, at seeing that which was planted and reared in common by the strong among her sons, destroyed and rooted up by one who trusts in mammon only. Which judgment, as if that unworthy one envied your authority alone, they say that attacker of the Roman diadem has resisted, and has set up that idol for the very reason, that your discretion saw that it should be opposed and broken down beyond others. In which how much appears to be detracted from the dignity of the Roman name, I leave to your prudence to be discussed: and would that that song may cease out of men's mouths, in which Winchester is extolled as more powerful than Rome. Why, they say, do we, who have a legate, go to the Apostolic see? What the lord [Bishop] of Rome orders and confirms, our legate, though a steward, perverts and weakens. Him whom the very wise Curia of S. Peter does not receive without a judgment, Winchester, evading that judgment, though promulgated, sets up and exalts. Let not then so patent an evasion pass into a precedent, lest the Roman dignity be torn by the hands of its assailants, and the authority of S. Peter absolutely fail before such injuries and new disgraces. In order therefore that the cause of religion in the Diocese of York may not grow lukewarm, or rather that it may not be dispersed and disappear altogether, strike heavily at the continuance of that headstrong person with the hammer of your severity, and for the mere love of true righteousness, break into pieces that idol, or rather the seat in which he unlawfully seeks to sit.

And if any one should come to Rome on their behalf to ask for the pall, firmly resist them, and condemn both Ananias and Sapphira together with their money, as it becomes your Holiness to do.

Furthermore, I am apprehensive and fear, as do also the whole body of Religious in the realm, lest that ancient seducer [the Bishop of Winchester] should in some way carry his point by the substitution of a new intermediary into the matter before disputed, or even into the fulness of power. Let your prudence therefore firmly resist this serpent who is working to bite both your heel and that of the whole kingdom; and bruise his head that the Church in that realm may not be entirely oppressed and fail altogether. May your Holiness have health and prosperity. [1]

---

[1] The date of this letter is fixed to A.D. 1144, by the fact that it is addressed to Pope Lucius II., whose brief pontificate began and ended in that year. The subject of it is rather indistinctly visible through the heated rhetoric of which it entirely consists; but is unquestionably the disputed election of William, nephew of King Stephen, to the Archbishopric of York, whose competitor was Henry Murdoch, Abbot of Fountains, and a former disciple of S. Bernard at Clairvaux. Respecting this dispute see Letters 235, 236, 238, 239, 240, 252; and note to the first named letter. The ' Dean ' referred to was William (called ' of S. Barbara '), the Dean of York: afterwards Bishop of Durham ; the Bishop of Winchester at that time was Henry of Blois (A.D. 1120—1174), who was the most powerful supporter of his kinsman William, and in fact, consecrated him to the see of York. Hence the invectives against him in the letter.   (E.)

LETTER CDLXXXIV.

To Pope Eugenius III. [1]
On the same subject.

. . . .

[I am importunate for the pronouncing of a judgment].
For you know that I speak with great confidence to the
heart of Jerusalem, nay, more, to the heart of him whom
the Lord hath set as the warden upon the walls of Jerusalem ; you yourself know the offences of that man *going
before the judgment*; nor is your prudence unaware what
such a person, so intruded and so reintruded, deserves.
If anyone should have suggested any other course to you,
whether I myself or an Angel from heaven, let him be
anathema from Him whom he does not fear to contradict,
the Lord whom you hear speaking among you.   For
He *speaks both unto His people and upon His saints*
(Ps. lxxxv. 8) : I speak of your brethren, if you think fit
so to speak of your own mother's sons, whom, as you
know so well, their zeal for Him makes to pine away,
because they see fearful things in the house of God, ex-
ecrable things in His sanctuary.   For behold how long
they are afflicted and groan ; they pine and almost
wither away for fear and expectation.   We beheld, and

[1] [The former half of this letter is identical with the well-
known letter of Bernard, No. 239, in which Bernard presses
for the deposition of William, Archbishop of York, as explained
in the last note.
The transcript of this letter has been made by the kindness of Mr. Plummer, Librarian of Corpus Christi College,
through the medium of Mr. Allnutt, of the Bodleian Library,
Oxford. (Hüffer's Note.) The same letter is also found in
Cod. 314 of that Library. The text is not clear in some
passages. (E.)]

there was no helper : we cried aloud, and there was no one to hear. But blessed be the Lord, who has given to us a Pontiff who compassionates our griefs, and who cannot but grieve over the affection of Joseph. To him therefore the poor cry out from the ends of the earth : but let him free his brethren from the hands of those who seek their lives, nor suffer them to be sold to Ishmaelite merchants. May the Lord be with your heart that you may not turn away your ear from our sobs and cries; that your bowels of mercy may be agitated by the sighs of the hearts of your brethren, and that you may set free their souls from so great a hazard and from a lot so extremely bitter. For it is not a temporal loss nor anything earthy that we deplore, but the souls which are under our care, which were once *purchased with a great price, not of corruptible things, such as silver and gold, but with the Blood of Jesus Christ, as of a lamb without blemish and without spot* (1 S. Peter i. 15) *and which it is not safe to give over to a new and shameless buyer.* We entreat you then for His sake by whom souls are redeemed; yea, indeed His Blood itself cries to you from Heaven, that you should not leave the rod of the wicked over the lot of the righteous lest the righteous put forth their hands unto iniquity (Ps. cxxv. 3). For He who cries out by us has bestowed power upon you, only let the will not be wanting. For even the Bishop of Tusculum, who, by the direction of your predecessor Pope Lucius, is acting as legate in that country, has already heard and ascertained (as we have been informed) of such great misdeeds committed by that man that, as it were, his nostrils are not able to endure their evil savour, if only the power to act was conferred upon him by his superior. This then is my request, my entreaty, this the desire of my heart, that you should bestow upon him plenary power to hurl down that idol without any subterfuge of appeal, if he shall find just and reasonable cause. I also supplicate your Excellency as before on behalf of the Archbishop of Canterbury, that he may be found worthy of your clemency in his just petitions, as well for the sake of his piety, as for your affection for me, in which he places great reliance. For he is a friend of our brethren, on whose behalf also I beg that his love for them may avail to obtain for him indulgence from you. Respecting other matters, how long will you hold our souls in suspense? We wait with quickened ears for your letters, but they do not come. I beg of you do not put off the matter from day to day. Make known to us both what you do and what you desire that we should do. May the Almighty God preserve you and multiply upon you His grace.

LETTER CDLXXXV. [1]

To all faithful Christians.

About the expedition to the Holy Land. He names the Feast of S.S. Peter and Paul, for the Crusaders to assemble at Magdeburg.

To the Lords and Fathers, the Reverend Archbishops, and the other Bishops, to the Nobles, and to all faithful Christian people, BERNARD, called Abbot of Clairvaux, wishes the spirit of strength and salvation.

I do not doubt that it has been heard in your country and commonly talked of, that God has aroused the spirit of Kings and princes to inflict vengeance among the na-

[1] *Boczek, Codex diplomaticus et epistolaris Moraviæ.* Olmütz 1836. 4to. Tom. I. p. 253. From an Olmütz MS. numbered cxxvi. and belonging to the fourteenth century.

tions and to root out from the land which bears the Christian name. . . . .[1]

Great is the good, abundant the richness of the Divine mercy! But the adversary sees this, and after his manner he envies it; he gnashes with his teeth and consumes away; he loses many from among those whom he held in bondage by various forms of wickedness and crime; those who were utterly sunk in perdition are converted, they have turned away from evil and are prepared to do good. But the adversary fears another and far greater loss from the conversion of the Gentiles, since he has heard that not only is the fulness of them about to enter in, but that all Israel also will be saved. The time for this appears to him to be now drawing near, and his practised malice is busying itself, with every kind of fraud, to hinder so great a blessing in every way possible. He has therefore stored up a seed of evil, the accursed pagans, whom (if I may be permitted to say so) the bravery of the Christians bore with too long, disregarding their stealthy attacks, and not crushing with armed heel their envenomed heads. But, because the Scripture saith: *Before destruction the heart is lifted up*; therefore their pride shall, God willing, be speedily humbled, and the road to Jerusalem be no longer impeded because of it. On this account the Lord (Pope) has committed this charge of proclaiming the Cross to my humility; and by the direction of the Lord King, and of the Bishops and nobles who met at Frankfort [2] I warn and declare to the strong and brave men among Christians that they take arms, and assume the Cross, the sign of salvation, against them and in order to destroy

[1] The MS. is apparently imperfect here. (E.)
[2] The scribe or copyist has written *Franconovort*, not Francofurtum. (E.)

or to convert those nations. And to those who shall
have set out upon the road to Jerusalem, I promise an
indulgence for their sins. Many indeed have signed themselves (with the Cross) on the spot; we now call others
to the same work: and we advertise those among Christian men who have not yet devoted themselves to this
expedition to Jerusalem, that they may, by doing so, obtain the same indulgence, provided that in it they observe
the directions of the Bishops and princes. But this we
forbid them absolutely, that they enter into any treaty
(with those heathen), either for money, or for tribute,
until with the Divine help, either their manner of worship
(be reformed), or the nation itself, be destroyed. To you
also who are Archbishops, and their fellow-Bishops we
speak : oppose it firmly, and give the greatest earnestness
and diligence in your power to ensuring that the enterprise be bravely accomplished; because you are ministers
of Christ in things relating to God, on that account a
strict reckoning shall be demanded from you; be watchful in the discharge in the duty which is entrusted to you.
And this we also earnestly beg and entreat of you in the
Lord. His army shall be, both in uniforms, arms, and
all equipment, arrayed with the same care and exactness
as that of another; inasmuch as those whom the same
return awaits. And furthermore, it has been determined
by all who were assembled at Frankfort, according to the
tenor of the letters despatched into all parts of the country
and which the Bishops and priests should make known to
the people of God, that they should sign and arm themselves against those enemies of the Cross of Christ, who
are without, with the Holy Cross in white [1] and that all

[1] Albi (sic).

ought to assemble at Magdeburg by the Feast of the Apostles Peter and Paul.

LETTER CDLXXXVI. (A. D. 1147. Boczek. From the same MS. as the preceding).

He invites all to the Expedition to the Holy Land, and commends the charge of the matter to a Bishop of Moravia.

To the Duke LADISLAUS, the Nobles, and the whole People of Bohemia, BERNARD, called Abbot of Clairvaux, wishes health in Christ.

I have to discourse to you on a matter belonging to the service of Christ, in whom alone is true salvation. Let the consideration which the Lord (Pope) has among you be my excuse for venturing to address you, and for the humble station of him who now writes to you; let me be excused because I am actuated by a motive of kindness towards you, and because my doing so may be to your benefit. I am indeed little in rank, but I desire you all not a little in the bowels of Jesus Christ. This zeal urges me to write to you, what I would more willingly labour to impress upon your heart by word of mouth, if the will to do so, which is not wanting to me, could supply me with the power so to do. For the spirit indeed is willing, but the flesh is weak. The corruptible body is not able to comply with the earnest desire of the soul, nor, earthly mass that it is, can it keep pace with the rapidity of the spirit. But may the ailments which I thus lament as my lot, be far from you: and my heart, I assure you, is enlarged so as to extend even to you, although the great distance detains my weighty body. Listen therefore, all of you, to the good news I have to speak; listen to the word of salvation; and let the liberal indulgence proffered to you be embraced with, as it were, the faithful and devoted arms of the soul. Nor is this time like those ages which have passed away, until now: for a new fulness of Divine mercy has come from heaven; blessed are those who are now living, and to whom has come the acceptable year of the Lord; the year of remission, yea, of jubilee! I say to you, that for no previous generation has the Lord done so greatly, nor have the gifts of His grace been poured forth so liberally upon our fathers. See what skill and care is employed to bring about your salvation; consider, O sinners, the abyss of the Divine goodness, and stand amazed: it creates, or it supposes, a necessity for its coming out of heaven to the help of your necessities: and that this enterprise is not from man, but from the heart of the Divine goodness. The earth trembled and quaked, when the Lord suffered His own Land to be lost. *His own Land*, I call it, in which he was beheld as a man for more than thirty years, and went to and fro among men. *His own Land*, which He honoured with His nativity, enlightened with His Miracles, dedicated with His Blood, consecrated with His burial; *His own Land* in which the voice of the turtle was heard, when He who was Son of a Virgin commended the zeal for chastity; *His own*, in which appeared the first blossom of His Resurrection. This land of the renewed Promise the wicked have begun to occupy; and if there had not been some to resist, the sanctuary itself of our religion would lie open to them; and the Sepulchre, in which He who was our Life, slept in death for our sakes, they would set about to defile; yea, to profane those Holy Places, which were purpled with the Blood of the immaculate Lamb. Furthermore, listen to a fact which ought to stir the heart of every Christian man, however hard it be. Our King is accused of treason: they say of Him that He is not God, that He falsely claimed to be what He was not. He among you who is His Lord's faithful servant, let him arise, let him defend his Lord against the infamy of this accusation; let him enter upon a conflict which is secure and safe, in which it is both glory to conquer, and gain to die. Servants of the Cross, to whom is wanting neither bodily strength nor wordly means; why do you delay? why do you hesitate? Take upon you the sign of the Cross; and the supreme Pontiff, the Vicar of him to whom it was said: *Whatsoever thou shall loose on earth shall be loosed in heaven,* he offers you a plenary indulgence for all sin, of which you shall have made confession with contrite heart. Accept then the gift which is offered you, and let each of you hasten to outstrip others in availing himself of this inestimable opportunity for indulgence, which is not likely to recur. I exhort and advise you, not to allow any affairs of your own to be preferred to the affairs of Christ; nor on account of those occupations, which have been attended to, or can be attended to, at other times, lose the opportunity for that which can never be afterwards obtained.

And in order that you may know when, in what manner, and by what road you are to set out, listen to a few more words. The army of the Lord will set out next Easter, and a considerable part of it, as it is determined, will pass through Hungary. It has also been ordained that no one in it should wear garments particoloured or trimmed with costly fur [1] or even made of silk: and that no trappings of gold or silver should be set upon the harness of the horses, but only upon the shields and the wood of the saddles which they use: though as the war

---

[1] GRISIIS = "Vair." See Du Cange, Glossary, in voc. *Griseum*; and S. Bernard. Ep. ii. c. 11. (E.)

goes on and battles take place, it will be permitted to those who will, to make use of gold and silver in that manner, that they may be resplendent in the beams of the sun; and by the terror of them, the courage of the heathen may be dissipated. It would be needful to enlarge on these matters more fully, if you had not among you the lord Bishop of Moravia, a man holy and learned, to whom I suggest that you should apply with the request that according to the wisdom which has been bestowed upon him by God, he should endeavour to instruct and exhort you all upon this subject. I have sent you also a copy of the letter of the Lord Pope, whose admonition you should listen to with attentive ear, and observe the directions he has given. Farewell.

LETTER CDLXXXVII. [1]

To G. . . . of Stopho [Staufen].

Bernard, called Abbot of Clairvaux, to his dear son in Christ, G. of Stopho, health and the assurance of his prayers.

Our very dear son, and your brother, Henry, has turned aside to us, and by my advice, has not laid aside the purpose which he had determined upon, of (taking) the sign of salvation. But far better than this: for as he was made poor for the sake of Christ who was poor, he has taken up his abode in the house of the poor of Christ, and under the habit of a religious. This ought not to seem to you either grievous or calamitous, because he

[Dom Gerbert. *Iter Alemanicum*, 1765, 8°. p. 216. (Migne Tome clxxxii. Col. 654)].

as Mary did, has chosen the better part, which shall not
be taken away from him; and has put on the garb of
one making pilgrimage to Jerusalem; not that which slew
the prophets, but that which is their common portion. Be
consoled therefore with these words, and remember the
last words which passed between you upon this subject.
And thus I give thanks with him for all things, as also
by us and by himself are given; and may you attain
mercy from God. Farewell, always beloved.

LETTER CDLXXXVIII. [1]

To N. . . . .

To his dear brother in Christ, N., Brother BERNARD
wishes that he may wholly put off in the Lord any remains
of the old man; that he may die to the world, and live
to Christ.

Since, my dear brother in the Lord, you have very
earnestly besought me, while I was still in retreat, that I
should visit you from time to time with some letters of
spiritual exhortation, I recognize, brother, that in saying
this, you heap coals of fire upon my head. For in affec-
tionately pressing upon my reluctance, you overcame with
your suppliant humility every feeling of pride that I had,
insomuch that I promised this to you, which you desired;

[1] [From Eugenius de Levis, Presbyter, *Anecdota sacra*,
sive *Collectio omnis generis opusculorum veterum*, S. S. *Patrum*,
etc. Augustæ Taurinorum [Turin] 178. . . 4to. p. 50. (Migne
Tom. i. Col. 653]. Who was this brother N. to whom S. Bernard wrote this letter, does not appear; nor is there any
indication to what place or monastery he belonged. The few
words in praise of solitude contained in par. 11, are insufficient to sustain the inference that he was a solitary. (E.)]

although it would be more fitting for me to receive such exhortation from you, than to address it to you. Yet the eagerness of your devotion has compelled me to become a fool in this respect, so that I shall try to do in some fashion, and according as I shall be able, what you request. Not indeed as writing unto you any other truths of the spiritual life, than those, however simple and elementary they will be found to be, which I had it in my mind to draw together.

But in the meantime I address myself to your affection, since no one, as you know well, is able to serve God perfectly, unless he shall separate himself wholly from the world. It behoves us, if we wish to follow God our Saviour, to hear the voice of the prophet, that we should *untie the knots, and loose the bonds, of impiety*, and thus follow our Redeemer, according to the testimony of the Apostle : *No man that warreth entangleth himself with the affairs of this life* (2 Tim. ii. 4). Never therefore let us permit our heart to be anxious on account of any created thing, unless insomuch as our affections are swayed and determined by the Divine love. For the vast variety of things which are perishing, if made more than needful, the subject of thought, give a fresh impulse to the body of death, not only by distracting the peaceful and welcome quiet of mind and soul, but also by generating troublesome and disturbing images or phantasms of things. But let us rather, after the burdensome weight of desires for all things earthly has been laid down, run, without grudging reflection upon the sacrifice of such things, towards Him who invites us, in whom is rich refreshment for souls, and peace supreme *which passeth all understanding. Come unto Me*, saith Jesus, *all ye that are weary and heavy laden, and I will give you rest.* O admirable condescension of our God! O loving gentleness, and ineffable

charity! Who among men has done actions like these?
Who has ever heard or seen the like? Behold, He invites
His enemies, He speaks kindly and encouragingly to
offenders, He attracts to Him those who are ungrateful!
Come, He says, *take my yoke upon you and ye shall find
rest* (S. Matt. xi. 29). O sweetest words, and full of harmony! words of Godlike quality, and more penetrating
than any two-edged sword, discovering the thoughts and
intents of the heart, filled with exceeding sweetness, and
extending to the dividing asunder of the soul. Arouse
thyself therefore, Christian soul, to the love of goodness
so great, to the fragrance and savour of sweetness so
exquisite. Assuredly I do not feel, that even when I
draw near to death, I shall be insensible to such words
as these. Kindle and glow, O my soul; I pray thee, grow
strong and fat in the mercy of thy God. Kindle and glow,
grow strong in its fatness and revel in its savour. Let
none hinder thee from drawing it to thee, from holding
it fast, and making proof of its taste. What more do we
ask for? What do we await? What do we even desire
beyond this? For in this alone we possess all good things.
But, alas, our astonishing folly! our miserable weakness!
our wicked madness! We are called to rest, and we pur-
sue labour; to blessedness, and we follow after grief; joy
is promised to us, yet we are ensnared by sorrow. Piti-
able is our weakness, most miserable our perversity! For
we are become, as it were, insensible, worse even than
dead images, having eyes, and seeing not: ears, and hearing not; reason, and yet are without discernment; putting
bitter for sweet, and sweet for bitter. O God! how shall
perversity so great in us find correction? Whence a satisfaction for so grave an offence? Assuredly none such can
be found in us, unless it be conferred upon us by Thy
mere goodness; Thou alone art able to make satisfaction

for our offences [1] who alone knowest the clay whereof
we are made, Thou art our redemption and salvation;
Thou who doest this in those alone, who seeing that they
are miserable and unhappy to their inmost hearts, yet
have faith that they can be raised up again by Thee; but
by Thee alone. Let us then lift up the eyes of our mind
straight to God, and let us realize in what condition of
prostration and helpfulness we are; for he who knows
not the need of his own condition, will surely not be
cured. Recognizing it therefore with fortitude, let us cry
unto God out of the depths, that He may stretch out to
us the helping hand of his mercy, which is never shortened
that it cannot save. Let us not, I pray, lose the confidence which has so great a reward. Let us present ourselves with full assurance at the throne of His grace,
receiving the end of our faith, which is the salvation of
our souls. Let there be in us no delaying, for now salvation invites us, and tribulation awaits us, so that we
are compelled to enter in. Why do we hesitate? Why
delay? Let us hasten to enter into that rest of eternal
joy, of supreme felicity, of inward refreshment, of which
the causes are great, wonderful, without number and
beyond understanding. Let our heart ascend into Jerusalem above. Let us sigh for our own country, which is
the mother of us all; and entering into the kingdom of
our Lord, let us behold our King, who is kindness itself,
ruling over all, and let our hearts grow tender with His
mercies. Let us thank Him with our whole heart, who
considering our weakness, has not withdrawn from us His
kind and merciful help; imparting to us His own desire
to run in the way of righteousness, which is not to be
accounted as a matter of debt, but reputed as of grace.

[1] *delectis* (Migne), but read *delictis* (E.)

Since he who was the chief of the prophets asserts that he earnestly desires this : *My soul longed earnestly to desire Thy righteous judgments at all times* [1] (Ps. cxix. 20 VULG.), and without this our want of zeal neglects this desire itself, and permits it, by a certain excessive tepidity to grow weary and fail. I have bethought me of noting down a few motives for this virtue, in a memorial form; in which are stated both what should be followed, and what avoided. Let us then practise these daily and with willing zeal; let us gird up the loins of our soul and give unwearied labour to these virtues; let us rise by grace to divine charity. Let *a desire for the everlasting hills* be perfected in us. These virtues then are many in number, and form, as it were, a ladder of salvation, by which those who are influenced by earnest faith, and sacred modesty, in all their words and actions, are able, without doubt, to reach the summit, and attain the perfection of virtues. Slowness in speaking, promptitude in obeying, frequency in prayer, the avoidance of inactivity, the confessing our weaknesses, sincerely and often, the giving of service willingly, prevent a community being without fruit. These are, as it were, shining pearls, which make their possessor to be in favour both with angels and men: and when it shall be according to His good pleasure who *separated thee from thy mother's womb* (Gal. i. 15) and called thee by His grace, to reveal in thee the image of His Son, to transfer thee from the miserable bondage of Egypt into the glorious liberty of the children of God ; when thou shalt have begun to use thy feet, as it were, upon the path of the new man, upon the footpath which is fixed between fear and the love of humility, you may

[1] *Concupivit anima mea desiderare justificationes tuas;* and S. Jerome is even more emphatic in the same sense : "*Desideravit anima mea desiderare.*" (E.)

be able to obtain greater heights (of virtue), and to move freely upon loftier eminences.

From which principles other precepts follow.

It is needful then:

1. Before all things to desire to follow the footsteps of the Saviour; that your entire hope should be fixed on the Lord, and that it should be wholly removed from all the things of this life.

2. That you should study to root out entirely from yourself, in so far as our human state will endure, all vices and evil concupiscences, to *purge out the old leaven of malice and wickedness, and to walk in newness of life* (1 Cor. v. 7) after Christ; because unless you shall have first broken through the chains of this unrighteousness, your soul, burdened and weighed down in the darkness, will be unable to rise upwards to heaven.

3. That you disembarrass yourself of every outward bond, that you may be united to the Lord in mind and soul.

4. That for the love of the Most High you should bear calmly all persecutions of the world, if it be possible; undergoing them as it were a vow, and filling up that which is behind of the afflictions of Christ (Col. i. 24); shrinking from earthly gladness, but rejoicing in tribulations themselves; regarding them as prepared for you, for the purgation of your sins, and grief as for the benefit of your soul.

5. That since you feel yourself as guilty before your Creator, you do not demand reason to be rendered to you for the things that are created.

6. That having disdain for your own self, and earnestly desiring that all should have it, preferring also a sacred poverty in all things, you should have in all things which concern you, hardness, commonness, and sparingness, to the utmost of your power. Yet you are not to require

this in others; but rather gladly and joyfully render to them every brotherly consolation, benefit and service, that may be needful, regarding them as worthy of all; not permitting in yourself any feeling of dislike or hatred of any, which would be without excuse, but grieving with, and compassionating them, from your inmost heart, to the utmost of your power.

7. That passing all your time in fear, you avoid altogether the flatteries, honours, glories and favours of the present world, and the breath of its vain glory, which are as poisoned draughts; standing always detached, as far as you are able, and holding yourself constantly in suspicion. For if you shall have attained this glory, no enemy within or without shall injure you.

8. That for the love of Him, who being the Lord of all things in heaven, and in earth, and under the earth, took for our sakes the form of the humblest servant, and subjected Himself voluntarily for the sins of men, you humiliate your own self; regarding every man as your superior, and you yourself as the vilest servant of men; and that in all things, and with regard to all persons, you regard yourself as a servant. Thus obtaining quietness and peace with all men, you shall not even know what it is to give scandal.

9. That of all those things, which do not conduce at all to spiritual improvement, you touch none whatever; that is to say, take no care for them, nor allow them to form a part of your life either inward or outward, in any manner, where you do not find benefit derived to your mind; nor allow yourself to be habituated to anything of this kind.

10. That you by every means enforce abstinence on your powers of sight and speech, and your other bodily senses; so as to make it your study not to see, to hear,

or to touch, anything that is not helpful to your soul: that you hold your tongue under perfect control, so as to speak nothing whatever, unless obliged by a question, or by necessity, or evident usefulness; and then to speak briefly, with reverence, fear, gentleness, and in a low voice; taking care also to avoid, if you can, prolixity of words, and cutting off every occasion for this beforehand.

11. That you hold fast all times, a grateful and sacred solitude; and that you hold it especially precious during your vigils; that you offer your prayers to God always with careful attention to the words, with fervent devotion and deep humility.

12. That when it is your duty to celebrate the Divine Office, you so do this as to retain no consciousness of earthly things, but to have your mind fixed and steady in the contemplation of things celestial; and that you discharge your ministry with such a degree of reverence, devotion, and fear, as becomes one who is set in the Divine Presence among the Choirs of Angels, and who offers like them a service pre-eminently of praise.

13. That holding at all times the highest feeling of veneration for the glorious Queen, the Mother of our Lord, you turn to her in the pressure of all difficulties and necessities; as to the one only and very safe refuge; entreating confidently the guard of her protection, and taking her, with the highest devotion, for your advocate: that you commit your. cause to her securely, who is the mother of mercy, and daily study to please her, and to show to her extreme reverence of spirit; and may your devotion to her be accepted, your reverence pleasing to her perfect purity; may every virtue both for mind and body, be poured upon you; and may you strive with all your powers, to follow the footsteps of her humility and gentleness.

14.   That you should at all times avoid all women and even youths, without there be a cause of some great and manifest utility; and everywhere that you may be, choosing for yourself one father; a man discreet, holy, gentle and pious; learned in his experience of work, and who has attained the high faculty of pastoral discourse; to instruct you by words, as also by inspiring and efficacious examples, in the Love of God, to whom you may be able to have recourse in all your necessities, for spiritual consolation.

15.   That you always repel from you inwardly with the greatest earnestness, all frigidity of melancholy, and bitter weariness, [1] in which lurks the way of confusion, which leads to death; and that you always maintain a peaceful outward demeanour.

16.   That you conform all your feelings and desires to the Divine Will; that the grace of God bountifully bestowed upon you may build you up in purity and innocence in all respects; and that you be not ever perturbed, more than is meet, by the defects of others, nor pollute yourself with others' uncleanness, adding iniquity to iniquity; lest while you desire to deliver others from the deep, you fall yourself instead into a deeper abyss.   Therefore leave those whom you are not able to benefit without doing harm, to that supreme wisdom, which knows how to bring good out of any evils whatsoever. So also equally in all good things as in evil, you will be able, with the permission of God, to find spiritual progress.

17.   That you may keep your heart in complete

---

[1] *Acedia*: that is an "immoderate weariness and bitterness of mind, which extinguishes spiritual joy, turns the mind in upon itself, and presents to it a sort of precipice of mental despair. It is called *acedia*, quasi *acida*, inasmuch as it renders all spiritual works sour and distasteful." *Cæsarius.*   (E.)

control, let it be given to spiritual exercises only, nor let
the image of any visible things be impressed upon (your
mind) by the processes of reflection; that being free from
all created things, you may be able to be wholly filled
by the Creator of all.

18. That being mindful of the Divine image and similitude in all men, you feel a love for all, and especially
for the sick; and this with the deepest feeling of charity;
and that of those who are poor and in need you charge
yourself with the care, provided that it do not become to
you hurtful and destructive, as regards spiritual things; as
a good mother loves and cares for an only and favourite
child.

19. That you so keep your mind constantly in relation
with God, that the entire time of your spiritual exercises,
be a continuous prayer as well of mind as of body; and
that you perform all those exercises, and all those services
and duties and especially those which are of a more mean
and common character, with such a fervour of charity, as
if you were rendering them to Christ present in the body,
as indeed you may and ought, to consider it the case;
and in this you will think truly, for Christ says in the
Gospel: *That which ye have done unto one of the least of
these My brethren, ye have done unto Me* (S. Matt. xxv. 40.)

20. That you show honour and devoted reverence to
all to whom it is due, and study to keep unimpaired as
the apple of your eye the most holy rule of obedience,
not only in great and difficult matters, but also in the
smallest details; that you be obedient, not only to elders
and those set in authority over you, but also that you
render yourself subject unto all persons whatsoever, deny-
ing your own self for Christ's sake in all things; and
studying earnestly to do His will, even when it differs
from your own. In no respect must you render yourself

16

burdensome to others; but rather as having affection for
all in the charity of Christ, render yourself agreeable to all
in common.   Take heed to avoid individual friendships,
courtesies, familiarities; and above all things beware that
you never, in your own person or in regard to another,
give cause or occasion to any, by word, action, or gesture,
for rancour, hatred, clamour, abuse, riot, murmuring, scan-
dalous detraction, or on the other hand, for flattery and
similar things.

21. That you study to conceal as far as you can, from
all, the virtues and spiritual graces, which by the Divine
bounty have been worked in you, or by your means; as
also your tribulations, spiritual conflicts, and similar expe-
riences; those only being excepted, which ought to be
disclosed to your own priest for your own accusation:
unless perhaps you should make them known to a proved
and spiritual friend of your own, whose advice and teaching you may suppose it wise to obtain with respect to
them, and for the sake of spiritual usefulness. Be also
everywhere careful to steal fragments of time, that you may
be able to find leisure for solitary prayer, and while sitting
solitary and silent, be raised in thought and desire to the
heavens above.

22. Make it your desire to be free of all things, and
to hold fast to nothing; nay, to hold in contempt all things
which were dear to you; that so great may be the fervour
of your mind, so earnest the effort, with which you direct
your will towards the Creator of all, that you become
forgetful of all lower things; where you may be standing,
what you may be doing, or with what affairs you may be
occupied day and night, because you have God so entirely
in all your consciousness at every hour and every moment.
Believe also, and reflect upon the fact, that you are most
truly in His Presence, and that He beholds you with all your

surroundings. Reflect upon it with the deepest reverence and circumspection, with fear and trembling. Prostrate yourself at one moment before the Feet of His incomprehensible Majesty, and entreat with bitter penitence pardon for your sins; at another, beholding the Son of God in His most sacred Passion, be pierced by the blade of His love and sorrow for us; be wounded with Him before His Cross, be full of tears and of mourning. At another, compare the straight line of righteousness with the downward oblique tendency of your whole life; at another, enumerate in your mind the great and numberless benefits bestowed upon you, and follow them with acts of thanksgiving; and again behold with stirrings of most ardent love, His mark upon all creatures. Now you will direct your attention to His power, now to His wisdom, now to His goodness and clemency; and you will give Him praise in all His works. Now you will be attracted by the desire of the heavenly country; and with sighs and groans, will pant to be there; now considering with joy and surpassing admiration the tenderness of His inestimable love towards us, heart and mind fail in Christ. Now (you behold Him) holding you fast in your headlong flight from Him; now you consider how ungrateful throughout all, you are found to be, and then the tenderness of the Divine mercies thus made manifest, which brings you to dissolve into floods of tears from mere depth of love towards him. Now there dawn upon your rapt gaze the deepest and the most secret, the loftiest and most wonderful of the hidden and awful mysteries of His justice upon all the wicked; while you constantly fall before Him in deep love and humble fear, venerating Him before all, and bearing in loving and constant memory His most sacred Passion.

23. That you may be watchful in guarding yourself at all times against the deceits of your ancient enemy, who

changing himself into the similitude of an angel of light, is frequently setting nets and snares in every path of men, that he may succeed in taking captive our souls; avoid as a sparrow with careful watchfulness the snares of the hunters; be thou of such extreme and holy humility in thine own eyes, that not even his most subtle and finely woven nets may be able to confine thee; and from these thou shalt surely then be able to escape unharmed. Keep before the eyes of thy mind the sight of God, and thou shalt become as Israel, whose guardian will neither slumber nor sleep.

24. That you may maintain unwearied the rigour of your holy Rule, and strive with holy ardour to attain heavenly desires, preserve undiminished the fairness of mental and bodily cleanness, the purity of innocence, and rectitude of conscience; and hold fast an earnest care, never to recede from a resolve. To this end, that you hold fast that which is good the more diligently and purely, examine your life with daily scrutiny, and even seven times in a day, and always after each of the canonical hours, whether you have walked before God, in righteousness and holiness worthy of Him. And because there is no one, who can so far keep righteousness and holiness, as never to neglect or omit anything; and therefore it is necessary that resorting very often to the laver of penitence, you should accuse yourself with grief and lamentation; in this accusation let your confession be wholly truthful and pure, without any screen or excuse or concealment. Recount all your defects in their turn unto the priest as unto God; relate the faults of omission of which you have been guilty in those things which relate to God, and especially as regards the mental act in prayer, and the faults of utterance in the observance of righteousness.

Then in the next place the faults of which you have been guilty, through ill custody of the senses, and the allied powers of thought and feeling. Which confession indeed ought to be accompanied with contrition and satisfaction. Strive to efface, not great offences only, but those which are less than great; and in lamenting a fault forbear to repeat it. Study always to cut off the causes and occasions of evil, in whatever degree they may appear to be joined to you by self-love. According to the just and holy saying of the Saviour, a right eye which causes to offend is to be plucked out : much more then the occasions of sin, though they may appear to us never so delightful, and even if the process be altogether repugnant to our feelings : and therefore it is that the struggle to do this is the most severe in the battle of this life. [1]

LETTER CDLXXXIX. [2] (Between A. D. 1132 and A. D. 1136. [3]).

Hatto, Bishop of Troyes, at the request of Hugo, Bishop of Auxerre (Burgundy; Yonne), and Bernard, Abbot of Clairvaux, grants the Church of Clerey and the Church of Faux-Fresnay to the Monastery of Monstier-Ramey.

[1] This remarkable letter was addressed to some one under monastic rule. But beyond this there are no internal evidences from which we can come to any conclusion as to the individual (E.)

[2] Migne Tom. iv. Col. 1919. The original is on parchment, without date : On the back is written : "A donation is made of the Churches of Clerey and Faux-Fresnay." The seal, which hung by a double strap in parchment, is wanting. Archives of L'Aube, Collection of Moutier-Ancey.

[3] This is the date given by the Editor of Migne's third edition. But it is clear from the mention of "Pope Innocent

In the name of the Holy and Indivisible Trinity, I, Hugo, by the grace of God, Bishop of Auxerre, [1] and I, Bernard, Abbot of Clairvaux, to the faithful in Christ.

Everyone who is of the truth willingly listens to the truth and bears testimony to it. On this account we note to the whole body of the faithful that Hatto, the venerable Bishop of Troyes, at our request and by our hand has made gift of the Church of Clerey and the Church of Faux-Fresnay, to the monastery of Monstier-Ramey; with the knowledge and approval of Manasses de Villemaur, and of Falco, his archdeacons. And that this gift may remain firm and unimpaired, the before-named Bishop, and we, by the apostolic defence of the Lord Pope Innocent II. of good memory . . . . That a truth so undoubted may not be either changed . . by any lapse of succeeding times, we have taken steps to confirm it by our. . . .

LETTER CDXC. [2] (A. D. 1143).

Hatto, Bishop of Troyes, at the request of Bernard of good memory, Abbot of Clairvaux, grants the Church of Lusigny to the canons of B. Lupus at Troyes.

II. of good memory," that it must be dated after the year 1138. For that Pope sat from A. D. 1130—1138. (E.)

[1] '*Antissiodorentis*', Migne. But read '*Autissiodorensis*' (E.)

[2] Migne, Tom iv. Col. 1920. The original is on parchment. On the back is endorsed: "A writing of Bishop Hatto respecting the Church and lesser tithe of Lusigny", and in characters of the fifteenth century: "Letter of donation of the Church of Lusigny, and tithe of the same." The seal, which was attached by a double strap, is wanting. Archives of L'Aube. Collection of S. Loup.

I. Hatto, by the grace of God, Bishop of Troyes, makes known to all people of the present age, and of future times, that Dom Bernard of good memory, Abbot of Clairvaux, has made request of us that we should grant the Church of Lusigny to the canons of the Blessed Lupus at Troyes. Now since we held the said Abbot in great veneration for his sanctity, and would not willingly refuse anything within reason, that he asked of us : We have granted the said Church for ever to the Canons before mentioned; that is to say to Dom Bernard the Abbot, and to the other brethren who serve God under his rule, and to their successors; yet saving our Episcopal rights. But since there is a certain knight named Galterus Piscator, who had anciently possessed and held even to our times, a third part in the small tithe, and in the oblations of the four great Festivals, and in the *census atrii*, we take the whole of this from the hands of the said knight by the vigour of our ecclesiastical authority, and add it to the gift of other things belonging to the same Church, which we make to the aforesaid Canons. But the matter shall be so settled, that it shall be permitted to the said Abbot and to his successors to select a chaplain, who may be either a regular or a secular (priest), to serve the said Church. Who, when he has selected a fit person, (*personam*) shall present him to the Bishop, and the Bishop shall institute (*præbebit*) him to the cure of the above named Church, without any contradiction. But the said chaplain shall make due response in all those things which belong to the Episcopal right, as in Visitations and Synods. The same Church is also bound to pay sixteen pence each year; namely, eight at the Paschal synod, and eight at that which is held in September; and every third year also five shillings. These therefore shall be paid by the presbyter, who shall be in the same Church, at the general Synod, according to the custom; but besides these, the same presbyter shall be and remain free from every exaction whatever. In the arrangement of this has assisted my beloved son and Archdeacon, Manasses de Villemaur, to whose charge the same Church belongs. Since then this gift has been made with deliberate intention, it behoves us to take the greater care that it should not be rendered of none effect by some future misstatement. Therefore we have caused the present writing to be made; which we have attested, not only with the impression of our own seal, but with the signatures of the various honourable persons whose names follow below.

These are the names of the witnesses, who have assisted at the execution of this document :

Dominus Guido, Abbot of the Monastery of Monstier-Ramey.

Dominus Theobald, Abbot of the Monastery of Monstier-en-Der.

Dominus Odo, Provost of S. Peter.

Manasses, Archdeacon of Rumilley.

Gibuin, Precentor and Archdeacon.

Stephen de Venisiaco (*de Venaissin*).

Garnier of S. Rémy, Presbyter and Canon of S. Peter.

Stephen Lupus, Canon of S. Peter and priest.

Eustache.

Hilduin of S. Paul.

Angelmer of Sezannia.

Stephen, son of Gerulf.

Milo de. . . . . Canon of S. Peter.

Guy, Count of Jouarre.

Dominus Helenus, Abbot of La Rivour.

Geoffrey of Peronne.

Geoffrey of Auxerre.

Gaucher of La Ferté, monk of Clairvaux.

Executed in this year 1143 of the Incarnation of Our Lord Jesus Christ, Epact xiii., in the reign of Henry, King of France, and during the tenure of the Countship of Troyes by Theobald. [1]

---

[1] There is a difficulty arising from the use of the words ' of good memory' as applied to Abbot Bernard *during his lifetime;* for the year of the Saint's death was 1153; while this document is plainly dated 1143. Can the words "*bonæ memoriæ*" have been added at a later period? (E.)

SERMONS FOR THE ECCLESIASTICAL YEAR.

(*DE TEMPORE.*)

FOR THE SEASON OF ADVENT.

SERMON I.

He shall be great, and shall be called the Son of the Highest. S. LUKE i. 32.

We celebrate to-day, brethren, the commencement of Advent. The name, like that of other seasons of the Church, is well known and familiar to all; but the reason of the name is not perhaps so familiar. For the children of Adam are so unwise as to neglect the truths which belong to their salvation, and devote themselves in preference to vain and transitory things. To whom shall we liken the men of this generation, whom we see unable to separate themselves, or to be separated, from worldly and fleshly pleasures? They are like people plunged into deep waters and struggling for life. See how they catch at everything that comes near them, though it be but a stick or a straw, and hold it fast, though it cannot be of the least use to them; and if anyone swims to their help, they will frequently seize them in such a grasp as to drown them with themselves. So the children of Adam perish in the vast and deep sea of this world: snatching at perishable things, and neglecting those abiding realities which they may grasp, and thus be able to keep afloat and to save their souls. For it is not of vanity, but of the truth, that it is said: *Ye shall know it, and it shall make you free* (S. John viii. 32). Do you then, brethren, to whom as little children, God has revealed those things which are hidden from the wise and prudent, meditate with care on those precious things. Consider now the reason of this Advent; who He is Who comes, whence He came, to whom He came, and why. Curiosity upon these points is praiseworthy and salutary; for the Church universal would not celebrate Advent with so great devotion, if it did not enshrine some great mystery.

2. First consider with the same wonder and admiration the greatness of Him who comes. He is, according to the testimony of the Angel Gabriel, the *Son of the Highest*, and He Himself is therefore the Most High. We dare not think the Son of God degenerate: He is of necessity of equal greatness and glory. The sons of Kings are themselves kings, and the sons of Princes of princely rank. But wherefore is it that of the Three Persons in the Supreme Trinity, whom we believe in, confess and adore, it is not the Father nor the Holy Spirit who comes to us, but the Son? There is doubtless some deep cause why this was so. But who has penetrated the design of the Lord? *Or who has been His counsellor?* (Romans xi. 34). Yet it was not without some deep purpose of the Holy Trinity that it was predestined that the Son should come into the world: and if we consider the cause of our exile, we may perhaps be able to understand in some degree how fitting it was that it should be the Son who should come to save us. For that Lucifer who was the Morning Star, having striven to make himself equal to the Most High, and by an outrage assumed that he was equal with God (which is the right of the Son), was therefore hurled headlong from heaven. The Father defended the glory of

His Son and declared as it were by his action: *Vengeance is Mine, and I will repay* (Romans xii. 19). Then *I saw Satan fall from heaven as lightning* (S. Luke x. 19). What right then hast thou to pride, thou who art dust and ashes? If God spared not the angels in their pride, how much less shall He spare thee, who art but corruption and a worm? Lucifer himself did nothing, effected nothing: only of a thought of pride was he guilty; and in a moment, in the glance of an eye, he was flung down without remedy into the abyss, because according to the Evangelist, he *abode not in the truth* (S. John viii. 44).

3. Fly then from pride, my brethren, I pray you. Pride is the beginning of every kind of sin. It was that which so swiftly plunged into the everlasting darkness that Lucifer, who shone the brightest among the stars. It changed him from being, not only an angel, but the first of angels, into a demon. Then envying the happiness of man in his heart, he contrived to bring to light the iniquity which he had conceived in his own; persuading him that by eating of the forbidden tree he would become as God, knowing good and evil. O unhappy one! What dost thou promise, what hope dost thou give to the man; when it is only the Son of the Most High who has the key of knowledge, yea, the *Key of David, which shuts and none can open* (Apoc. iii. 7). In Him are all the treasures hidden of wisdom and knowledge (Col. ii, 3); wilt thou then steal them, to impart them to the man? You see how according to the saying of the Lord, *he is a liar and the father of a lie* (S. John viii. 24). For he was a liar when he said *I will be like unto the Most High* (Is. xiv. 14). And was he not the father of a lie when he poured into the heart of man the poisoned germ of his own falsehood, *Ye shall be as God* (Gen. iii. 5). And thou also, O man, when thou sawest a thief consentedst unto him; for you heard, my brethren,

what was read from Isaiah this night, where the Lord said: *Thy princes shall be unbelievers* or as another translation has it: *disobedient and companions of thieves* (Isaiah i. 23).

4. Thus then our first parents (*principes*) Adam and Eve, the founders of our race, are disobedient and companions of thieves; since they attempt, by the counsel of the serpent, or rather of the devil who used the serpent as his instrument, to snatch at that which is the right of the Son of God only. Nor did the Father pass over the injury to His Son, *for the Father loveth the Son* (S. John v. 20), but on the instant visited the man with just judgment; and His Hand weighs heavy upon us still. For in Adam have we all sinned and in him have been condemned. What shall be the part of the Son, seeing that the Father visits with judgment on His account, and will spare no created being? Behold, He says, because of me my Father loves the creatures He has made. The first of the angels desired to usurp the greatness which was Mine, and has found adherents among his fellows: but instantly the justice of My Father has stricken him, and his followers with dreadful punishment, with an incurable wound. The knowledge also which pertained to Me man wished to steal, and My Father has had no pity upon him, nor has His eye spared him. *Doth God take care for oxen* (1 Cor. ix. 9). Yet he had made two noble creatures to whom He had equally imparted reason, and had made them capable of blessedness, namely, the Angel and Man. But behold, He has lost because of Me a multitude of angels and all men. But that they may know that I love My Father, let Him recover by means of Me those whom on My account He seems to have lost. *If because of Me this tempest has arisen*, said Jonah, *take me up and cast me forth into the sea* (Jon. i. 12). All look upon Me with

envy. Lo I come, I will show Myself to them in such a condition that whosoever envies me, whosoever takes in hand to imitate me, their envy shall become salutary consolation, their endeavour shall turn to their good. But I know that the angels have deserted the right path, have done so through gratuitous malice and wickedness, and have not sinned through any ignorance or weakness. They therefore as refusing to repent, must of necessity perish. For the love of the Father, and the honour of the supreme Sovereign require justice.

5. This is why He also created men in the beginning that they might supply the place of those and restore the ruins of Jerusalem. For he knew that for the angels no way of return lay open. He knew the pride of Moab *that he is very proud* (Is. xvi. 6): and pride does not admit of the remedy of penitence and consequently not of pardon. But in the place of man God has created no other creature, wishing to show by this that man is still capable of restoration. He was ruined by the malice of another, and therefore the love of another was able to do him service. So, O my God, I entreat that it may please Thee to raise me up, because I am powerless of myself, and because I have been cast down by fraud from my first state and although innocent have been cast into this place (Gen. xl. 15). Innocent indeed I was not altogether : but in comparison of him who seduced me I was well-nigh innocent, I was made to believe a lie. O Lord, let the Truth come that falsehood may be taken away, that I may know the truth and the truth make me free; if only I shall renounce the falsehood when it is made clear to me, if I shall cling to the truth when it is made known. Otherwise it will not be a human temptation nor a human sin, but a diabolic obstinacy. For to persevere in evil is a thing diabolic, and whosoever con-

tinue in their sin, like the devil, are worthy to perish with him.

6. You have heard, brethren, who it is that comes. Consider now whence He comes, and to whom. He comes, that is to say, from the Right Hand of His Father into the bosom of the Virgin Mother: He comes from the highest heaven into the lower parts of the earth. But why? Is it not because we human beings, had our life appointed upon the earth? Yes, but on condition that He remained there. For where could it be otherwise than well where He is? *Whom have I in heaven but thee? and there is none upon earth that I desire in comparison of thee. God is the strength of my heart and my portion for ever* (Ps. lxxiii. 25, 26). *Though I walk through the valley of the shadow of death, I will fear no evil,* if only *thou art with me* (Ps. xxiii. 4). Well we see to-day, that He has descended, not only into the earth, but also into the place of departed spirits itself; not as a captive bound, but as free among the dead; as the Light which shined in darkness, though the darkness comprehended it not. Wherefore His soul was not left in hell, nor did His holy Body see corruption in the earth. For Christ, who descended, is He who also ascended upon high that He might fill all things; of whom it is written: *He went about doing good, and healing all who were oppressed of the devil* (Acts x. 38) and in another place: *He rejoiced as a giant to run his course: his going forth is from the height of heaven, and his circuit even unto its height again* (Ps. xix. 5, 6). Rightly therefore does the Apostle proclaim: *Seek those things which are above, where Christ sitteth at the right hand of God* (Col. iii. 1). It would be in vain that He strove to raise our hearts on high, if He did not show us that the Author of our salvation was there. But let us proceed; for although the

matter we have to treat is abundant and fruitful, the shortness of our time does not admit a corresponding length of discourse. Thus when we have considered *Who He is that comes?* we have found that He is a Guest of great and unspeakable majesty. When we have looked up to see *Whence does He come?* a prospect has unrolled before our eyes extending into the far distance, according to that which was testified beforehand by the prophetic Spirit 'Behold the Name of the Lord comes from far' (Is. xxx. 27). Finally if we enquire *To whom He comes?* we recognize the honour inestimable, and almost inconceivable, which He has deigned to do to us in descending from so high into the horror of this prison-house.

7. Now who can doubt that it must have been for some great cause that one of so great Majesty should deign to descend from so far into a place so unworthy of Him? Unquestionably the motive must have been entirely great, because it is nothing less than a great mercy, a grand compassion, an overflowing charity. To what end is it to be believed that He came? It is that which we have now to examine. Nor is there need of much search in this respect, since His words and His actions declare aloud what was the motive of His coming. It was to seek the hundredth sheep which had wandered that He hastened to descend from the celestial mountains; it was on our account and that His mercies might make known the Lord more clearly to His people, and His wonders to the sons of men, that He came. Wonderful the condescension of God in seeking man, great the dignity of man to be thus sought! If anyone should desire to boast of this, assuredly he would not be wrong in so doing; not because he would appear to be anything in his own self, but because He who has done this is one of rank so exalted. All the riches and all the glory of the world and

whatever can seem desirable to us here below, all this is little, or rather it is absolutely nothing, in comparison with this honour and with the worth of man himself. Lord, what is man, that Thou glorifiest him? Or why does Thy heart yearn towards him?

8. And yet I ask of myself why He has willed that He should come to us, rather than that we should have gone to Him. For ours was the necessity; but it is not the custom of the rich to come to the poor, even if they wish to do them good. It is true, brethren, that it would have been more proper for us to go to Him, but there was a double hindrance in our way. In the first place our eyes were darkened that they could not see; and He, He dwelt in *the light that no man can approach unto* (1 Tim. vi. 16): while we, lying paralysed upon our couch, were entirely unable to draw near to that Divine brightness. Because of this, our most kind Saviour and Physician of our souls descended from His high place and softened His glory, to suit our weak eyes. He clad Himself, as it were, with a lantern, with that Body, glorious and most pure from every stain, which He took upon Him. This is indeed that light and effulgent cloud, upon which the Prophet had predicted that the Lord should mount in order to go down into Egypt (Is. xix. 1).

9. We must now also consider the *time at which* the Saviour came. This was, as you know, not at the beginning, or in the middle, but at the end of time. Nor was it determined without reason, but on the contrary, with abundant reason, by the Supreme wisdom, that it would bring help to men only when their necessity was at the greatest, as not being ignorant of the proneness to ingratitude in the sons of Adam. It may be truly said that already the day was far spent and the evening was drawing near, the Sun of Righteousness had declined in some de-

gree towards the horizon, and diffused over the earth only
lessened warmth and enfeebled brightness.   For the light of
the knowledge of God had become very feeble, at the
same time that as iniquity abounded, the fervour of mutual charity had grown cold.   No Angel any longer appeared, no Prophet raised his voice, it seemed as if, overcome by the excessive hardness and obstinacy of men,
they had ceased to appear or to speak: but then spake
the Son: *I said, Lo I come* (Ps. xl. 7).   Thus, while all things
were sunk in deep silence, and night proceeded on her
course, Thy Almighty Word, O Lord, came from Thy royal
throne (Wisd. xviii. 14, 16) as in the same sense said the
Apostle: *When the fulness of the time was come, God
sent forth His Son* (Galat. iv. 4). Without doubt the fulness and abundance of temporal things had produced a
forgetfulness of and scarcity in things eternal. For to pass
over other things, temporal peace itself was at that time
so wide spread, that at the bidding of one man a census
of the whole world was carried out (S. Luke ii. 1).

10.   You have now considered who He is that comes,
and to what place: also the cause and the time of His
coming.   One thing remains to consider, the road by which
He came; and this also we must diligently inquire into,
that we may be able to go to meet Him, as it is right
we should do.   But as He came once upon this earth in
visible flesh to work out our salvation, so He comes daily
in the Spirit and invisibly to save our souls, as it is written:
'Christ our Lord is a Spirit before our eyes.' And in order that you may know that this spiritual coming is secret
it is said: *In His shadow shall we live among the heathen*
(Lam. iv. 20). On this account it is suitable that even if
the sick man is not able to go very far to meet the
coming of so great a Physician, he should at least make
an effort to lift his head and raise himself up a little to-

wards Him who comes. It is not needful for thee, O man, to sail across the seas, to rise up into the clouds, to cross the mountains, in order to meet thy God. The way that is shown to thee is, I say, not long; thou hast but to enter into thy own soul to meet Him. For His word is very nigh thee: it is in thy mouth and in thy heart (Rom. x. 8). Go then to meet Him even as far as the repentance of the heart and confession of the mouth, so that at least thou mayest come forth from the dunghill of thy defiled conscience; for it were an unworthy thing that the Author of purity should enter there. And let these few words suffice concerning that Advent in which He deigns to enlighten the mind of each of us by His invisible presence.

11. But it is needful also to consider the way of His visible Advent, since *His ways are ways of pleasantness and all His paths are peace* (Prov. iii. 17). *Behold*, says the Spouse, *my beloved comes leaping upon the mountains, bounding over the hills* (Cant. ii. 8). You see Him, O beautiful one, when He comes, but you were not able to behold Him before, when He was reposing. For then thou didst cry out: *Tell me, O thou whom my soul loveth, where thou feedest thy flocks, where thou liest down* (Cant. i. 6). While He rests, they are the angels whom He feeds throughout endless eternities, whom he satiates with the vision of His eternal and unchangeable existence. But do not slight thyself, O beautiful one, for that marvellous vision is produced from thee, and by thee it is strengthened and yet thou art not able to reach it. Yet behold, He has come forth from His holy place, and He who while resting, nourished the angels, begins a new work and applies Himself to cure our ills. He shall be seen coming and strengthened, who before when resting and nourishing the angels, could not be seen. For He comes leaping upon the mountains, bounding over the hills. By mountains and

hills understand Patriarchs and Prophets; and in the book
of the genealogy you may see how He has come leaping
upon the one and bounding upon the other: Abraham
begot Isaac, Isaac begot Jacob, etc. (S. Matt. i. 2). You
will find that from those mountains came forth the root
of Jesse, from whence, according to the Prophet, came forth
the shoot, and from it uprose the flower upon which rested
the sevenfold Spirit (Is. xi. 1—3). It is that which the
same Prophet explains to us in another place, saying:
*Behold a Virgin shall conceive and bear a Son, and His
name shall be called Emmanuel, which being interpreted,
is, God with us* (Is. vii. 14). Thus what in the former
he called a shoot, he explains in the latter by calling a
Virgin. But it is needful to reserve to another day a
consideration of this very deep mystery; it is a subject
very worthy of a separate sermon, especially as the discourse of to-day has extended to a considerable length.

SERMON II.

*Ask thee a sign of the Lord my God; ask it either in
the depth or in the height above. But Ahaz said, I will not
ask, neither will I tempt the Lord.*   Is. vii. 11.

1. We have in this the prophet Isaiah advising King
Ahaz to ask a sign from the Lord, either in the depth below
or the height above. We hear also his reply, having
indeed a form of piety, but not the power of it : and because
of this he deserved to be reproved by Him who reads
the heart, and to whom the thoughts of man lie open.
Ahaz was filled with pride because he was exalted upon
a throne, and his words show the astuteness of human
wisdom. Esaias then had heard from the Lord : 'Go, say
to that fox that he seek from the Lord a sign in the
depth.' For a fox has his burrow, but even if he shall

descend into the depth of hell, He is there who taketh the wise in their own craftiness : also Go, saith the Lord, say to that bird that he seek a sign in the height above. For the bird hath his nest, but even if he shall climb up into heaven, He is there who resisting the proud, tramples under foot by His strength the necks of the proud and exalted ones. But he pretended not to wish at all to ask of God a sign of His power in the heavens, or of His incomprehensible wisdom in the depth : because of this the Lord Himself promises a sign of His goodness and love for the house of David, so that those whom neither power nor wisdom strike with terror, the display of his love may win over. It is possible also I allow, that in the phrase *"in the depth"* He may have wished to speak of that love that no one has ever exceeded, which made Him die for His friends and descend for them into the depth of Hades : so that King Ahaz might be taught to tremble at the Majesty of Him who reigns on High, or to embrace the love of Him who descends into the depth. Whosoever then has no impulse to tremble at the Majesty of God, nor thinks with gratitude upon His love, is insupportable not only to man but also to God. *Therefore* He says, *the Lord Himself shall give you a sign*, in which both His Majesty and His glory shall be plainly set forth. *Behold, a Virgin shall conceive and bear a Son and call his name Emmanuel, which being interpreted, is, God with us.* Do not seek to fly, O Adam, because it is God who is with us. Do not fear, O man, nor tremble at hearing the name of God : because He is with us, though He is God. With us in likeness of flesh, with us in unity of nature. He comes on our account, He comes as one of us, like us in appearance and equally subject to pain.

2. He says finally : *Butter and honey shall He eat.* As if he said : He shall be an infant, and eat infants' food.

That He may know to refuse the evil and choose the good.
Here also we are told of the good and the evil, as before
of the forbidden tree, the tree of disobedience. But He
the second Adam, made a far better choice than the first;
choosing the good, He rejected the evil, not like him
who delighted in cursing and it came unto him, who
delighted not in blessing and it was far from him (Ps.
cix. 17). In the words which precede ' Butter and honey
shall He eat,' we may understand the choice of this Child.
Now His grace comes to our aid and enables us (which
is a matter of great importance) to think rightly of Him,
and to bring His words suitably to our understanding.
There are two things in milk, butter and cheese; butter
is soft and rich; cheese on the contrary is hard and dry.
Wisely then does this child know how to choose, when
he prefers the first and leaves the second. Who then is
the hundredth sheep who wandered (S. Matt. xviii. 12)
and who speaks in the Psalm: I have gone astray as a
sheep that is lost (Ps. cxix. 176)? Even the human race :
which the Good Shepherd seeks, while the other ninety-
nine are left upon the mountains. In this sheep then are
found two things also : one nature sweet and good, even
very good; that is the butter : and the corruption of sin,
that is the cheese. Notice then how excellently our Child
has chosen, in that He has taken our nature without any
corruption of sin. For it is said concerning sinners under
the Law : *Their heart has been curdled like milk* (Ps. cxix.
70 VULG.) inasmuch as the ferment of malice, the curd of
iniquity, has corrupted the purity of the milk.

3. So also with regard to the bee : if it possesses sweet
honey, it has also a sharp sting. But it is the bee which
feeds among lilies, which dwells in the flowery land of the
Angels. There it took its flight towards the village of
Nazareth (which means a flower) it reached and remained

upon the sweetly perfumed blossom of perpetual virginity. Of its honey and its sting he is not ignorant, who sings with the Prophet, of *mercy and judgment* (Ps. ci. 1). And yet when coming to us, he brings the honey and not the sting, that is mercy and not judgment : for when His disciples begged that the city which would not receive Him, should be destroyed with fire from heaven, He replied, The Son of man has not come to judge the world, but to save it (S. Luke ix. 54—56). Our bee had not then a sting, he was as it were disarmed, when enduring such unworthy treatment. He responded with mercy only, not with judgment. But do not rest your hope on iniquity, do not commit iniquity in that hope. For there shall be a time when our bee shall retake his sting and plunge it deep into the marrow of sinners : since the *Father does not judge any, but hath committed all judgment unto the Son* (S. John v. 22). But at the present the Holy Child eats butter and honey, since He unites in His own Person all that is good in human nature with the mercy which is in God, that He might be truly Man, yet without sin : God merciful and gracious, and not yet showing Himself in judgment.

4. From all this it is clear, what is the stem proceeding from the root of Jesse, what is the Flower upon which rests the Holy Spirit. The Virgin, the *Genitrix Dei*, is the stem, her Son the Flower. Yes, the Son of the Virgin is that Flower *white and glowing red, chiefest among ten thousand* (Cant. v. 10); the Flower upon which the Angels come to gaze, of which the perfume restores life to the dead; and as He Himself declares, a flower of the field, not of the garden (Cant. ii. 1). For the field blooms with flowers without human help; it is not sown nor tilled, nor enriched with nourishment. Thus it was with the womb of the Virgin : inviolate, untouched, it brought forth, as a prairie of living green, this Flower of immortal

fairness, whose glory shall never fade. O, Virgin, lofty
stem, to what an exalted height dost thou attain! even to
Him who sitteth upon the throne, unto the Lord of Glory.
Nor is this strange, since thou sendest deeply into the
ground the roots of humility.

O plant truly heavenly, more precious and pure than all
others, truly the tree of life, which was found worthy to
bear the fruit of salvation! Thy cunning, O malignant serpent, has overreached itself; thy falseness is made evident.
Two charges thou hadst brought against the Creator; of
untruth, and of envy: and in each thou hast been shown
to have lied. He, to whom thou didst say, *Thou shalt
by no means die* (Gen. iii. 4), dies from the beginning;
and the truth of the Lord endureth for ever (Ps. cxvii.
2). Tell me, if thou canst, what tree there is whose fruit
can be an object of envy to him, to whom God has not
denied this chosen stem and its lofty fruit? *He who
spared not His own Son, how shall He not with Him
also freely give us all things?* (Rom. viii. 32).

5. You have now understood, I think, that the Virgin
is that royal way. by which the Saviour came to us;
proceeding from her womb, as a bridegroom from his
chamber. Pursuing then the way, which we began to
investigate, if you remember, in my former sermon, let
us endeavour, brethren, to ascend to Him by it, as by it
He descended to us: and by it to come into His grace,
who by it descended to share our unhappiness. By
thee let us have access to thy Son, O thou who wast
blessed in finding grace, and becoming the mother of the
Life and the Salvation. May He who was given to us
by thee, by thee receive us also. May thy holiness excuse with Him the fault of our corruption, and thy humility, pleasing to God, plead for pardon of our vanity. May
thy abundant charity conceal the multitude of our sins,

and thy fulness make us fruitful also in good works. Our
Lady, our mediatrix, our advocate, reconcile us, commend
us, represent us to thy Son. Do so, O blessed one, by
the grace which thou hast found by the prerogative which
thou hast merited, by the mercy of which thou art mother;
so that He who has deigned to become, by thy means,
a sharer of our weakness and our misery, Jesus Christ thy
Son, our Lord, may at thy intercession, make us sharers
of His glory and blessedness, who is above all, God blessed
for ever. Amen.

SERMON III.

OF THE THREEFOLD COMING OF THE LORD, AND OF THE SEVEN COLUMNS WHICH WE OUGHT TO RAISE UP IN OURSELVES.

*He was in the world, and the world was made by Him,
and the world knew Him not.* S. JOHN i. 10.

1. In the Advent of the Lord which we are celebrating,
if I look on the Person of Him who comes, I cannot grasp
the excellence of His Majesty; and if I regard those to whom
He came, I tremble at the greatness of His condescension.
Certainly the Angels themselves are astonished at the
newness of the prodigy, as they see below themselves
Him, who being above them, they continually adore, and
as they ascend and descend to the Son of Man. If I
consider for what reason He came, I embrace to the utmost of my poor powers, the wide reach of His priceless
charity. If I regard the manner of His coming, I am
struck with the ennoblement it effected in the human
condition. In fact, He who is the Creator and Lord of
the universe, comes to men, comes on account of men,
comes as Man. But someone will say: 'In what way can
He be said to have *come*, who has always been everywhere? It is very true that *He was in the world, and the*

world was made by Him, and the world knew Him not.
(S. John i. 10). He did not then come into the world as
if He had ever been out of the world, but He became
visible there who had before been invisible. That is why
He took upon Him a human form in which He might
be known by others, since He dwelt in *the Divine Light
which none can approach unto* (1 Tim. vi. 16). Nor was
it altogether inglorious to the Majesty of God, to show
himself in His own likeness which He had made in the
beginning, nor unworthy of God to allow Himself to be
beheld in a bodily form by those who were not able to
behold Him in His substance. So that He who had made
man in His own image and likeness, should Himself when
become man, be made manifest to man.

2. It is then the Advent of so exalted a Majesty, an
Advent of so profound condescension, of so great charity,
and also of a glory so great for us, that the whole Church
solemnly celebrates the remembrance of, once each year. But
would that it were so celebrated now, as it will be always
in eternity. That would be more worthy of it. For how
great a folly is it, that after the coming of so great a thing
men should wish or should dare to busy themselves with
other things; and not rather to lay other things aside and
employ themselves wholly in His worship, so as not to bear in
mind anything else in his Presence? But all men are not
of those of whom the Prophet says: *They shall abundantly utter the meaning of Thy great goodness* (Ps. cxlv.
7). Nor do all bear this in memory, for no one speaks
of that which he has not tasted, or has only just tasted;
and the mouth exhales the odour of that only with which
the man is filled and satiated. Those whose mind and whose
life is entirely of this world, never exhale the sweet odour
of these spiritual truths, even although they recall them to
memory; and they observe such days as these without devo-

tion or affection, by the force of lifeless custom. Lastly, the very memory of this inestimable condescension is taken (which is most shocking) for an occasion to the flesh, so that men may be seen on these solemn days full of anxiety about the splendour of vestments, and preparing more delicate food, as if Christ sought these things, or things of this kind, in His Nativity, and as if it were more worthily commemorated, the more things of this kind were carefully prepared. But hear what He Himself says: *he who hath a proud look and a greedy heart, with him I will not eat* (Ps. ci. 5). Why do you prepare vestures with such ambition for the day of My birth? I detest pride, I will not endure it. Why do you lay up with such anxious care, stores of dainties for that time? I condemn and will not accept the delights of the flesh. Evidently you are insatiable in heart, to procure for yourself so many things and from so great a distance: since the body would be satisfied with fewer, and those more easy to be procured. Though, then, you are celebrating my Advent, you are honouring Me only with your lips, and your heart is far from me. It is not I whom you worship, but your god is your belly, and your glory is your shame. Altogether unhappy is he who seeks for the pleasures of the senses, and honours the vanity of this present world. *Blessed is the people whose God is the Lord* (Ps. cxliv. 15).

3. *Brethren, fret not yourselves because of evil doers, nor be envious against the workers of iniquity* (Ps. xxxviii. 1). Rather look to the end which awaits them, pity them in your heart, and pray for those who are surprised into some transgression. Those unhappy ones act thus because they are ignorant of God. If they had known Him, they would not so madly provoke against themselves the Lord of glory. But we, dear brethren, have no excuse on the score of ignorance. It is certain that you, who-

soever you are, have come to know Him, and if you should say, I know him not, you would be like worldly people, deceitful. For if you have not known Him; who brought thee hither or why art thou here? If you do not know Him at all, how have you been brought to renounce spontaneously the affection of your friends, the pleasures of the flesh, the vanities of the world, and to devote all your thoughts to God, to lay every care that you have upon Him, if your conscience bears you witness that you have deserved nothing good, or rather so much evil, at his hands. Who could have persuaded you (I ask again) if indeed you knew Him not, how good the Lord is to those who trust in Him, to the soul that seeks Him; and if you had not known for yourself how sweet and gentle is the Lord, how full of mercy and truth? But whence have you come to know this, if not because He has come, not only to you but also within you?

4. The coming of Christ is in fact threefold; to men, within men, against men. He has come to all men without distinction; but not so within all men or against all men. The first and the third kind of coming are well known, since they are open to all eyes; as to the second, which is secret and spiritual, listen to what He Himself says: *If a man love Me, he will keep my words, and my Father will love him, and We will come unto Him and make our abode with Him* (S. John xiv. 23). Blessed is he, O Lord Jesus, in whom thou makest Thy abode. Blessed is he in whom Wisdom builds for herself a house and hews her out seven columns. Blessed is the soul which is the abode of Wisdom! But what is that soul? It is the soul of the righteous. How should it be otherwise, since it is justice and judgment which prepare for wisdom her seat! Who is there among you, brethren, who desires earnestly to prepare in his soul a habitation for Christ? Behold what silken

hangings, what rich carpets, what a softly cushioned couch it is needful to prepare for Him! *Justice,* He says, *and judgment, are the habitation of Thy seat* (Ps. lxxxix. 14). Justice, because it is the virtue which renders to each that which is his own. Render therefore to three sorts of persons that which is theirs, and that which is their due from you; to your superiors, to your inferiors, and to your equals; and then you will celebrate worthily the Advent of Christ, and prepare for Him His seat in justice. Render, I say, the reverence due to him who is set over you, and obedience; of which the former is a virtue of the heart, the latter of the body. It is not sufficient to yield to our elders in action only, unless in the depth of our hearts we have feelings of respect for them. If it should happen that the life of a superior should be so manifestly unworthy, as not to admit of being passed over, nor of being excused; even then, because of Him from whom comes all power, we ought to have respect even for such a superior; if not because he merits it himself, at least by consideration for the order established by God, and for the dignity of the charge which he bears.

5. So also we owe to the brethren among whom we live, our counsel and our help, by the double claim of human association and of brotherhood. For these, we on our side, desire that they should bestow upon us : advice to instruct our inexperience, and help to supply our weakness. But perhaps there is someone among you who will silently reply to this : What advice can I give to my brother, when I am not permitted to say a simple word to him without licence? Or what help can I render to him, not being able to do the least thing beyond the law of obedience? To which I reply : You will always find something to do for your brother, if you have a feeling of brotherly kindness for him. No advice, I suppose,

could be better for him than that you should study to
instruct him by your good example, what he ought to do
and what he ought to avoid : animating him to better
things, and advising him, not by tongue or by word,
but by deed and in truth. Can any help be more
useful and efficacious than to pray earnestly for him,
not to neglect to reprove his faults, and not merely
to avoid putting in his way any occasion of falling,
but to remove such out of his way to the utmost of
your power, as an angel of peace; taking away scan-
dals from the Kingdom of God, and also the occasions of
such? If you afford to your brother such assistance and
such counsels, you will discharge your debt in his behalf,
nor will he have any right to complain of you.

6. But are you placed over others? then indeed you
owe to them the duty of a fuller solicitude ; and they
require of you vigilance and discipline. Vigilance, that
offences may be prevented; discipline, that whoever offends,
may not escape unpunished. But if you have none
other under your authority, you have at all events yourself, and towards yourself you ought to exercise both
vigilance and discipline. Without doubt it is the appointed
task of your soul to direct your body; you ought then
to be vigilant over it, so that in it sin may not reign,
nor make your members instruments of iniquity. You
ought to discipline it, that it may be mortified and rendered obedient, and bring forth worthy fruits of penitence.
Yet the debt of those who have to answer for many souls
is more weighty and perilous. Miserable man that I am,
whither shall I go, if I am too careless in guiding so great
a treasure, so precious a deposit as (a soul) for which
Christ thought good to shed His blood! If it had been
permitted to collect at the foot of the Cross the Blood of
Jesus as It dropped from His wounds, and if It were

stored in a vase of crystal that it behoved me to carry about wherever I went; what apprehensions should I not feel for the danger I ran? And it is certain that I have received into my charge such a treasure, for which a wise merchant, indeed Wisdom Himself, gave His own Blood. More than this, the treasure is in fragile vases, exposed to many more dangers than those of glass. It adds to the burden of my care and the weight of my anxiety, that although I have the charge of my neighbour's conscience as well as my own, I have no certain knowledge either of the one or the other. Each of them is an unfathomable abyss, a dark mystery, to me, nevertheless the safe custody of each is required of me, and I hear a voice which calls to me: *Watchman, what of the night? Watchman, what of the night?* (Is. xxi. 11). It is not for me to reply with Cain, *Am I my brother's keeper?* (Gen. iv. 9), but to confess humbly with the prophet: *Unless the Lord keep the city, the watchman waketh but in vain* (Ps. cxxvii. 1). I am to be held excused in this, only by the care with which I have discharged the duty which, as I have said before, I owe, equally, of vigilance and of discipline. If these four things are not wanting: reverence and due obedience to superiors, counsel and help to equals, all of which justice requires, then Wisdom will not find her seat unprepared.

7. We may perhaps call these six out of the seven columns which she hews out in the house which she has built for herself: let us now consider what is the seventh, if Wisdom will deign to enable us to find it. As, then, the six were found in justice, why should not the seventh be understood of judgment? For not justice alone, but *justice* it is said, *and judgment are the preparation of thy seat.* Finally, if we render to our superiors, to our equals, to our inferiors that which is due to them, shall we render

nothing to God? But of a certainty, no one can repay unto Him the whole of our obligations, because He has heaped upon us the treasures of His mercy; so great is the multitude of our faults, so weak and insignificant are we, while He is great and sufficient to Himself, and needs nothing that we can give. Yet I have heard one to whom He had revealed the secrets and the mysteries of His wisdom, say that *the honour of the King loveth justice* (Ps. xcix. 4). He asks for nothing from us which He does not find in Himself : only let us confess our iniquities and He will justify us freely, so that His grace may be made manifest. He loves the soul which considers and judges its own condition constantly and without pretence, as in His sight. This judgment He demands of us for our own sake : because if we judge our own selves, we shall not be judged. Therefore he who is wise, suspects his own doings, examines and weighs them with care, and judges them without prejudice. That man honours the truth, who acknowledges without reserve and confesses in all humility that which he finds himself to be. If you would be convinced that God demands of us all judgment according to justice, hear what He says : *When you shall have done all that is commanded to you, say, we are unprofitable servants* (S. Luke xvii. 10). This is, as far as man is concerned, a worthy preparation for the Lord, of His throne of majesty ; that he should both study to observe the commandments of righteousness, and should acknowledge his endeavour and himself to be imperfect and unprofitable.

SERMON IV.

Of His twofold Advent; and of the zeal we ought to
have for true virtue.

*The foolish said unto the wise, Give us of your oil, for
our lamps are gone out.*   S. MATT. xxv. 8.

1. It is proper, brethren, that you should celebrate the
Advent of the Lord with all possible devotion, that you
should be cheered by so great a consolation, should
realize so vast a condescension, and be moved to gratitude
by such Divine love.

But be not content to think only of the first Advent,
in which He came to seek and to save that which was
lost, but think also of the second, in which He shall come
and take us to be with Him. Would that you were
unceasingly occupied in meditating upon those two Advents, in making yourselves familiar in thought with all
He has done in the first, and all that He promises in the
second. Would that you slept as it were between these
two heritages. For these are the two arms of the Bridegroom, of which the bride reposing said: *His left hand
shall be under my head, and His right hand shall embrace
me* (Cant. ii. 6). For indeed, as we read elsewhere, *In
His left hand are riches and glory, and in His right, length of
days* (Prov. iii. 16). O sons of Adam, ambitious and
greedy race, listen to this: *In His left hand are riches
and glory.* Why do you strive for earthly and temporal
glory, which are not really what they claim, nor belong to
you at all? What are gold and silver, but red earth and
white earth, which only the error of men makes to be, or
rather thinks to be precious? Again if these things were
truly yours, you could take them away with you when you
die. But no, when man perishes, he takes with him none of

those things, nor shall his glory follow him into the tomb.

2. The true riches do not consist in treasures, but in virtues; which the conscience of a man bears with him and renders him rich for ever. As for glory, the Apostle says of it: *Our glory is this, the testimony of a good conscience* (2 Cor. I. 12). This is indeed true glory, which is from the Spirit of truth. *For the Spirit Himself beareth witness with our spirit that we are the sons of God* (Rom. viii. 16). But the glory which they who seek not the glory which comes from God alone, receive from each other in turn, is vain; since the children of men are themselves foolish. O foolish man, who storest thy merchandise in a sack full of holes, who makest the mouth of another thy treasure house! Dost thou not know that that chest cannot be made fast, and has no bolts? How much wiser are they who themselves guard their treasure and do not confide it to others: Will they indeed keep it safe always? Will they hold it always hidden? A day shall come when the secrets of the heart shall be revealed, and those things which have been merely pretended, shall vanish altogether. Hence it is that when the Lord is coming, the lamps of the foolish virgins are gone out (S. Matt. xxv. 8) and those are not owned by the Lord who have received their reward in this world (S. Matt. vi. 17). Wherefore I say to you, dear brethren, that if we have anything precious, it is better to hide it, than to make a show of it. We must do as beggars when they ask alms: they do not display costly garments, but limbs half naked, or ulcers if they have them, so that compassion may be more excited in the mind of the spectator. The observance of this rule of conduct the publican in the Gospel followed much better than the Pharisee: therefore he returned to his house justified rather than the other (S. Luke xviii. 14), that is, in preference to him.

3. It is time, brethren, that judgment should begin at the house of God. What shall be the end of those who do not obey the Gospel of Christ? What judgment for those who do not rise up in this judgment? Those who have no wish to have part in this judgment, which is now, in which the prince of this world is cast out, have reason to expect, or rather have reason greatly to fear, the Judge who will cast them out themselves with their prince. But as for us, if we are perfectly judged now, we may await with entire security the coming of the Lord Jesus Christ, *who will change the body of our humility and make it like to the body of His glory* (Phil. iii. 21). Then shall the righteous shine, the unlearned equally with the learned; they shall shine forth as the sun in the kingdom of their Father (S. Matt. xiii. 43). And then the *brightness of the sun shall be sevenfold* (Is. xxx. 26) that is, as the light of seven days.

4. The Saviour then, when He comes, shall transform the body of our humility, and make it like unto the body of His glory, provided that our heart has been previously transformed and made like unto the humility of His heart. Therefore He said: *Learn of Me, for I am meek and lowly in heart* (S. Matt. xi. 29). Remark on this subject that there are two kinds of humility, as the words of the Saviour indicate; the one of conviction, the other of feeling or, as it is here called, *of the heart*. By the first we are enabled to recognize our nothingness; and this we can learn by ourselves alone, and even in our own weakness; by the second we are enabled to trample under foot the glory of the world; and this we learn from Him *who emptied Himself and took upon Him the form of a servant*, (Phil. ii. 7). Who, when he was sought for to be made a king, fled; and when He was sought for to endure the shameful, ignominious punishment of the Cross, presented

Himself of His own accord. If then we wish to sleep between the two heritages, that is to say, between the two Advents of Christ, we need to have the wings, covered with silver, of a dove (Ps. lxviii. 13), that is to say, that we should hold fast that model of virtues which Christ when he was in the flesh, taught by word and by example. For we may not improperly understand by those words "covered with silver," His Humility, and by "Gold" His Divinity.

5. Thus then all our virtue is as far from true virtue as it is different from that model of virtue shown us in Christ; and (so to speak) the wing is of no value if it be not "covered with silver." A wing of great power is that of poverty, by which we fly so quickly into the kingdom of heaven. For to all the other virtues which come after it, promises are only made for the future; but to poverty it is not promises for the future that are given, but an actual gift in the present. He says: *Blessed are the poor in spirit, for theirs is the kingdom of heaven* (S. Matt. v. 3), whilst in speaking of the other virtues it is said, "They shall inherit, they shall be comforted, etc" and similar words. For we see some poor people who, if they had a true poverty, would not be so sorrowful and fearful, since the kingdom of heaven would be their portion. Such are they who are willingly poor, provided that they want for nothing: and who love poverty on the express condition that they are called upon to endure no privation. Such are those also who are gentle, but only as long as nothing is said and nothing is done contrary to their will; for it will soon appear how far they are from true gentleness, if a slight provocation should occur. How could such gentleness as this have part in a heritage, which fails before the heritage appears? I see others also who have the gift of tears: but if these tears proceeded from

the heart, they would not so easily give place to laughter. But now when thoughtless and abusive words flow more abundantly from their lips than tears did before from their eyes; I cannot conclude, that it is to tears of this kind that Divine consolation is promised, since they are so easily dried by weak and silly consolations. Others inveigh so violently against the offences of others that one might believe that they have truly a hunger and thirst for right-eousness; but they are far from regarding their own faults with the same severity: *now divers weights are an abomination unto the Lord* (Prov. xx. 23). Again there are those who abuse others with a violence as impudent as it is useless, while they flatter themselves with as much folly as falseness.

6. There are some persons who are benevolent with goods which do not belong to themselves, who are scandalized if abundant charity is not distributed to all, provided that they do not themselves suffer in the smallest degree. If they were truly benevolent, it would be from their own goods that they would give alms; and if they were not able to bestow temporal goods, they would at least give with good will their forgiveness to those who perhaps are thought to have offended them. They would at all events bestow a sign of goodwill, a kind word, which is worth more than the best present, in order to excite the minds of those offending them to regret. In short they would pour out willingly compassion and prayer both upon these and upon all whom they knew to be in sin. Otherwise their pity is of no value, and they attain unto no true pity. Also those who so confess their sins, as to make it appear that they are actuated by the desire of making their conscience clear (since all faults are washed away by confession of them), yet are not able to hear with patience the avowal by others of similar offences to those they themselves

confess. These, if they truly wished to be purified, as they seem to do, would not treat those harshly who avow to them their failings, but forgive them. There are those also who will take great pain to appease any one who is angry and irritated, even about a small thing, and so may pass for true peacemakers: yet if anything is said or done against themselves, are very slow and reluctant to forgive it. But if they truly cared for peace, they would seek it also for themselves.

7. Let us then cover (as it were) our wings with silver by communion with Christ, as the holy Martyrs made their robes white by union with His Passion. Let us imitate as far as we are able, Him who so loved poverty that when the whole earth was in His power, He *had not where to lay His Head* (S. Luke ix. 58); Him whose disciples, as we read, were obliged to rub the ears of corn between their hands to satisfy their hunger, as they went through the cornfields (S. Luke vi. 1); *Who was led as a lamb to the slaughter, and as a sheep is dumb before the shearer, so He opened not His mouth* (Is. liii. 7); Who wept, as we read, over Lazarus and over Jerusalem (S. John xi. 35, S. Luke xix. 41). and Who passed whole nights in prayer. Who is never recorded to have either laughed or jested; Who so hungered for righteousness that though He had no sins of His own to atone for, He made so great a satisfaction to expiate ours. Even upon the Cross He thirsted for nothing else than righteousness; He did not hesitate to die for His enemies, and prayed even for His executioners; He did no sin, and bore patiently the sins of others which were laid upon Him; Who endured so great sufferings, that He might reconcile sinners to Himself.

SERMON V.

OF THAT COMING OF THE LORD WHICH IS BETWEEN HIS FIRST
ADVENT AND HIS LAST: AND OF THE THREEFOLD RENEWAL.

All flesh shall see the salvation of God. S. LUKE iii. 6.

1. I have already said that the two inheritances between
which those are to rest, who have covered their wings
with silver, signify the two Advents of Jesus Christ: But
I have not yet said where is the place of their rest. For
there is a third coming which is midway between the
other two, and in this they who know him may rest with
gladness. The two others are visible, the third is not. In
the first Advent Jesus showed Himself upon the earth and
went about among men; when, as He Himself bears witness,
they both saw Him and hated (S. John xv. 24). And
in the last *all flesh shall see the salvation of our God*
(S. Luke iii. 6), and *they shall behold Him whom they
have pierced* (S. John xix. 37). But there is a coming
between these, in which only the elect behold the Saviour, in
their own souls, and are saved. Thus in the first Advent
He came in our flesh and in our weakness; in the second
in the spirit and in power; in the last in glory and majesty. By power He attains to glory; for the Lord of
Power *He is the King of glory* (Ps. xxiv. 10). And again
that I may see Thy power and Thy glory (Ps. lxiii. 2).
The second coming then is, as it were, the way which
conducts from the first to the last. In the first Christ
was our Redemption; in the last He shall appear as our Life;
in the second, that we may rest between these two heritages, He is our rest and our consolation. That you may
not suppose that what I say of this second coming is an
invention of my own; listen to His own words. *If any
man love Me he will keep My words: and My Father will*

love him and we will come to him (S. John xiv. 23). But
what does He mean by these words? For I read elsewhere,
He that feareth the Lord will do good (Ecclus. xv. 1):
but I think that something more is said of him who loves
God, viz., that he will keep the words of God. But where
are they to be kept? In the heart, without doubt, as says
the Prophet: *Thy word have I hid in my heart that I
might not sin against Thee* (Ps. cxix. 11). But how are
they to be preserved in the heart? Or is it sufficient to
preserve them only in the memory? But the Apostle
says to those who thus preserve them, *Knowledge puffeth
up* (1 Cor. viii. 1). And besides, that which is committed
only to the memory is easily forgotten. We ought then
so to keep the word of God as we are able to keep the
food of the body, and we can do this more easily, as that
word is itself the Bread of Life, the food of the soul.
Earthly bread, whilst it is in the chest, may be stolen by
a thief, may be gnawed by the mice, may be corrupted
by age. But when you have eaten it, you need fear none
of these dangers. In this way then keep the Word of God:
For blessed are they who hear it and keep it (S. Luke
xi. 28). Let it be deposited in the inmost parts of your
soul, let it pass into your affections and into your character. Feed upon this good food to the full, and your
soul shall delight itself in fatness. Do not forget to feed
upon this your bread, that your heart may not become
exhausted; but let your soul be filled with its fatness.

2. If you keep the word of God thus, without doubt
you will be kept by it. For the Son shall come to you
with the Father, that great Prophet shall come who will
rebuild Jerusalem and will make all things new. His coming
will work this effect upon us, that *as we have borne the
image of the earthly we shall also bear the image of the
heavenly* (1 Cor. xv. 49). And just as the old Adam was

spread through the entire man and occupied him wholly, so Christ shall possess us wholly, as He created us wholly, redeemed us wholly, and shall glorify and save the whole man in the great Sabbath of the world. Once the old man was in us, that deceiver was in us, so that he acted by our hands, spoke by our mouths and felt in our heart. With our hands doubly, by sin and by shame; by our mouth also, by pride and by envy. And in our heart also, by the desires of the flesh and the desires of worldly glory. But now, if we have become a new creature in Christ, the old things have passed away, and instead of sin and shame we have innocence and purity. In our mouth, in place of pride, we have humble confession, and words of edification have taken the place of detraction. In our hearts, instead of the desires of the flesh, there is charity; and humility instead of the thirst for worldly glory.

See now in these three renewals the way in which each one among the elect receives Christ the Word of God. To them He says; *Set me as a seal upon thy heart, as a signet upon thy arm* (Cant. viii. 6). And in another place: *The word is near thee, in thy mouth and in thy heart*, (Rom. x. 8).

SERMON VI.

OF THE THREEFOLD COMING OF THE LORD, AND OF THE RESURRECTION OF THE BODY.

We look for the Saviour, the Lord Jesus Christ, who shall change the body of our humiliation, that it may be made like to the body of His glory.   Phil. iii. 20—21.

1. I am unwilling, brethren, that you should be ignorant of the time of your visitation, and especially of the object with which God visits us in this time of our probation. Our souls, not our bodies supply the reason for this visit-

ation : for the soul being far more worthy than the
body, claims by the very excellence of its nature to be
the first object of care. And since it appears to have
been the first to fall, it is also the first to be raised up
again. For the soul commenced to be corrupted when
it fell into sin; and it was the cause why the body also
was made liable to corruption as a penalty. So then, if
we wish to be found true members of Christ, we must
without doubt follow Him our Head : and must have it
chiefly at heart to make good the injuries of our souls,
for which He has already come into the world, and whose
disease He first devoted Himself to heal. But as for the
care of our body, we must put it off, and reserve it to
that day when the Saviour shall come, and shall Himself
take up the task of transforming it, as the Apostle declares :
*We look for the Saviour, the Lord Jesus Christ, who
shall change the body of our humiliation that it may be
made like to the body of His glory.* At the time of His
first Advent, S. John Baptist, being truly His herald and
forerunner, cried unto men : *Behold the Lamb of God,
who taketh away the sin of the world* (S. John i. 29).
He does not say, the diseases of the body; not, the
infirmities of the flesh; but *sin ;* and sin is the disease of
the soul, the corruption of the mind. This He takes away
from the hands, from the eyes, from the neck, and in short
from the whole of our flesh, in which it is deeply rooted.

2. He takes away sin from the hands, blotting out the
sins they have committed : from the eyes, purifying the
intention of the mind : He takes it from the neck, by
destroying the tyrannical yoke which weighed upon it,
according as it is written : *Thou hast broken the sceptre
of his oppressor, as in the days of Midian* (Is. ix. 4), and
also : *The yoke shall be destroyed because of the anointing*
(Is. x. 27). The Apostle also well says : *Let not sin*‧

reign in your mortal body (Rom. vi. 12). And the same
in another place : I know that in me (that is in my flesh)
dwelleth no good thing : and again : *O wretched man that
I am! who shall deliver me from the body of this death?*
(Rom. vii. 18, 24). For he knew that he would not be
delivered from that calamitous germ of sin, which was
deeply rooted in his flesh, as long as he was not freed
from the body itself. Wherefore he desired to be *released
and to be with Christ* (Phil. i. 23) : knowing that sin,
which separates between us and God, cannot altogether
be done away, until we are freed from the body. You
have heard of that man whom the Lord delivered from
the demon, who tore and tortured him grievously, before
He came out at the bidding of the Lord. Therefore I
say to you that the particular kind of sin which so often
destroys the peace of our souls (I mean concupiscence
and evil desires) can be and ought to be, by the grace of
God, overcome in us, so that it should not reign in us
any longer, nor make our members to be weapons of iniquity
unto sin; but it cannot be altogether done away except
by death, when we are so torn asunder, that our soul is
separated from our body.

3. You know for what purpose Christ has come, and
that the Christian ought to endeavour to attain that same
purpose. Therefore do not, O my body, preoccupy my
time : for you may well hinder the salvation of my soul,
but your own salvation you cannot accomplish. *For all
things there is a time* (Eccles. iii. 1). Let the soul strive
now on its own behalf, and do you become even its fellow labourer : since if you suffer with it, with it you
shall also reign. Insomuch as you hinder its salvation,
in the same degree you hinder your own : for not until
the image of God is restored in it, can you be restored
to your original excellency. You have a noble guest, O

body, a noble guest indeed, and all your well-being depends upon it. Give honour then to so great a guest. You dwell in your own land : but your soul is a stranger and a foreigner, to which you have given shelter. What peasant is there, let me ask you, who, if some powerful and noble seigneur wished to take up his abode in his cottage, would not most willingly receive him, and himself lie down to sleep in some corner of his house, under the stairs or on the very hearth, in order to yield his place of rest, as was proper, to his illustrious guest? Do you then do likewise : count for nothing your privations and your sufferings; think of only one thing, that your guest should be treated honourably as long as he remains in your house. It is an honour to you to expose yourself to discomfort, as long as he shall remain with you.

4. And in order that you may not despise the guest you are sheltering, or think less of it than it deserves, precisely because it is a stranger and an exile; notice carefully, of how great advantage to you its presence is the cause. For it is because this living soul is present with you, that sight is given to your eyes : it is this inmate who supplies speech to your tongue, taste to your palate, motion to all your limbs. If there is any life, any sensibility, any beauty in you, remember that you owe it all to the presence of this your guest. In short, its departure gives proof of the benefits that its presence bestowed. For when the soul departs, instantly the tongue will become silent; the eyes will no longer see, the ears will no longer hear, the countenance will grow pale, and the whole body rigid. Then in a short space of time, there will be only a corpse falling into offensive corruption, and your beauty will be changed into foulness.

Why then do you distress and wound by your carnal delights, this your guest, when you would not be able even to feel anything except by its means? When this exile, driven from the face of God because of enmity, is restored to it by reconciliation, of how great service will it be to you! Do not hinder, O body, that reconciliation, because a great glory is being prepared from thence for you. Suffer all things patiently and gladly: and do not shrink from anything that may help on the reconciliation. Say to your guest: When your Lord shall remember you, and restore you to your former place, remember me, I pray you (Gen. xl. 14).

5. If you will serve it well, it will certainly remember you for good: and when the guest shall have reached the presence of its Lord, he will plead for you for good, in gratitude for the good he has received from you, saying: When your servant was in exile for his fault, a certain poor man with whom I lodged, had mercy upon me: would that my Lord would reward him for it. In the first place he put himself and all that he had at my disposition, not sparing himself on my account, in frequent fasts, in labours and watchings beyond measure, in hunger and thirst, in cold and nakedness. What then? The scripture tells us truly: *He will fulfil the desire of them that fear Him: He will hear their cry and will help them* (Ps. cxlv. 19). O my body, if you could only taste of that sweetness: if you could only form an idea of that glory! What I am about to say, will perhaps surprise you; yet there is nothing more certain, nothing less doubtful to those who are faithful. The God of Hosts, the Lord of Power, the King of Glory, shall Himself come from the height of heaven, to change our bodies, and to render them like unto the body of His glory. What shall be that glory, that ineffable joy, when the Creator of the world, who was hidden under a humble exterior, when He came to save souls, shall appear manifest in all His glory

and His majesty, and no longer in weakness, in order to glorify thee, O miserable flesh! Who can think [without gladness] of the day of His Advent, when He shall come down in the fulness of light, preceded by angels, and with such a sound of trumpets as shall summon from the dust our bodies, and we shall be caught up to meet Christ in the clouds?

6. How long then will the unhappy flesh, foolish, blind, thoughtless and almost insane, seek transitory and failing delights which ought rather to be called desolations, so as to cause it to be rejected, and judged unworthy of this glory, or rather I should say, to be exposed to unspeakable torment for ever? Let it not be so with you, I pray you, brethren; but rather let our soul delight itself in these Advent thoughts; let our flesh rest in this hope, and wait for our Saviour the Lord Jesus Christ, who shall change it, and make it like to the body of His glory; for thus says the Prophet: *My soul thirsteth for Thee, my flesh longeth for Thee* (Ps. lxiii. 1). The soul of the prophet longed for the first Advent, by which it was to be redeemed, but much more still did his flesh long for the latter Advent, to be glorified. Then our desires shall be fulfilled, and all the earth be filled with the glory of the Lord. To that glory, to that felicity, to that peace which passes all understanding, may He in His mercy bring us; and may the Saviour for whom we wait, JESUS CHRIST our LORD, who is blessed above all for ever, let us not be disappointed in our hope.

SERMON VII.

OF THE THREEFOLD FRUIT OF THE ADVENT OF CHRIST.

If God be for us, who can be against us?   ROM. viii. 31.

1. If we celebrate with devotion the Advent of the

Lord, we only do that which we are bound to do : since He who needs nothing of us, has come, not only to us, but on our account. The greatness of His condescension shows clearly the greatness of our need. For as the peril of a disease is indicated by the costliness of the cure, so the number of diseases is shown by the multitude of the remedies to which recourse is had. For why such a diversity of graces, if there was not a corresponding diversity of needs? It is difficult to pass in review in a single discourse all the needs which we experience : but at present three occur to my mind which are common to all, and may be regarded as our chief needs. For there is no one among us who has no need sometimes of guidance, of aid, and of protection; and this may be called the threefold need of all human beings. Whosoever we are, who walk in this valley of the shadow of death, in weakness of body, and in constant liability to temptation, if we reflect seriously, we shall see that we are unhappily liable to this threefold trouble. For we are easily open to be led into evil, we are weak in doing good, and have little power to resist temptation. If we try to distinguish between good and evil, we make mistakes; if we try to do good, we fail; if we try to resist evil, we are cast down and overcome.

2. On that account the coming of the Saviour was needful; and the presence of Christ is still needful, because of the condition of men. May God grant that He may not only come to us in the fulness of His grace, but dwelling in our hearts by faith, may enlighten our darkness, may help our weakness, and casting the shield of His protection over us, may supply our need of strength. If He is in us, who will be able to lead us in error? If He is with us, of what shall we men not be capable, in Him who strengtheneth us? *If He is for us, who can be against*

us? He is a faithful counsellor, who cannot be deceived, nor is able to deceive: He is a strong helper who does not know fatigue; He is a prevailing protector, who is able to tread Satan himself under our feet, and to bring to nothing all his devices. For He is the very Wisdom of God, who is able to make the ignorant wise: He is the Power of God, who is able both to succour the fainting and rescue those involved in danger. Therefore, brethren, in every time of doubt, let us have recourse to this wise councillor: let us invoke this strong helper in all that we have to do: let us commit our souls in every time of struggle to this faithful defender. For this very purpose He came into the world, that He might dwell in men, with men and for men; that He might enlighten our darkness, that He might relieve our troubles, and might protect us against the dangers by which we are threatened.

SERMON VIII. [1]

The Angel Gabriel was sent from God unto a city of Galilee, named Nazareth, to a virgin espoused to a man whose name was Joseph, of the house of David; and the Virgin's name was Mary.   S. Luke i. 26, 27.

1. With what intention did the Evangelist in this place enter so significantly into the enumeration of so many

---

[1] *Note on the four following Homilies.* These four Homilies are one of the earliest works of S. Bernard, and are usually entitled "Upon the *Missus est*" (S. Luke i. 26), but are sometimes entitled "Of the Praises of the Virgin Mother". See Preface, also Letter 18 to Peter the Cardinal Deacon; also Letter 77 to Hugo, c. 5 (Treatise concerning Baptism), where he explains a statement in this first discourse, and defends it from objection.

[2] Hom. I., on the Vigil of Our Lord's Nativity.

proper names? Without doubt, it was in order that we might give to his recital a degree of attention equal to the care which he himself showed in making it. You see that he mentions the names of the messenger who was sent, of the Lord by whom he was sent, of the Virgin to whom he was sent, and of the betrothed of that Virgin: and furthermore he mentions the name of their nation, their village and their province. And are we to suppose that all this was done without special purpose? By no means. For if not a leaf falls from a tree without cause, if a sparrow does not fall to the ground without permission of our Heavenly Father (S. Matt. x. 29), I cannot suppose that a single word flowed uselessly from the mouth of a holy Evangelist, especially in the sacred history of the Word; I cannot, I repeat, believe it. All these details are full of heavenly mysteries, and exhale a celestial sweetness, if they have a diligent reader who knows how to suck honey from the rock, and collect oil from the flinty stone. For *in that day the mountains dropped sweetness, and the hills flowed with milk and honey* (Joel iii. 18); it was the day when the skies dropped dew from above, and the clouds gave the Just One to descend like a refreshing shower; when the earth opened and brought forth the Saviour (Is. xlv. 8); when the Lord gave His blessing and our land yielded her increase (Ps. lxxxv. 12); when mercy and truth met together on the lofty and fertile mountains, and righteousness and peace kissed each other (Ps. lxxxv. 10). At that time also a chief one among these mountains (I mean this holy Evangelist) relates to us sweetly and eloquently the long desired commencement of our salvation, as with the breath of the south wind, and under the shining beams of the Sun of righteousness pouring forth spiritual odours. May God now send forth His Word and cause them to fall around us; may He

19

breathe upon us with His Spirit, and cause us to comprehend the words of the Gospel: may He render them
sweeter than honey and the honeycomb, more longed for
by our hearts than gold and precious stone!

2. He says then: *The Angel Gabriel was sent from
God.* I suppose that this angel was not one of those of
lesser dignity, who are sent frequently upon the earth to
discharge ordinary missions: his name is given, as it is
said to mean, *Strength of God:* also he does not come as
is usual, at the order of a spirit of higher rank than himself, but is said to be sent by God Himself. And we
must understand by these words *by God,* that the counsel
of God was revealed to no other of the blessed spirits,
before the Virgin, excepting only the Archangel Gabriel;
who was alone found worthy among the rest of the angels
of a similar rank, of the name which he received, and of
the mission which was intrusted to him. Nor is the
name without relation to the mission. For what angel
did it better befit to announce the coming of Christ, Who
is the Power of God, than he whose very name signifies
Strength of God? For what else is power than strength?
Nor let it seem unbecoming or unsuitable that the Lord
and the messenger should bear the same name; since
although they are similarly named, that is not for similar
reasons. For Christ is called the strength or the power
of God in one sense, and the angel in another. It is only
a matter of appointment (*nuncupative*) that the angel is
so called, but Christ is called so, according to His nature
(*substantive*); He both is and is called the Power of God
(1 Cor. i. 24); He is the stronger man armed spoken of
in the Gospel, who has overthrown by His own power
the armed man who kept his house in peace, and has
taken from him his spoils. But the angel is called the
strength of God, either because he had been honoured

by the office to announce the Advent of that same Strength, or because it was needful that he should strengthen a Virgin naturally timid, simple and retiring, and whom the novelty of a miracle might cause to tremble. And this he did, saying: *Fear not, Mary, for thou hast found favour with God* (S. Luke i. 30). And the same angel is not unreasonably believed to have strengthened also her betrothed; a man no less humble and apprehensive, although his name is not in that instance mentioned by the Evangelist. *Joseph, son of David, fear not to take unto thee Mary, thy wife* (S. Matt. i. 20). Most fittingly therefore Gabriel was chosen for the work which he had to fulfil, or rather it was because he had it to fulfil, that he was called Gabriel.

3. The angel Gabriel then was sent by God. Whither? *To a city of Galilee, named Nazareth.* Let us see, as Nathanael said, *whether any thing good can come out of Nazareth* (S. John i. 46). Nazareth is interpreted, *a flower*. It seems to me that there is a certain germ of the Divine thought, cast as it were from heaven upon the earth, in the addresses and promises made from on high to the Fathers, Abraham, Isaac and Jacob; of which germ it is written: *If the Lord of Sabaoth had not left us a germ, we should have been as Sodom, and we should have been made like unto Gomorrha* (Is. i. 9). This germ shot forth in the marvellous deeds which were shown when Israel went out of Egypt, in the figures and emblems of their journey over the Desert and unto the Promised Land, and after that in the visions and predictions of the Prophets, in the establishment of the Monarchy and the Priesthood until Christ.

But Christ is rightly regarded as the fruit of the germ of these flowers, according to the word of David: *The Lord shall give His benediction, and our land shall give*

her increase (Ps. lxxxv. 12) and that other: *Of the fruit
of Thy body will I set upon Thy throne* (Ps. cxxxii. 11).
Christ then is declared by the angel to be about to be
born in Nazareth, because to the *flower* it may be hoped
that the *fruit* will succeed. When the fruit appears, tha
flower falls; so also when the Truth appears in the
flesh, the type passes away. Wherefore Nazareth is called
a city of Galilee, that is to say, (mystically) of *trans-
migration*. In fact, at the birth of Christ, all of which
I have spoken above and of which the Apostle said: *All
these things happened to them in a figure (in figura*
1 Cor. x, 11 VULG.), passed away. And we, who now enjoy
the fruit, see that these flowers have passed; and even
while they still seem to be in vigorous life, it was foreseen
that they would one day pass away. So David says:
*As the grass which passeth away, in the morning
it flourishes, in the evening it withers, falls and is
dried up* (Ps. xc. 6). Now by the evening we are to
understand the fulness of time in which God sent His only
begotten Son, made of a woman, made under the law
(Gal. iv. 4), saying: *Behold I make all things new* (Apoc.
xxi. 5). Old things have passed away and disappeared,
even as flowers fall and dry up when the fruit begins to
grow. Also it is said in another place: *The grass withereth, the flower fadeth, but the Word of our God shall endure eternally* (Is. xl. 8). There can be no doubt, that
by the "Word" is meant the fruit; but the Word is Christ.

4. Thus the good fruit is Christ, who shall endure
eternally. But where is the grass that withereth? Where
is the flower that fadeth? Let the Prophet reply: *All flesh
is grass and all its glory as the flower of grass* (Is. xl. 6).
If all flesh is as grass, then the carnal people of the Jews
would necessarily be consumed as the flower of the field,
and is this not in fact the case? Is not that same people

deprived of all the fatness of the Spirit, so that they hold to the dryness of the letter? Has not the flower of the nation fallen, while their glorying, which they had in their Law, has passed away? If their flower has not fallen, where is their monarchy, their priesthood, their Prophets, their Temple, and all those great and wonderful things of which they were wont to boast, and say: *How great things have we heard and known, and our fathers have declared to us:* and again: *How great things did He command our fathers, that they should make them known unto their children* (Ps. lxxviii. 3, 5). Such are the reflections which are suggested to me by these words: *Unto Nazareth a city of Galilee.*

5. To that city then was sent the Angel Gabriel by God; but to whom was he sent? *To a Virgin, espoused to a man whose name was Joseph.* Who is this virgin so worthy of reverence as to be saluted by an Angel: yet so humble, as to be betrothed to a carpenter? A beautiful combination is that of virginity with humility: and that soul singularly pleases God in which humility gives worth to virginity, and virginity throws a new lustre on humility. But of how great respect must she not be thought worthy, in whom maternity consecrates virginity, and the splendour of a Birth exalts humility? You hear her, a virgin, and humble: if you are not able to imitate the virginity of that humble soul, imitate at least her humility; Virginity is a praiseworthy virtue; but humility is more necessary. If the one is counselled, the other is commanded; and if you are invited to keep the one, you are commanded to practise the other. Of the one it is said: *He who is able to receive it, let him receive it* (S. Matt. xix. 12); but of the other *Except ye become as this little child ye shall not enter into the Kingdom of heaven* (S. Matt. xviii. 3). The one then is rewarded; but the other is absolutely

required. You can be saved without virginity: but not
without humility. The humility, I say, which mourns over
the loss of virginity, is pleasing to God; but without humility, I am bold to say, not even the virginity of Mary
would have been so. *Upon whom*, He says, *shall My
Spirit rest, but upon one that is of a humble and quiet
spirit?* (Is. lxvi, 2). *Upon one that is humble.* He says not,
Upon one that is a Virgin. If Mary had not been humble,
the Holy Spirit would not have rested upon her. It is
then evident that she conceived by the Holy Ghost, just
because, as she herself declares: *God regarded the humility of His handmaiden* (S. Luke i. 48), rather than her
virginity: and I conclude without doubt that it was rather
by her humility than by her virginity (where both were
pleasing) that she pleased God and was chosen by Him.

6. What say you to this, O virgin who art proud?
Mary forgets her virginity and dwells only upon her humility: And you think only of flattering yourself about your
virginity, while neglecting humility. *The Lord*, she said,
has had regard to the humility of His handmaid. Who was
she who speaks this? A virgin holy, prudent and pious.
Would you claim to be more chaste, more pious than she?
Or do you think that your modesty is more acceptable
than the purity of Mary, since you think that you are able
by it to please God without humility, whilst she was not
able? The more honourable you are by the singular gift
of chastity, the greater is the injury you do to yourself,
by staining it with an admixture of pride. It were better
for you not to be a virgin, than to grow haughty about
virginity. It is not granted to all to live in virginity; but
to much fewer to do so with humility. If then you are
only able to admire (not to imitate) the virginity of Mary,
study to admire her humility, and it suffices for you. But if
you are a virgin and are also humble, then you are truly great.

7. There is something still more admirable in Mary: namely, her maternity joined with virginity. For from the beginning was never such a thing heard, as that one should be at the same time Mother and Virgin. If you consider also of whom she is Mother, to what degree will not your admiration of such a marvellous advancement soar? Will you not feel that you can hardly admire it enough? Will not your judgment or rather that of the Truth, be, that she whose Son is God, is exalted even above the choirs of Angels? Is it not Mary who says boldly to God, the Lord of Angels, *Son, why hast thou thus dealt with us?* Who of the Angels would dare to speak thus? It is sufficient for them, and they count it for a great thing, that they are spirits by nature, that they were made and called Angels by His grace, as David testifies: *Who makes His Angels Spirits* (Ps. civ. 4). But Mary, knowing herself to be Mother, with confidence names Him Son, whom they obey with reverence. Nor does God disdain to be called by the name which He has deigned to assume. For a little after the Evangelist adds: *And He was subject unto them* (S. Luke ii. 51). Who, and to whom? God, to human beings; God, I say, to whom the Angels are subject, whom Principalities and Powers obey, was subject unto Mary; and to Joseph also for her sake. Admire then both the benign condescension of the Son and the most excellent dignity of the Mother; and choose whether of the two is the more admirable. Each is a wonder, each a miracle. God is obedient to a woman, an unexampled humility! a woman is in the place of ancestor to God, a distinction without a sharer! When the praises of virgins are sung, it is said, that they follow the Lamb whithersoever He goeth (Apoc. xiv. 4), of what praise shall she be thought worthy, who even goes before Him?

8. Learn, O man, to obey; learn, O dust and ashes,

to abase thyself and submit. The Evangelist, speaking of thy Creator, says : *He was obedient to them*, that is, to Mary and Joseph. Blush then, O ashes, that darest to be proud! God humbles Himself, and dost thou raise thyself up? God submits Himself unto men, and dost thou lord it over thy fellow creatures, and prefer thyself to thy Creator? Would that God, if ever I should nourish such an inclination, would deign to reply to me as He once reproached His Apostle : *Get thee behind Me, Satan, for thou savourest not the things which be of God* (S. Matt. xvi. 23). For as often as I desire to raise myself above men, so often I am wishing to raise myself above my God ; and then most truly I do not savour the things which are of God ; for of Him it was said : *He was subject unto them*. If thou disdainest, O man, to imitate the example of man, at least it will not be unworthy of thee to follow in the steps of thy Creator. If thou art not able to follow Him wheresoever He goeth, at all events deign to follow Him where He condescends to thy littleness. That is, if you are not able to tread the lofty path of virginity, at least follow thy God by the perfectly safe way of humility : from the strict following of which not even virgins can deviate, I say emphatically, if they would follow the Lamb whithersoever He goeth. Without doubt, even a sinner, if he be humble, follows the Lamb ; and a virgin, though she be proud, follows him also ; but neither follows Him *whithersoever* He goeth ; because neither is the one able to attain to the purity of the Lamb, who is without spot, and the other does not know how to descend to the humility and gentleness of Him Who was silent, not before the shearer, but before the murderer. Certainly the sinner has taken a surer path to follow His steps, in tracing the footpaths of humility, than the soul which prides itself upon its virginity, since while the humble penitence of the one purifies its uncleanness, the pride of the other defiles its purity.

9. But happy was Mary: to her neither humility was wanting, nor virginity. And what a virginity was that, which Maternity did not violate, but honoured. And what an incomparable maternity, which both virginity and humility accompanied. Is there anything here, which is not admirable, incomparable and unique? Will not anyone hesitate in deciding which is the more worthy of admiration, which is the more wonderful, the Birth from a Virgin or Virginity in a Mother: the exalted rank of the Son, or the great humility in exaltation: except that, without doubt, the whole is to be preferred to any of its parts, and that it is incomparably more excellent and more happy to obtain the whole, than any part of it. And what wonder is there, if God, Who is *wonderful in His saints* (Ps. lxviii. 35. Vulg.), has shown Himself still more wonderful in His Mother? Reverence then, O you who are married, the purity of the flesh in corruptible flesh: you also, holy virgins, admire the Motherhood in a Virgin: and all ye who are men, imitate the humility of the Mother of God. Holy angels, honour the Mother of your King, ye who adore the Son of a Virgin of our race, Who is at once our King and yours, the Restorer of our race and the founder of your State. To Him, among you so exalted, among us so humble, be given equally by you and by us, the reverence which is His due, the honour and glory for His great condescension for ever and ever. Amen.

SERMON IX. [1]

Same Text.

1. No one doubts that the new song which shall be given to be sung in the Kingdom of God by Virgins alone, shall be sung by her, the Queen of Virgins, with the rest or rather first among the rest. I imagine to myself, that besides that song, which though for virgins alone, yet shall be common to all virgins, she will rejoice the City of God by some more sweet and beautiful canticle, whose heart-searching modulations, no other among virgins shall be found worthy to catch and to repeat; because it shall belong to none but her to sing it, who alone was honoured with the glory of Maternity and of the Divine Son. But if she glories in her maternity, it is not in herself, but in Him who was born of her. He who was born of her is God: and He shall bestow upon His Mother special glory in heaven, as she was prevented with special grace on earth, so that she conceived and bore miraculously and as a virgin. For the only kind of birth which befitted God, was to be born of a virgin, and it befitted the Virgin that Him whom she should bring forth should be God. And the Creator of men, when He desired to become Man and to be born into the world, had of necessity to choose His Mother from among the human race; or rather to form her for Himself such as should be worthy of Him, and as He should approve. He willed therefore that she should be a pure virgin; from whom a pure offspring should proceed, to purge the sin of all. And He willed that she who should give to the world Him who is meek and humble in heart, should herself be humble, since He

[1] Homily ii. on the *Missus est.*

would show in Himself an example as salutary as necessary to all men, of those virtues. He therefore who had before inspired in her the determination of virginity, and the merit of humility, He bestowed upon her, being a virgin, the honour of maternity. This is shown by the fact that the Angel proclaimed her to be full of grace, which he would not have been able to do, if she had had only so small a degree of excellence, as was not the fruit of grace.

2. So then, that she who should conceive and bring forth the Most Holy One, might be holy in body, she received the gift of virginity; and that she might be holy in mind, she received that of humility. Adorned therefore with the jewels of these two virtues, conspicuous by double beauty, both of body and mind, like the dwellers in heaven in sweetness and grace, the royal Virgin obtained for herself the approval of the King, who sent to her from on high a heavenly messenger. We learn this from the Evangelist, when he tells us that an Angel was sent of God to a virgin. 'From God' he says 'to a virgin': that is from the lofty to the lowly, from the Lord to the servant, from the Creator to the creature. What condescension by God! and what excellence in the Virgin! Come, maidens and mothers; all who since Eve and because of Eve have brought forth and are still bringing forth, in sorrow. Come to that virginal couch; enter if you can, that modest chamber of your sister. For behold, God sends to the Virgin, and an Angel addresses Mary. Lend your ear and listen to what he announces; and what you hear, may perhaps console you.

3. Rejoice, O father Adam; and do thou, O Eve our mother, exult even more. As ye are the parents of all, so ye have been their destroyers; and, unhappy as ye are, their destroyers before they had even come into

the world. Be consoled now, because of this your
daughter, and that she is of such excellence. Be consoled the first, thou from whom the evil first began,
and from whom it has fallen back upon all women.
For the time draws near when that ancient reproach
shall be done away, and man shall have no longer anything
to reproach to woman: man, I say, who did not hesitate
to excuse himself as rashly as cruelly in accusing her:
*The woman whom Thou gavest to be with me, she gave
me of the tree, and I did eat* (Gen. iii. 12). Wherefore
hasten, O Eve, to Mary; hasten, O mother to daughter;
let the daughter answer for the mother, take away her
reproach and afford to her father for her a just satisfaction.
For if it was by woman that man fell, it is by woman
also that he is raised up. What hadst thou, O Adam, to
say of thy sin? *The woman whom Thou gavest to be with
me, she gave me of the tree, and I did eat.* But these are
words of malice, and by them thy fault is increased, not
removed. But Wisdom has overcome malice; when it
found in the treasury of unfailing bounty, the occasion
for pardon which God in questioning thee sought to elicit;
but sought in vain. A woman is rendered for a woman,
but a wise in place of a foolish, a humble for a proud.
This one, instead of offering the fruit of a tree which
brings death, brings thee to taste of the Fruit of the Tree
of Life; and in place of the bitterness of that poisonous
food, prepares for thee the sweetness of the fruit of eternal
happiness. Change therefore the words of unjust accusation into those of returning thanks, and say: 'Lord, the
woman Thou gavest me, has given to me of the Tree of
Life, and I have eaten; and because in that fruit Thou
hast bestowed upon me life, it is sweeter than honey to
my mouth.'

For behold, with this purpose was the Angel sent unto

the Virgin. O Virgin, truly admirable and most worthy of all honour; woman singularly to be venerated, admirable above others, who repairest the ill which thine ancestors have caused, and art the means of restoring life to their descendants.

4. *An Angel,* says the Evangelist, *was sent unto a Virgin;* a virgin in body, in mind, in intention; in a word such as the Apostle describes, *holy both in body and in spirit* (1 Cor. vii. 34); not found newly nor by chance, but chosen from the beginning, foreknown by the Most High and prepared for His work, kept safe by Angels, indicated by Patriarchs and foretold by Prophets. Search the Scriptures, and you will approve what I say. Do you desire that I should adduce some testimonies drawn from thence? To mention a few out of very many, what other does God seem to have predicted, when He said to the serpent: *I will put enmity between thee and the woman?* And if you hesitate to believe that He spoke of Mary, hear what follows: *She shall bruise thy head* (Gen. iii. 15). To whom was that victory reserved, if not to Mary? Without doubt she bruised the envenomed head, who trampled under foot every suggestion of evil, whether from the pride of mind, or the allurements of the flesh.

5. To what other did Solomon refer, when he said: *Who can find a virtuous* (or brave) *woman?* (Prov. xxxi. 10). For the wise man knew the weakness of that sex, a delicate body, a changeable mind: but since he had read that God had promised, and it seemed also to himself befitting, that he who had overcome by means of woman, should be vanquished by means of one, he asked in great wonder, *Who shall find that brave woman?* As if he had said: 'If your salvation and that of all the restoration of our innocence and the defeat of our enemy hangs thus from the hand of a woman, it is most necessary that a

woman should be provided who shall be brave, that she
may be fit for so great a work'. Who then can find that
brave woman? But that he might not be thought to have
despaired in this enquiry, he adds prophetically, Her price
is from afar and from the end of the earth. [1]

That is to say, she is no thing of little value, no thing
mean or common, not in short similar to what may be
found upon the earth; but the price of this brave woman
is from Heaven, nor yet for the lowest, but from the
highest Heaven will her going forth be.

What again signified that ancient bush of Moses which
shot forth flames, but was not consumed (Exod. iii. 2),
except Mary bringing forth without sorrow? What again that
rod of Aaron which flowered without having been watered
(Num. xvii. 8)? Is it not Mary who conceived, though
"she knew not a man?" It was from that great marvel
that Isaiah predicted a mystery greater still, when he said,
There shall come forth a Rod out of the stem of Jesse
and a branch shall grow out of his roots (Isaiah xi. 1).
The rod meaning the Virgin; the flower the bringing forth.

6. If it seems to you that we cannot see Christ in the
flower without being in contradiction to that which has
been said above, in which it was maintained that He was
pointed out, not by the flower appearing from the Rod,
but by the fruit from the flower; take note that in that
Rod of Aaron, which produced not only flowers, but leaves
and fruits, Christ is signified not only by the flowers and
the fruit, but also by the Leaves themselves. Take note
also that with Moses it is not the fruit of the Rod of which
one stroke divided the waters of the sea, to leave a
passage for the Children of Israel, or by which water was made
to gush forth from the rock for them to drink, which is a

---

[1] [Her price is above rubies. *Eng. vers.*]

figure of Christ (Exod. xiv. 16). After all it is in no
wise inconvenient that for different causes Christ should
be typified in different manners. Thus the Rod is the
sign of His power, and the flower represents the sweetness
of His character, the fruit how dear He is to those who
know Him; the leaves recall the perfect protection which
He extends over them, the shadow of His wings with
which He does not cease to protect those who fly to Him,
whether from the storm of carnal desires or from the
attacks of the wicked who persecute them. Jesus affords
a welcome and valuable shelter under His wings, where
is a safe refuge to the fugitive and a welcome repose to
the weary. *Be merciful unto me, O God, be merciful
unto me, for my soul trusteth in Thee, yea, in the shadow
of Thy wings will I make my refuge, until these calamities
be overpast* (Ps. lvii. 1). Yet in this passage of Isaiah, by
the flower we are to understand the Son, by the stem of
it the Mother; since both the stem flowered without seed
and the Virgin conceived, but not of man. Neither did the
sending forth of the flower injure the freshness of the
stem, nor the birth of the Virgin's Son affect her virginity.

7. Let us bring forward some other passages of Holy
Scripture referring to the Virgin Mary and her Divine
Son. What does the fleece of Gideon (Judges vi. 37)
signify? It is shorn from the skin of the lamb, but the
skin itself remains without wound; it is stretched upon
the sand and at one time it is the fleece, at another time
it is the sand which receives the dew of Heaven; what
else is this than the human flesh which was taken from the
flesh of the Virgin, without affecting her virginity? Was
it not into her womb that the fulness of the Divinity
descended, as the Heavens let fall their dew? It is of that
fulness that we have all received, and without it we should
in truth be nothing (as it were) than dry earth. To that

incident in the life of Gideon seems to answer very well that phrase of the Psalmist : *He shall come down like the rain into a fleece of wool* (Ps. lxxii. 6), since that which follows, *even as the drops which water the earth*, appears to refer to the same thing as the sand of Gideon which was found all soaked with dew. As the soft and plentiful showers which God has reserved for His heritage, it falls placidly and without sound of human intervention, and penetrates by its secret operation the Virgin's womb : but afterwards it was diffused over the whole world by the mouths of preachers, no longer as the dew upon a fleece of wool, but as drops falling upon the earth with sound of words and resonance of miracles. Thus it is recorded that when those clouds which carry the rains in their bosom, (that is, the Apostles) were being sent forth, the command was given to them : *what I tell ye in darkness, that speak ye in light : and what ye hear in the ear, that preach ye upon the housetops* (S. Matt. x. 27). Which they all did : *for their sound is gone out into all lands, and their words to the end of the world* (Ps. xix. 4).

8. Let us listen also to Jeremiah, who adds new prophecies to old; and not being able as yet to show us the Saviour, he looks forward with earnest desire to His future coming, and announces it with confident assurance : *The Lord hath created a new thing in the earth : a woman shall compass a man* (Jer. xxxi. 22). Who is the woman spoken of? And who the man? Or if a man, how compassed by a woman? or if compassed by a woman, how a man? And to speak more plainly, how a man, and at the same time in the womb of his mother? For this is what must be understood by the phrase, a woman shall compass a man. Those whom we call men have passed through infancy, boyhood, youth and early manhood, have reached the maturity nearest to old age. Who

then having reached such a time of life, could be compassed by a woman? If it has been said, a woman shall
compass an infant; or, a child; it would not have seemed
either new or wonderful. But as on the contrary, a *man*
is named, we ask in wonder what is this novelty which
God has done in the earth? what is this miracle?

For can a man, as Nicodemus asks, *enter the second
time into his mother's womb, and be born?* (S. John iii. 4).

9. I turn to the conception and bearing of the Virgin;
and I inquire if among the many new and wonderful
things which anyone who carefully considers them, dis-
covers, I find the novelty which I have brought forward
from the Prophet. There is recognized, length which is
bounded, breadth narrowed, loftiness lowered, profundity
made level. There is recognized, light which lightens not,
a stammering Word, water which has thirst, and bread
which hungers. You will see there, if you closely examine,
power governed, wisdom instructed, power sustained; God,
who strengthens Angels, Himself strengthened by milk;
and Him who consoles the unhappy, lamenting as an
infant. You will see joy made sorrowful, confidence trembling, health feeling pain, the life dying, strength rendered
weak. But which is not less wonderful, you will also see
sorrow inspiring joy, fear encouraging, endurance saving,
death giving life, weakness strengthening. Who does not
notice at once that which I sought? Among all these wonderful
paradoxes, who does not at once recognize that a woman
compasses a man, when you see Mary bear in her womb
Jesus, the Man approved by God? For I should say that
Jesus was a Man, not only when He was called *a prophet
mighty in deed and word* (S. Luke xxiv. 19), but even
when as a tender infant He was carried in the arms of
His mother, or even borne in her womb. Jesus was then a

Man even before His birth; but by wisdom not by age; by strength of soul, not by bodily powers; not by development of the limbs, but by perfectness of senses. There was no less Wisdom in Jesus, or rather Jesus was no less Wisdom when conceived, as when born; and when less of stature, as when greater. Whether then He was hidden in the womb, wailing in the cradle, interrogating the Doctors, as a young Boy in the temple or as a man of full age teaching the people, He was always equally filled with the Holy Spirit, nor was there any hour in his life at any age in which He had any more or less of that fulness than He received at the moment of His conception in the womb. From the beginning He was perfect; from the beginning, I say, He was filled with the spirit of wisdom and understanding, with the spirit of counsel and strength, of knowledge and of the fear of the Lord. (Isaiah xi. 2).

10. Nor let this astonish you that you read concerning Him in another passage; Jesus increased in wisdom and stature and in favour with God and man (S. Luke ii. 52.) For in what is here said of wisdom and grace, the Evangelist is to be understood as speaking, not according to the actual fact, but according to the appearance: not because He acquired something which was new to Him, day by day, which He had not before; but that He appeared to acquire, when it was His will that it should so appear. As for you, O man, when you make progress, you do not make it just when you wish or as much as you would wish: on the contrary your progress is determined and your life ordered without your own knowledge; but as for the Child Jesus, He who now orders your life ordered then His own; and He appeared wise, and wiser, when He willed it, and to whom He willed it, and Divinely wise

when and to whom He willed, although to Himself he
was never anything but Divinely wise. Similarly also never
having ceased to be filled with every grace, whether the
grace He had towards God, or that which it became Him
to have towards men, He allowed this to be visible only
according to His good pleasure; sometimes more, sometimes
less, according as the merit of those who beheld Him
deserved, or as He knew was expedient for their salvation.
It is then quite certain that Jesus had always a manly
soul, although He did not appear always to be a man in
body. Wherefore should I doubt after this that a man
could have existed in the womb (of a Virgin) when I do
not hesitate to believe that God was there? Evidently it
is less wonderful that a man should be there than that
God should be.

11. But let us see if Isaiah does not throw a great light
upon this novelty of Jeremiah, as he has just now explained the sense of the newly bloomed flowers in the Rod
of Aaron. He says, *Behold a Virgin shall conceive and
bear a Son.* Here is mentioned a woman, namely, a virgin.
You wish to know now to what man there is here reference? *And His Name shall be called Emmanuel, that is,
God with us* (Isaiah vii. 14). Therefore the woman who
shall compass a man, is the Virgin who conceives Him
who is God. You see how exactly and how beautifully
the mystical saying and the wonderful facts answer to
each other. You see how great and marvellous is this
miracle performed from the Virgin and in the Virgin,
which so many prophecies foretold, so many miracles preceded. It is because all the Prophets are of one Spirit;
and although differing one from the other in manners,
signs and periods, they foresaw and predicted the same
great fact, by the same Spirit. That which Moses saw

in the burning bush; Aaron in the Rod that budded and
bloomed; and Gideon in the dew upon his fleece of wool:
that which Solomon predicted in his saying of a brave woman
and her value, Jeremiah celebrated more openly in his prophecy of woman and man, and Isaiah revealed with perfect
plainness in his prophecy concerning God and the Virgin,
that Gabriel at length showed forth in saluting that Virgin
herself. For it was she of whom the Evangelist wrote:
The Angel Gabriel was sent from God to a Virgin betrothed.

12. *To a Virgin*, he says, *betrothed*. Wherefore betrothed? Since she was, I say, a Virgin elect, as was shown,
to this wonderful Conception and Birth, it is strange that
she should be betrothed, though not to be wedded (in the
ordinary course). But who will imagine that this happened
by chance? Not by chance, because it was commended
by a good reason; useful and even necessary, and worthy
of the Divine Wisdom. I will state what occurs to me
upon this point, or rather what occurred before me, to the
Fathers. In principle the reason for the betrothal of Mary
is the same as for the doubting of Thomas. The custom
of the Jews was, that from the day of the betrothal to
that of the nuptials, the future husband had the care of
the future wife: and the more scrupulously the one preserved the modesty of the other, the more faithful a spouse
he might hope to have, just as doubting Thomas, by
touching Our Lord, became the firmest witness of the
Resurrection: so also Joseph by betrothing Mary to himself, and by carefully watching and approving her demeanour during the whole time she was in his custody, became
the most faithful witness of her purity. Of each of these
circumstances, both the doubt of Thomas, and the betrothal
of Mary, the convenience was signal. We might be taken
in the net of a similar error, so as to bring us to suspect

faith in the one : chastity in the other ; but on the contrary, by the kindness and prudence of God, certitude is firmly established in our mind by the very means which might have endangered it. For as relates to the Resurrection of the Son, I should rather have believed, weak as I am, in Thomas doubting at first, and then touching the Risen Lord with his own hands, than in Peter who heard and immediately believed : and as relates to the continence of the Mother of Jesus, in her spouse who had watched over and convinced himself of it ; than in the Virgin defending herself from the testimony of her conscience alone. Tell me, I pray you, who seeing her with child while yet unmarried, would not have regarded her rather as a woman of ill life than a virgin? But it would have been unbecoming that such a thing should be said of the Mother of the Lord. It was more tolerable and more honourable that Christ should be thought at the time to be born in wedlock, than by fornication.

13. But you ask, perhaps, whether God could not have given some plain sign, and thus prevented both any suspicion being thrown on the mother, or any slight on the birth! He could have, no doubt ; but then demons would not have been ignorant of what men knew. But it was expedient that the mystery (*sacramentum*) of the Divine plan should be hidden, at least for a time, from the prince of this world: not because God, if He should will to carry out this plan openly, would fear that He could be hindered by a demon ; but because He, doing all things as He wills, wisely as well as powerfully, is accustomed to observe in all His works certain fitnesses of times and circumstances, because of the beauty of order. This is why, although able to effect this in some other way, had He chosen, He yet preferred to reconcile man to Himself in the same

manner, and in the same order, in which He knew him
to have fallen. So that as the devil had first deceived
woman, and afterwards through her had overcome man;
so he should first by a woman be deceived, and afterwards
openly vanquished by a Man, that is, Christ. Thus while
on one side, pious art outmanœuvred the fraud of the
malicious one, the virtue of Christ broke down his resist-
ance; and not only the power, but the wisdom of God,
showed themselves greater than that of the devil. It was
fitting that incarnate Wisdom should overcome spiritual
wickedness, in order that not only should she *reach from
one end to another mightily*; but also *sweetly order all
things* (Wisd. viii. 1). For it reaches from one end to the
other, that is from heaven to hell; for according to the
Psalmist: *If I climb up into heaven, thou art there: if
I go down into hell, Thou art there also* (Ps. cxxxix. 8).
And in either place He acts with strength; for from the height
of heaven He hurled down the proud, and in the depth of hell
He spoiled the spoiler. It was then quite suitable that He
should dispose all things with sweetness, in the heaven and on
the earth: inasmuch as in hurling down that restless spirit
from thence, He left the others in peace; and when about to
vanquish that envious one here, He first began by leaving to
us an example greatly needed, of humility and gentleness.
For what would it have profited that the devil had been overcome, if we had remained proud? Mary was therefore of
necessity betrothed to Joseph; since by this not only was a
holy mystery withdrawn from the dogs, and the virginity of
Mary approved by her spouse, but also the modesty of
the Virgin was spared, and her reputation provided for.
What could have been more wisely done, or more worthily
of Divine providence? By this means the secret designs
of God were provided with a witness, while yet the enemy
was excluded from the knowledge of them, and the fair

fame of the Virgin mother was preserved unstained. If it had been otherwise, would Joseph have been just in sparing an adulteress? For it is written: *Joseph her husband, being a just man, and not willing to make her a public example, was minded to put her away privily.* (S. Matt. i. 19). Thus, it was because he was just that he was unwilling to expose her to shame and punishment: but he would have been far from just, if knowing Mary to be in fault, he had concealed it; and similarly he would not have been just, if knowing her innocence he had nevertheless condemned it. As therefore he was just, and was unwilling to put her to open shame, he wished to put her away privately.

14. Wherefore did he wish to put her away? Upon this point I will give you not my own opinion, but that of the Fathers. He wished to do this, because of the same reason which made Peter repel the Lord from him: *Depart from me, for I am a sinful man, O Lord* (S. Luke v. 8) and the Centurion discourage Him from entering his house, saying: *Lord, I am not worthy that Thou shouldest come under my roof* (S. Matt. viii. 8). Thus also it was that Joseph, thinking himself a sinner and unworthy, said to himself that he ought not to live longer in the closest companionship with a woman so holy and so noble, whose dignity, so far surpassing his own, made him tremble. He saw by certain signs, and was struck with fear by, the Divine Presence which she bore; and as he was unable to penetrate the mystery, he wished to send her away. Peter trembled at the greatness of His power, the Centurion at the Majesty of His presence. So Joseph, being only a simple man, was appalled at the novelty and greatness of the miracle, and the depth of the mystery: and therefore he wished to send her away secretly. Can you won-

der that Joseph felt himself unworthy of the society of
the Virgin during this time, when you hear that the holy
Elizabeth was not able to bear her presence without fear
and respect? For she said: *Whence is this to me, that
the Mother of my Lord should come to me?* (S. Luke i.
43). This is why Joseph wished to dismiss her; but wherefore should he have intended to do so secretly and not
openly? No doubt in order that the cause of the divorce
might not be enquired into, and the reason demanded. For
what would a righteous man have had to reply to a stiff-
necked people, a people unbelieving and contradicting? If he
said, as he thought, that he had proof of the purity of
Mary, would not the incredulous and cruel Jews at
once have laughed him to scorn, and have stoned her?
How would they have believed the Truth still silent in
the womb, whom afterwards they despised when He spoke
to them in the temple? To what excess would they have
dared to go against Him whom they had not yet seen,
when afterwards they laid wicked hands upon Him even
resplendent with the fame of miracles? Rightly therefore
did that just man, that he might not be obliged either to
lie or to slander an innocent person, desire to send her
away privately.

15. But if anyone thinks otherwise, and contends that
Joseph doubted as an ordinary man, but because he was
just, though he did not wish to dwell with her on account
of the suspicion, and yet (being good) was not willing to
throw suspicion on her, and so wished to send her away
privately; I reply briefly, that the doubts of Joseph, such
as they may have been, were worthy of being dissipated
by an oracle from on high. For thus it is written: *While he
thought on these things* (that is, of dismissing her secretly) the
Angel of the Lord appeared unto him in a dream saying;

Joseph, thou son of David, fear not to take unto thee Mary thy wife: for that which is conceived in her is of the Holy Ghost (S. Matt. i. 20). Therefore, because of these reasons, Mary was espoused to Joseph, or rather, as the Evangelist describes it, *to a man whose name was Joseph.* He names him, not because he was the husband of Mary, but as a man of virtue. Or rather, because, according to another Evangelist, he was called not simply as a man, but as one standing in that relation to her; and it was right that he should be called by the title which of necessity he seemed to bear. He was then called the husband of the Virgin, because he was necessarily thought so; just as, though he was not the father of the Saviour, yet he was thought to be, and therefore called so, even by the Evangelist: *And Jesus Himself began to be about thirty years of age, being (as was supposed) the son of Joseph* (S. Luke iii. 23). He was not then the husband of the mother, nor the father of her Son, although by a certain and needful dispensation (as was said) he was supposed at the time to be, and was spoken of as being both.

16. Yet imagine from the very appellation by which (though by a dispensation) he was honoured by God with being called; imagine from the word itself, which was doubtless a farther honour; who, and what kind of man, this Joseph was. Remember also the patriarch of that name who was sold into Egypt (Gen. xxxvii. 27): and gather from the fact that even the name was not one chosen by chance, but that it indicated in this case, as in the former, purity, integrity and grace. For the former Joseph, sold by the envy of his brethren, and taken into Egypt, prefigured the selling of Christ; this Joseph, flying from the envy of Herod, carried Christ into Egypt (S. Matt. ii. 14.) The one, remaining faithful to his master, refused

to commingle with his mistress: the other, recognizing the Virgin as the mother of his Lord, entitled to be respected, observed faithfully towards her the law of continence. To the one was given understanding in the interpretation of dreams: to the other was granted to know and to co-operate in the mysteries of the purposes of God (S. Matt. i. 20). The one kept in store the corn which was to feed, not himself, but the whole people: the other received the guardianship of the Heavenly Bread, as well for himself, as for the whole world. There is no doubt then that this Joseph, to whom the Mother of the Saviour was espoused, was a man good and preëminently faithful. A prudent and faithful servant he was, I say, whom the Lord placed beside Mary to be her protector, the nourisher of His human body, and the single and most trusty assistant on earth in His great design. To this is to be added that he is said to have been of the house of David. Truly did Joseph, that man of noble birth, but of still more noble heart, show that he was of the house of David, and truly descended of royal blood. Evidently he was the true son of David, a son who had not degenerated from his father; nor was this merely according to the flesh, but also in faith, holiness and devotion: whom the Lord found as another David, *a man after His own heart*, to whom He might safely commit the most secret and sacred mystery of His heart: to whom as to another David, the manifested the hidden arcana of His wisdom, which had been known to none from the beginning of the world: to whom, in fine, it was given to know, what many prophets and kings had desired to see, and had not seen; to hear, and had not heard; and not only was it given to him to see and to hear it, but also to carry in his arms, to lead by the hand, to nourish and to watch over the infant Saviour. We must believe also that Mary as well was of

the House of David, since she would not have been espoused to a man of that royal line if she had not belonged
to it herself. They were then both of the royal House
of David; but it was only in Mary that the promise was
verified which the Lord sware unto David; while Joseph
was but the witness and confidant of its fulfilment.

17. The verse of the Evangelist ends thus: *And the
Virgin's name was Mary.* Let us say a few words upon
this name also. The word Mary means *Star of the Sea*,
which seems to have a wonderful fitness to the Virgin
Mother. For she is fitly compared to a star; for just as
a star sends forth its ray without injury to itself, so the
Virgin, remaining a virgin, brought forth her Son. The ray
does not diminish the clearness of the star, nor the Son
of the Virgin her Virginity. She is even that noble star
risen out of Jacob, whose ray enlightens the whole world,
whose splendour both shines in the Heavens and penetrates
into Hell: and as it traverses the lands, it causes minds
to glow with virtues more than bodies with heat, while
vices it burns up and consumes. She, I say, is that
beautiful and admirable star, raised of necessity above
this great and spacious sea of life, shining with virtues
and affording an illustrious example. Whosoever thou art
who knowest thyself to be tossed about among the storms
and tempests of this troubled world rather than to be
walking peacefully upon the shore, turn not thine eyes
away from the shining of this star, if thou wouldst not
be overwhelmed with the tempest. If the winds of temptation arise, if you are driving upon the rocks of tribulation,
look to the star, invoke Mary. If you are tossed upon
the waves of pride, of ambition, of envy, of rivalry, look
to the star, invoke Mary. If wrath, avarice, temptations
of the flesh assail the frail skiff of your mind, look to

Mary. If you are troubled by the greatness of your crimes, confused by the foulness of your conscience, and desperate with the horror of judgment, you feel yourself drawn into the depth of sorrow and into the abyss of despair; in dangers, in difficulties, in perplexities: invoke and think of Mary. Let not the name depart from heart and from lips; and that you may obtain a part in the petitions of her prayer, do not desert the example of her life. If you think of and follow her you will not go wrong, nor despair if you beg of her. With her help you will not fall or be fatigued; if she is favourable you will be sure to arrive; and thus you will learn by your own experience how rightly it is said: *The Virgin's name was Mary.* But now let us stop for a little, that we may not have merely a passing glance at the lustre of the great light. For to use the words of the Apostles *It is good for us to be here;* it is a happiness to be able to contemplate in silence what a laboured discourse could not sufficiently explain. But in the meantime the pious contemplation of that brilliant star will give us new ardour for what remains to be said.

SERMON X.

[HOMILY III. ON THE *Missus est.*]

And the Angel came in unto her and said, Hail, thou that art highly favoured, the Lord is with thee: blessed art thou among women. S. Luke i. 28—32.

1. I willingly make use of the words of the Saints, where I see that they harmonize with my subject, in order that whatever I shall present to the reader with respect to it may be rendered more acceptable by the beauty of

the words which form its setting. At present I will begin from the Prophet's words: *Woe is me*, not indeed, as the prophet, *because I have kept silence*, but because I have spoken, *because I am a man of unclean* lips (Is. vi. 5). Alas, how many vain, even false and unseemly words I reflect that this my mouth most impure as it is, has uttered, in which, I now venture to take word relating to heavenly things!

Greatly do I fear, that I may one day hear spoken to me the reproach: *What hast thou to do to declare My statutes or that thou shouldest take My covenant in thy mouth?* (Ps. l. 16). Would that to me might be brought from the heavenly altar, not indeed a single coal only, but an entire globe of fire, great enough to burn away the thick and obstinate rust from my lips, insomuch that I might be held worthy to recount in my discourse, such as it is, the noble and pure converse of the angel to the Virgin and of the Virgin in turn to him.

The Evangelist therefore says: *The angel came in unto her*, that is to Mary, and he said: *Hail, thou that art full of grace:* [1] *the Lord is with thee.* Whither did he enter in? I imagine that it was into the retirement of the modest chamber, where she with the door fast closed was praying perhaps in secret to her Father. Angels are wont to stand by those who pray, and to take delight in those whom they see lifting up holy hands in their worship: it rejoices them to present unto God the offering of a secret savour, the pure burnt-offering of a saintly devotion. The angel indicates how acceptable the prayers of Mary were in the sight of the Most High, by saluting her so reverently on his entrance. And it was not difficult for him to enter into the retirement of the Virgin though

---

[1] [VULG. The E. V. is *'thou that art highly favoured.'*]

the door were shut; since the nature and fineness of his material substance is such, that iron bars cannot hinder its ingress, wheresoever it wills to go. Thus walls are no obstacle to angelic spirits, but all things visible give them way: and all bodies, however thick or solid, are penetrable and passable to them. It is not to be supposed therefore, that the angel entered at some little door which the Virgin had left open; since undoubtedly it was her purpose to escape from the society, and to avoid the converse, of men; so that the silence of her devotion might not be troubled, nor her purity offended.

In that hour then, the Virgin, most prudent, had closed her small dwelling around her; against men; but not against Angels. For although an angel was able to enter, to no man would an entrance have been easy.

2. The Angel then when he had entered, said to her: *Hail, thou that art full of grace, the Lord is with thee.* We read in the Acts of the Apostles, that Stephen too was full of grace [1] and that the Apostles were filled with the Holy Ghost (Acts ii. 4); but these very differently from Mary: inasmuch as neither in him as in Mary, dwelt the fulness of the Godhead bodily: nor did those conceive of the Holy Ghost, as did Mary.

Hail! thou that art full of grace, the Lord is with thee. What wonder that she, with whom the Lord was, should be full of grace? But this is a thing far more wonderful, that He, who had sent the Angel to the Virgin, was found by the Angel with the Virgin. Was God then so much swifter even than an Angel, that He outstripped his messenger though he hasted to the earth? But it is not

---

[1] [Acts. vi. 5. The E. V. is 'full of the Holy Ghost'. But 'full of grace' is supported by ℵ, A, B, D and Syr. as well as by the *Vulg.* (E.)]

strange that it should be so. For when the King was in His seat, (Cant. i. 12), the ointment [= the prayers] of the Virgin gave forth its sweet odour, and the smoke of its sweetness rose into the sight of His glory, while those who stood around cried out: *Who is this that cometh out of the wilderness like a pillar of smoke, with the odours of myrrh and frankincense* (Cant. iii. 6). And immediately the King coming forth from His holy place, rejoicing as a giant to run a race: though His going forth be from the highest heaven (Ps. xix. 6, 7); His great love outstripped His messenger to the Virgin whom He had loved and chosen, and in whose excellent beauty He had pleasure. The Church rejoices and is glad as she beholds Him coming from afar, and says: *Behold, He cometh leaping upon the mountains, skipping upon the hills* (Cant. ii. 8).

3. Rightly therefore did the King desire the beauty of the Virgin. For all that she did had been long before prophesied by her father David, saying to her: *Hearken, O daughter, and consider, incline thine ear; forget also thine own people and thy father's house.* And if thou shalt do this: *the King shall have pleasure in thy beauty* (Ps. xlv. 10, 11). She heard then and saw, not as some, who hearing do not hear, and seeing do not understand; but she heard and believed, she saw and understood. She inclined her ear to obedience and her heart to discipline; she forgot also her people and her father's house; she did not regard the hope of posterity among her people, nor of heritage in the house of her father; and whatever honour among the people, or possessions of earthly things in her paternal house might have been hers, all these she counted as dung that she might win Christ. Nor was she disappointed in her hope; since Christ came, without doing any violence to her modesty,

to be to her a Son. Well therefore she may be said to
be full of grace, who both retained the grace of virginity,
and added to it besides the glory of offspring.

4. *Hail*, he says, *O full of grace; the Lord is with thee.*
He did not say, the Lord is in thee; but *the Lord is
with thee.* For God, who is wholly in every place equally
in His uncompounded Nature, yet is in rational creatures
after one manner, and in others after another manner;
and of the former He dwells effectively in the good,
otherwise than in the evil. So indeed it is in irrational
creatures, but these have no consciousness of Him. For
all rational creatures indeed have a consciousness of God
by the understanding; but only the good by the affections
also. Therefore with the good alone it is the case, that
He is with them because of the agreement of their will
with His. For when they thus subject their wills to
righteousness, that what God thinks fit to will, that they
will also; inasmuch as they disagree in no respect from
the will of God, they join themselves specially to Him.
This is the case with all saints, but in an especial degree
with Mary; since so complete was her self-devotion, that
she associated with the Divine purpose not only her will
but also her body; and of her Virgin substance was
formed or rather came into being, the one Christ; who
although He was not wholly from God, nor wholly from
the Virgin; yet was wholly of God, and wholly of the
Virgin; nor were there two Sons, but one Son of both
the One and the other.

He said therefore, *Hail, O full of grace, the Lord is
with thee.* Not only the Son, whom thou clothest from
thy human body: but also the Holy Ghost, by Whom
thou conceivest: and the Father, by Whom He was
begotten Whom thou conceivest. The Father, I say,

is with thee, who makes His Son to be also thine. The
Son is with thee, Who in order to bring about in thee
a wonderful mystery, opens for Himself marvellously the
womb, and yet preserves to thee the sign of virginity.
The Holy Spirit is with thee, who with the Father and the
Son, sanctifies thy womb. Truly the Lord is with thee.

5. *Blessed art thou among women.* We may add here
what Elizabeth, whose words these are, added: *And blessed
is the fruit of thy womb* (S. Luke i. 42). Not because
thou art blessed, is the fruit of thy womb also blessed;
but because He has prevented thee with the blessings of
sweetness, therefore art thou blessed. For truly the fruit
of thy womb is blessed, in Whom all nations of the earth
are blessed; of Whose fulness thou also hast received with
others, though in a different manner to others. And
therefore thou indeed art blessed, but among women:
but He is blessed, not among men, not among Angels,
but is, as says the Apostle, *over all, God blessed for ever*
(Rom. ix. 5). A man is called blessed; a woman, the
earth, bread or any such created thing may be said to be
blessed; but the fruit of thy womb is blessed in a manner
peculiar to Himself; since *He is above all, God blessed
for ever.*

6. *Blessed* then *is the fruit of thy womb*; blessed in
look, in taste, and smell. He described the fragrance of
this odorous fruit, who said: *Behold, the odour of my
son, is as the odour of a field which the Lord hath
blessed* (Gen. xxvii. 27). Is he not truly blessed, on whom
the Lord hath bestowed His blessing? Of the sweetness
of her fruit a certain man who had tasted of it [1] bursts
forth thus and says: *O taste and see how sweet is the Lord*

---

[1] [Or, of that which he had tasted, *quod gustaverat.*]

(Ps. xxxiv. 8), and in another place : *How great is thy sweetness, O Lord, which Thou hast laid up for them who fear Thee* (Ps. xxxi. 19). And yet another says : *If so be ye have tasted that the Lord is gracious* (1 Peter ii. 3). And He Himself, the Fruit, when inviting us to come to Him, says of Himself : *They that eat Me shall yet be hungry, and they that drink Me shall yet be thirsty* (Ecclus. xxiv. 21 and see S. John vi. 35 sqq.). This he said on account of the exceeding sweetness, which when once tasted, does not fail still further to excite the appetite. This is a good fruit indeed, which is both food and drink and even righteousness to hungry and thirsty souls. You have heard of the fragrance, you have heard of the sweetness : hear now of the beauty of this Fruit. For if that mortal fruit was not only, as Scripture bears witness, sweet to the taste, but also *pleasant to the eye* (Gen. iii. 6); how much more ought we not to desire the reviving beauty of this life-giving fruit upon which, as another Scripture declares, even *the Angels desire to look?* (1 S. Pet. i. 12). He saw in the spirit this perfect beauty, and desired to see it in the body, who said: *Out of Sion is the perfection of His beauty* (Ps. l. 2). And that he may not seem to you to have praised a merely common degree of beauty, compare with it what you read in another Psalm : *Thou art fairer than the children of men : full of grace are Thy lips, therefore God hath blessed Thee for ever* (Ps. xlv. 2).

7. *Blessed* then *is the fruit of thy womb*, whom God hath blessed for ever; from whose blessing thou also art blessed among women; because an evil tree cannot bring forth good fruit. *Blessed,* I say, *art thou among women* who hast escaped that universal curse, by which it was said, *In sorrow thou shalt bring forth children* (Gen. iii. 16);

and nevertheless art free of that other, *Cursed is the barren in Israel* (Exod. xxiii. 26 and Deut. vii. 14) ; who hast obtained that unique blessing, of not remaining barren, and of at the same time, bringing forth without sorrow. Hard the necessity, and heavy the yoke, that lies upon all the daughters of Eve ! if they bring forth, they endure anguish, and if they do not, they incur malediction. The pang renders painful their bearing, and the curse forbids them to be barren. Hearing this and reading this, O prudent Virgin, whether of the two wilt thou choose? Difficulties, she said, surround me : but it is better for me to remain chaste, though under the curse of barrenness, than first to conceive by concupiscence, what afterwards I shall deservedly bring forth in sorrow. In the one I see malediction, but no sin; in the other both sin and suffering. For is this malediction anything else, than the contempt of men ? Is the barren in fact called cursed for anything but this, that she is exposed to opprobrium and contempt, as unfruitful and useless? and this is in Israel only. But with me it is a very small thing that I should displease men, while I am able to present myself as a chaste Virgin to Christ. O Virgin prudent and devoted, who has taught thee that virginity is pleasing to God? What law, what righteousness, what page of the Old Testament has taught or exhorted, or counselled to live in the flesh not according to the flesh, but to lead upon the earth an Angelic life? Where didst thou read, O blessed Virgin, *The wisdom of the flesh is death* (Rom. viii. 6), and *Make not provision for the flesh, to fulfil its desire* (Id. xiii. 14)? Where didst thou read of Virgins that *they sing a new song, which none can sing, but they who follow the Lamb whithersoever He goeth* (Apoc. xiv. 4)? Where didst thou read that they are praised, *who have made themselves eunuchs for the Kingdom of Heaven's sake* (S. Matt.

xix. 12)? Where didst thou read *Though we walk in
the flesh we do not war after the flesh* (2 Cor. x. 3),
and: *He who giveth his virgin to marriage, doeth well;
but he who doth not, doeth better* (1 Cor. vii. 38)? or, *I
would that all men were even as I myself* and *It is
good for a man to remain thus, according to my counsel?
Concerning virgins*, he says, *I have no precept, but I
give a counsel* (1 Cor. vii. 40, 25 VULG.). But thou
hadst no precept, nor counsel, nor even an example:
only an anointing taught thee about all things, and the
Word of God, quick and powerful, was a teacher to thee,
before a Son, and informed thy mind, before He clad
Himself with thy flesh. Thou makest vow then to show
thyself a virgin to Christ: and art ignorant that it behoves
thee to show thyself to Him a mother. Thou choosest to
be despised in Israel; and that thou mayest please Him
to whom thou hast committed thyself, to incur the curse
of unfruitfulness: but behold the curse is changed into
blessing, the sterility into fruitfulness.

8. Open, O Virgin, thy bosom, prepare thy womb: for
He who is mighty shall do for thee great things, insomuch
that in place of being for a curse in Israel, all generations
shall call thee blessed. Nor do thou, O prudent Virgin,
distrust thy fruitfulness, since it shall not take away
chastity. Thou shalt conceive, but without sin: shalt be
with child, but without the burden and fatigues of that
state: [1] shalt bring forth, but not with sorrow: thou shalt
know not a man, yet shalt bear a Son! And what a Son!
Thou shalt be the mother of Him, Whose Father is God.
The Son of the Brightness [2] of the Father shall be the
crown of thy chastity. The Wisdom of the Heart of the

---

[1] *Gravida eris, sed non gravata.*

[2] *Charitatis;* otherwise *charitatis;* or *majestatis.*

Divine Father shall be the fruit of a virgin womb. Thou shalt conceive of God, and shalt bring forth Him who is God. Be of good comfort then, O fruitful Virgin, chaste giver-of-birth, [1] spotless Mother: for thou shalt no longer be held a disgrace in Israel, nor numbered among the barren. And if thou even still art spoken ill of by Israel according to the flesh, not because they see thee barren, but because they envy thee fruitful: remember that Christ also endured the curse of the Cross, who blessed Thee His Mother, in heaven; but even on earth thou art blessed by the Angel, and by all generations of the earth thou shalt deservedly be called blessed. Blessed then art thou among women, and blessed is the fruit of thy womb.

9. *When she had heard this, she was troubled at his saying, and cast in her mind what manner of salutation this might be.* Virgins, who are really virginal, are always apprehensive, never secure: they shrink from what is harmless, and are fearful of what is safe, knowing that they have a precious treasure in earthen vessels, that it is difficult to live the angelic life among men, to dwell on earth in a heavenly manner, and while in the flesh to live unwedded. And consequently in whatever is new or sudden, they suspect a snare, and think that the whole is directed against them. Therefore Mary also was troubled at the saying of the Angel. Troubled, but not overwhelmed. *I am so troubled*, says one, *that I cannot speak: I have considered the days of old, and borne in mind the eternal years* (Ps. lxxvii. 4, 5.) Thus Mary too was troubled and spoke not, but considered what manner of salutation this might be. That she was troubled was a mark of virginal modesty: that she was not overwhelmed, of fortitude; that she held her peace and pondered, of prudence. She

[1] [*Puerpera.*]

knew, as a prudent virgin, that often a messenger of Satan transforms himself into an Angel of light: and inasmuch as she was humble and full of simplicity, she hoped nothing at all of such a kind from the holy Angel, and therefore pondered what manner of salutation this might be.

10. Then the Angel, very easily comprehending the doubtful looks of the Virgin, understanding that she was revolving various thoughts in her mind, consoles her affright, removes her doubts, and calling her familiarly by her name, kindly persuades her not to fear. *Fear not, Mary*, he said, *for thou hast found favour with God*. Here is no snare, no deception. Suspect not here any fraud or artifice. I am not a man, but a spirit: an angel of God, not of Satan. *Thou hast found favour with God*. If thou knewest how pleasing is thy humility to the Most High, how high it raises thee before Him, thou wouldest consider thyself unworthy neither of angelic address nor respect. For why shouldest thou consider that the favour of Angels is not due to thee, who hast found favour with God? Thou hast found that which thou didst seek, that which none before thee was able to find, thou hast found favour with God. What favour? Peace between God and men, the destruction of death, the renewal of life. This then is the favour which thou hast found with God. And this is the sign of it to thee: *Behold thou shalt conceive and bear a Son, and thou shalt call His Name Jesus*. Learn then, prudent Virgin, from the name of thy promised Son, how great and special is the favour which thou hast obtained before God. *Thou shalt call His Name Jesus.* Another Evangelist states the reason of this name, an Angel thus explaining it: For He shall save His people from their sins (S. Matt. i. 21).

11. I read that two Saviours preceded Him of whom

we are now speaking, of whom they were types, and that both were of great service to their nation. The one of these led forth his people from Babylon (Hag. i., Ezra v. 1—5) the other introduced his people into the land of Promise (Joshua i.). They indeed defended from their enemies those over whom they ruled; but it could not be said that they saved them from their sins. But He, our Jesus, both saved His people from their sins, and has brought them into the land of the living. Who is this, who even forgives sins? Would that the Lord Jesus would deign to number me, a sinner, among His people, that He may save me from my sins!

For truly blessed is the people, whose Lord God is Jesus, because He shall save His people from their sins. But I fear lest many profess themselves to be of His people, whom He will not own: I fear lest there be many more, who seem to be, as it were, even among the more devout of his people, to whom He will one day say: *This people honoureth Me with their lips, but their heart is far from Me* (S. Matt. xv. 8). For the Lord Jesus knows those who are His: He knows whom He has chosen from the beginning. *Why call ye Me Lord, Lord*, He says, *and do not the things which I say?* (S. Luke vi. 46). Do you then wish to know whether you belong to His people, or rather do you desire to belong to them? Do what Jesus commands; and He will count you among His. Do what He bids in the Gospel, in the Law and the Prophets, and by the mouth of His ministers who are in the Church: submit yourself to His vicars who are set over you, not only to the good and gentle, but also to the froward. Learn from Jesus Himself, for He is meek and lowly of heart; and you shall belong to the happy and honourable company of His people, whom He has chosen to Him to be His inheritance; whom the Lord of Hosts has blessed, saying: *Thou art the work of Mk Hands, Israel Mine inheritance* (Is. xix. 25): to whom, lest you should envy Israel according to the flesh, He bears witness, saying: *A people whom I have not known, have served Me; as soon as they heard Me, they obeyed me* (Ps. xviii. 43, 44).

12. But let us hear what the same Angel thinks respecting Him upon whom, while not yet conceived, He bestows such a name. For he says: *He shall be great, and shall be called the Son of the Highest.* He may well say that One shall be great who shall merit to be called the Son of the Highest; *and of whose greatness there is no end* (Ps. cxlv. 3). And *who is great*, he says, *as is our God?* (Ps. lxxvii. 13). He is evidently great, whose greatness is as the Highest, because He is the Highest. The Son of the Highest will judge it no robbery to be of equal Nature with the Highest (Phil. ii. 6). Yet One would be rightly judged to have devised robbery, who having been brought from nothing into being in Angelic form, should compare himself with his Maker, and arrogate to himself that which is the exclusive right of the Son of the Highest, who was not made, but begotten by God, and in the form of God.

For God the Father, who is the Highest, although He is omnipotent, is not able either to make a creature equal to Himself or to beget a Son unequal. He has indeed made the Angel great, but not as great as Himself: and therefore not the Highest. But the Son alone He has not made, but begotten, the Omnipotent by the Omnipotent, the Highest by the Highest, the Coeternal by the Eternal; and He is able without usurpation or injury to compare Himself in all things with God. It is rightly said therefore that He shall be great, who shall be called the Son of the Highest.

13. But, wherefore is it said *He shall be* and not rather *He is* great; since He is always great equally,

so that He can increase in nothing, nor can be greater after His conception than He is, or has been, before it? Perhaps the Angel said *He shall be*, in order to indicate that He who was great as God, shall be great as man? Yes, He shall be truly great; great as Man, as Teacher, as Prophet. For thus it is spoken of Him in the Gospel: *That a great prophet has risen up among us* (S. Luke vii. 16). And in fact, that a great Prophet should come was promised by a prophet of lesser rank; "Behold a great Prophet shall come, and He shall renew Jerusalem." And thou indeed, O Virgin, shalt bear, and nourish, and bring up a little child: but seeing Him little, reflect that He is great. For He shall be great, because God shall so magnify Him that all kings and peoples shall worship and do Him service. Let thy soul too magnify the Lord, because *He shall be great and shall be called the Son of the Highest.* He shall be great, and He who is mighty shall do for thee great things, and holy is His Name. For what name can He be called by more holy, than the Son of the Highest? And we also who are humble shall glorify the Lord who is great; who that He might make us great, Himself became a child. *Unto us*, says the Prophet, *a Child is born: unto us a Son is given* (Is. ix. 6). Yes, He is born for us, not for Himself; and having received before time a birth much more noble from His Father, He needed not to be born in time of a mother. Nor did the Angels, who beheld Him in His greatness, need that He should become a little child. For us then He was born, to us He was given, since to us He was necessary.

14. It only remains that we should do for Him who was born for us and given to us, that, for which end He was born and given. Let us avail ourselves of our Saviour to our own good; let us work out, by the Saviour, our

salvation. Behold. He is brought into our midst as a little child. O Child, the Desire of all children! truly Childlike, but in malice, not in Wisdom! Let us study to become such as He is: let us learn of Him, for He is meek and lowly in heart: so that He who is the great God may not have become a humble man, have been crucified, and died, all to no purpose. Let us learn His humility, let us imitate His gentleness, let us embrace His Love, let us partake His Passion, and be cleansed by His Blood. Let us present Him as the propitiation for our sins; since for this it is that He is born for us and given to us, let us present Him before the eyes of His Father and before His own: For the Father *spared not His own Son, but delivered Him up for us all* (Rom. viii. 32) and the Son emptied Himself of His glory and *took upon Him the form of a servant* (Phil. ii. 7). He gave up His soul to death, He was counted with the transgressors. He bore the sins of many, and made intercession for the transgressors (Is. liii. 12). Those cannot perish for whom the Son intercedes, and that they might live, the Father delivered up His Son unto death. Pardon may then be hoped for equally from the one and from the other, since the Mercy of each is equal in goodness, the Power equal in will, and one the Divine Nature in which, in the Unity of the Holy Spirit, God liveth and reigneth for ever and ever. Amen.

SERMON XI. [1]

He shall be great, and shall be called the Son of the Highest.   S. Luke i. 32.

1. There is no doubt, that whatever we say to the praise of the Mother, we say also to that of the Son:

[1] [Homily iv. on the *Missus est.*]

and again, when we honour the Son, we do not detract
from the glory of the Mother. For if, according to Solomon,
A wise son is the glory of his father (Prov. x. 1). how
much more glorious is rendered the mother of Him who
is Wisdom itself! But why do I venture upon the praises
of one, whom the Prophets extol as praiseworthy, whom
an Angel distinguishes, and with whom the Evangelist fills
his page? I do not then praise, because I do not dare
to do so: I am content to repeat with reverence what the
Holy Spirit has explained by the mouth of the Evangelist.
He goes on to say: *And the Lord God shall give to Him
the throne of His father David.* These are the words of
the Angel to the Virgin concerning the Son promised to
her: and who, he assures her, shall possess the Kingdom
of David. That the Lord Jesus came of the House of David,
no one doubts. But how, I ask, did God give to Him
the throne of David His ancestor, seeing that He did not
reign in Jerusalem, that when the crowd desired to make
Him King, He did not yield to their wishes (S. John vi. 15),
and that before Pilate He protested: *My Kingdom is
not of this world* (Id. xviii. 36)? And after all, what great
matter was it to promise to Him who sits throned upon
the Cherubim (Ps. lxxx. 1), whom the Prophet saw *seated
upon a throne high and lifted up* (Is. vi. 1), that He
should sit upon the throne of David His father? But we
know that here another Jerusalem is signified, much more
noble and more rich than that city which is now, and in
which David once reigned. That therefore I suppose to
be meant here, according to the habitual usage of the
sacred writers, who constantly put the sign for the thing
signified. Then God truly gave to Him the throne of His
father David, when *He set His King upon His holy hill
of Sion* (Ps. ii. 6). But here the Prophet seems to have
indicated more distinctly of what kingdom he had spoken,

in saying not in *Sion*, but *upon Sion*. Therefore perhaps the word *upon* was used, because David indeed reigned *in* Sion : but His realm is *over* Sion, of whom it was said to David : *Of the fruit of thy body will I set upon thy seat* (Ps. cxxxii. 11); and of whom it was said by another prophet ; *Upon the throne of David and upon his kingdom he shall sit* (Is. ix. 7). Now do you see why you find this word *upon* everywhere? *Upon Sion, upon the throne, upon the seat, upon the Kingdom.* The Lord God will then give to Him the throne of David his father, not a typical, but a real one ; but eternal and heavenly, not temporal and earthly. And that is called, as it is here, the throne of David, because that upon which David sat in this world, was a type of that eternal and heavenly one.

2. *And He shall reign over the house of Jacob for ever; and His Kingdom shall have no end.* Here also, if we take the words of the temporal house of Jacob, how can He reign for ever in it, since it does not endure for ever? We must then look for another house of Jacob, which shall endure for ever, in which He shall reign with a never-ending dominion. And did not that (former) house of Jacob in its fury deny Him, and in its foolishness repudiate Him, before Pilate, when that governor said to them : "Shall I crucify your King" (S. John xix. 15)? and did not they reply with one voice "We have no king but Cæsar". Inquire then of the Apostle, and he will enable you to distinguish between him who is a Jew in secret, from him who is one openly : the circumcision in the spirit from that which is only in the flesh ; those who are sons of the faith of Abraham, from those who are his sons only according to the flesh. *For they are not all Israel, who are of Israel: neither, because they are the seed of Abraham, are they all children.*

(Rom. ix. 6, 7). Apply the same principle then and say: Not all who are of the blood of Jacob, are to be reckoned as of the house of Jacob. Jacob himself is he who was called Israel. Only those then who shall be found perfect in the faith of Jacob shall be counted as of his house; or rather it is only those who are truly of the spiritual and everlasting house of Jacob over whom the Lord Jesus shall reign eternally. Who is there of us who, according to this meaning of the word Jacob, will cast out of his heart the devil, will struggle with his vices and concupiscences, so that sin may not reign in his mortal body, but that on the contrary, Jesus shall reign in him now through grace, and through eternity in glory? Happy those in whom Jesus shall for ever reign, for they shall reign at the same time with Him; and His Kingdom shall have no end. O how glorious is that kingdom in which Kings are gathered to praise and glorify Him who above all others is King of kings and Lord of lords; in the glorious beholding of whom the righteous *shall shine forth in the kingdom of their Father* (S. Matt. xiii. 43). Oh! if the blessed Jesus would deign to remember me, a sinner, when He shall come into His Kingdom! O if He, in that day when He shall deliver up the Kingdom to God and His Father, if He would visit me with His salvation, that I may see the felicity of His chosen ones, and rejoice in the joy of His people, that I too may praise Him with His inheritance! (Ps. cvi. 4 and 5), But come, Lord Jesus, even now, take away the offences out of Thy Kingdom, that is, my soul; so that Thou mayest reign in it, as it is Thy right to do. For Avarice has come, and claimed a throne in me: Boastfulness seeks to rule over me; Pride desires to be my lord: Luxury says, I will reign: Ambition, Detraction, Envy and Anger strive within me, whose I shall be? As for me, I resist them as far as I am able, and struggle

against them to the best of my Power. I call upon Jesus,
my Lord; I defend myself for Him, because I feel that
His is the right over me. I hold to Him as my Lord and
my God, and I say: I have no King but Jesus. Come
then, O Lord, scatter them in Thy strength, and do
Thou rule over me, for Thou art my Lord and my God,
who art the salvation of Jacob.

3. *Then said Mary to the Angel, How shall this be,
seeing I know not a man?* First she prudently held her
peace, while she pondered in doubt, of what nature that
salutation was; preferring humbly not to reply, than to
speak rashly of what she knew not. But having well
reflected and being reassured (for while the Angel addressed
her outwardly, God influenced her inwardly) and thus strengthened, faith having put fear to flight, and joy diffidence,
she asked of the Angel: *How shall this be?* She did not
doubt of the fact; but she inquires respecting the manner
and the order in which it would take place: not whether
it should do so, but in what way. It is as if she had said:
As my Lord, who is the witness of my conscience, is aware of
the vow of His servant not to know a man, by what means,
and in what order, will it please Him that this shall take place?
If it shall be needful that I should break my vow, in order
to become the mother of such a Son; though I rejoice
for the Son, yet I grieve for the means proposed: yet
His will be done. But if as a virgin I may conceive and
bring forth a son, which will not be impossible for [Him,
if He shall so please: then I know in truth, that He has
had respect unto the lowliness of His servant. *And the
Angel answered her: The Holy Ghost shall come upon thee,
and the power of the Highest shall overshadow thee.* She
was just now said to be *full of grace:* and now in what
way is it said *The Holy Ghost shall come upon thee?*

How could she be filled with grace, and yet not have the Holy Spirit, who is the Bestower of graces? If on the contrary, she already had the Holy Spirit, how could the Angel promise that the Holy Spirit should come upon her, as it were, anew? Perhaps it was on this account that it was not said simply "He shall come", but "He shall come upon", [1] because He was indeed already in her through much grace, but is now announced to superabound (supervene) because of the fulness of more abundant grace, which He was about to pour upon her? But how could she receive more grace, being already filled? If on the contrary, she was able to receive more, how can she be understood to have been previously filled? Could it be that formerly grace filled her mind, but is now to sanctify her womb for its appointed function: inasmuch as the fulness of the Divinity which was in her previously, as in many of the Saints, dwelt in her *spiritually;* but is now about to dwell in her *corporeally,* as it had done in none of the Saints?

4. He continues then: *And the power of the Highest shall overshadow thee.* He who is able to comprehend the meaning of this, let him do so. For who, she alone being excepted who had the immense happiness of knowing by her own experience what it signified, is capable of understanding, or even of forming an idea, how that Brightness inaccessible was poured into the chaste womb of the Virgin; and how the latter was able to endure the approach of the inaccessible, when the Spirit vivified instantaneously a minute portion of the same body, of which He overshadowed the whole? And perhaps because of this chiefly it was said *shall overshadow thee,* because the matter was altogether a mystery, which the holy Trinity willed to

[1] [*Superveniet* = ἐπελεύσεται, in the sense of coming in greater degree or power. (E.)]

bring about alone and with Mary alone; and which was given to her alone to know, to whom alone it was given to be experienced. Let then the words, *The Holy Ghost shall come upon thee*, be thus explained: shall render thee fruitful by His power: and *the power of the Highest shall overshadow thee* as thus: the manner in which thou shalt conceive of the Holy Ghost, Christ, the power of God and the wisdom of God, shall be so closely veiled and so deeply hidden in the impenetrable shadow of His secret counsels, that the mystery shall be known only to Himself and thee. It is as if the Angel had replied to the Virgin: Why dost thou question me upon a matter which thou shalt soon thyself have experience of. Thou shalt indeed know it, and that happily; but He who brings about the mystery shall be the teacher to bring it to thy knowledge. I have been sent only to announce to thee thy Virginal conception, not to bring it about. It can be taught only by Him who effects it; none but she in whom it shall be brought about, can comprehend it. *Therefore also that Holy Thing which shall be born of thee shall be called the Son of God.* That is to say: Since thou shalt conceive, not of man, but of the Holy Spirit, [1] but thou shalt conceive the very Power of the Highest, that is, the Son of God; *therefore, that Holy Thing which shall be born of thee, shall be called the Son of God.* That is to say, not only He who is in the Bosom of the Father, coming thence into thy womb, shall overshadow thee, but He shall also, taking of thy substance, unite it with Himself; and from this He shall be then called Son of God. Even as it is He who was begotten by the Father before all worlds, and therefore called Son of God; so He shall hereafter be called thy Son. For thus

[1] [Another reading is: *Since that which thou shalt conceive, is not of man, but of the Holy Spirit.*]

He who was born of the Father is thy Son, and His Son shall be born of thee; yet not that there are two Sons, but one Son. And although one be of thee, another of Him; yet shall there not be to each His own, but one Son, both of the one and of the other.

5. Notice, I pray you, how reverently the Angel spake it; *that Holy Thing which shall be born of thee*. Why does he say simply *that Holy Thing*, without adding more? I believe because there was no name by which he could properly and worthily designate that noble, exalted and reverend being to be formed by the uniting of the soul, and the body drawn from the most pure flesh of the Virgin, with the Only Begotten Son of the Father. If he had said "the holy body", "the holy man" or "the holy child" or any expression of that kind, he would seem to have spoken inadequately. Therefore no doubt, he used the indefinite expression, *that Holy Thing*: because whatever were the fruit born of the Virgin, it was without doubt holy and even uniquely so, both through the sanctification by the Spirit, and through its assumption by the Word.

6. Then the Angel added: *Behold, thy cousin Elizabeth she hath also conceived a son in her old age*. Why was it necessary to announce to the Virgin that this barren woman had also conceived a son? Was it perhaps in order to convince, by the news of a miracle so recent, the Virgin whom he saw to be still doubtful and incredulous? By no means. For we read that Zacharias was punished for such incredulity by this very Angel: but we do not read that Mary was in any respect blamed. On the contrary, we know that her faith was praised by Elizabeth speaking prophetically. *Blessed is she that be-*

lieved: for there shall be a performance of those things which were told her from the Lord. But the reason that the Angel made known to Mary the conception of her cousin, hitherto barren, was to complete her joy by adding miracle to miracle. Moreover, it was needful that she who was soon about to conceive the Son of the Father's affection, with the joy of the Holy Spirit, should in the first place be animated by no slight degree of love and joy: since it was only a heart as full of gladness as of perfect devotedness that was capable of receiving the fulness of happiness and joy. Or it may be that the conception of Elizabeth was announced to Mary, because it was fitting that a fact which was soon to be known to all, should be declared beforehand to the Virgin by an Angel, rather than made known to her by the mouth of men, and the mother of God appear to be a stranger to the counsels of her Son, if she had remained in ignorance of the events which were taking place so near her upon earth. Or, more probably, the conception of Elizabeth was announced to Mary in order that, being made aware already of the coming of the Saviour, and now of that of His Forerunner, and knowing the order and the time of each, she would better be able at a later period, to declare the truth to the Sacred Writers and the preachers of the Gospel, as having been fully instructed from on high in all these mysteries from the very beginning. Finally, it is possible that it was made known so that Mary, on learning that a relative already advanced in age was pregnant, she who was still young, should hasten as a matter of dutiful attention, to visit her; and thus occasion be given to that infant Prophet, to pay to his Lord, still younger than he, the first fruits of his duty; and that while the two mothers met, the consciousness felt by the children of each other's presence, should add to one miracle another still more marvellous.

7. But take care not to suppose that all these events so wonderful, which you hear foretold by the Angel, are to be brought to pass by him. If you inquire by whom, listen to the Angel himself. *For with God*, he says, *nothing shall be impossible*. As if he had said; All these things that I promise you so faithfully, rest not upon my power, but upon His by whom I have been sent. And with Him nothing shall be impossible: for what can be impossible to Him who has done all things by His Word? And I am struck by this in the Angel's speech; that he markedly says *not* "no action", but "no *word*" is impossible with God. [1]

Does he employ this phrase in order to enable us to understand that while men are easily able to say all that they please, but by no means able to do what they please; God is able as easily and with incomparably greater ease to carry out in action whatsoever they are able to express in words? I will explain myself. If it were as easy for men to do what they wished as to say it: then to them also no word would be impossible. But now, according to a saying as ancient as well-known, "there is a great difference between saying and doing"; and that is so with men, but not with God; for with God alone it is the same thing to do what He shall say, and to express what He wills; most truly then "no word" shall be impossible with God. For example: the Prophets were able to foresee and foretell that a sterile Virgin should conceive and bring forth: but were they able to cause her to do so? But God, who gave them the power to foresee, as easily as He was able to predict what He pleased through them, just so easily was able now when it pleased Him, to fulfil what He had

---

[1] The Vulgate reads "*quia non erit impossibile apud Deum omne verbum*". The Greek word here, ῥῆμα, has the sense both of *factum* and *verbum*. (*E.*)

caused to be predicted. And in fact with God, neither does the word differ from the intention, because He is truth; nor the act from the word, because He is power; nor is the manner unsuitable to the act, because He is wisdom. Thus it is that with God no word shall be impossible.

8. You have heard, O Virgin, the announcement of that which is about to take place; and the manner in which it will take place; in each there is matter for wonder and rejoicing. Rejoice then, daughter of Sion, daughter of Jerusalem. And since you have heard news of gladness and joy, let us too hear from you the glad response for which we wait, so that the bones which have been humbled by sorrow may leap for joy. You have heard, I say, the fact and have believed, believe also in the manner in which it shall be accomplished. By the operation of the Holy Spirit not of a man, shalt thou conceive and bear a Son; and the Angel waits only for the reply, to return to God who sent him. We too, O Lady, we who are weighed down by the sentence of condemnation, wait for the word of pity. The price of our salvation is offered to you: soon shall we be freed, if you consent (to give yourself to the Divine plan.) Alas! we, who all are the creatures of the Eternal Word of God, are perishing; we are to be restored by your brief response, and recalled to life. Unhappy Adam with his miserable progeny exiled from Paradise, Abraham also and David, entreat this, O pious Virgin, of you. Others join in the entreaty, holy Fathers and ancestors of your own, who also dwell in the valley of the shadow of death. The whole world prostrate at your knees, waits for your consent; and not without reason; since upon your lips hangs the consolation of the unhappy, the redemption of the captives, the freedom of the condemned; in fine, the safety of the children of Adam, of the whole human race. Reply

quickly, O Virgin: give the word which the earth, hell
and the heavens themselves wait for. He, the King and Lord
of all things, waits for the word of your consent, by means
of which He has proposed to save the world, inasmuch as
He has approved of your graces. He whom in silence you
have pleased, you will please still more by speech, since
He cries to you from Heaven; O fairest among women,
let me hear thy voice (Cant. ii. 15). If then thou doest
this, he will cause thee to see our salvation. Is not this
what you desire, what you long for, what you sigh for
in daily and nightly prayers? What then! are you she to
whom this was promised, or do we look for another? On
the contrary, it is you yourself and not another. You, I
say, are that promised, expected and desired one, from
whom your holy ancestor Jacob, already drawing near to
death, hoped for everlasting life, saying: *I wait for Thy
salvation, O Lord* (Gen. xlix. 18). In whom, in short, and
by means of whom, our God and King Himself purposed
before time began to bring about a salvation in the midst
of the earth. Why do you hope for that from another
woman, which is offered to you? Why do you expect
that to be done by means of another woman, which will
be speedily made manifest by means of you, provided you
reply and yield your assent? Reply then quickly to the
Angel, or rather by the Angel to the Lord. Speak a word,
and receive the Word, utter but your transitory word, and
conceive the Word Divine and Eternal. Why do you fear
and delay? Believe, consent and conceive. Let humility
become bold, let your timidity have confidence. In no wise
is it needful even now, that virginal simplicity should forget
prudence. In this matter alone, O prudent Virgin, you
need not fear presumption; for although reserve is prized
by its silence, yet now charity should speak. Open, blessed
Virgin, your heart to confidence, your lips to consent,

your bosom to its Creator. Behold the Desire of all nations knocks at its door. If He should pass away while you are delaying, and you should begin again with grief to seek Him whom your soul loveth! Arise then, hasten and open to Him. Rise by faith, hasten by devotion, open by giving consent. [1]

9. *Behold*, she said, *the handmaid of the Lord, be it unto me according to thy word.* The virtue of humility is always found closely associated with Divine grace: *for God resisteth the proud, but giveth grace unto the humble* (S. James iv. 6). She replies then with humility, that the dwelling of grace may be prepared. *Behold*, she says, *the handmaid of the Lord.* How sublime is this humility, which is incapable of yielding to the weight of honours, or of being rendered proud by them! The Mother of God is chosen, and she declares herself His handmaid. It is in truth a mark of no ordinary humility, that even when so great an honour is done to her, she does not forget to be humble. It is no great thing to be humble when in a low condition; but humility in one that is honoured is a great and rare virtue. If, for my sins or for those of others, God should permit that the Church, deceived by my pretensions, should elevate such a miserable, and humble man as I to any, even the most ordinary honour; should not I immediately, forgetful of what I am, begin to think myself such an one as men (who do not see the heart) imagine me to be? I should believe in the public opinion, not regarding the testimony of my conscience, not estimating honour by virtues, but virtue by honours; I should believe myself to be the more holy, the higher was the position I occupied. You may frequently see in the Church men sprung from the lower ranks who have attained to the

[1] [A similar expression will be found in S. Augustine, Tom. V., Sermon 120, Appendix.

higher, and from being poor, have become rich, beginning to swell with pride, forgetting their low extraction, being ashamed of their family and disdaining their parents, because they are in humble condition. You may see also wealthy men attaining rapidly to ecclesiastical honours, and then at once regarding themselves as men of great holiness, though they have changed their clothes only and not their minds; and persuading themselves that they are worthy of a dignity to which they have attained by solicitation: and that which they owe (if I dare to say so) to their wealth, they ascribe to their merits. I do not speak of those whom ambition blinds, and for whom even honour is a matter for pride.

10. But I see (much to my regret) some who after having despised and renounced the pomp of this world in the school of humility, habituating themselves still more to pride; and under the wings of a Master who is meek and humble in heart, become more and more insolent and impatient in the cloister, than they had been in the world. And, which is a thing still more perverse, there are very many who while in their own homes they would have had to bear contempt, cannot endure to do so in the house of God. They would not have been able to obtain honours in the world, where all desire to possess them: and yet they expect to be loaded with honours, where all have made profession to despise them. I see others (and it is a thing not to be seen without grief) after having enrolled themselves in the army of Christ, entangling themselves anew in the affairs of the world, and plunging again into worldly objects: with earnest zeal they build up walls (*muros*), but neglect to build up their own characters (*mores*); under pretext of the general good, they sell their words to the rich and their salutations to matrons; but in

spite of the formal order of their Sovereign, they cast covetous eyes on the goods of others, and do not shrink from lawsuits to maintain their own rights; not listening to the proclamtion made by the Apostle, as a herald bidden by the King; *This is the very fault among you, that ye go to law one with another. Why do ye not rather endure wrong?* (1 Cor. vi. 7). Is it so that they have crucified themselves to the world, and that the world is crucified to them, that those who before had scarcely been known in their town or village, are now seen traversing provinces, frequenting courts, cultivating a knowledge of kings and the friendship of the great? What shall I say of their religious habit itself? In it they require not so much warmth as colour: and they have more care of the cleanness of their vestment than the culture of their virtues. I am ashamed to say it, but mere women are surpassed in their study of dress by monks, when costliness in clothing is studied more than utility. At length every appearance of the religious state is laid aside, and the soldiers of Christ strive to be adorned, not to be armed. Even when they are preparing for the struggle, and ought to oppose to the powers of the air the ensign of poverty (which those adversaries greatly fear) they rather prefer to present themselves in carefully studied dress, the sign of peace, and thus willingly to give themselves unarmed and without the striking of a blow, to their enemies. All these evils only come when, renouncing those sentiments of humility which have caused us to quit the world, and finding ourselves thus drawn back to the unprofitable tastes and desires for worldly things, we become like dogs returning to their vomit.

11. Whoever we are who find inclinations in ourselves, let us mark well what was the reply of her who was chosen

to be the mother of God, but who did not forget humility. *Behold*, she said, *the handmaid of the Lord; let it be to me according to thy word. Let it be to me* is the expression of a desire, not the indication of a doubt. Even those words "according to thy word" are to be understood more as the feeling of one wishing for and desiring, than as the expression of the doubt of one uncertain. We may understand *let it be to me* as words of prayer. And certainly no one prays for anything unless he believes that it exists, and hopes to obtain it. But God wills that what He has promised should be asked of Him in prayer. And perhaps therefore He in the first place promises many things which He has resolved to give us, that our devotion may be excited by the promise: and that thus our earnest prayer may merit, what He had been disposed to bestow upon us freely. This it was that the prudent Virgin understood, when she joined the merit of her prayer with the prevenient gift of the promise freely bestowed upon her, saying: *let it be to me according to Thy word.* Let it be to me according to Thy word concerning the Word. Let the Word which was in the beginning with God become Flesh from my flesh according to Thy word.

Let the Word, I pray, be to me, not as a word spoken only to pass away, but conceived and clothed in Flesh, not in air, that He may remain with us. Let Him be, not only to be heard with the ears, but to be seen with the eyes, touched with the hands and borne on the shoulders. Let the Word be to me, not as a word written and silent, but Incarnate and living: that is, not traced with dead signs upon dead parchments; but livingly impressed in human form upon my chaste womb: nor by the tracing of a pen of lifeless reed, but by the operation of the Holy Spirit. Finally, let it thus be to me, as was never done to anyone before me, nor after me shall be done. God hath indeed

formerly spoken in divers manners to the fathers by the
Prophets: and the word of God is recorded to have been
produced in the ear of some, in the mouth of others
and in others, again, by the hand: but I pray, that the
Word of God may be formed in my womb according to
Thy word. I desire that He may be formed, not as the
Word in preaching, not as a sign in figures, or as a
vision in dreams: but silently inspired, personally incarn-
ated, found in the body in my body. Let the Word
therefore deign to do in me and for me, what He needed
not to do and could not do, for Himself; according to Thy
word. Let it be done indeed generally for the sake of
the whole world, but specially let it be done unto me,
according to thy word.

*Excuse of S. Bernard, because he had taken upon him,
after many other expositors, to treat of this passage of the
Gospel.*

I have expounded this passage of the Gospel, as well as
I was able; I am not unaware that my manner of doing so
will not be pleasing to all, and I know that, on the contrary,
I shall draw upon myself the criticism of many. By some
my work will be thought useless, by others I shall be regarded
as presumptuous, in that I have dared to set my hand to
explain in my turn a passage which has been the subject of
abundant exposition by the Fathers. But if what I have
written, though after the Fathers, is not in contradiction to
them, or as sitting in judgment on what they have said, I
do not think that anyone has the right to be displeased with
me for writing. If I have repeated what I have learned from
the Fathers, provided that the sign of presumption be absent,
so that it may bring forth the fruit of devotion: I shall listen
with equanimity to those who call it superfluous. Yet I beg
to say to those who taunt me with having given a useless
and superfluous explanation, that my purpose has been not
so much to expound the Gospel, as to take occasion from
the Gospel to speak of truths which it is a delight to me to

enlarge upon. But if I have been wrong in this, that I have followed the impulses of my own devotion, more than I have sought the common good, the pious Virgin will be powerful with her merciful Son, to excuse this my wrong doing: to whom I dedicate this my little treatise, such at it is, with the greatest devotion.

SERMON XII. [1]

On the words of the Martyrology "Jesus Christ the Son of God, was born in Bethlehem of Judea." [2]

1. A Voice of joy has sounded upon our earth, of salvation and of gladness in the dwellings of sinners. Good tidings have been heard, a word of consolation, a message of great joy, worthy of all acceptation. Sing praise, all ye mountains; and all ye trees of the woods, applaud before the Lord; for He comes. Hear, O heavens, and give ear, O earth; wonder and praise, O all creation, but thou especially, O man: "Jesus Christ, the Son of God, is born in Bethlehem of Judea." What man is there of heart so stony-hard, that he is not softened at these words? What sweeter news could be announced to us? or what could be welcomed more? What such news did the world ever hear or receive? *Jesus Christ, the Son of God, is born in Bethlehem of Judea.* A brief phrase indeed to express the Word in His humility, but how full it is of heavenly sweetness! The grateful soul labours and strives to express more completely that sweet fulness of delight, and finds no words to do so: and such is the worth of these few

[1] [Sermon I. For the Eve of the Nativity].

[2] These words are read in the Martyrology of Usuardus, which all, or almost all, the Churches of France, and even the Churches of Rome, made use of at that period.

words, that if only one *iota* be changed, the meaning of the whole message is instantly diminished. O Birth of inviolate sanctity, honourable to the whole world, precious to men for the greatness of the benefit which it brings, which even Angels desire to look into for the depth of its sacred mystery, and the newness of its singular excellence; since before it there was nothing like unto it, nor after it shall be such. O Birth alone without sorrow, or shame, or corruption; which did not open, but consecrated, the sanctuary of a Virginal womb! Nativity that was above nature, but on behalf of nature; surpassing it by the excellence of its miracle, but repairing it by the mysterious virtue which was in it. My brethren, who can narrate such a Birth as this? An Angel announces it, the power of the Highest overshadows it, the Holy Spirit intervenes: a Virgin believes, conceives by faith, brings forth, yet remains virgin: who does not wonder? The Son of the Highest, God of God, begotten before the worlds, is born in time: the Word born as an infant: who can wonder sufficiently?

2. Nor is that nativity unnecessary, nor that condescension of the Divine Majesty unfruitful. *Jesus Christ, the Son of God, is born in Bethlehem of Judea.* Ye who are in the dust, rise up and render praise to God. Behold, the Lord comes with salvation: with anointing He comes and with glory. For *Jesus* comes not without *salvation:* the Christ not without *anointing,* nor the *Son* of God without *glory:* and indeed He Himself is salvation, anointing and glory, as it is written: *A wise son is the glory of his father* (Prov. x. i.). Happy the soul, which having tasted the fruit of His salvation, is drawn by and runs willingly after the perfume of His sweetness, that it may behold His glory, the glory as of the Only Begotten of the Father.

Breathe more freely, ye lost ones; for Jesus comes to seek and to save that which was lost. Return to health, ye who were stricken with death : Christ comes to heal with the balm of His mercy those who are of contrite heart. Rejoice and exult, ye, whosoever ye are, who long for high destinies; the Son of God comes down to you, to make you coheirs of His Kingdom. So heal me, I beseech Thee, O Lord, and I shall be healed : save me, and I shall be saved; glorify me, and I shall become glorious. Bless the Lord, O my soul, and all that is within me bless His Holy Name, who forgiveth all mine iniquities, who healeth all my diseases, who crowneth me with loving kindness and tender mercies! (Ps. ciii. 1, 3, 5).

These three reflections, dearly beloved, occur to me, as suggested by the news that Jesus Christ the Son of God, is born upon the earth. Wherefore do we call His Name Jesus, unless that *He shall save His people from their sins?* (S. Matt. i. 21), or why has He willed to be named Christ [*the Anointed One*] except because *He shall cause the yoke to be destroyed because of the anointing?* (Is. x. 27). Wherefore has the Son of God been made man, but that He may make men the sons of God? But then, who shall resist his will? It is Jesus who justifies us, who can condemn us? It is Christ who makes us whole, who could possibly wound us, the Son of God who exalts us, and who can humiliate us?

3. It is the Birthday of Jesus: let each one rejoice, whom his conscience condemns as a sinner, and deserving eternal damnation; for the Love of Jesus overpasses the sins of every offender, whatever be their number or their weight. It is the Birthday of Christ: let each who is struggling with his former vices, rejoice and be glad; for no disease of the soul, however inveterate it be, can continue, in presence of the unction which Christ imparts.

It is the Birthday of the Son of God: let all those who aspire to high destinies rejoice because the great Rewarder has come. My brethren, here is the Heir of the Father: come let us welcome Him loyally, and *His inheritance shall be ours*; for *He who has given His own Son for us, how shall He not with Him freely give us all things?* (Rom. viii. 32). Let no one doubt, let no one hesitate; we have a sure testimony: *The Word of God was made Flesh, and dwelt among us* (S. John i. 14). The Only Begotten Son of God has willed to have brethren, that *He might be the Firstborn among many brethren.* He did not scruple at the fragility and weakness of humanity, before He became the Brother of men, He became the Son of Man, He became Man. If man regards this as impossible, let him see and he will believe.

4. *Jesus Christ was born in Bethlehem of Judea.* Notice the condescension of this. Not in Jerusalem, the royal city; but in Bethlehem, which is the least among the thousands of Juda. O Bethlehem! who art small, but rendered great by the Lord! He, who though so great, has deigned to be made small in thee, has rendered thee great. Rejoice then, Bethlehem, and let the festive Alleluia be sung along all thy ways. What city in the world, on learning this great news, will not envy thee that stable, and the glory of that manger? In the whole world thy name is already famous; and all generations call thee blessed. Everywhere glorious things are spoken of thee, O city of God: everywhere the words are chanted: *A Man was born in her, and the Most High has established her* (Ps. lxxxvii. 5). Everywhere, I say, it is proclaimed and preached that *Jesus Christ, the Son of God, is born in Bethlehem of Judea!* Nor is it useless to add the word 'Judea' since it reminds us of the promise made unto the

fathers: *The sceptre shall not depart from Judah, nor a lawgiver from between his feet, until He who is to be sent forth, and who is the Desire of the nations, shall come* (Gen. xlix. 10). For salvation is of the Jews; but a salvation for the whole earth. *Judah*, says the Patriarch, *thy brethren shall praise thee, and thy hands shall be upon the necks of thy enemies;* and the rest, which we never see accomplished in that Judah. but which is fulfilled in Christ. For He is the Lion of the tribe of Judah: of whom it is added: *Judah is a lion's whelp: unto the prey, my son, thou hast gone up (Ibid.)* That great spoiler who *before he knew how to call by name his father and his mother, takes away the spoil of Samaria* (Is. viii. 4), is no other than Christ. Christ is that spoiler, *who ascending up on high, led captivity captive:* but as for Himself He has taken from none; but rather has given gifts unto men. These words then "in Bethlehem of Judah" recall to my mind these and similar prophecies which are fulfilled in Christ, of whom indeed they were spoken long before: nor do they leave it doubtful that some good thing should come out of Bethlehem.

5. But now as to what immediately concerns us, we learn from this, in what manner He, who willed to be born at Bethlehem, desires to be received by us. The King of glory might no doubt have thought that it became Him to seek out lofty palaces, where He might be received with glory: but it was not for such an end that He had descended from His royal throne. *In His left hand are riches and glory, and in His right length of days* (Prov. iii. 16). He possessed all things in abundance in the heavens, but poverty was not found there. Moreover, this abounded and superabounded on the earth, and man knew not its value. This therefore the Son of God loved, and came

down that He might choose it for Himself, and make it
precious in our eyes also by the esteem in which He held
it. Deck thy bridal couch, O Sion; but with humility, with
poverty. In these marks of poverty He takes delight: and
according to the testimony of Mary, these are the silken
robes in which it pleases Him to be wrapped. Therefore
sacrifice to your God the abominations of the Egyptians.

6. Consider finally, that *He is born in Bethlehem of Judea:*
and strive to become yourself, in a sense, another Bethlehem, that He may condescend to be received also in thee.
Bethlehem signifies *the house of Bread;* Judah signifies
confession. [1]

If then you fill your soul with the bread of the Divine
Word; and receive with all the faith of which you are
capable, however unworthily, that Bread, which came down
from heaven, and giveth life unto the world, the Body,
that is, of the Lord Jesus: that new body of the Resurrection shall sustain and renew your former natural body
and enable it to contain the new wine [of everlasting life]:
and if you live by faith, you need not lament because
you have forgotten to eat your bread: you have become
a Bethlehem, truly worthy to receive the Lord, if only
you have not failed in confession. Let Judea then be your
sanctification. Put upon you an honorable confession, which
is the vestment in which the ministers of Christ are most

[1] [Juda (יְהוּדָה) from (אוֹדֶה ôdeh) = I will praise (Gen.
xxix. 35) means *praised.* Ἰουδας in the Greek form of the
name, as it occurs in the lxx. and New Testament = a confessor of Jehovah (see Rev. ii. 9 and iii. 9). Hence F. Hiero-
nymus Lauretus (*Sylva Allegoriarum, sub voce*) takes the
symbolic meaning of the word to be *laudatio sive confessio*
(Gen. xxxviii. 26): and in the latter *typus est fidei* (Ps.
lxviii. 27). (E.)].

acceptable to Him. Lastly, the Apostle briefly commends to you both the one and the other in these words : *With the heart man believeth unto righteousness, and with the mouth confession is made unto salvation* (Rom. x. 10). Righteousness in the heart, is as bread in the dwelling. For righteousness is bread; as it is said *Blessed are they that hunger and thirst after righteousness, for they shall be filled* (S. Matt. v. 6). Let then righteousness be in your heart, the righteousness which is of faith : for this alone has glory before God: and by your mouth let confession be made unto salvation. Then you may safely receive Him who is born in Bethlehem of Judea, Jesus Christ the Son of God.

SERMON XIII. [1]

O Judah and Jerusalem, fear not: to-morrow ye shall go forth, and the Lord will be with you. 2 Chron. xx. 17.

1. I am addressing those who are truly Jews, not in the letter, but in the spirit: the seed of Abraham, which is multiplied according to the promise that we read was made to him. For *not the children of the flesh, but the children of the promise are counted for the seed,* (Rom. ix. 8). Similarly I do not speak here of that Jerusalem which killed the Prophets. How, in fact, could I be able to console her, over whom the Lord wept (S. Luke xix. 41) and which has been given over to destruction? But I speak of that new Jerusalem, which descends from heaven. *Fear not, O Judah and Jerusalem!* No, fear not at all, ye who are true confessors, who confess the Lord, not only with

---

[1] [Sermon II. for the Eve of the Nativity].

your mouth, but with your whole being: who are clad
with that confession as with a robe, yes, your whole inward natures confess the Lord, whose very bones say:
Lord, who is like unto Thee (Ps. xxxv. 10), not like those
who *profess that they know God, but in works they deny
Him* (Tit. i. 16). You confess Him truly, my brethren,
if all your works are His works and confess Him. Let
them confess Him in two ways, let them be clad, as it
were in a double robe of confession, that is, of your own
sins, and of the praise of God. For then you shall be true
Jews [= confessors of Jehovah, Rev. ii. 9] if your whole lives
confess that you are sinners, and deserving of the greatest
punishments: and that God is supremely good, who fore-
goes the eternal penalties which you have deserved,
for these slight and transitory pains. For whosoever
does not ardently desire penitence, seems to say by his
actions, that he has no need of it, and thus does not
confess his fault: or that penitence is of no service to him,
and thus does not confess the Divine goodness. Do you
then be true Jews and a true Jerusalem, that you may
fear nothing. For Jerusalem is the Vision of peace; the
Vision of it, not the possession; on whose borders the
Lord hath established peace: but not at the setting out,
nor at the midway thither. If then you have not perfect
peace, which indeed you are not able to have in this
world, at least behold it, look forward to it, meditate
upon it and desire it. Fix upon it the eyes of your mind,
let your intention direct itself towards peace, do all your
actions with a view to attain that peace *which passeth
all understanding* (Philip. iv. 7) and in all you do propose
to yourself no other end, than to be reconciled with God
and have peace with Him.

2.   It is to those who do this that I say: *Fear not.*

Those I console; and not those who have not known the way of peace. For if to them it is said, *To-morrow ye shall go forth;* that is not to console, but to threaten. In truth, only those who behold peace, and know that if the earthly house of their habitation were dissolved, they shall have another of God's building; — it is only such that desire to be dissolved and depart: not such as are turned towards folly and delight in their chains. Of such as die in this disposition, it cannot be said that they go forth into light and liberty, but rather that they enter into darkness, into prison, into hell. But to you it is said: *Fear not, to-morrow ye shall go forth:* and there shall be no fear any longer in your borders. You have it is true, numerous enemies; *the flesh,* than which no enemy can be nearer to you: *the present evil world* which surrounds you on all sides: and lastly the princes of darkness, who are ambushed in the air to beset your road. Nevertheless fear not, to-morrow ye shall go forth; that is, in a short time: for to-morrow means in a short time. Thus also the holy Jacob said: *In time to come my righteousness shall answer for me* (Gen. xxx. 33). For there are three epochs, and of these we read: *After two days He will revive us, and the third day He will raise us up* (Hos. vi. 3). One is under Adam, another in Christ, the third with Christ. Wherefore also it is there added: *We shall know, and shall follow to come to the knowledge of the Lord* (Ibid.), and as it is said here, *To-morrow ye shall go forth and the Lord will be with you.* For these words are addressed to those, who have divided their days, for whom the days in which they were born have perished: that is, the day of Adam, the day of sin, on which Jeremiah called down a malediction, saying: *Cursed be the day on which I was born* (Jer. xx. 15). All of us were in fact, born in that day: would that in all of us too it might perish: that day of darkness and gloominess, of storm and tempest, which Adam has brought about for us, which is due to that enemy which said: *Your eyes shall be opened* (Gen. iii. 5).

3. But behold the day of a new redemption for us has dawned, of the ancient plan of renewal, of an eternal felicity. *This is the day which the Lord hath made, let us rejoice and be glad in it* (Ps. cxviii. 24), for *to-morrow we shall go forth.* And from whence? from our sojourn in this state of existence, from the prison-house of this body, from the fetters of necessity, of restless inquiringness, of vanity, of pleasures which entangle, in spite of ourselves, the feet of our desire. What is there really in common between our spirit and earthly things? Why does it not desire, and seek, and appreciate spiritual things? O my soul, since thou art from above, what hast thou to do with these lower objects? *Seek those things which are above, where Christ sitteth at the Right Hand of God. Set your affection on things above, not on things upon the earth.* (Coloss. iii. 1, 2). But *the corruptible body presseth down the soul and the earthy tabernacle weigheth down the mind, that museth upon many things* (Wisd. ix. 15). Many unhappy necessities of the body hold us back. The wings of the soul are clogged with carnal desire and delight, so that they cannot soar; and if even the mind is raised above the earth, it speedily falls back again. Yet fear not, *to-morrow ye shall come forth* from this abyss of misery, of foul slime; for the Lord, in order that He might draw you forth thence, has Himself plunged into it: and ye shall come forth from a state of mortality and from every corruption of sin. Spend that day then in Christ, that ye may walk as He walked: for *he that says that he abideth in Him, ought himself also so to walk, even as He walked* (1. S. John ii. 6). *Fear not, then, for to-morrow ye shall*

go forth, and so ye shall be ever with the Lord. Perhaps those striking words *and the Lord shall be with you,* are to be understood thus; that while we are in the body, we are able to be with the Lord, that is, in unity of will with Him; but not He with us, in the sense that He should be at one with our will. For we would wish to be freed; we earnestly desire to be released and go forth, but hitherto for a certain cause, He delays to grant our wish. But to-morrow, we shall go forth, and the Lord shall be with us, so that whatever we wish He will wish with us, and His will and ours will be in complete accord.

4. Therefore Judah and Jerusalem, fear not, if you are not yet able to obtain the perfection which you desire: but let the humility of confession of your imperfection supply what is wanting in your daily life; since that imperfection is not hidden from the eyes of God. If he has commanded that His precepts should be diligently kept (Ps. cxix. 4) it is in order that, seeing our constant imperfection and our inability to fulfil the duty which we ought to do, we may fly to His mercy, and say: *Thy mercy is better than life* (Ps. lxiii. 3) and that, not being able to appear clad in innocence or righteousness, we may be at least covered with the robe of confession. *For confession and beauty are in the sight of the Lord* (Ps. xcvi. 6. VULG.) if only (as we have said) it proceeds not from our lips only, but from our whole nature; if all our bones say: *Lord, who is like unto Thee,* and that in the pure prospect of, and desire of reconciliation with God. For to such as feel thus is the saying: *Fear not, O Juda and Jerusalem, to-morrow ye shall go forth;* that is to say, speedily your soul shall go forth from the body; all its affections, all its desires, which now like so many bonds, hold it still fast to the things of the world, shall be dissolved; it shall go forth from this clogging hindrance; *and the Lord shall*

be with thee. Perhaps the time may seem to you very long, if you have regard only to yourself, and not to those things which are in relation with you. For is not the whole world in such relation? The creation was made subject to vanity: and on the Fall of man, whom the Lord had set over His house as its ruler, and the prince of His whole possession, the whole heritage was infected with him. Thence are extremities of heat and cold in the atmosphere, the soil being cursed in the labours of Adam, and the subjection of all things to vanity.

5. Nor indeed, will the heritage be re-established, until the heirs of it return to their first state. Wherefore, according to the testimony of the Apostle, *it groaneth and travaileth in pain together until now* (Rom. viii. 22). It is not to the eyes of this world alone, but to those of Angels and of men [departed] that we are made a spectacle. *The righteous*, saith the Psalmist, *wait for me, until Thou shalt restore me* (Ps. cxlii. 7. VULG.). And thus the martyrs, when they earnestly besought the day of judgment, not as being desirous of vengeance, but because they longed for the perfection of blessedness, which they shall then obtain, received from God this response: *Endure yet for a little while, until the number of your brethren be made up* (Apoc. vi. 11). Each of them indeed received a white robe; but they will not be vested in a second, until we too shall be vested with them. We hold as pledges and hostages their very bodies, without which their glory cannot be consummated, nor will they receive those until the time when we shall receive ours with them. Wherefore the Apostle says of the Patriarchs and Prophets: *God reserving some better thing for us, that without us they might not be perfected* (Heb. xi. 40). O if we could comprehend with what earnest and eager desire they expect and await

our coming! how anxiously they enquire about, and how willingly listen to, any good actions that we do!

6. Yet why do I speak of these, who have learned compassion by the sufferings they have themselves endured, when our coming is desired by the holy Angels themselves? Is it not from such poor worms of the earth, and from such dust that the walls of the heavenly Jerusalem are to be raised again! Have you any idea of the ardour with which the citizens of that heavenly country desire the rebuilding of the ruins of their city? With what solicitude do they await the coming of the living stones, who are to be built in together with them? How they pass to and fro between us and God, bearing to Him most faithfully our groans and complaints, and bringing back to us His grace with admirable zeal! Unquestionably they will not disdain to have us for companions, whose helpers they have already become. For *are they not all ministering spirits, sent forth to minister unto those who shall be heirs of salvation* (Heb. i. 14). Let us hasten then, beloved, I entreat you, let us hasten, since the whole multitude of the heavenly host awaits us. We cause the Angels to rejoice, when we have turned to penitence; let us come forwards now and hasten to fill them with joy on our behalf. Woe to you, whoever you are, who art meditating a return to the mire, and the vomit. Do you suppose that you will thus render favourable to you at the day of judgment, those whom you wish to deprive of a joy so great, and so much hoped for? They have been glad when we came to penitence, as over those whom they saw turning back from the very gates of hell. What will now be their affliction, if they see returning from the gates of paradise and taking the backward road, those who had already one foot within its threshold? For if our bodies are still below, yet our hearts are already in heaven.

7. Hasten, then, my brethren, hasten; for not the
Angels alone, but the Creator of the Angels awaits you.
The marriage feast is prepared, but the house is not yet
full of guests: those who shall fill the places at the feast
are still being waited for. The Father awaits you and
desires your coming; not only because of the great love
wherewith He loved you (wherefore also the only Begotten
Son, who is in the Bosom of the Father, Himself declared
The Father loveth you (S. John xvi. 27), but because of
His Own Self, as He speaks by the Prophet: *Because of
my own Self I will do this, not because of you* (Ezek.
xxxvi. 22. Vulg.). [1]

Who can doubt that the promise shall be fulfilled which
He made to the Son, saying, *Ask of Me, and I will give
Thee the nations for Thy inheritance* (Ps. ii. 8). And in
another place: *Sit Thou on My Right Hand; until I shall
make Thine enemies Thy footstool* (Ps. cx. 1). Now all
His enemies would not be subdued, as long as they shall
continue to attack us who are His members. Nor will
this promise be fulfilled, until the last enemy shall be
destroyed, which is death. For who knows not, how
greatly the Son longed for the fruit of His Incarnation,
and of the whole Life which He lived in the flesh; in
short, the fruit of His Cross and Passion, the price of His
Precious Blood? Will he not hereafter give over to God the
Father the Kingdom which He has acquired? Will He not
bring back to communion with Him, His creatures, for whose
sake the Father sent Him into the world? The Holy Spirit
also awaits us. For He is that Charity and loving kindness,
in which we have been predestinated from all eternity: nor
is it doubtful, that He wills His predestination to be fulfilled.

---

[1] [S. Bernard was no doubt quoting from memory, and not
quite exactly: *Non propter vos Ego faciam, domus Israel, sed
propter Nomen sanctum Meum.* (E.)].

8. Since then the wedding feast is prepared, and all the hosts of the heavenly court are waiting for and desiring our coming: let us, my brethren, run our Christian course not as uncertainty, let us run with earnest desire, and striving after virtue. To set out, is to make progress. Let each of us say: *Look upon me, and have mercy upon me, as Thou usest to do unto those who love Thy Name* (Ps. cxix. 132). Have mercy upon me, not as I have deserved, but as They have decreed. Let us say also: *Let Thy will be, as it is done in heaven;* or simply *Thy will be done* (S. Matt. vi. 10). For we know that it is written: *If God be for us, who can be against us?* and again: *Who shall lay anything to the charge of God's elect?* (Rom. viii. 31, 33). *Is it not lawful for Me,* He says, *to do what I will with mine own?* (S. Matt. xx. 15). Let these words be our consolation, my dear brethren, until we go forth from this world, and may the Lord be with us to the end. May He, in His great mercy, bring us to that blessed departure and to that glorious *to-morrow;* may He, in that *to-morrow* which is near each of us, deign to visit us and to be near to help us; so that those who find themselves perhaps entangled and held back by some temptation, by his mercy who comes to preach deliverance to the captives, may be able in that *to-morrow* to go forth free; let us, in the joy of salvation, accept the crown of our new-born King; by His help, Who with the Father and the Holy Ghost, liveth and reigneth, God, for ever and ever. AMEN.

SERMON XIV.

To-morrow the Lord shall come; and in the morning ye shall behold His glory.   Exod. xvi. 6, 7. [1]

1. Dwellers on the earth, children of men, hearken: ye who sleep in the dust, awake and sing the praises of God: for One shall come, who is to the sick a Healer, to those who are sold into slavery a Redeemer, to the wandering a Guide, and life to the dead. Yes, He comes who shall cast all our sins into the depth of the sea, who shall heal all our infirmities, who shall bear us upon His own shoulders to our own original greatness. Great is His power, but His mercy is more wonderful still; that He who was able to help should have been willing thus to come. *To-morrow*, says our text, *the Lord shall come*. These words have indeed their own first fulfilment in place and time recorded in the Scripture; but our mother Church has not unfitly adapted them to the Vigil of our Lord's coming in the flesh. The Church I say, who has with her the guidance and the Spirit of Him who is God and her Spouse, who is the Well-beloved, and rests upon her bosom, which He alone possesses and makes His throne. It may be said that she, opening her heart, has plunged the eye of her contemplation into the deep abyss of the secret purposes of God, so as to prepare for Him a perpetual habitation in her heart, and for herself in His. When then she either transfers or varies the words of Holy Scripture, that transference is even of as much more

[1] (Serm. III. for the Eve of the Nativity.)

weight than the original sense [1] as the truth is more than the figure, the full light than the shadow, the mistress than the servant.

2. *You shall see then even to-day that the Lord will come.* In my opinion these words give very clearly the idea of two kinds of days: the first has begun with the Fall of the first man, and continues even until the end of the world; a day on which the saints have often poured their maledictions. For on that day Adam was driven out from that brightness of light in which he was created; and being thrust upon the things of this world, he entered upon a day of darkness, and was deprived almost wholly of the light of truth. We are all born into this day when we come into this world, if indeed it ought not rather to be called night, not day, except that the sovereign mercy of God has left to us the light of reason, as it were a certain glimmering of day. But the second day shall be that of the glory of the Saints, and shall endure throughout endless eternities, when that peaceful morrow shall dawn, which is the obtaining of the promised mercy, when death shall be swallowed up in victory: when clouds and shadows shall be dispersed, and all things both within and without, above and below, shall be equally filled with the splendour of the true light. Thus a saint says: *Cause me to hear Thy loving kindness in the morning* (Ps. cxliii. 8), and *In the morning we were filled with Thy mercy* (Ps. lxxxix. 14). But let us return to our day, which for its shortness is called a watch of the night, a shadow and a nothing, by the inspiration of the Holy Spirit: *My days*

[1] So great weight did Bernard attach to the decrees of the Church universal, as to recognize an authority even in her accommodation of the sense of Scripture, such as she herself assuredly never claims!

are as a shadow that declineth; they are consumed like smoke (Ps. cii. 3). *Few and evil have the days of the years of my life been* (Gen. xlvii. 9) says that holy Patriarch who saw the Lord face to face, and talked with Him as with a friend. And indeed in this day God has endowed man with reason, He has left to him intelligence; but it is needful for man that when he goes forth from this world he should be enlightened by God with the light of the knowledge of Him, lest if he should leave this prison-house quelled, as it were, by the completeness of its gloom, he should be for ever unable to receive the light. Therefore it was that the only begotten Son of God, the Brightness of Righteousness, has enlightened and warmed the prison-house of this world, as it were, with a torch of brilliant and unmeasured light: so that all who desire to be enlightened may be fired by His glory, may be united to Him so closely that nothing may intervene between. For it is our sins that come between us and God. Let them be taken away, and we are at once enlightened by the true Light, are united, and as it were absorbed into Him. Thus if an extinguished light be brought near to one still burning and shining, so that nothing intervenes between, it is at once relighted. So by an example taken from visible things, we may learn the working of the invisible.

3. Let us follow then the counsel of the prophet (Hos. x. 12; lxx.); let us light up for ourselves the light of knowledge at this star so great and so refulgent, before we go forth from the shadows of this world, that we may not pass away into the darkness which is eternal. But what is that knowledge? Plainly it consists in knowing that the Lord will come, though when He will come, we cannot know. This is all that is asked of us. But you reply, that knowledge belongs to all. For who is there,

being a Christian even in name only, who knows not that the Lord will come; that He will come to judge the quick and the dead, and to render to every man according to his works? No, my brethren, that knowledge does not belong to all: it belongs even to few, because in truth there are few that are saved. Do you think, for example, that those who are happy when they have done wrong, who take pleasure in the worst of actions, that they either consider or know that the Lord will come? If they should say that they do so, do you not believe them: for *he that says I know God, and keepeth not His commandments, is a liar* (1 S. John ii. 4). *They confess*, says the Apostle, *that they know God, but in works they deny Him* (Tit. i. 16); for *faith without works is dead* (S. James ii. 20). They would not thus pollute themselves with every kind of impurity, if they knew or feared that the Lord would come; on the contrary, they would watch, and not suffer their consciences to be wounded thus grievously.

4. For this knowledge works, in the first place, in the soul penitence and sorrow. It changes laughter into weeping, songs into groans, joy into sorrow. It causes those things to displease you in which you had before taken extreme pleasure; and to have a special horror of those which you were wont specially to desire. For thus it is written, *He who increaseth knowledge increaseth sorrow* (Eccles. i. 18), so that the consequence which follows true and holy knowledge is sorrow. In the second stage it brings about correction; so that you no longer employ your members as instruments of iniquity unto sin; you restrain gluttony, you strangle luxury, you lower pride, and make your body, which before had been the slave of iniquity, the servant of holiness. For penitence profits not without correction, as says the wise man: *If one builds and another*

destroys, of what profit is their labour? If one prays and another curses, whose voice shall the Lord hear? If one who is washed after having touched a dead body, again touches it, his washing profits him nothing. (Ecclus. xxxiv. 28—30). It is on the contrary to be feared, according to the word of the Saviour Himself, that a worse thing will happen to a man who does this (S. John v. 14). But as these two conditions cannot be long maintained, unless the mind watches and strives in all things with unwearied circumspection ; knowledge in the third stage produces solicitude, so that a man begins to walk with continual care in his God, and to examine himself in every part, lest he should offend in the smallest matter the sight of His awful majesty. Thus repentance lights up the soul, correction makes it earnest, solicitude gives it brightness and light ; and thus the whole man is renewed both within and without.

5. But here he begins to breathe a little from the depression and griefs which his sins have caused him, and to temper the extremity of his fear with spiritual joy, that he may not be swallowed up with overmuch sorrow on account of the greatness of his crimes. Hence, although he fears his judge, he has good hope in his Saviour ; and since fear and joy exist together in his soul, they conflict and war with each other ; often fear prevails over joy, but still more frequently joy triumphs over fear, by its secret strength. Happy is the conscience in which such a conflict goes on without ceasing, until mortality is swallowed up in life ; until fear, which is only in part, shall be done away, and joy which is complete and perfect shall take its place ; for its fear is but for a time, but its joy eternal. But the soul, though thus burning and shining with the fire of love, must nevertheless not as yet believe itself to be in the House where the lighted torch of Love

may be ever borne, without any fear of hostile winds; it
must remember that it is still under the open sky, and
carefully shield with either hand the light which it carries,
and distrust the winds, even though the air seems peaceful. For suddenly, and at an hour when he expects it
not, a change will come: and if he shall have removed his
sheltering hand ever so little, the light will be extinguished.
Even if the heat of its flame should have burned (as sometimes happens) the hands of him who bears it, he prefers
rather to endure this, than to withdraw his hands; because he knows that in a moment, in a twinkliug of an
eye, the flame may be blown out. If we were in that
house not made with hands, which is eternal in the heavens, where no enemy enters, and no friend goes forth,
there would be nothing to fear. But now we are exposed
to three winds most malign and strong; the world, the
flesh and the devil; which strive to extinguish the light in
the conscience, blowing upon our hearts with evil desires,
unlawful impulses, and so disordering us with sudden
trouble, that we scarcely know any longer whence we
came or whither we go. Two of these fierce winds are
often at rest: but from the blasts of the third none is
ever free. This is why we ought to protect our soul,
with the hands as it were, both of the heart and of the
body, lest the light of the soul, once lit up, should be
extinguished; we must neither yield to the tempest, nor
recoil before it, even though the extreme violence of temptations has broken upon either element of our human
nature; but we must say with the Psalmist: "*My soul is
always in my hands*" (Ps. cxix. 109). Let us rather endure
the pain, than yield to the temptation. And as we cannot
easily forget that which we hold in our hands: so let us
never forget the care of our souls, but apply ourselves
earnestly and with all our powers, to carry it out perfectly.

6. With our loins girded, therefore, and with lamps burning, let us, during the watches of this night, keep under strict control the multitude of our thoughts and actions; so that the Lord when He shall come, whether it be in the first, or the second, or the third watch, may find us ready. The first watch is rightness of action; and it consists in endeavouring to fashion your whole life according to the Rule which you have sworn to observe; in not transgressing the limits which your fathers have laid down in all the details of duty and of this your calling, not declining to the right hand nor to the left. The second is purity of intention, so that your eye being without guile may render your whole body full of light, in so far that whatsoever you may do you shall do it as unto God, and so the graces which you have received will return again to their source and come back to you anew. The third consists in the preservation of unity amongst yourselves, so that being placed in a community you should study to prefer the wishes of others to your own wishes; thus you will live with your brethren not only without quarrel, but also with good understanding and kindly feeling; each one praying for all the rest, so that it may be said of each of us: He is a lover of the brethren and of the people of Israel, he has much at heart the good of his people and of the holy city Jerusalem (2 Macc. xv. 14). Thus, then, on this day the coming of the Only Begotten Son lights up in us the flame of a true knowledge; of that knowledge, I say, which teaches us that the Lord will come, and is a constant and firm foundation of goodness in us.

7. *And in the morning ye shall behold His glory.* O what a morning! O day which art in the courts of the Lord, and better than a thousand passed elsewhere! When shall we see month succeed to month and Sabbath to

Sabbath, when shall the splendour of light and the glow of charity enlighten the dwellers upon the earth, even to the discerning of the loftiest wonders of God? Who shall presume to think of Thy wonders, much less to speak of them? Yet in the meanwhile, brethren, let us build up our faith, that if we cannot behold those wonders which God has reserved for us, we may at least contemplate some small part of the marvels which are done on our account upon the earth. The Almighty Majesty of God has done three things, accomplished three blendings [1] in taking our flesh; so uniquely wonderful and so wonderfully unique that nothing similar was ever done or is to be done again upon the earth. That is to say, there were joined closely together: God and man, (the characters of) mother and virgin, faith and a human heart. Marvellous indeed are those blendings, but that which is more marvellous than any miracle is the manner in which things so diverse in character and so mutually distinct from each other are yet able to be mutually conjoined.

8. And in the first place consider the creation, the position, and the arrangement of things. What great power, that is to say, is manifested in their creation, what great wisdom in their position, what great goodness in their arrangement! In creation see how many things were created, and with how great power; in position, with what wisdom all things were placed; in arrangement, with what goodness, with what wonderful and engaging love, things which were highest were united to those which were lowest. For to the dust of the earth He has united a vital force which, in the trees, for example, causes beauty to arise in the leaves, brilliance in the flowers, taste and healthful qualities in the fruits. And not being content with this He has added to our

---

[1] [*Mixturas*].

dust another power still, that of feeling, as in the lower animals, which have not only life, but also rejoice in a five-fold power of sense. Again, He did something more; and honoured our dust by giving to it the power of reason that we see in men who not only have life, and have feeling, but who also are able to discern between what is fitting and what is unfitting, between good and evil, between what is true and what is false. He willed after that to raise up our weakness to a more lofty glory still, and His Majesty emptied itself so as to unite to our dust that which was loftiest in Him, that is to say, Himself, and to unite in one and the same person God and the dust of the earth, majesty and weakness, loftiness so exalted and lowness so extreme. For nothing is higher than God, nothing lower than the dust of the earth: and yet with condescension so great God descended to the dust, and with such great elevation the dust arose to God; so that whatever God did in our dust it might be believed by our faith that it was done even by our dust; and whatever our dust suffered and went through God might be said to have gone through in it, by a mystery as unspeakable as it is incapable of being grasped. And remark again, that as in the one and only God there is a Trinity of Persons, but a Unity of Substance; so in this unique blending there is a Trinity of Substance, but a Unity of Person; and as in that the three Persons do not destroy the Unity nor the Unity diminish the Trinity: so also in this, the Unity of Person does not cause a confusion of Natures; nor the Natures take away the Unity of Person. The Supreme and blessed Trinity has thus put before us a trinity; a work wonderful and surpassing all things, and which among all things stands absolutely alone. For the Word of God, a soul, and a body, unite to form one Person: and these Three are One, and this One is Three, not by confusion

of Substance, but by Unity of Person. This is the first
and supremely excellent blending; and it is first among three.
Consider, O man, that thou art dust, and be not proud:
consider also that thou art united to God, and be not ungrateful.

9. The second blending is that of [the characters of]
virgin and mother: a wonderful event indeed, and obviously unexampled. From the beginning of the world has
it not been heard, that there was a Virgin who was a
Mother, or a Mother who remained Virgin. Never in the
ordinary course of things is virginity found, where fecundity exists; nor fecundity where virginity remains intact.
There is only this instance, in which virginity and fecundity have met each other. In this one case was that done
which had never been done before, nor ever shall be done
again; it had no precedent, nor shall have any repetition.
The third blending is, of faith and a human heart: it is
no doubt inferior to the first and second, but perhaps
not less as a proof of power. For that a human heart has
entertained faith is wonderful, as well as that God could be
believed to be Man, and that one who has become a mother
should have remained a virgin. Just as iron and clay are
not capable of being united; so these two cannot be blended,
unless by the uniting power of the Spirit of God. Is it
then to be believed that He is God great and boundless,
who is laid in a manger, who weeps in a cradle, who
endures the pains of infantile necessities, who is scourged,
spit upon, crucified, laid in the sepulchre and enclosed
between two stones? Shall she be a virgin, who suckles
her child, whose husband shares her table and couch,
leads her into Egypt, brings her back thence, making alone
with her a journey so long and so solitary? How could the
human race, and the whole world, be persuaded of this?

And yet it was persuaded; so easily and so powerfully, that the multitude of believers in it makes it credible to me. Young men and maidens, old men and children, have chosen rather to die a thousand deaths, than to fall from that faith even for a moment.

10. This first blending is indeed excellent, the second more so, but the third surpasses these. The ear has heard the first, but the eye has not seen it: because that great mystery of piety is heard and believed even to the ends of the earth; but yet the eye of man has not seen, O God, none has seen but Thou, in what manner Thou hast united to Thyself a body similar to ours, in the narrow space of a Virgin's womb. The second blending, the eye of man has seen; because that Queen highly favoured saw herself fruitful and yet a virgin, as she kept in memory all these words, and pondered them in her heart: Joseph too, who was the witness as well as the guardian of so wonderful a virginity, had knowledge of it. Finally, the third has found place in the heart of man, because he has believed that which was done, as having been done: since we give greater credence to the voice that speaks to us from above than to our own sight, [1] when we hold and most firmly believe, nothing doubting, what was done and handed down to us. See then in the first mystery what God has given to you; in the second, by what means He has given it; in the third, for what motive He has given it. He has given to you Christ by means of Mary, in order to restore you to spiritual health. In the first blending is a remedy: a remedy, [2] God-and-man, to heal all your spiritual ills.

[1] [*Oraculo quam oculo*].

[2] [Lit. *cataplasma confectum est ex Deo et homine*. It does not often occur that S. Bernard pushes his metaphors to the length of bad taste. (E.)]

The two were crushed and mingled in the womb of the Virgin, as in a mortar; and the Holy Spirit, as it were a pestle, gently mingled them. But as you were unworthy on whom He should be bestowed, He was given to Mary, so that you might receive of her whatsoever you might have: and Mary, inasmuch as she is a mother, has brought forth for you Him who was God: and inasmuch as she is a virgin, she has, for her reverence, been heard in your cause and in that of the whole human race. If she were only a mother, it would suffice for her that she should be saved through the generation of her children; if she were only a virgin, it would suffice for her: but the fruit of her womb would not be blessed, nor the price of the world's [redemption]. Since then in the first mystery there is a remedy, in the second the remedy is applied; since according to the will of God, all that we have received comes to us by means of Mary. But in the third, merit is found, since when we firmly believe these things, then we have a degree of merit: and in faith there is salvation; for *he who believes the same shall he saved* (S. Mark xvi. 16).

SERMON XV. [1]

Rejoice in the Lord alway: and again I say, Rejoice.
Phil. iv. 4.

1. The custom of our Order does not require a sermon to-day: but as the Celebration of Masses will occupy us longer than usual to-morrow, and the short time remaining will not admit of a sermon, I think it not amiss to prepare your hearts to-day for a solemnity so great; espe-

[1] [Serm. IV. for the Vigil of the Nativity. On the healing in the Left Hand of the Most High, and the delights in His Right Hand.]

cially as in considering the profundity and the immeasurable height of this great mystery, it seems nothing less than a source of living water, of which we may drink the more abundantly, that it can never be exhausted. And as I know how greatly your tribulation for Christ's sake abounds, I would that your consolation through Him should abound also: since I am neither able, nor desirous, to offer you the consolation of the world. That is of no value, and of no utility: and (which is a thing more to be feared) it is an obstacle to true and salutary consolations. Therefore it is that He who is the delight and the glory of the Angels has made Himself the salvation and the consolation of the unhappy. He who, being great and highly exalted in His heavenly city, made the citizens of it perfectly happy, has come as a poor and humble Child into the exile of this world, and brings great joy unto us exiles: and He who in the highest heaven is the glory of the Father, upon earth is made Peace to men of goodwill. He is given, a lowly Child, to us who are lowly, so that we may become great and receive Him in His real greatness: and that those whom as a Child He justifies, He may at a later time, make great and glorious when He shall have resumed His glory. Hence without doubt that vessel of election, who had received of the fulness of that little Child [for although He were a child He was filled, filled with grace and truth, and in Him dwelt all the fulness of the Godhead bodily (Col. ii. 9)]; hence, I say, no doubt S. Paul spoke those words of blessed meaning which during these days have been frequently sounding in our ears. [1] *Rejoice in the Lord al · ay: and again I say. Rejoice.*

[1] [In the English Prayer Book, as in the Sarum Use, these are the opening words of the Epistle for the Fourth Sunday in Advent, and thus would immediately precede the Christmas Festival, as the words of S. Bernard seem to intimate. In the

Rejoice, he says, for the blessing that is before your eyes, and rejoice for that which is promised in the future: since the fact accomplished, and the future promised, are alike full of joy. Rejoice, because from the left Hand of God you have already received gifts; and from His Right Hand also you hope for them. *His left hand,* it is said, *shall be under my head, and his right hand shall embrace me* (Cant. ii. 6). The left hand sustains us, the right hand lifts us up: the left hand heals and justifies: the right blesses in embracing. In the left are contained merits (to redeem); in the right promises (to sanctify): in the right, delights: in the left, remedies.

2. But notice how good and how wise is our Physician. Consider diligently how new the remedies which He brings; and not only new, but costly and beautiful: not only priceless for the restoration of health, but sweet to the taste and pleasant to the eye. Think of the first remedy which He brings in His left hand: you will find it to be His Miraculous Conception. Reflect what a wonderful and novel a fact that is, 'as well as how admirable and lovable. What more admirable, than a holy generation? what more glorious than a conception holy and pure, unstained by shame or corruption? But as we should be perhaps less struck by admiration of this new thing, however welcome, if our mind were not delighted by the thought of the usefulness and salvation which comes with it: that conception manifests itself to us as not only glorious in outward appearance, but also precious in inward virtue: since in it is found, according to that which is written, *in the left hand of the Lord riches and honour* (Prov. iii. 16); the riches of salvation, the honour of newness. For who can make pure

modern Roman Use, they have been transferred to the Third Sunday. (E.)]

that which is conceived of an impure stock, but He who alone was conceived without evil concupiscence? In my very root and origin I was infected and defiled: in sin was I conceived: but He by whom it is taken away, upon Him did it fall.

3. I have then the riches of salvation, the most pure conception of Christ, by which I am redeemed from the stain of my own conception. Add to these, O Lord Jesus, abiding signs, unchanged marvels: for the first have lost their wonder by our very familiarity with them. For although the sun's rising and setting, the fruitfulness of the earth, the alternation of the seasons, are evidently miracles and great ones: yet they are so often renewed before our eyes, that no one now notices them. But *behold*, He says, *I make all things new* (Is. xliii. 19). Who says this? It is the *Lamb who sat upon the throne* (Rev. xxi. 5). The Lamb who is altogether sweetness and delight, who is in short, the Anointed One; for this is the interpretation of the name CHRIST. To whom can He appear harsh or stern, when not even to His mother at His birth did He bring injury or suffering? These were marvels truly new! without sin was He conceived, and without pain born. In our Virgin the malediction of Eve was changed; for without sorrow she brought forth. A malediction was changed, I say, into a benediction, as it was foretold by the angel Gabriel: *Blessed art thou among women* (S. Luke i. 28). O woman happy in being blessed not cursed, alone free from the general malediction, and exempted from the pains of childbirth! Nor is it strange, brethren, that He should bring no sorrow to His mother, who bore the sorrows of the whole world; who, according to the saying of Isaiah, *Himself carried our sorrows* (Is. liii. 4). There are two things which human weakness fears, shame and suf-

fering. Each of these Christ came to take away, wherefore
He bore both the one and the other, when (not to speak
of other endurances) He was condemned by wicked men
to 'a shameful death. Therefore, that He might give us
confidence that He would preserve us from these evils,
He first preserved His mother in safety from each: and
thus she conceived without sin and brought forth without
suffering.

4. Riches still increase, glory is augmented, new
signs appear, miracles change their nature. Not only
is the Son of Man conceived without stain, but brought
forth without suffering, and His Mother is without corruption. O novelty truly unheard of! A Virgin has brought
forth, and after childbirth has remained a virgin, has obtained fruitfulness in posterity while retaining integrity of
the flesh, and has both the joy of maternity and the honour
of virginity. Now I await with confidence the promised
glory of incorruption in my flesh, since by Him incorruption has been preserved in His Mother. It will be easy
for Him, who did not suffer His Mother to see corruption
in bringing forth a Son, to make me, the corruptible, to
put on incorruption, when He raises me from the dead.

5. Yet you have riches greater and glory more abounding
even than this. A woman becomes Mother without loss
of virginity; a Son is born without any stain of sin. Upon
that Mother the malediction pronounced upon Eve does
not fall; the Child born of her is also free from the
common lot of which the prophet speaks: *None is free
from the stain of uncleanness, not even the infant, whose
life upon the earth is but of one day* (Job xiv. 4, 5 ; lxx.).
Behold an Infant without spot, alone true among men,
who is even more—the very Truth itself. *Behold* the Lamb
without spot, *the Lamb of God, who taketh away the sins*

of the world (S. John i. 29). For who can better take away sins than He upon whom sin has not descended? He is without doubt able to cleanse me from sin, who is evidently free from any. Let His Hand, screened in clay, yet which is alone without earthly stain, purge my eyes from their darkness (cf. S. John ix. 6). Let Him who has no beam in His eye, pluck forth the mote out of mine: yea, rather, let Him pluck forth the beam from mine, who has not in His own the smallest grain of dust.

6. We have seen in truth the riches of Life and salvation: we have seen His glory, glory as of the Only Begotten of the Father. If I am asked, of what Father? I reply in the words of the prophet: *And He shall be called the Son of the Highest* (S. Luke i. 32). It is plain who is meant by 'the Highest.' But that there may be no place for hesitation about this, the Angel Gabriel himself says to Mary: *That Holy One who shall be born of thee shall be called the Son of God* (Ibid. v. 35). O truly Holy One! *Thou, O Lord, shall not suffer Thy Holy One to see corruption,* who hast kept corruption even from His mother (Ps. xvi. 10). Miracles grow greater and greater, the treasure house of grace is opened, and its riches are poured forth in profusion. She who bears, is mother and yet Virgin: He who is born, is God-and-man. But are holy things to be given to dogs, or pearls thrown unto swine? Let our treasure then be [that] hidden in a field, our money kept safely in the purse. Let the miraculous conception be sheltered by the betrothal of the Mother; the painless Birth by the wails and suffering of the Child. Let the purity too of the newly made mother be hidden by undergoing the purification of the Law, and the innocency of the Child by the accustomed circumcision. Hide, I say, O Mary, hide the splendour of that Sun newly rising: lay

thy Infant in the manger, fold around Him the swathing bands: for they are our riches. The bands which bound the Saviour are more precious than any purple, and this manger more filled with glory than the gilded thrones of Kings; in fine, the poverty of Christ is more costly than all riches and treasures. For what is found richer or more precious than the humility by which grace is acquired and even the Kingdom of heaven attained? as it is written, *Blessed are the poor in spirit, for theirs is the Kingdom of heaven* (S. Matt. v. 3); and by the Apostle: *God resisteth the proud, but giveth grace unto the humble* (S. James iv. 6). In the Nativity you have humility commended by God Himself. For in it He emptied Himself, taking upon Him the form of a servant, and was found in the likeness of man.

7. Do you seek riches more precious still, and a glory still more excellent? You have it in the love shown in His Passion. *Greater love hath no man than this, that one should lay down his life for his friends* (S. John xv. 13). This riches and glory of salvation, is the Precious Blood wherewith we have been redeemed; and the Cross of Jesus, in which we glory with the Apostle. *God forbid,* he says, *that I should glory, save in the Cross of our Lord Jesus Christ* (Gal. vi. 14): and again: *I determined to know nothing among you, but Jesus Christ, and Him crucified* (1 Cor. ii. 2). The Left Hand of God (in the text) is then Christ Jesus, but Him crucified: and the Right Hand is still Christ Jesus, but Him glorified. We ourselves, perhaps, are the Cross, upon which we are told that He was nailed: for man has himself the form of a cross; and more manifestly, when he extends his hands. For Christ says in the Psalm: *I am sunk in the deep mire where there is no standing* (Ps. lxix. 2). It is plain that

the mire is nothing but ourselves, for we are made of the dust of the earth: though then we were of the dust of Paradise, but now of the dust of the abyss. *I am sunk in it*, He says: not, I have passed through it, or, I have come out of it. *I am with you even to the end of the world* (S. Matt. xxviii. 20). For He is Emmanuel, God with us. He is with us indeed, but as it were, by the left hand. Thus we see that once when Tamar was in labour, and Zara first put forth his hand, it was bound with a thread of scarlet, which is a symbol of the Lord's Passion.

8. We hold fast then now by the Left Hand of God: but yet it is needful for us to cry: *Stretch out, O Lord, Thy Right Hand to the work of Thy Hands* (Job xiv. 15), for *at Thy Right Hand there are pleasures for evermore* (Ps. xvi. 11). Lord, stretch [1] out to us Thy Right Hand, and it suffereth us.

Glory, he says, *and riches are in his house* (Ps. cxii. 3), that is to say, of him who fears the Lord; but in Thy House, O Lord, there is the voice of praise and the giving of thanks. *Blessed are they who dwell in Thy House* etc. (Ps. lxxxiv. 4). For eye hath not seen nor ear heard, neither have entered into the heart of man, the things which God hath prepared for them that love Him (1 Cor. ii. 9). For there is light inaccessible, peace which passeth all understanding; a spring which never waxes nor wanes. The eye hath not seen the inaccessible light; the ear hath not heard the peace which cannot be comprehended. *Beautiful indeed are the feet of those who bring good tidings of peace* (Romans x. 15), but their sound hath gone forth into the whole world; while the peace which passeth all understanding is far from being comprehended in its

---

[1] [Or, *ostende*, show.]

fulness by men, nor has it entered into their ears. For
Paul himself says: *Brethren, I count not myself to have
apprehended* (Phil. iii. 13). *Faith cometh by hearing* indeed,
and hearing by the word of God (Rom. x. 13): but faith
not sight: the promise of peace, not the manifestation of
it. And indeed there is peace even now to men of goodwill,
even upon the earth: but what is that peace to the plenitude
and fulness of that farther gift? Wherefore the Lord Himself also says: *My peace I give unto you, peace I leave with
you* (S. John xiv. 27). That peace of mind indeed which passeth all understanding, and is a peace above peace, you are not
capable of experiencing; wherefore I give unto you the land
of peace, and leave to you in the meantime the way of peace.

9. But why these words, *Into the heart of man it hath
not ascended?* Doubtless because it is a spring and does
not flow upwards. For we know that the nature of springs
is to follow the streams of the valleys and to fall from
the steeps of the mountains, as it is written: *Who sendeth
the springs into the valleys which run among the hills.*
(Ps. civ. 10). For this is why I study frequently to admonish your charity that *God resisteth the proud, but giveth
grace to the humble*, for a spring does not rise higher than
the spot where it takes its beginning. It might at first
sight appear that according to this rule, the paths of grace
are not hindered by pride: especially because he who was
the first to be proud, whom Scripture calls the *King over
all the sons of pride* (Job xli. 34), is not said in the Scripture
to have declared, 'I will be higher than I am', but 'I will
be like unto the most High' (Is. xiv. 14). And yet the
Apostle was not wrong in saying that *he exalteth himself above
all that is called God or that is worshipped* (2 Thess. ii.
4). Man cannot hear the statement without a shudder of
horror: but would that he shuddered equally at evil thoughts

and sentiments. For I say to you, that not the evil one alone, but every one that is proud exalteth himself against God. For the will of God is that what He commands should be done: and the proud desires to do his own will. These two things may seem to be equally legitimate: but notice how different are the conditions of the two. God does indeed will that His commands should be obeyed, but in those particulars only which reason approves (as reason always does approve the holy commands of God): he who is proud on the contrary, desires that his will should be done, whether it be conformable to reason or not. Do you not see how high he holds himself, and that the streams of grace are not able to reach him? *Unless ye be converted*, it is said, *and become as little children* (He says this who is the Source of Life, in whom dwelleth and from whom floweth forth the fulness of all graces) *ye shall not enter into the kingdom of heaven* (S. Matt. xviii. 3). Prepare then the channels, level the barriers of proud and earthly thoughts, become like, not to the first man Adam, but to the Son of Man: because the source of grace does not ascend into the heart of man while it remains carnal and earthly. Purify thine eye also, that it may be able to behold the purest light; and incline thine ear to obedience, that thou mayest sometime attain to perpetual peace, which is above all peace. That is light which is the cause of serenity, peace which possesses tranquillity, and a fount, that which is a source of eternal and full satisfaction. By the source understand the Father, from whom is born the Son, and from whom proceeds the Holy Spirit: by the Light the Son, who is, as it were, the splendour of Eternal Life, and the true Light, which lighteth every man who cometh into the world: by the Peace the Holy Spirit, who rests upon the heart that is humble and peaceful. But I do not say this as if these qualities were the *propria* of the several Persons:

for the Father is Light also, as the Son is Light of Light; and the Son is Peace, He is our peace, who has made both one: and the Holy Spirit is a Source of living water, which springeth up unto eternal life.

10. But when shall we reach this? When wilt Thou satisfy me, O Lord, with the joy of Thy countenance? We indeed rejoice in Thee, because Thou hast visited us, as the Son rising from the height of heaven: and again we rejoice in the blessed hope of Thy Second Advent. But when shall come the fulness of joy, not from Thy remembrance, but in Thy presence; not from expectation, but in the fulfilment of our hope? *Let your moderation*, says the Apostle, *be known unto all men; the Lord is at hand* (Phil. iv. 5). For it is proper that your moderation should be known to all, as was that of the Lord. For what is more incongruous that man, who cannot but be conscious of his own weakness, should act pretentiously when the Lord of Glory has shown Himself unpretending among men? *Learn of me*, He says, *for I am meek and lowly in heart* (S. Matt. xi. 29), that so your moderation may be known among men. By the words which follow, *the Lord is at hand*, are to be understood His Right Hand: as when He says, *Lo, I am with you always, even to the end of the world* (Id. xxviii. 20) the words are to be understood of His Left. The Lord is at hand, brethren, therefore be anxious for nothing: He is very near, and shall speedily come to our sight. Fail not, be not wearied: seek Him while He may be found, call upon Him while He is near. *The Lord is nigh unto them that are of a broken heart* (Ps. xxxiv. 18); He is near to them that wait for Him, that wait for Him with true hearts. Finally, would you know *how near* He is? Listen to the song of the Bride when she speaks of her Bridegroom: *Lo, He standeth*

behind our very wall (Cant. ii. 9). By that wall, understand thy body, which is the hindrance interposed, so that though He is near, yet thou art not able to behold Him. Because of this Paul desired to be dissolved and to be with Christ (Phil. i. 23); and elsewhere he exclaims in sorrow: *O wretched man that I am, who shall deliver me from the body of this death?* (Rom. vii. 24). So also the Psalmist: *Bring my soul out of prison that I may praise Thy Name* (Ps. cxlii. 7).

SERMON XVI. [1]

Sanctify yourselves and be ye ready: for to-morrow ye shall see the glory of the Lord in you. [2]

1. Now that we are about to celebrate the ineffable mystery of the Birth of Our Lord, it is with great fitness that we, my brethren, are warned to sanctify ourselves and to be ready. For He who comes to us is the Holiest of the holy: it is He who said: *Be ye holy; for I the Lord your God am holy* (Lev. xix. 2). For otherwise how could that which is holy be given to dogs, and pearls cast before swine, unless they have previously cleansed themselves, the one class from their iniquity, the other from their unlawful pleasure; unless they fly with all care, these from their vomit, those from their wallowing in the mire? When Israel after the flesh were once about to receive the commandments from God, they prepared for it by purifying their bodies, by various washings, by gifts and sacrifices; which nevertheless had no power to make perfectly clean the conscience of him who practised them.

---

[1] [Sermon V. for the Vigil of the Nativity.]
[2] [*Respons. in Vigil. Nativ. Dom.*, and see Exod. xiv. 13.]

But all these things have passed away; nor indeed were they intended to last beyond the season of Redemption, which now has come. From this we may properly learn that a complete sanctification is needful for us, an inward washing, and spiritual purity required of us, according to the words of the Lord: *Blessed are the pure in heart, for they shall see God* (S. Matt. v. 8). It is for this end that we live, brethren, for this end we were born, to this we are called; to this, finally, the Festival of to-day has given us light. Once a night reigned, in which none could do these works: a night which was universe over all the world, before the rising of the true Light, before the Birth of Christ. Similarly there was a spiritual night to each and every one of us before his conversion and inward regeneration.

2. Was it not the case, too, that the whole face of earth was covered with the profoundest night, and deepest shadows, when, formerly, our fathers worshipped gods which their own hands had made, and with sacrilegious folly adored divinities of stone or of wood? Was not each of us in a night just as deep and gloomy, when we lived, as it were, without God in this world, when we walked after our own lusts, when we yielded to and followed the pleasures of the flesh and the objects of this world, when we yielded our members as instruments of iniquity unto sin, when the iniquity of the past obliged us to go on to iniquity in the future, unto works of darkness for which now we are rightly ashamed? *Those who sleep*, says the Apostle, *sleep in the night; and those who are drunken are drunken in the night* (1 Thess. v. 7). And such were some of you: but you are awakened, you are sanctified, if you are sons of the light and of the day, not of the night nor of darkness. In truth, he was the herald of the

day who has said: *Be sober, be vigilant* (1 Pet. v. 8).
And on the day of Pentecost he said to the Jews, speaking
of his fellow-disciples: *These are not drunken, as ye suppose,
seeing it is but the third hour of the day* (Acts ii. 15).
And his co-apostle said: *The night is far spent, the day is
at hand. Let us therefore put away the works of darkness, and put upon us the armour of light. Let us walk
honestly as in the day* (Rom. xiii. 12, 13), The works of
darkness; that is, sloth and drunkenness, (since as we said
above, those who sleep and who are drunken, are so in
the night), that we may walk, not sleep, now that it is
day: and walk honestly, not as those whom drunkenness
makes to totter. Do you perceive a man whose soul is
weary and has distaste to everything that is good, and
slumbers; you may be sure that he is still in the night and in
darkness. Do you perceive another (as it were) intoxicate
with absinthe, not disposed to sobriety, wise above that which
is meet; of whom the eye is not satisfied with seeing nor
ear with hearing: who loves money or something that
resembles it, with an insatiable hunger and thirst like that
of one who is afflicted with dropsy. He too is a son of
night and of darkness. Nor are these two vices easily
separated: as says the Scripture: *Every slothful man is
full of desires.* Let us then be sanctified to-day, let us
be made ready by shaking off the bonds of sleep: let us
be sanctified, as in the day we are freed from the bondage
of night, by restraining the violence of evil passion. Upon
these two commands hang all the Law and the Prophets,
viz., to refrain from evil and to do good.

3. But this is the task of to-day: for to-morrow is
the day not of sanctification, nor of preparation, but of
beholding the Divine Majesty. "*To-morrow*," he says, "*ye
shall see the glory of the Lord among you.*" This is what

the patriarch Jacob says: *To-morrow my righteousness shall answer for me* (Gen. xxx. 33). To-day righteousness is practised, to-morrow it bears witness for us: to day it is cultivated, to-morrow it will bear fruit. For how should man reap that which he has not sown? He who in the meantime despises the holiness, will not then behold the glory: the Sun of splendour will not arise unto him, to whom the Sun of righteousness has not risen: nor will that *to-morrow* make him to rejoice with its light, on whom to-day has not shined. For He who is to-day made our righteousness by God the Father, is the same who to-morrow shall appear as our Life, so that we shall appear with Him in glory. To-day He is born among us as a little Child, that man may have no ground for boasting, but that we may rather be converted and become as little children. But to-morrow He shall be known to us as the great God, worthy of all praises, so that we too may receive glory and praises, since then shall every one have praise of God. For to-morrow He will glorify those whom He shall have justified to-day, and to the perfecting of holiness shall succeed the vision of Glory. Not an empty vision, which consists only in similitude or likeness: for we ourselves shall be like unto Him, seeing Him as He is. That is why it is said, not simply "*you shall see the glory of the Lord,*" but it is added expressly "*in you*". At the present time we see ourselves in Him as in a mirror, and He receives of us: but then we shall behold Him in ourselves, when He shall bestow upon us of His gifts, when He shall show Himself to us, and draw us to Himself. It is there that He has promised to come forth and serve us (S. Luke xii. 37), of whose fulness in the meantime we receive, not indeed glory for glory, but grace for grace; as it is written, *the Lord will give grace and glory* (Ps. lxxxiv. 11). Do not then despise the former gifts, if

you desire those that are to follow; do not disdain the
first instalment, if you wish to obtain those succeeding: or
refuse to take what is offered, for the sake of the vessel
on which it is offered. For He who is our Peace has
made for Himself a Body incorruptible; upon which He
ministered to us the Food of salvation. *Thou shalt not
suffer*, it is said, *Thy Holy one to see corruption* (Ps. xvi.
10); and certainly He is referred to of whom the Angel
Gabriel made mention to Mary: *That Holy one which shall be
born of thee, shall be called the Son of God* (S. Luke i. 35).

4. Let us then be sanctified now by that Holy One,
that we may, when His day shall come, behold His glory:
inasmuch as that sacred day has dawned for us, the day
of salvation, though not of glory or felicity. And until
the Passion of the Holy One is brought before us, who
suffered on the day of preparation, it is right for us to say to all
"*Sanctify yourselves and be ye ready.*" Sanctify yourselves
in making progress more and more from virtue to virtue:
and be ready by steady perseverance. But in what shall
we be sanctified? I have read of some one in the Scripture, whom the Lord *made holy in faithfulness and meekness* (Ecclus. xlv. 4). For it is as impossible to please
men without meekness, as it is to please God without
faith. Rightly then are we warned to be ready in these
respects, that in them we may be pleasing to God, whose
glory we are about to behold: and also to ourselves, that
we may see His glory reflected even in us. Wherefore it
behoves us to provide things good not only before God,
but also before man; that we may be acceptable both to
our King, and also to our fellow-citizens and fellow-soldiers.

5. And indeed before all things faith is to be sought,
of which we read: *Purifying their hearts by faith* (Acts

xv. 9). *Blessed are those who are pure in heart, for they shall see God* (S. Matt. v. 8). Trust yourselves then to God, commit yourselves to Him, cast all your care upon Him, and He shall nourish you, so that you may trustfully say: *The Lord hath care for me* (Ps. xl. 17). Of this experience those men know nothing who love their own selves, half-experienced, anxious on their own account, who accomplish all the desires of the flesh, who are deaf to the voice of Him who says: *Casting all your care upon Him, for He careth for you* (1 S. Peter v. 7). To trust in your own self, is not really trust, but distrust: to have faith in yourself, is not confidence, but diffidence. He is truly faithful, who neither believes in (his own goodness) nor trusts to his own exertions: who seems to himself as a vessel of destruction, but who so loses his life, that he may preserve it to life eternal. Only a heart full of humility is able to do this, to prevent the faithful soul from relying upon itself: but rather quitting its own self, to rise and come up, as it were, from the desert leaning on the Beloved, and therefore filled with consolations.

6. But that our sanctification may be perfect, we must learn from the most Holy One the grace and gentleness suitable to the common life; as He Himself says: *Learn of Me, for I am meek and lowly in heart* (S. Matt. xi. 29). Why should we not say that a man who has done this, who is sweet and gentle and full of mercy, who is made all things to all men, who spreads over all his neighbours, so to speak, that oil of meekness and gentleness wherewith he is himself so anointed, so penetrated and saturated, that he seems to exude it drop by drop everywhere, is similarly saturated with happiness and joy? Happy is he who is prepared by this double sanctification to say: *My heart is ready, O God, my heart is ready* (Ps. lvii. 7). For he

has even now his fruit to sanctification, and shall hereafter have the perfection of it unto eternal life. He shall behold the glory of God, in which consists eternal life, as the Truth Himself has declared: *This is Life eternal, that they might know Thee, the only true God, and Jesus Christ whom Thou hast sent* (S. John xvii. 3). The just judge shall bestow upon him a crown of glory in that day, which shall be followed by no other. Then he shall behold and overflow with joy; his heart shall expand with wonder and happiness. How far shall it expand? Until it shall behold the glory of God in itself. But do not think, brethren, that I can possibly explain to you by means of words the fulness of that promise.

7. Sanctify yourselves then, and be ye ready : to-morrow you shall see, and rejoice, and your joy shall be full. For what is there that the glory of God will not fill? It will even overfill and saturate; when *good measure pressed down, and shaken together and running over, shall be given into your bosom* (S. Luke vi. 38). It shall superabound to such a degree, that it shall surpass in height, not merely your merits, but even your prayers: for God is able to do much more than we can ask or even comprehend. All our wishes and prayers may seem to be summed up in these three things : that which is honourable, that which is useful, and that which is agreeable. These are the things which we desire; and every one of us desires them all; but some have greater desire for one of these, and others for another. This man is so given over to the desire for what is agreeable, that he does not sufficiently wish for either the honourable or the useful: that man dwells more on the prospect of usefulness, and passes over both that of honour and of gladness: while a third is too neglectful, alike of pleasure and of usefulness: and thinks

only of the obtaining of honour. Nor is there anything really reprehensible in the desire for these things: and if we should seek them in God we should in truth find them. For where they truly exist they are combined into one; so that the very same thing is at once the highest good, the highest utility, the greatest honour and extremest pleasure. And these very things as far as we are capable of obtaining them at the present time are held forth to us as the object of our expectation; and a promise is made that the glory of God shall be seen in us; so that God shall be all in all; all joy, all blessedness and all glory.

SERMON XVII. [1]

On the Annunciation of Jesus Christ.

Unto you is born this day in the city of David a Saviour, who is Christ the Lord. S. Luke ii. 11.

1. We have heard a word full of grace, worthy of all acceptance: "Jesus Christ, the Son of God, is born in Bethlehem of Judæa." My soul is melted within me and my spirit bounds at hearing it; it hastens to make you sharers, as you are accustomed to desire, of its joy and gladness. Jesus signifies Saviour. Who so necessary as a Saviour to those who are lost? so desirable to the unhappy, so precious to the despairing? Without Him, whence could salvation be sought, and whence could there be any, even the smallest, hope of safety under the law of sin, in a mortal body, in these evil days and this abode of affliction? This hope was of necessity new to us and unexpected. But you, though you desire your salvation, yet are perhaps so penetrated by the consciousness of the

[1] [Sermon VI. for the Vigil of the Nativity.]

SERMONS.

gravity of the evil and of your own weakness, that you shudder with fear that the remedy may be too painful to support. But fear not: the Saviour is meek and gentle and full of mercy, anointed with the oil of gladness above His fellows, that is to say, those who have received a share in the fulness of His anointing, though not the completeness of it. But when you hear that the Saviour is kind, do not suppose that He is weak and inefficient, for He is also the "Son of God". For such as is the Father, such also is the Son, and all things are subjected to Him according to His will. Or when you hear that He is anointed with the benefit and joy of salvation you perhaps murmur, I know not what, in your care for His honour. You rejoice that the Saviour draws near to you, inasmuch as you are like the paralytic lying upon his pallet, or even more like the man who was left half dead in the road between Jerusalem and Jericho. But you have still greater cause of rejoicing that your Physician is not stern, that He does not employ severe medicines nor cause the brief process of cure to seem more unendurable than even the long suffering of the disease. Yet thus it is, even in our own day, that many perish because they fly from the Physician; they know indeed the name of Jesus, but they know not Christ the Redeemer and they estimate [the difficulty and trouble of the cure which is prepared for them by their own feeling of the number and the malignity of the diseases with which they are affected.

2. But if you are assured that you have a Saviour and if you recognize also without doubt that He is Christ the Anointed One, that He uses not the cautery, but balm; that He cures not by burning, but by anointing: I suppose that one sentiment only will occupy the mind of every created being of noble nature; it is that perhaps (though

God forbid) the person of this Saviour does not seem sufficiently worthy of Him. Yet I suppose that you are not so ambitious and desirous of vainglory, not so tenacious of the point of honour that you would scorn to receive this grace at the point of need, even from any one of your fellow-servants, if he were able to restore you to health. If he were an angel or archangel, or if he were one from some higher order of blessed spirits, your vanity perhaps would have much less of which it could make cause of complaint. This Saviour ought then to be received by you with so much the greater devotion as Jesus Christ the Son of God hath by inheritance so much greater a Name than any of these. See now if there are not plainly three things which the angel who spoke to the shepherds at Bethlehem announced unto them as glad tidings of great joy; He told them: *There is born unto you this day a Saviour who is Christ the Lord.* Let us rejoice then, brethren, in this Nativity, let us give earnest thanks for the great value of this salvation, for the sweetness of this grace, for the glory of the Son of God which is displayed in a manner so astonishing before our eyes; so that nothing is wanting of all those desires which men most prize, neither joy, nor usefulness, nor honour. Let us rejoice I repeat, in inward reflection and mutual congratulation upon that sweet word, that joyful saying, "Jesus Christ the Son of God is born in Bethlehem of Judea."

3. Let not any one with as little piety, as gratitude or religion, say to me in reply: This is nothing new: this happened and has been heard of long ago, it was long ago that Christ was born. I too agree that it was long ago and before our time. Nor will any one wonder at this, who recalls the prophetic saying: "[The Lord shall reign] *for ever and ever*" (Exod. xv. 18). Our Christ

was then born, not merely before our time, but before all time. That Birth is lost in the night of time, or rather it has its dwelling in the light that none can approach unto, in the Bosom of the Father, on the mountain covered with cloud and thick darkness. That He might make this known in some degree, He was born; born in time and of flesh, and being born in the flesh, the Word became flesh. Is there then anything wonderful that the Church in speaking of Him of whom it was said so long before His Birth, *Unto us a Child is born* (Is. ix. 6), should say unhesitatingly to-day: ' Christ, the Son of God, is born?' Long ago this saying began to resound in the ears of Saints, who were never tired of hearing it: inasmuch as *Jesus Christ is Son of God, yesterday, to-day and for ever.* Hence without doubt it was that the first man, the father of all living, enunciating a great mystery, which, long after, an Apostle showed forth as applying to Christ and the Church, said: *A man shall leave his father and his mother and cleave unto his wife: and they two shall be one flesh* (Gen. ii. 24, and Eph. v. 31).

4. Similarly it was because of this that Abraham the father of the faithful, rejoiced to see that day, and he saw it and was glad (S. John viii. 56). And when he ordered his servant to put his hand under his thigh, and thus to swear to him by the God of Heaven, did he not do so as foreseeing that the very God of Heaven should be born of his loins? This design of his Heart God revealed to the man after His own Heart, to whom He swore a faithful oath and will not shrink from it: *of the fruit of thy body will I set upon thy seat* (Ps. cxxxii. 11). Wherefore also [Jesus] is born in Bethlehem of Judæa, in the city of David, as saith the angel: namely, for the sake of the truth of God and to accomplish the promises made unto the Fathers. This also was revealed many times and in divers

manners, unto other Fathers and Prophets (Heb. i. 1). Be it far from us to suppose that it was ever negligently listened to by those who loved God: though he who said, *I beseech Thee, O Lord, send whom Thou wilt send* (Exod. iv. 13), might seem to shrink from the task committed to him: or to be averse to it, as he who cried: *O, that Thou wouldest rend the heavens and come down* (Is. lxiv. 1), and other similar sayings. After them come the holy Apostles who saw with their eyes and heard with their ears, and touched with their hands the Word of Life, Who said to them with truth: *Blessed are the eyes which see the things which ye see* (S. Luke x. 23). Finally, the same truth has been committed to us who are among the faithful to whom the treasures of the Faith have been entrusted; and of whom the Lord Himself says: *Blessed are they who have not seen, and yet have believed* (S. John xx. 29). This is our part in the Word of Life; nor is it to be undervalued, or it is by the faith that we live, and by faith that we overcome the world. It is in fact said by the Prophet: *The just lives by faith* (Hab. ii. 4): and again, *This is the victory which overcometh the world, even our faith* (1 S. John v. 4). This [Divine Purpose] it is, which, like eternity, embraces at once the past, the present and the future, in its vast expanse, so that nothing precedes it, nothing is out of its scope, and nothing outlasts it.

5. Rightly then did you, in reliance on the testimony of our faith, when the sound of this Annunciation was in your ears, rejoice with great joy. Rightly did you give thanks, did you prostrate yourselves and adore, hastening to take refuge under His wings, and to be safe under the shadow of His feathers. Has not each of you, at the news of the Saviour's Birth, said in his heart, *It is good for me to hold me fast by God* (Ps. lxxiii. 28), or rather, as

the same Prophet says, *My soul wait thou only upon God?*
(Ps. lxii. 5). He is to be pitied whose worship was only
feigned, who has bent down his body, but with unbent
heart. For there is a wicked man who hangeth down
his head sadly, but inwardly he is full of deceit (Ecclus.
xix. 26). For whosoever considers too little his own spiritual need and his imperfections, who fears too little the
perils to which he is exposed, who has recourse with too
little piety to the remedies of salvation thus begun, who
submits himself with too little willingness to God, and
has but doubtful faith, when such as he sing: Lord, Thou hast
been our refuge (Ps. xc. 1): their adoration is less pleasing,
their worship less truthful, their humility less humble and
their victory less complete, inasmuch as their faith is less
powerful. For why is it said, *Blessed are those who have
not seen and yet have believed*, except that to believe
appears to be in a sense, to see? Notice to whom and
under what circumstances it was spoken; it was to that
Apostle who was blamed because he had believed only
when he had seen. For it is not at all the same thing to
have seen, and on that account to have believed, as
to have seen in and by believing. Otherwise in what
manner must we suppose that Abraham your father saw
this day of the Lord, if it were not by faith? And again,
in what manner are those words to be understood which
you have sung to-night, "Sanctify yourselves to-day and
be ye ready; for to-morrow ye shall see the glory of God
in you": if it is not meant that we should see in mind,
that we should represent to ourselves with pious devotion,
and adore with faith unfeigned, that great mystery of the
great love of Christ, that He was manifested in the flesh,
that He was justified in the spirit, that He appeared unto
angels, was preached unto Gentiles, was believed on in the
world, was received up into glory? (1 Tim. iii. 16).

6. This mystery is always new because it always renews souls; nor is it ever old, because it never ceases to bring forth fruit which to everlasting shall not wither. For this is that Holy One who is not suffered to see corruption. He is the new man who is never capable of age and decay, who restores to a true newness of life those whose every bone has withered with age. Therefore it is that even in the present most joyful Annunciation it is said, if you notice carefully, not "has been born", but "is born": *Jesus Christ, the Son of God, is born in Bethlehem of Judea.* For as in a certain sense He is sacrificed daily as often as we speak of His death, so also He appears to be born while we represent by faith the mystery of His birth. To-morrow then we shall see the glory of God, but observe, in us, not in Himself, that is to say; His glory in humility, His strength in weakness, God in man. For He is Emmanuel, which is interpreted, *God with us.* And here it is expressed even more plainly. *The Word was made flesh and dwelt among us* (S. John i. 14). Finally then, and thenceforth we have beheld His glory, the glory as of the Only Begotten of the Father, that is full of grace and truth. For it is not the glory of power or of dignity, but the glory of goodness of the Father, the glory of grace of which the Apostle says: To the praise of the glory of His grace (Eph. i. 6).

7. Thus then He is born. But where? "In Bethlehem of Judea." Nor ought we to pass over this mention of Bethlehem without notice. *Let us now go even unto Bethlehem*, say the shepherds, not "let us pass through Bethlehem." Why? Is it not a poor little village? Is it not the least in Judea? Even if so, it is not unsuitable to Him who, though He was rich, yet for our sakes became poor, and though He was the Lord full of greatness and

glory, was born as a little infant for us; to Him who said, *Blessed are the poor in spirit, for theirs is the Kingdom of Heaven* (S. Matt. v. 3); and also, *Unless ye be converted and become as little children ye shall not enter into the Kingdom of Heaven* (S. Matt. xviii. 3). Wherefore He also made choice of a stable and a manger, of a house built of mud, a mere lodging for cattle, that you might know that is He who raises the poor man out of the dunghill and who saves both men and beasts.

8. Would to God that we might be as Bethlehem in Judea, and that Jesus would deign to be born in us also; and that we might be worthy to hear said to us: *To you that fear My Name shall the Sun of Righteousness arise with healing in His wings* (Mal. iv. 2). For perhaps these words which we have cited above signify that there is need to sanctify ourselves and to be ready in order to see the glory of the Lord in us. For, according to the Prophet, *Judah became his sanctification* (Ps. cxiii. 2. VULG.), which implies that by confession of sins all are purified. As to the word Bethlehem, which signifies *House of Bread*, it seems to me to have the meaning of *preparation*. For in what respect is a person prepared to receive so great a guest, who says: *In my house there is no bread* (Is. iii. 7). It was because he was thus unprepared, that a certain man in the Gospel was obliged to go in the middle of the night to knock at the door of a friend, and say, *A friend of mine is come to me in his journey and I have nothing to set before him* (S. Luke xi. 6). It is no doubt of the righteous man that the prophet says: *His heart is fixed, trusting in the Lord. His heart is established, he shall not be afraid* (Ps. cxii. 7, 8). There is no heart prepared which is not established. Now we know from the testimony of the same prophet that *it is bread which*

the great Covenant, an Angel announced that good tidings of great joy.

9. The three Magi also perhaps are types of those who come not from the East only, but also from the West, to sit down with Abraham, Isaac and Jacob. It seems perhaps that to Ephraim (which word signifies Fruitfulness [1]) it belonged not unfitly to offer incense: for to offer incense, an offering of sweet savour, is the proper duty of those whom the Lord has set to go and to bring forth fruit, that is, to the rulers of the Church. As for Benjamin (= son of the right hand), he necessarily offers gold, that is, the substance of this world: just as the faithful people who are placed at the right hand of the Judge, merit to be told by Him: *I was an hungred and ye gave Me meat, etc.* (S. Matt. xxv. 35). Furthermore, Manasseh, if he has desired that it should be he to whom God should appear, would offer the myrrh of mortification, which I consider to be especially required from those of our profession. And these remarks are made, so that we may belong not to that part of the tribe of Manasseh which remained on the east side of Jordan, but that we may forget those things which are behind, and press forward to those which are before.

10. Now let us return even to Bethlehem, and see that which has taken place there; which the Lord has done and has revealed unto us. It is the *House of Bread*, as we have said: therefore it is good for us to be there. For where the Word of God is, there is not wanting that bread which strengthens the heart, as says the prophet:

[1] [Ephraim אפרים signifies *fruitful*: though Josephus (Ant. II. 6. § 1) interprets the word as meaning "restorer, because he was restored to the freedom of his forefathers". (E.)]

Strengthen Thou me with Thy Words (Ps. cxix. 28).
Without doubt, man lives by every word which proceedeth
out of the mouth of God: he lives in Christ and Christ
in him. There is He born, there He manifests Himself:
He loves not the heart that is inconstant and vacillating,
but that which is firm and stable. If anyone murmurs,
hesitates, wavers, meditates returning to his vomit and
being again wallowing in the mire, renouncing his vow
and changing his purpose of life, he is not that Bethlehem,
the House of Bread, in which Christ is born. For famine
only, famine the most severe, obliges him to descend into
Egypt, to feed the swine, to live upon husks, because he
is dwelling far from the house of bread, the house of the
Father: in which, as is well known, even the hired servants
have bread enough and to spare. Christ is not born in the heart
of such an one to which is wanting a warm faith, which is
the very bread of life, according to the statement of
Scripture, *The just shall live by faith* (Hab. ii. 4), that is
to say, the true life of the soul (which is Jesus Himself)
does not, at the present, dwell in our hearts except by
faith. How can Jesus be born in him, how can salvation
arise for him, when the true and perfectly certain declaration is *Whosoever endureth to the end, shall be saved*
(S. Matt. x. 22)? Plainly, Christ will not be found in
him, nor will he be of those of whom it is said, *ye have
an unction from the Holy One* (1 S. John ii. 20); from
which it plainly appears, that his heart is doubtless dried
up and withered, from the moment that he has forgotten
to eat of this his bread. Much less does one who is of
this character, belong to the Son of God, who is such,
that His Spirit rests only upon the soul which is peaceful
and humble and which trembles at His word (Isaiah lxvi.
2); nor can there be any fellowship between unchanging
eternity and such inconstancy; between Him who is (the

same for ever) and one who never remains in the same
state. But, furthermore, however firm we are and strong
in the faith, however well prepared, however abounding
in the bread of life which He bestows upon us liberally,
to Whom we say daily in our prayers, *Give us this day
our daily bread*; we need always to add to our prayers,
Forgive us our trespasses (S. Matt. vi. 11, 12). For if
we say that we have no sin we deceive ourselves and the
truth is not in us. (1 S. John i. 8). Now the Truth is He
who is born not simply in Bethlehem, but in Bethlehem of
Judea, Jesus Christ, the Son of God.

11. Let us hasten then to present ourselves before the
Face of the Lord in confessing our sins, that we may be
found both prepared and sanctified, and that we may have
the happiness to see the Lord born in us, as in Bethlehem
of Judea. But if there be any soul which has so far made
progress in the spiritual life (which indeed is a matter of
much consequence to us) that it is as it were a virgin
become fruitful, the star of the sea, the soul full of grace
and having the Holy Spirit which has come upon it; I
think that Christ will deign not only to be born in it, but
also from it. But let no soul presume to arrogate that
distinction to itself except those whom He has designated
by a special indication and, as it were, has pointed out
with his finger, saying: *Behold My Mother and My brethren*
(S. Matt. xii. 49). Listen now to the words of one of
these chosen souls: *My little children*, he says, *of whom I
travail in birth a second time until Christ be formed in
you* (Gal. iv. 19). If Christ seems to be born in them
when Christ was formed in them; how can any one presume to say that He is not similarly born of him who in
a certain sense travailed in birth with them? But thou
indeed, O ungodly Synagogue, hast brought forth this son

for us, having the office if not the affection of a mother. Thou hast driven him forth from thy bosom, expelled him from thy city, and lifting him up between heaven and earth hast, as it were, said both to the Church of the Gentiles and to the Church of the first-born whose names are written in Heaven: "Let Him be neither thine nor mine, but let Him be divided. Divided, I say, not that He may be shared between us both, but that both may share in the deed." For after having driven Him forth from thy bosom thou hast seized Him and lifted Him into the air; yet thou hast only done this that He might be no longer within thy walls and might not touch the earth any longer; then thou hast bound Him with iron bonds that He might not move to one side or the other. This was thy desire, that when separated from thee He might belong neither to the one church nor to the other. O cruel mother, thou hast striven to make Him, as it were, an untimely birth and that there might be none to receive Him when thus driven forth. See then how far thou hast succeeded, or rather recognize that thou hast not succeeded at all. All the daughters of Sion come forth to see their King Solomon wearing the diadem with which thou hast crowned Him. Leaving His mother, He cleaves unto His spouse, that they two may be one flesh; driven forth from thy city and lifted up from the earth, He draws all things unto Him, since it is He who is over all, God blessed for ever. AMEN.

SERMON VIII. [1]

On the Saviour as a Fount of Grace.
Do not I fill Heaven and Earth? saith the Lord.

Jer. xxiii. 24.

The Festival of the Lord's Nativity, brethren, is indeed a great solemnity: but it is on that account a short day,

[1] [Sermon I. on the Nativity of our Lord.]

and requires a shorter sermon. Nor is it strange that I should limit my discourse, when God the Father limited His Word. Would you know how great He is, yet how little He made Himself to be? He, the Word, says, *Do not I fill Heaven and earth?* But now that He is made Flesh, He is laid in a narrow manger. *From everlasting to everlasting,* says the Prophet, *Thou art God* (Ps. xc. 2), and lo! He has become an Infant of a day old. Now for what purpose was it, brethren, that He thus emptied Himself; or what necessity was there that the Lord of Glory should so humiliate, so limit Himself? Was it not that He might leave you an example to do likewise? He begins already to cry to you by His example what He would afterwards preach to you in His word, *Learn of Me, for I am meek and lowly in heart* (S. Matt. xi. 29). So that He who says that *Jesus began both to do and to teach* [1] (Acts i. 1) states only what is exactly true. And I earnestly beg and intreat you, brethren, not to suffer an example so precious to be placed before your eyes in vain, but that you conform yourselves to it and be renewed in the spirit of your mind. Give yourselves to the study of humility, which is the foundation and the guard of all the virtues; follow it, which alone is able to save your souls. For what is more unworthy, more blameable and deserving of greater punishment, than that after seeing the God of Heaven humbling Himself to become a little child, man should attempt to magnify himself and lift himself up above the earth? It is a proof of intolerable effrontery, for a miserable worm to be puffed up with pride where the majesty of God emptied Itself.

2. This then is the reason why He did so, taking upon

---

[1] [*I. e.*, that the teaching *by action* preceded that *by word.* (E.)]

Him the form of a servant, He who was in the form of God and equal with the Father; but if He emptied Himself, it was of His power and His glory, not of His goodness and mercy. For what says the Apostle: *After that the goodness and mercy of God our Saviour towards man appeared* (Titus iii. 4). His power had previously appeared in the creation of the world, His wisdom appeared in its government: but the goodness of His mercy now appeared most clearly of all, in His Humanity. His power had been made known to the Jews in signs and wonders; wherefore you will find frequently occurring in the Law the words: *I am the Lord, I am the Lord.* His glory had made Itself evident to philosophic minds also by abundant proofs; according to the words of the Apostle, *that what is known of God, has been manifested to them* (Rom. i. 19). But on the one hand the Jews trembled at the thought of His power, and the philosophers were oppressed in their meditations upon God, by the thought of His glory. Power demands submission: and glory admiration; but neither commands imitation. Let Thy goodness, O Lord, be displayed, so that man, who was created in Thy image, may be conformed unto it: for we are not able to imitate, and ought not to envy, Thy majesty, Thy power and Thy wisdom. How long is Thy mercy straitened in the case of the Angels; and does Thy justice engross the remainder of it equally with the whole human race? *Thy mercy, O Lord, is in the heavens and Thy truth reacheth into the clouds* (Ps. xxxvi. 5) condemning both the whole earth, and the powers of the air. Let Thy mercy enlarge its boundaries, extend its limits, expand its folds, and stretch with power from one end of the world to the other, ordering all things with gentleness. Unbind, O Lord, Thy bosom, closed to us by justice, and come to our help with pity and abounding charity.

3. Why do you fear, O man, why do you tremble at the thought of the presence of the Lord who comes? He comes, not to judge the world, but to save it. Once you were persuaded by some unfaithful servant, to take away secretly the crown from His head and to put it upon your own. Why did you not fear, when taken in the theft? why did you not fly from His presence? for perhaps the sword of justice already glittered in His hand. Now you are dwelling in exile, now you eat your bread in the sweat of your brow; and lo, a voice is heard in the earth, that its Ruler approaches. Whither will you go from His Spirit? and whither will you fly from His Presence? But do not fear nor fly. He does not come with the armed hand; nor does He call for you to punish, but to save. And do not now say again: *I heard Thy voice, and I hid myself* (Gen. iii. 10), for He comes as a little child, who has no words. The voice of a wailing child is more to be pitied, than feared: or if it is terrible to any, it is not so to you. He has become a little Child: His Virgin Mother binds His tender limbs with swathes: and do you still tremble with fear? Even from this you may learn that He comes not to destroy you, but to save: not to enslave you, but to deliver you from bonds. Already He contends against your enemies; already He who is nothing less than the Power and Wisdom of God, sets His foot upon the necks of those proud and lofty ones.

4. You have two enemies, Sin and Death: that is, the death of the body and that of the soul. He has come to subdue each of these, and to save you from them; therefore fear not. Already in his own person He has conquered sin, in assuming human nature without any stain of it. Great is the blow given to sin, and striking the defeat it has experienced, when human nature, which it boasted

itself to have entirely occupied to overcome, is found in Christ entirely free from sin. From that moment He follows after these your enemies, and overtakes them; nor will He turn back until he has destroyed them. As He wars against sin in His life, so He opposes it equally by word and example, He has bound it like the strong man armed in the Gospel, and taken its spoils. Then, continuing His victory, He triumphs over death also; first in His own Person when He rises again, the first-fruits of them who sleep, the first-born from the dead; and afterwards shall subdue it equally in all of us, when He shall raise up our mortal bodies, and death itself the last enemy, shall be destroyed. That is why He is clad with glory in His Resurrection, not wrapped in swathing bands as at His birth. Therefore He who at first gave forth freely of the affluence of His mercy, and judged no man: when He has risen again, draws tight, as it were, the girdle of His justice, and gathers in the flowing folds of His mercy; since then He is prepared for the judgment, which shall take place at our resurrection. For as He came the first time as a little child, that He might bestow freely His mercy; so at the end it shall go before the future judgment, to temper it.

5. For although He has come to us as a little child, it does not at all follow that what He has brought to us or has bestowed upon us, is little. If you ask what He has brought: first of all, He has brought mercy; secondly, He, as the Apostle says, *has saved us* (Tit. iii. 5). Nor did that profit those only, who were in the world when He came: but He is, as it were, a fountain which cannot be exhausted. For the Lord Christ is as a Fountain in which we may be cleansed, as it is written: *who loved us and washed us from our sins* (Apoc. i. 5). But it

is not the only use of water to remove our defilements; it also quenches our thirst. 'Blessed,' says the wise man, 'is he that doth meditate good things in wisdom and will meditate in righteousness' (Ecclus. xiv. 22). And again 'She shall make him drink the salutary water of wisdom' (Ecclus. xv. 3). Well is it said of *salutary* wisdom; for the wisdom of the flesh is but death, and the wisdom of the world is even enmity towards God. Only the wisdom which is of God is salutary, which, according to the definition of S. James, is *first pure, then peaceable*, (S. James iii. 17). For the wisdom of the flesh is given to pleasure and is not pure; and the wisdom of the world is tumultuous, not peaceable. But that which is of God is first pure, seeking not her own, but those things which are of Jesus Christ; and it brings every one not to do his own will, but to consider what is the will of God; and next, it is peaceable, not insisting upon his own opinion, but acquiescing more in the opinion and decision of others.

6. The third use of water is for irrigation: which is absolutely necessary for new plantations; and without which they either perish altogether through dryness, or their growth is seriously checked. Let those then who have sowed the seed of good works seek for the water of devotion: that they may be irrigated from the fountain of grace; so that the garden of a good life may not grow dry, but flourish in perpetual verdure. It is for this that a prophet prays: *Let thy burnt-offering be fat* (Ps. xx. 3. VULG.). So in the praises of Aaron you read, that the fire consumed his sacrifice every day. In all of which nothing but this seems to be understood, that our good works ought to be seasoned by the fervour of devotion and the sweetness of spiritual grace. Shall we be able

to find the fourth fountain, and thus recover that Paradise which was rendered most delightful by the waters of four fountains? For if we have lost all hope of recovering the Earthly Paradise, how should we preserve the hope of possessing the kingdom of heaven? *If I have told you heavenly things*, says our Lord, *and ye believe not, how shall ye believe when I tell you heavenly things?* (S. John iii. 12). Now since the sight of things present strengthens the expectation of things future; we have a Paradise much better and more delightful than that which our first parents possessed; and our Paradise is the LORD CHRIST. In him we have already found three fountains; let us now seek the fourth. We have the fountain of mercy, the waters of remission for cleansing our faults; we have the fountain of wisdom, the waters of discretion for quenching our thirst; we have the fountain of grace, the waters of devotion, for irrigating the plants of our good works: let us now seek the waters that boil, the waters of zeal which are useful for cooking our food. For these season and warm our affections, and boil forth from the fountain of charity. Wherefore the prophet says, *My heart grew hot within me, and while I was musing the fire burned* (Ps. xxxix. 3); and in another place: *The zeal of Thy house hath eaten me up* (Ps. lxix. 9). And in fact whosoever is led by the sweetness of devotion to the love of righteousness, is also led by the love of charity to hatred of iniquity. Does it not perhaps seem as if Isaiah spake beforehand of these fountains: *Ye shall draw water with joy out of the fountains of the Saviour* (Is. xii. 3. VULG.). In order that you may know that this promise has reference to the present life, not the future, mark the words which follow: *In that day shall ye say, praise the Lord and call upon His name* (v. 4) For invocation and prayer have relation to the present time, as it is written: *Call upon me in the day of trouble* (Ps. l. 15).

7. Furthermore, with regard to these four fountains, [1] three of them seem to answer exactly to the three orders of the Church, each to each. For the first state is common to all the faithful. For in many things we offend all, and we all need the fountain of mercy therefore, in order to cleanse us from our defilements. We all, I say, have *sinned and come short of the glory of God* (Rom. iii. 23): both prelates and monks and those who are married, and *if we say that we have no sin we deceive ourselves* (1 S. John i. 8). But if no one is pure from sin, then the fountain of mercy is needful for all, and Noah, Daniel and Job must hasten to this fountain, with equal ardour as others. With regard to the second, Job had indeed great need of the fountain of wisdom, since he found himself in the midst of the snares of the enemy, and it would have been very surprising if he were able to escape from every kind of sin. And so Daniel also had need of the fountain of grace, since the grace of devotion was necessary to render him earnest in the works of penitence and the labours of abstinence. For it behoves us also, and that greatly, to do all things with cheerfulness: *for the Lord loveth a cheerful giver* (2 Cor. ix. 7). For our land (that is our nature) is far from being fertile in producing that sort of crop which we may call a holy life: and therefore easily becomes dry and sterile if it be not helped by frequent waterings. This is the reason why we ask in the Lord's Prayer, for this grace under the name of "our daily bread." And it is

[1] [Cf. Sermon 96, "De Diversis", where he explains these fountains in a different way].

quite right that we should do this, if we wish to escape the terrible malediction of the prophet : *Let them be as the grass upon the housetops, which withereth afore it groweth up* (Ps. cxxix. 6). But the fountain of zeal seems to answer specially to Noah, since it becomes prelates above all to have zeal. Finally, JESUS CHRIST affords in His Own self these four fountains to all those who are still living in the flesh. As for the fifth, which is the fountain of life, that is promised to us after death, and it was this which the prophet desired, when he said, *My soul thirsteth for God the fountain of life* (Ps. xlii. 2). Perhaps again it is these four fountains which represent the four Wounds which CHRIST received on the Cross while He was still living : the fifth was rendered in type by that stroke of the lance with which He was pierced through the Side when He gave up the Ghost. For He still lived when both Hands and Feet were pierced, and so opened to us the four fountains of grace which flow from Himself, and which we profit by while we are still living ; but He endured the fifth wound when He had already expired, and thus opened to us a fifth fountain in Himself, but after death. But lo ! while speaking of the mysteries of the Nativity of our Lord, I have been suddenly drawn on to examine those of His Passion. But yet it is not wonderful that we should seek in the Passion that which Christ brought to us in His Nativity. For in the former, the strings of the purse, as it were, which held the riches of His grace, were cut ; and the riches flowed forth to be the price of our redemption.

SERMON XIX. [1]

On the three chief works of God, and on the triple mingling.

The works of the Lord are great. (Ps. cxi. 2).

1. This is the saying of the prophet David. His works are indeed great, brethren, as He Himself is great: but those among them which seem to be greatest of all, are those which relate to ourselves. And that is what the same prophet declares, saying: *The Lord hath done great things for us* (Ps. cxxvi. 3). How gloriously He has dealt with us, is shown with especial clearness by three things particularly: in the beginning, by our creation: in the present age, by our redemption: and in the future, by our glorification. How glorious, O Lord, are Thy works towards each of us. It belongs to Thee to declare to Thy people the power of Thy works, but we will at least not be silent respecting the works themselves. It is our task, brethren, to consider the threefold connexion between these three works made by Divine power and by interposition from heaven. For in the first of His works which related to us, God made man out of the dust of the earth, and breathed into his nostrils a living soul. What a skilful worker is this, what a uniter of [diverse] things, who could so closely bind together at His mere will, the dust of the earth and a living soul! The former indeed had been previously created, when in the beginning God created the heaven and the earth: but the soul was not constituted in common with the rest, but has a conditionment peculiar to itself: nor was it created in the mass, but inspired with a certain unique excellence. Recognize, O man, thy own dignity: recognize the glory of thy condition

[1] [Sermon II. on the Nativity of Our Lord.]

as man. Thou hast a body in common with the universe: for it is suitable that he who is set at the head of the entire world of bodily existences should have some point of similarity with it. But to thee belongs something more elevated in quality, and which does not permit you to be confounded with other creatures. In thee are allied and compacted together flesh and spirit: the one shaped by His power, the other inbreathed by His spirit.

2. But of what importance is this mingling [of body and spirit]? and whom does this union profit? For according to the wisdom of the sons of this world, where things of a lower order are associated with those of a higher, that which is the more powerful is the ruling factor in the alliance, and uses the other as it thinks fit. The strong is overcome by the stronger, the ignorant laughed to scorn by the wise, the simple deceived by the cunning, the weak despised by the powerful. But it is not so in Thy work, O Lord, not so in the unison which Thou hast made; not to this end hast Thou associated spirit with clay, the lofty with the lowly, Thy excellent and worthy creature with matter abject and comparatively worthless. Who of you, brethren, does not see how much the soul excels the body in worth? would not the body, without the soul, be merely a senseless block? From the soul comes beauty, growth, clearness of vision and power of speech; in short, every sense has its seat in the soul. That union of body and soul urges me to charity; I read charity in the first page of this our human state: and that which the infinitely beneficent hand of the Creator not only preaches at once in the very beginning, but also presses upon me, is Charity.

3. Assuredly, dear brethren, this was an admirable conjunction [of body and soul], if it had remained unaltered.

But, alas, although fortified with the Divine seal [for God made man in His own image and likeness] the seal has been broken, the true unity dissipated. That worst of robbers approached and broke the seal, while it was, so to speak, still warm: and thus losing the Divine likeness, unhappy man was compared unto the beasts that are without sense, and was made like unto them (Ps. xlix. 13). For God made man upright: and in His similitude, of which it is written: *The Lord our God is upright, and there is no unrighteousness in Him* (Ps. xcii. 16). He made man just and truthful, as He is Himself justice and truth: nor was that union capable of being dissolved, unless the seal placed upon it were destroyed. But a forger came upon the scene, and promising to ignorant men a better seal, he broke the seal, alas, which had been impressed by the Hand of God Himself. *Ye shall be*, he said, *as Gods, knowing good and evil* (Gen. iii. 5). O evil and malevolent one, to what purpose that mere pretence of knowledge? Let them be as God, upright and just: let them be truthful as God in whom is no sin. Then the seal will remain untouched, and the original union will still subsist. But now, alas! we unhappy ones know by experience, to what the cunning of diabolical fraud has persuaded us. For when the Divine seal was broken there followed for us a bitter separation, a sad division. What has become of the promise which that wicked one made, *By no means shall ye die!* For we are all in a state of death; there is no man who liveth and shall not see death.

4. But, Lord God, wilt Thou never restore Thy work, and shall man, who has fallen, not be helped to rise again? Only the Maker can repair His work. Therefore *because of the oppression of the poor, because of the sighing of the needy, now will I arise, saith the Lord: I will set him in safety, I will deal faithfully with him* (Ps. xii. 5. VULG.)

inasmuch as *the enemy shall not gain advantage over him,
nor the son of wickedness approach to hurt him* (Ps.lxxxix.22).
I will make then, He seems to say, a new union, on which
I will place a seal clearer and more strong; a seal not
made after My image and likeness, but which is My
likeness itself; the brightness of My glory, the figure of
My substance; not made, but begotten before all ages.
And do not fear that this shall be broken as was the
other; for hear the Prophet: *My strength is dried up as
a potsherd* (Ps. xxii. 16), but a potsherd which the entire
universe, were it a hammer, could not by any means shatter.
The first union was composed but of two elements, the
second of three; and we are thus reminded of the mystery
of the Holy Trinity. The Word, which was in the beginning with God, and was God: the Soul, which was created,
and did not before exist: the Flesh, which was separated
by a Divine operation from the mass of corruption, but
without any corruption whatever, and such as no flesh
ever previously existed; these three elements come together
and are joined by an indissoluble bond into a Unity of
Person. You have here a triple act of power: that which
was not, has been created: that which had perished, has
been renewed: and that which was above all things, made
to be a little lower than the Angels. Here are the three
measures of meal of which we read in the Gospel (S. Matt.
xiii. 33), of which the whole were leavened, that they
might become the bread of angels, for man to eat the bread
that strengthens man's heart. Happy and blessed among
all women she in whose chaste bosom was matured that
bread [1] by the resting upon her of the fire of the Holy
Spirit. Happy, I say, is she who mingled in these three
bushels of meal as it were the leaven of her faith. For

---

[1] [*Or* the Bread of Life].

indeed by faith she conceived and by faith she brought
forth; and, according to the word of Elizabeth, Blessed is
she that believed, for all things were perfected in her which
were told her from the Lord (S. Luke i. 45). Do not
wonder that I should say, that the Word was united to
flesh by means of her faith, since it was of her flesh that
He took upon Him His own. Nor is there anything to
conflict with the present exposition in the fact that the
Kingdom of Heaven should be compared to those three
measures; for it does not seem unsuitable that the Kingdom
of Heaven should be compared to the faith of Mary by
which it was retrieved or recovered.

5. The bond then of this union no creature whatever is
able to dissolve: for the prince of this world has nothing
whatever [of power] over Christ, nor was John himself
worthy to unloose the latchet of His sandal. Nevertheless
it is certainly needful that union should in a certain degree
be dissolved, and without this that other union which was
broken, could not be re-united. Of what service are bread
which is never broken, a treasure which is kept concealed,
wisdom which is known to none? S. John might well weep
that no one could be found to open the Book and to
undo the seals thereof (Apoc. v. 4); for while it remained
closed none of us could succeed in attaining that knowledge
of God. But do Thou, O Lamb of God, who art truly
meek, Thyself open the Book. Present Thyself to the Jew
that Thy Hands and Feet may be pierced, and thus that
treasure of Salvation, that full and free Redemption which
in them is hidden may pour forth. Break, O Lord, Thy
Bread to men who are hungering: it is only Thou who
art able to break it, Thou who art able to cause that which
was broken to stand firm and strong again: and even
during that severance, art alone able to lay down Thy life,

and to take it again. In Thy mercy therefore let this temple be in a certain degree taken down, but not altogether destroyed. Let the Body be separated from the soul, but let the Word preserve Thy Flesh in incorruption, and Thy Soul in the fullest liberty: so that among the dead, It alone may act freely, and bring forth from their prison-house the souls which were bound there, which sat in darkness and the shadow of death. Let Thy Soul lay down Its Flesh immaculate, but only to take it again on the third day: so that in dying it may destroy death, and that the life of men may rise again with it in its resurrection. This was in fact what was done: and that it was done we, dearly beloved, rejoice. In His Death was destroyed death itself; and we have been born again into a good hope of everlasting life, through the Resurrection of Jesus Christ from the dead.

6. But that third union, who can say what it shall be? *Eye hath not seen, nor ear heard, nor hath it entered into the heart of man to conceive, what God hath prepared for them that love Him* (1 Cor. ii. 9). That will be the consummation, when Christ shall have delivered up the Kingdom to God, even the Father : and They two shall be one, not indeed in flesh, but in spirit. For if, in taking a body, the Word was made Flesh; much more He who is united so closely to. God, shall be one Spirit with Him. And indeed in this union is shown humility which is the means of it, a humility than which nothing can be greater : but in that which we long for and await, is contained for us (if only it be for us) a far more exceeding and eternal weight of glory. If we have not forgotten, then, in the first conjunction, in which soul and body unite to form a man, it is charity which is commended to us: in the second, that which is rightly most conspicuous is humility, because it is only the virtue of humility which is able to repair the

injury to charity. But the union of a reasonable soul to
a body formed of the dust of the earth is not wholly
the work of· humility : since it is not of its own deliberate choice that it is found united with a body of flesh ;
but it is sent into that union immediately upon its creation, and is created in sending. Not so indeed that
supreme Spirit, Who being infinitely good, has united
Himself to a Body undefiled, at the good pleasure of His
will. In conclusion then, it is with good right that the
glory of heaven should follow charity and humility : since
on one side without charity no good result could be
reached : and on the other, it is only he who humbles
himself, that shall be exalted. (S. Luke xiv. 11).

X.

ERRATA ET CORRIGENDA TO VOL. I. [1]

P. xiii., Note 2. Two notes have been blended here. The second part, beginning "This is the *Liber de modo*, etc. applies to No. 6, in the list above.

p. 68, line 15. For "Passagiens" read "Passagii."

p. 77, line 13. For "Clairvaux" read "Citeaux."

p. 78, line 23. For "Godfrey" read "Geoffrey."

p. 80, line 30. Add (A. D. 1137.)

p. 89, line 21. Add as note [But qy. — was this in 1152?]

p. 98, line 17. For "Godfrey" read "Geoffrey."

p. 105, line 30. For "Godfrey" read "Geoffrey".

p. 109, line 37. Insert "Has he not his reason for a teacher, his own conscience for a rod of judgment, and his natural modesty as a rule of conduct?"

p. 110, line 16. For "his superiors" read "the chief [or prince] himself of the Priors."

p. 110, line 18. Add "He deceives the shepherds, who took him for a sheep; and alas! alas! brought him, wolf as he was, into the company of a young lamb,

---

[1] The Editor has to thank the Reviewers of Vol. I. for pointing out various inaccuracies, which are here, it is believed, set right. With regard to Letters I. and II., which supplied the greater part of these, it is as well to explain that in view of the prolix style of the Letters, and the many repetitions, it was his original idea to prune and condense them in translation to a certain extent. This idea was, however, abandoned after Letters I. and II., and a literal translation adopted: but, as time went on, the various *lacunae* in these two letters escaped notice, until referred to as above. They are now all supplied. (E.)

who did not fly from the wolf, because he did not recognize him as such."

p. 111, line 2. Insert "The sinner, as a victor returning from the fight, is praised and encouraged in the desires of his soul."

p. 111, line 16. Insert "and indeed no objector was waited for."

p. 111, line 22. Insert "the tenor of these letters, the substance of this judgment, the conclusion of the whole affair, is that those who have taken away this young man may continue to keep him, and those who have lost him must keep silence."

p. 111, line 31. Insert "He will certainly come, who by the mouth of His prophet utters the threatening: *When I shall have taken my time, I will judge according to justice* (Ps. lxxv. 2. VULG.). What will He do with unjust judgments, He who will judge justice itself (*justitias quoque ipsas judicabit*)? He will come, I repeat, the day of judgment will come: in which pure hearts will be of more avail than cunning words, and a good conscience than a full purse: and then that judge will neither be deceived by words, nor influenced by presents."

p. 113, line 21. Insert "Unless they who say to you There, there! (Ps. xl. 15) will persuade you that to act as you have done is not to look back. But, my dear son, if sinners entice thee, consent thou not (Prov. i. 10). Believe not every spirit (1 S. John. iv. 1). Be at peace with many: nevertheless have but one counsellor of a thousand (Ecclus. vi. 6). Avoid occasions of evil, repulse blandishments, shut thine ears to flatteries, and question thine own heart, since thou knowest thyself better than another person does."

p. 114, line 5. Insert "Then I nourished you with milk, because you were still a young child, and could take nothing else: but I should have given you bread also, had you waited until you were grown. But alas! how hastily and unseasonably thou wert weaned! And I fear lest he whom I should have cherished with blandishments, strengthened with exhortations, sustained by prayers, should be chilled, and failing, and on the point to perish: I sadly fear, not only for the loss of so much labour, but also for the unhappy fate of my lost child."

p. 114, line 11. Insert "You also have been taken away from my bosom, and snatched from my arms. I mourn the loss of a son violently torn from me, and seek to recover him. Can I forget my own bowels? The little that remains to me of them cannot but suffer pain for the loss of that no small part which has been torn away."

p. 114, line 13. Insert "Whose hands are full of blood (Is. i. 15), whose sword has pierced through my soul (S. Luke ii. 35), whose teeth are spears and arrows, and their tongue a sharp sword (Ps. lvii. 4)".

p. 114, line 24 (end). Insert "O cruel charity, O hard necessity! They cared so much for your salvation, that they endangered mine. And would that they may save you, even without me; yea, would that I may die, so that you may live."

p. 116, line 24. Insert "If during the day you have given yourself to manual labour, as you are bound to do by your profession; hard indeed will be the food which you do not eat willingly."

p. 117, line 6. Insert "But otherwise, if you are so timid, why do you fear where there is nothing to be feared, and yet are without fear where there is more real reason for fearing?"

p. 117, line 25. Insert "Doubtless when a man passes without interval from gloom to the sunlight, from repose to labour, everything commenced seems heavy and burdensome: but after he has begun to accustom himself to leave off the one and to practise the other, custom makes every difficulty disappear, and he . finds that easy which he had before supposed impossible."

p. 118, line 1. Insert "By flight you can lose it, by death you cannot: yea, you are even blessed if you die in the combat, because when you have scarcely uttered your last sigh, you shall receive the crown."

p. 118, line 5. Insert "and there he found in thee no improvement in these respects."

p. 121, line 2. Insert "Although injured, she does not wish to use reprisals: but scorned as she was, recalls you to her: thus showing by her conduct that it is written truly of her, *Charity suffereth long and is kind* (1 Cor. xiii. 4)."

Although she is injured, although she is offended, if you will return to her, she will return to meet you, as if you had always honoured her as a mother. She will forget your contempt and rush into your arms: she will rejoice that he who was dead, is alive again, that he who was lost is found (S. Luke xv. 32).

p. 122, line 18. Insert "There, shameful to say, he who was thought the better of the two fled, while he who was considered the inferior bravely overcame."

p. 128, line 35. For "wine" read "swine daily."

p. 129, line 14. Insert "May the youth for whom we are concerned be saved from this:"

p. 147, line 5. After "wholly" read "good."

p. 150, line 33. For "then listen. . . . His side" read "He from whose Side it flowed hears it."

p. 151, line 7. After "word" read "even."

p. 151, line 18. Read the sentence thus: "in which nothing is ordered plainly contrary to the Divine laws."

p. 151, line 21. "and freedom frankly to set it at naught."

p. 151, line 26. Read "or if he wished to be pushed headlong into the fire or into the water by you, would you obey?"

p. 152, line 1. Read "coöperate with him in a graver offence."

p. 152, line 2. Read "by whom it has been said'

p. 154, line 2. After "of" read "such a."

p. 169, line 3. For "accident" read "quality."

p. 172, line 37. For "so" read "the case."

p. 174, line 11. For "sometimes" read "most often."

p. 182, line 29. Fot "But" read "has."

p. 182, line 30. *Dele* "He."

p. 184, line 26. Insert "5."

p. 189, line 26. For "commands" read "commends."

p. 190, line 18. Transfer "3." to line 14.

p. 191, line 9. *Dele* "hindering"; after "perspiration" read "being delayed."

p. 195, line 23. Add the following note at foot: "The same words are read in the third letter of Nicholas of Clairvaux, which he wrote in the name of S. Bernard to the Bishop of Luçon."

p. 208, line 6. For "would it" read "it would."

p. 208, line 8. *Dele* the "?"

p. 225, line 10. For "belong" read "belonged."

p. 243, line 16. For "but" read "that."

p. 246, line 7. For "is" read "his."

p. 247, line 13. Add "BERNARD heartily wishes health."

p. 247, line 15. For "know" read "have heard."

p. 264, line 25. Insert To his very dear RAINALD, BERNARD, not his father and lord, but his brother and fellow-servant, wishes health, as to a very dear brother and faithful fellow-servant.

p. 267, line 19. Add "But I am digressing too far."

p. 290, line 30. For "rather" read "not so much."

p. 290, line 31. For "than" read "as."

p. 330, line 28. Omit "always."

p. 336, line 6. Insert "2."

p. 336, line 29. For "2." read "3."

p. 337, line 22. For "3." read "4."

p. 338, line 12. For "4." read "5."

p. 339, line 9. For "5." read "6."

p. 339, line 31. For "6." read "7."

p. 340, line 14. For "7." read "8."

p. 341, line 18. For "ask" read "asked."

p. 351, line 35. Add "Count on me to be prepared to aid your flight, by meeting you with the bread of hospitality."

p. 354, line 13. Omit "in the good" and read "need is there."

p. 363, line 8. *Dele* the first "for" and read "of."

p. 363, line 9. *Dele* "for" and read "of."

p. 421, line 22. For "King" read "Duke."

p. 430, line 28. For "sweetly" read "providently."

p. 441, line 24. For "facts" read "fasts."

p. 447, line 3. For "the King of terrors" read "fearful death."

p. 447, line 27. For "1130" read "1137."

p. 447, line 27. For "Clearmont" read "Clermont."

p. 448, line 22. Add "and your endeavours."

INDEX TO VOL. III.

A.

B.

C.

D.

E.

F.

G.

X. Y. Z.